THE SYNODAL POPE

THE SYNODAL POPE

The True Story of the Theology and Politics of Pope Francis

Jean-Pierre Moreau

Translated by Jeanne Smits

TAN Books
Gastonia, North Carolina

Cover design by David Ferris—www.davidferrisdesign.com

Cover image: Pope Francis celebrates the 'Via Crucis' procession at Colosseum in Rome on April 18, 2014. Photograph by giulio napolitano. Used with permission. Shutterstock.

ISBN: 978-1-5051-3317-2

Published in the United States by
TAN Books
PO Box 269
Gastonia, NC 28053
www.TANBooks.com

Printed in the United States of America.

CONTENTS

Appendix

Foreword

by the publishers of the original French version

I t is often said that Pope Francis is as pragmatic as he is unpredict-able, because he lacks structured thought and has no true intellec-tual mentor—let alone a concern for liturgy. How else are we to explain his openness to the "Amazonian Rite" and his rejection of the traditional Latin Rite? How are we to understand his contradictory statements, for example, on the subject of the Abu Dhabi Document on Human Fraternity, in which he speaks of the diversity of religions as "willed by God in his wisdom," while he privately asserts that this is merely God's permissive will, the same that permits evil?

More questions arise: Why does Francis seem obsessed by the issues of our material world—climate, pollution, health, poverty, migration, and so on—while relegating the proclamation of the Faith to the back seat? Why is this pope prepared to take the risk of changing the doctrine of the Church by placing so-called pastoral concerns at the forefront of his speeches and actions?

This book argues that there is in fact a unifying factor, a "red thread" to follow in Francis's thought.

Jean-Pierre Moreau, a keen observer of liberation theology, many of whose leading figures he personally met when he was a special cor-respondent for the *Figaro-Magazine* in the 1980s, has made a close study of the personal and intellectual itinerary of Jorge Mario Bergo-glio, described by his closest supporters as professing the "theology of the people."

Drawing on his encyclopedic knowledge of the ideological shifts that have affected so many areas of Catholicism in Latin America, the author provides insights from his own encounters and readings: the theology of the people, he shows, is a spin-off of oft-condemned "liberation theology." Stripped of the most obviously Marxist-Leninist aspects of the latter, it places "the people of God" (and above all the poor as a "people" replacing the Communists' "oppressed class," but now with a messianic dimension) at the center. It promotes "the people" to the role of a "theological locus," in other words, an eminent source of knowledge of God and His "word."

This is why Pope Francis puts so much emphasis on the "signs of the times" and on history. These are the new tools at the service of a doctrine that is inherently evolutionary.

Jean-Pierre Moreau establishes clear links between modernism as denounced at the beginning of the twentieth century by Saint Pius X on the one hand and, on the other, Jesuit thought and its profound influence on "conciliar" innovations in particular, as well as the "praxis" of the Latin American Church. He shows the latter to have been the true testing ground for the application of Vatican II in the way those who prepared and piloted it intended.

This modernist, progressive thinking, strongly advocated by Fr. Pedro Arrupe, who became superior general of the Jesuits in 1965, was supported on a practical level by Bergoglio's own Peronism.[1] One of the great merits of this book is that it shows, with supporting evidence, how Bergoglio drew inspiration from both the Argentine dictator's relationship with "the people" and his military strategies and tactics. He used them to gain and retain power, to serve his own ascent within the Church.

It was Arrupe who drew up the plans for the revolution that was to give birth to the Church of tomorrow; Bergoglio, and even more so Francis, put them into practice with all the determination, skill, and know-how with which his political hero, Juan Perón, had inspired

---

[1]   Juan Domingo Perón was an Argentine politician who served as president from 1946 to 1955. Peronism is a political movement based on his ideas and has been described as a vague blend of nationalism and laborism.

him; such is the essence of this book. But there is much more to it than this summary: it offers a wealth of facts and quotations that support these claims.

The strength of this book lies in its solid and convincing documentation (we have been able to verify the accuracy of all quotations and the reality of the facts evoked, insofar as they are in the public domain). It uncovers the guiding principles of the pope's thought and action, showing that these have hardly changed—even at the time when he was thought to be a conservative.

Jean-Pierre Moreau highlights the unbroken continuity of Pope Francis's religious and intellectual options with those of the thinkers behind the theology of the people; he provides their names and describes their thinking, disclosing the facts and Hegelian ideas that are only too often ignored by the public. These help to bring clarity to a seemingly elusive pontificate.

Portraits abound, and quotes are revealing, from Lucio Gera, the young Bergoglio's theology teacher, to Leonardo Boff, a defrocked priest, a convinced "liberationist," and today a promoter of ecologism who has been praised by Pope Francis on several occasions. Thanks to Jean-Pierre Moreau, the extent of the subversion that was at work in Argentina is here exposed—and also the way in which Cardinal Bergoglio supported and justified the action of the movement of third world priests who were responsible for its spread.

Jean-Pierre Moreau also focuses on the work and ideology of the Latin American Bishops' Conference (CELAM), where liberationists, Jesuits, and Bergoglio himself played a leading role from the early 2000s onwards.

This book sheds light on the real Bergoglio and the real influences behind him. It is anything but a catalogue of trivia about Pope Francis's governance; rather, it shows his deep-rooted coherence and true affiliations (which go back further than is generally imagined), and more importantly, it reveals the truly revolutionary nature of his leadership.

Preface

The French title of this book, *La conquête du pouvoir* (The conquest of power), did not come out of thin air. It was inspired among others by a statement from the man who serves as a reference for the current pope, the ex-Franciscan Leonardo Boff. On March 15, 2015, the Argentine daily *Clarín* published an interview of Boff, the inventor of "ecotheology," by Marcello Larraquy. The interview wound up with the following dialogue:

> *Two years into his pontificate, can you already say what will be the legacy of Francis?*
>
> *Leonardo Boff:* In my opinion, he will create a dynasty of popes from the Third World, from Asia, Africa and Latin America, who will bring new blood to antiquated European Christianity, which is old and wrinkled (*envejecida*), and practically dead (*agónica*). His legacy will be that of a Church that is no longer centralized in Rome, but an immense network of communities throughout the world, and the Pope will go from one to the other. It will not be a Church only of the West. It will be a global church.

Boff's reply to the previous question had already hinted at the direction the pontificate would take:

> *There are some who fear that the process of reform will eventually dismantle the doctrinal edifice of the Church.*

> **Leonardo Boff:** There are two competing models. The doctrinal model, with the dogmas of canon law, is what has worked until now. The other, that of the people of God, is a Church accompanied by a true pastor, that has respect for the fallibility and the weakness of the human being. One of these Churches has a pastor; the other, a "doctor." The Pope's position is very clear. The Church must journey along with history and discover the signs of the times.

We could also have chosen to quote Cardinal Kasper, who said that the scope of current reforms is such that several pontificates will be needed to bring them to fruition. In view of what we know and see today, Kasper and Boff are two first-class experts on what is happening before our very eyes.

―――――

The Catholic Church is experiencing a cataclysm of such magnitude as has not occurred in two thousand years. In the face of an extraordinary situation, it is the duty of commentators to seek out its main cause, if any, and then, if possible, its secondary causes. Today, many are looking to the apocalypse to discern the final catastrophes that will accompany the end of the world.

The Second Vatican Council encouraged the faithful to discover and read the signs of the times. These mysterious signs are purported to contain the explanation of the world as they unfold, allowing those who are attentive to them to catch a glimpse of the future of the Church and of our societies. On a more prosaic level, we have chosen to observe the signs of the past, which can also shed light on the present gloom.

We belong to a generation that read Jean Madiran's *L'hérésie du XXe siècle* (The Heresy of the 20th Century). We have observed the global spread of Marxism-Leninism and its dialectics even to the heart of Catholic movements and associations. Under the pretense of justice, this social revolution accompanied the guerrilla wars of the Third World as well as the struggles against colonialism organized by the USSR or Mao's China.

We had accepted the idea that liberation theology in Latin America was one of the driving forces behind these bloody conflicts. The best historians described this in detail. But the fall of the Soviet Union did not slow down this tragic process, insofar as the same revolution has continued to this day under different names.

This is a fact that compels us to consider that liberation theology was not merely an expression of class struggle but that it was also something else. It is, in reality, a sort of fulfillment of modernism, which has been rampant in the Catholic Church for a very long time. Liberation theology masqueraded in Argentina as the "theology of the people." It shed its Bolshevik garb and donned the trappings of modernism through the thinking Lamennais and Yves Congar, Maurice Blondel, Karl Rahner, and Jean-Luc Marion. One of the people behind this "extraordinary transformation" was Fr. Juan Carlos Scannone, an Argentinean Jesuit and one of Jorge Bergoglio's professors during his novitiate. Scannone once said that it is "the *theology of the people* that inspires the actions of Pope Francis." This is surprising, because as a rule, an elected pope abides by Catholic theology, regardless of his preferred school of thought.

The only French-language book on the subject is Juan Carlos Scannone's *La théologie du people: racines théologiques du pape François*, published by the Jesuits of Belgium (it was issued in English in 2021 under the title *Theology of the People: The Pastoral and Theological Roots of Pope Francis*). This work has not been subjected to any serious criticism. The reader therefore has no way of forming an objective opinion about it.

This allegedly Latin American theology has a European and conciliar pedigree. All the Latin American theorists of liberation theology and theology of the people attended universities in France, Germany, and Belgium, not to mention the Jesuit University in Madrid. This multifaceted version of modernism might never have moved beyond the stage of being an intellectual and theological exercise. But with Father Arrupe, the general of the Society of Jesus, it ceased to be a mere subject of dissertation, instead becoming the ideological mask for radical change in the Catholic Church. It was Arrupe who appointed the youngest provincial in the history of the Society to head the powerful province of Argentina: Fr. Jorge Bergoglio.

From 1943 to 1955 and from 1972 to 1974, General Juan Domingo Perón ruled over Argentina. His impact on the course of the events under our consideration has been confined to anecdotes provided by cursory research. The truth, however, is altogether different.

Many other issues have failed to attract the attention of commentators, and yet . . .

In his first apostolic exhortation, *Evangelii Gaudium*, Pope Francis laid out four principles that have shaped all his speeches since his election. Where do these four principles, which are presented as the essential principles for reform of society and of the Church, actually come from?

The answer appears to have slipped even Pope Francis's mind.

No one seems to have been able to find the origin of these four principles in Catholic literature or theology. But they actually do have a source that is never quoted.

One of the young Jesuit Bergoglio's theology professors, Lucio Gera, was a revolutionary priest who was among the most active in the Movement of Priests for the Third World. He was buried in the cathedral of Buenos Aires by order of Cardinal Bergoglio. Why?

Similarly, the story of the famous sickle and hammer sculpture associated with the crucifix that Pope Francis received as a gift in Bolivia has not been properly investigated.

As a rule, those who report on these subjects fail to carry out proper research. And many who claim to have studied the matter leave out anything that would undermine their hagiographic approach.

This book does not presume to answer every possible question. Its documentary, evidence-based method simply aims to point out a few interesting clues to understanding how the youngest provincial in the history of the Jesuits became "Francis the First."

Hopefully, they will be useful in helping to understand the crisis that the Church is going through. Behind the most extraordinary propaganda apparatus ever seen in the Vatican, organizing the constant praise of Francis the First, a radical, systematic, and organized "law of silence" is in force.

It has been operating in Argentina since the 1970s. Its purpose is to conceal the true origins of an unprecedented ascent to power and to circulate far-fetched anecdotes or cleverly crafted deceptions.

Francis the First is someone who disturbs, disrupts, and initiates processes. The hagiography he has inspired exceeds anything seen or heard in the past. Even Pope John Paul II, at the height of his popularity, never received such acclaim. One of the most recent books to have contradicted this chorus of praise is *The Dictator Pope*. It lifts a corner of the veil on the true Francis, yet it does not fundamentally change the way the whole world perceives the Francis phenomenon. The new Dicastery for Communication and the 2018 Wim Wenders film on Francis commissioned by the pope himself have reinforced this stranglehold on the media.

The endless list of laudatory adjectives praising his unfailing popularity is echoed by networks whose universal reach is unparalleled in history. For example, Zenit.org, issued in ten languages, publishes four to six photos of the pope every day. Nunciatures all over the world now subscribe to the Jesuit magazine *Civiltá Cattolica*. This publication, founded in 1850, has become the semi-official newspaper of the Vatican, under the leadership of Father Spadaro, a close friend of the pontiff. It now has a French and even a Korean edition.

The main books that have appeared, including the one published in Italy in 2020, *Jorge Mario Bergoglio, Una biografia intellettuale - Dialettica e mistica*, share similar structures, being based on an interview with the pope. The latter leads the writer in a given direction, and the writer thus limits himself to writing only along those lines. It is difficult to imagine the fate of anyone who would dare to make even a minor objection. The same is true of the first book to be published on "Francisco" in Latin America, which, by the way, was presented as the work of the bishop of Rome, *Conversaciones con Hernán Reyes Alcaide*.

Typical of this kind of work is French author Dominique Wolton's *Politique et société* (*The Path to Change: Thoughts on Politics and Society*). The author was granted twelve interviews with the pope, each lasting two hours. An article by Caroline Pigozzi, a famous Vatican expert who writes for *Paris-Match*, was headlined by a statement by Dominique Wolton himself: "The Pope's unrestricted confession." Who would dare argue with the pope's confession?

Most books draw heavily on *The Great Reformer* by Austen Ivereigh, one of Pope Francis's champions who is also his authoritative biographer. Oddly enough, the French title of the translation was shortened to *Le Réformateur*, "The Reformer," even though the English author gives the strong impression that Pope Francis will surpass Luther. From the very first page of the English edition, the reader is told what to expect: "Well written, full of information; this is the best biography of Pope Francis to date."

In our eyes, the only reliable work to date is *The Political Pope* by George Neumayr, published in 2017. It is full of significant anecdotes, yet it fails to provide the key that connects Father Arrupe to Francis. It also ignores General Perón, Lucio Gera, and Juan Carlos Scannone. The liberal and progressive left do not suffice to account for what really was afoot.

The greatest difficulty has been to gather meaningful documentation among an abundance of sources that never run dry, covering fifty-five years. We have searched for the events and texts related to the formidable current that brought the provincial Bergoglio to the chair of Peter. His election owes nothing to chance.

We have deliberately made little use of studies that concentrated only on the Marxization of the Latin American Church. Great historians such as Ricardo de la Cierva focused on these approaches, whereas from our point of view, this Marxization is only one of the temporary components of a far older and more profound destabilization and transformation of the Catholic Church. The theory of history and Marxist dialectics have never been decisive elements in the birthing of the new Church. They were destabilizing factors. It must be said, to be precise, that philosophical and theological modernism as well as liberation theology stem from the same ancient and modern sources, from Heraclitus to Teilhard de Chardin, by way of Hegel and Maurice Blondel.

I wrote this essay so that others may continue on the path of this research on Francis's accession to the throne of Saint Peter, which is widely acknowledged to be absolutely unique in over two thousand years of Christianity. The Argentines should be the first to embark on this task.

Writing about the Society of Jesus and its "refounder," Fr. Pedro Arrupe, was also a daunting task. But this challenge proved even more hazardous insofar as the aim of this work was to understand the thoughts and actions of the first Jesuit pope in the history of the Church. The height of the challenge was reached when the case for the beatification of the general of the Jesuits—whom we consider to be the main inspirer of the great reform of the Church—was opened in Rome.

According to one of his official biographers, Fr. Gianni La Bella, SJ, Father Arrupe "was one of the greatest actors of post-conciliar Catholicism." We have certainly taken a great risk in reading this statement in its most obvious sense.

We are well aware of the immense turmoil and confusion that reign in the Catholic Church because of Francis: his secret agreement with the government of Communist China is only one of its features.

The election of Francis the First is the result of a full-scale electoral campaign aimed at seizing the power of the keys of Saint Peter: it included the setting up of an ideological corpus, a manifold communication system, agents in crucial positions, and unlimited funding. His election has made it possible to discover a hidden past and to understand what is happening today before our eyes. We were perhaps too quick to forget that all the cardinals who elected him could not have ignored the fact that he had been the candidate of the "Sankt-Gallen Mafia" in 2005, against Cardinal Ratzinger.

———

The heresiarchs of old imposed themselves thanks to the support of princes who saw in them the means to consolidate their own power.

Henry VIII subjugated the Church in order to satisfy his own compulsions. Luther succeeded in finding those German princes who similarly were seeking both to get their hands on the wealth of the Church and to satisfy their passions. Without complicit princes, there would have been no major spread of heresy.

Today, the battlefront has been reversed on the basis of a very different objective. Luther proclaimed: "*Los von Rom*," which can be translated as "Anything rather than Rome." Those who contributed to the establishment of Francis do not want a new Church in competition with the Church of Rome. They want a new mode of being for the Church of Rome herself.

The reasoned timeline presented in this book constitutes the incomplete history of what happened to the largest Catholic continent in the world, Latin America. Every event, every actor, every piece of writing, and every word wove the meshes of a net that has finally ensnared the Catholic Church in its entirety, leading to an agony that has been all too protracted.

Jorge Mario Bergoglio is a fascinating character. Once stripped of his gangue of praise and his spectacular humility, we see him as the central character of an adventure that appears to be carrying him forward, while in truth, he is its main actor. His appetite for power, his suspicious nature, and his art of communication place him on a par with the greatest leaders who have set out to conquer the world. Both an adulator of the people and a tyrannical ruler, he has taken over the oldest institution in the world, the Catholic Church, to the point of making some of the faithful wonder about the continuance of the divine assistance that accompanied the Church for two millennia.

In order to make our case, we have been compelled to present numerous texts because this story is generally unknown.

We must confess that Francis's accession to power was a blessing for us because, without him, we would never have known about the real, the only revolution that has been taking place in Latin America since the 1960s. We would never have known about the true situation of the Catholic Church today.

Introduction

At the start of it all, the Vatican Council

It would be of great interest to explore the twists and turns of the theology, philosophy, and general lines of thought of those who promoted the election of Pope Francis. Such an endeavor would, in our opinion, be very useful to a universal history of the Catholic Church in the twentieth and twenty-first centuries. However, the main factor in the unprecedented disruption we are witnessing has been the remarkable organization that linked Europe to Latin American hotbeds for the development of the ideology of the Second Vatican Council. From the moment it was announced, the council has been an inexhaustible catalyst for all things modernist that have flourished since the 1930s. In Germany, France, Belgium, Spain, and Italy, where all the major Latin American figures of the conciliar revolution were educated, a communications network of unusual intensity was set up. The only examples that can convey any idea of such a mechanism are those related to the preparation of the French Revolution of 1789 and the Bolshevik Revolution of 1917. In his book *The Second Vatican Council —An Unwritten Story*, Prof. Roberto de Mattei observed: "For information about the numerous para-conciliar groups, it is indispensable to consult the research of Salvador Gómez y Catalina, *Grupos 'extra aulam' en el Concilio Vaticano y su influencia* (three books in nine volumes, for a total of 2,585 pages!)."[2]

---

[2] Mattei, *Vatican II, une histoire à écrire*, n. 79, p. 378.

1

The advent of this revolution—and its timeline offers irrefutable proof of this—owes nothing to ideological developments borrowed from Marxism-Leninism or from class struggle. What prevailed among the conscious part of the progressive bishops and the myriad of experts assisting them was a unanimous determination to change the Church. All the reforms they undertook had this sole purpose. Ultimately, liturgical reform was based only on the intent of breaking with the sacramental tradition of the Church.

The traditional Offertory included this prayer: "O God, Who in creating man didst exalt his nature very wonderfully and yet more wonderfully didst establish it anew." It offers an admirable proclamation of the divine origin of our dignity and of its restoration! The intensity of these words expressing the *Gesta Dei* during the Holy Sacrifice carries an incredible force that surpasses all discourse. It was purely and simply suppressed in the "new Mass," at a time when we are awash with speeches on man-centered human dignity from the United Nations.

The source of this great upheaval is to be found especially in *Gaudium et Spes*. Drafted by experts in the field of revolution, it contained the very essence of modernist ideology, which would go on to be endlessly explored. It was later complemented by the encyclicals *Populorum Progressio*, *Ecclesiam Suam*, and *Evangelii Nuntiandi*, among others.

The initial work that nourished the thinking of the Council Fathers was that of a French worker priest, Paul Gauthier: *Christ, the Church and the Poor*. These words were copied and transformed because all revolutions need a slogan that strikes the imagination.

From Marx to Hélder Câmara

In 1848, Marx and Engels made their famous appeal at the end of their manifesto: "Proletarians of the world, unite."

The Second Vatican Council made an appeal that was every bit as powerful and decisive as that of *Das Kapital*. It had been so well prepared, so methodically organized, and spread by such a powerful network of strong supporters within the council and beyond that it continues to roam the world today. It has been echoed countless times by all the actors who appear in this book, including Francis in his *Letter to Priests* of August 4, 2019. It was a cry voiced by Leonardo Boff and updated by him in 1995 in *Ecology and Poverty: Cry of the Earth, Cry of the Poor*.

At the Vatican Council, The Church of the Poor, a group led by the Brazilian bishop Dom Hélder Câmara and the Chilean bishop Manuel Larraín, teamed up with the famous Bologna Working Group. They were all driven by the desire to transform the institutional Church, presented as arrogant and over-rich.

Fr. Paul Gauthier was a member of this group. It was he who circulated a firebrand pamphlet to all the Council Fathers calling for a definitive reform of the Church.

This Frenchman, who had been "exiled" to the Holy Land and was a worker-priest in Palestine, was considered by Leonardo Boff to be the father of liberation theology. In *L'Église et la subversion* (The Church and Subversion),[3] Guillaume Maury described this character's subversive activities in detail, but he was not aware of Gauthier's links with the Bologna Group. Paul Gauthier would later abandon the priesthood and marry.

The first meeting of the Working Group took place at the Belgian College on October 26, 1962, in the presence of the bishop of Tournai, Charles-Marie Himmer. Twelve bishops, including Cardinal Gerlier and Cardinal Lercaro, archbishop of Bologna, there resolved to intervene in the council aula. It was Lercaro who, on December 6, 1962, lit the fuse that would never be extinguished.

> What did the cardinal say? That the mystery of Christ in the Church is more than ever "the mystery of Christ in the poor." Following the words of John XXIII, the Church is "the Church of all men, but above all the Church of the poor." The cardinal expressed surprise at the complete absence of this aspect from the schemas of the Council, although it was "the essential and

---

3   Maury, *L'Église et la subversion, le CCFD*, pp. 28–29.

primary element of the mystery of Christ, who lived it out himself throughout his earthly life." For this reason, he urged that
the Council should establish "as the very center and soul of its
doctrinal and legislative work the mystery of Christ in the poor
and the evangelization of the poor."[4]

Father Rouquette, SJ, would later underscore: "This address by the
Cardinal of Bologna was the boldest and most reforming of all those
heard during the first session; perhaps it will open up a new path."[5]

Poor people of all countries, unite with the Church that liberates!

From that moment onwards, the "poor" lost their "evangelical" status
and became the "ideological poor," the equivalent of the proletariat.
On the poor, a new Church, faithful at last to its founder, could be
built. A female Argentinian theologian, a friend of the pope, went so
far as to speak of "recategorization."

In September 1964, Cardinal Lercaro developed this new conception of the Church together with eleven bishops. Their agenda would
receive its first concrete expression with the Pact of the Catacombs,
which some forty bishops signed on November 16, 1965.

The Church of Latin America had become the Church of the poor;
from then on, not a single meeting or encounter would fail to mention this call to battle. On May 25, 2019, the cardinal of Buenos Aires,
Archbishop Mario Aurelio Poli, forcefully reiterated the "preferential option for the poor" by quoting Bishop Enrique Angelelli, who
preached under the flag of the "Montoneros," a Peronist Argentine
political-military organization of the 1970s.

In this context, the agents fighting the "structures of sin" are the
religious institutes that are engaged in social ministry or in the struggle
for social justice. Among these, the Jesuits were by far the most active
and best organized. They asserted themselves by piloting political and

---

4   Sauvage, CIRTP, Acte 10, 4 June 2013.
5   *Etudes*, February 1963.

social choices, thereby becoming a "parallel temporal magisterium." In the name of faith and of the poor, they supplanted "the laity." Being a spiritual power—because of their religious status—they governed through proxy associations and groups of influence. They shaped the decisions of the temporal powers by designating the enemy of the poor.

This is visible today in the Vatican's policy regarding immigration, the death penalty, ecology, or "coexistence." The pope told a Mexican television station on May 28, 2019, that Trump's wall between the United States and Mexico is like the Berlin Wall. He also slammed the walls around Ceuta and Melilla but never mentioned the one built by Israel in Palestine. In Romania, he canonized martyred bishops without ever using the word *communism*. Was he trying not to offend the Chinese communists?

Not so long ago, religion was dismissed as a private matter; nowadays, it associates with globalist powers and has its throne in the political arena. Ours is a time of confusion, where totalitarian powers refuse to distinguish between the temporal and the spiritual. The combination of the sickle and hammer with the crucifix, or the politicization of the "Way of the Cross of Solentiname" by the revolutionary poet Ernesto Cardenal in Nicaragua, are just a few examples of this major disruption.

However, this overview would be out of step with reality if we were to ignore the ecological turn taken by the pontificate. Two years after the election of Francis, the Church entered into the "ecological" era. Leonardo Boff revealed in an interview given on March 17, 2015, that Pope Francis had asked him for his writings to help prepare *Laudato si'*; Boff sent him two sets of documents. He specified that as early as the 1980s, he had launched the idea that the earth was the "*Great Poor*" and that he had been the first to speak of the "ecotheology" of liberation.

The Amazonian Indians are the latest "poor" in the process that began at the council. It is a process that cannot be measured in ordinary electoral time frames. This is a long-term project.

Vatican expert Sandro Magister was the first, on December 9, 2015, before the Amazon synod was even announced, to predict that after the issue of remarried divorcees at the family synods, that of marriage for priests would be brought to the fore. He made the connection with Amazonia, where some are calling for this in the name of promoting an indigenous clergy.

All this is forcing us to consider the full meaning of Leonardo Boff's pronouncement about Francis: *"He has made liberation theology the good of the Church and has caused it to spread."*[6]

CHAPTER 1

The Second Vatican Council and Its Repercussions in Latin America

No one can truly grasp the work and thinking of Pope Francis without a brief mention, at least, of the ecclesial context in which he has functioned since the close of the Second Vatican Council. The major upheavals that took place in Latin America as a result of recommendations made by leading figures of the council have been decisive in this regard. We have moved from one religion to another without having, even today, genuinely explored the ways and means of this process. Some of the effects are well-known, but the principle has never been affirmed as such. We feel it is essential to give a synthetic analysis of the impact of the council in Latin America, and especially in Argentina.

The council marked the beginning of a major crisis in the Latin American continent, and it remains difficult today to imagine what its final outcome will be.

Literature on this subject is overabundant and includes thousands of articles and books. We will summarize it here with a few quick expressions and recurring judgments that demonstrate the existence of an unfailing consensus. Those who failed to subscribe to the general enthusiasm in Latin America, France, and Europe were totally sidelined and played only a minor role in the course of events.

In his apostolic letter *Novo Millennio Ineunte*, Pope John Paul II called the council "the great grace bestowed on the Church in the twentieth century": "there we find a sure compass by which to take our bearings in the century now beginning."

Latin American analysts think exactly that—but they do not have the same compass.

Ricardo Miguel Mauti, an Argentine, wrote in *Vatican Council II: event and theology*:

> The names of Chenu, Congar and de Lubac are *characteristic* of the dramatic tension that existed in the various paths of Catholic theology from the 1930s onward. They were all *involved* in the *groups* in favor of ecclesial renewal that were preparing Vatican II, but at the time they were *under suspicion* and had to face being misunderstood, slandered and silenced. The *summons* of Pope John XXIII turned them into experts, which not only led to their personal *rehabilitation* but also to the acknowledgement of the *Catholic* character of their theology. Their *Diaries* are a living testimony of their *passion* and love for the Church; with assertive realism, they proved that the Council was a true *springtime of the Spirit*, who at every moment assisted the assembly of the Fathers and the theologians' work. But they also show the *historical* character of the faith, revealing the *human dimension* of the assembly, which is by no means negligible, through which the Spirit fulfills his work of renewal.[7]

The same author quoted the Argentinian priest and "expert" Jorge Mejía as telling the same Father Congar: "The position of many [bishops] is that the Holy Father prepared the Council, that the texts are the best that could be hoped for, and that we should say: Amen. Many believe in a simplistic ecclesiology: the Pope has studied things and teaches what needs to be said; all we have to do is follow. For them the Council has no precise objective."

But was this council truly one of blind trust?

---

[7]   Mauti, "El Concilio Vaticano II: acontecimiento y teología"; italics in the original text.

Virginia Raquel Azcuy—also from Argentina, and in our opinion one of the best specialists on our theme—similarly quoted
Father Congar in an article written in 2013 for the *Revista Teología*: "*La
recepción del Concilio Vaticano II en el Pueblo de Dios*" (The Reception
of the Second Vatican Council in the People of God). She there refers
to an article published by Congar in 1972 in *Concilium*: "Reception
as an Ecclesiological Reality," of which he was to publish a more complete version in the *Revue des Sciences Philosophiques et Théologiques*
soon afterward: "According to Congar reception involves something
very different from what the scholastics understood as obedience . . . ;
reception implies a distinctive contribution of consent and of incidental judgment, thus expressing the life of a body that brings its original
spiritual resources into play."

Angel Anton, also quoted by Virginia Azcuy, saw the council as
"an indirect stimulus for creating a new consciousness and praxis of
reception, starting with the re-reception of previous councils." Anton
propounded an ecclesiological notion of reception which would
include both "the deposit of faith and also the sense of faith of the
entire body of the faithful."

Virginia Azcuy provides a similar assessment of Cardinal Walter
Kasper's opinion: "Kasper's orientation could be summarized as follows: the reception of Vatican II requires consent to its true content—
letter and spirit—so that it can be put into practice in the Church;
reception is also an interpretation that calls us to learning in order to
understand, to conversion in order to put into practice, and to witness
in order to proclaim."

Similarly, the Venezuelan Bishops' Conference stated in 2008: "It
should be made clear that the Council was the inspiring and enlight-
ening principle of the Medellín Conference." In the eyes of the Latin
American bishops, all things need to be interpreted in the light of the
Second Vatican Council in order to bring about a profound renewal,
and this necessarily involves a greater presence to the world and also
a conversation with the world in the light of the Gospel, the council,
and the papal magisterium. In Latin America, the Church scrutinizes
and interprets *the signs of the times*.

The council prompted widespread enthusiasm that continues to this day. In Peru, José Manuel Rodriguez wrote in 2013, "In our opinion, the Second Vatican Council brought forward three main lines of action that have been adopted in a particularly forceful way in Latin America: *aggiornamento*, the promotion of the laity and dialogue with people of good will, which are considered necessary for the proclamation of the Good News."

The impulse given by the council was classified by Leonardo Boff, from Brazil, in several categories. These are summarized below:

"First of all, all the CELAM Conferences, from Medellín (1968) to Aparecida (2007), adopted the preferential option for the poor. This option has become the trademark of the Latin American Church and of Liberation Theology."

It is the council that gave concrete expression to the Church as the People of God. "Vatican II placed this category ahead of that of the Hierarchy. For the Latin American Church, 'People of God' is not a metaphor."

The council opened itself to human rights—that is, the right to life (*which has nothing to do with pro-life*), to work, to health, and to education.

The council welcomed ecumenism among the Christian churches. "All the Churches together committed themselves to the liberation of the oppressed. It is an ecumenism based on the mission."

Lastly, it established "dialogue with the other religions, in which it recognized the presence of the Spirit who arrived before the missionaries; they are to be respected with their particular values."

It is safe to say that the reception of the council was a triumph in all the Latin American nations. All anticipated that it would bring about the realization of their deepest aspirations, in accordance with their personal choices regarding mission, ecclesiology, and/or politics.

There lies the source. Alongside the vast majority of bishops, clerics, and lay people who were willing to adhere to everything in a spirit of fidelity to the Church, other bishops, clerics, and lay people had taken hold of the council before it had even begun.

The council: a catalyst for modernism and progressivism

The council was not the cause of the great upheaval in the Church. It simply enabled the organization and expansion of all the heterodox currents with which the Church was already teeming. The history of Catholicism in Europe and South America abundantly proves this. The initial moments of the council, with their rejection of the schemas prepared under the authority of the Curia, together with the unprecedented act of Cardinal Alfrink cutting off Cardinal Ottaviani's microphone while the latter was defending the use of Latin in the liturgy, announced *urbi et orbi* that the source of power in the Church was no longer where it had been until then.

Admittedly, the older power would still exist, but it would dwindle, get blocked, and pass into other hands. The reform of the Curia by Pope Francis is but the most recent development of those memorable days at the beginning of the council.

The Latin American Church has been nourished by European modernism and progressivism. All of its leaders studied in the most revolutionary "Catholic" faculties in Europe: Paris, Lyon, Louvain, Frankfurt, Madrid, Tübingen, and so on.

Thus, the Colombian priest Camillo Torres, who died leading the guerrilla in his country, had studied in Louvain under Canon François Houtart, who would later present himself on the internet as a "*Marxist Canon.*" This was the same priest who taught the Cubans and then communist Vietnam how to manipulate the Catholic religion in order to serve the worldwide Marxist revolution.

That story has yet to be told.

From the moment Pope John XXIII announced his decision to convene the council, three figures who would become the initial and most important agitators of the revolution in the Latin American Church made their appearance: Hélder Câmara, Ivan Illich, and the aforementioned François Houtart.

The name of Dom Hélder Câmara is widely known. On May 3, 2015, Archbishop Saburido of Olinda-Recife proclaimed the opening of the diocesan phase of investigation of his heroic virtues. The decisive step toward his beatification was recently made public.

At this point, it seems important to recall that Dom Hélder Câmara violently opposed Pope Paul VI on *Humanae Vitae* and that he was in favor of a second religious marriage following a divorce.

After having been seduced in his youth by Nazism, he became an active agent of the radical transformation of the Catholic Church. On October 14, 1952, Hélder Câmara was appointed auxiliary bishop of Rio de Janeiro. He remained in that position until 1964.

In 1952, he was also behind the creation of the National Conference of Brazilian Bishops (CNBB), of which he would remain secretary for twelve years, until 1964. In 1955, he also participated in the creation of the General Conference of Latin American Bishops (later known as CELAM) under the presidency of a Chilean, Bishop Larraín, and was the representative of the Brazilian episcopate at CELAM until 1992.

Pope John XXIII announced the opening of an ecumenical council on January 25, 1959.

At that time, Dom Hélder Câmara was already in touch with Ivan Illich and François Houtart, who had worked together from 1958 to 1962 to organize and produce a forty-three-volume study on the history and sociology of Catholicism in Latin America. This monumental opus was to serve as a work of reference for all future liberation theology studies and for all subsequent research. It truly became the matrix for all later developments.

François Houtart once admitted that Dom Hélder Câmara was not an intellectual but a remarkable maneuverer with a considerable degree of arrogance and seduction. It was his idea to write a summary of the forty volumes of the history of Catholicism in Latin America. It was immediately implemented, and the summary was distributed to all the bishops at the council in 1963.

An abridged version of the book by the French priest Paul Gauthier, *Christ, the Church and the Poor*, which is a model for all liberation theology, was also distributed at the council.

1961

The strategy of intervention at the council had made it necessary to hold a meeting between the main agents who would transform the Assembly of Bishops into a "destruction and reconstruction" machine. It took place in Rio de Janeiro, with the presence of Ivan Illich, François Houtart, Father Poblete, SJ, Bishop Larraín, and Dom Hélder Câmara.

Illich became Cardinal Suenens's theologian at the council, and Houtart was one of the main redactors of *Gaudium et Spes*.

Illich and Houtart, joined by Lucio Gera from Argentina and Alex Morelli, OP, would later publish *Del subdesarrollo a la liberación* (From Underdevelopment to Liberation) in Madrid in 1974 under the banner of the Catholic Popular Propaganda association.

Ivan Illich's and François Houtart's writings foreshadowed all present-day demands. Illich would abandon the priesthood, and Houtart's last years were marred by an accusation of child abuse.

1964

In March, at the request of Ivan Illich, a meeting was held in Petropolis, Brazil, about fifty kilometers from Rio de Janeiro. Gustavo Gutiérrez, Juan Luis Segundo, Lucio Gera, and Enrique Dussel, among others, took part in this meeting. It was at this point that the theology of liberation began to flood the Latin American continent. The Second Vatican Council was in full swing.

According to the historian Enrique Dussel, Segundo spoke about "the theological problems in Latin America"; Gera addressed the "sapiential and not only rational character of '*what should be done*' from the point of view of theology" and the need for theologians to be committed to the aspirations of the people; Gutiérrez analyzed the function of theology in connection with the majority masses, the intellectual elites, and the conservative oligarchy.

According to Dussel, this was a foundational meeting. Pope Francis's theology professor, Juan Carlos Scannone, agreed: "That is where it all began."

From that point, the speakers split up the workload. Segundo Galilea and Luis Maldonado stopped over in Havana from July 14 to 16, 1965. Juan Luis Segundo and Casiano Floristan were in Bogotá from July 9 to 14 of the same year. Ivan Illich went to Cuernavaca in Mexico, where he was soon joined by Segundo Galilea, from July 4 to August 14.

Similar meetings mushroomed throughout the continent for years and led to the creation of training, distribution, and consultation networks that still exist today under different names.

Their mission was and is straightforward: to revolutionize society and the Church.

1965

On November 16, on the sidelines of the council and less than a month before its conclusion, the Pact of the Catacombs was signed under the impetus of Dom Hélder Câmara (see the full text at the end of this book): it constitutes a full-scale catalogue of the "duties" of the Church's hierarchy toward the poor. It not only propounded a new lifestyle for the hierarchy but above all a new way of governing the Church. This will be discussed in more detail in the course of this work. Five hundred bishops are said to have signed it over the years.

1967

This was the year in which Dom Hélder Câmara launched a new appeal, the Message of the Bishops of the Third World, a rallying call to work for the Revolution in the Church and in society. The appeal called on the French Revolution of 1789 as a model for a beneficial revolution. It was signed by seventeen bishops.

The declaration reached Argentina in French. It was translated into Spanish locally and led to the creation of the most important movement of revolutionary priests on the continent, the Movimiento de Sacerdotes para el Tercer Mundo (MSTM, Movement of Priests for the Third World). The MSTM spread everywhere under different names and through numerous meetings, books, and pamphlets, so much so that in 1968, it was the MSTM and its affiliated bishops that controlled the CELAM Assembly in Medellin. Lucio Gera became a member in 1968. As will be shown later, the movement was to become the spearhead of the revolution of the clergy in Argentina and throughout the continent.

1968

In Chimbote, Peru, a month before the great assembly of CELAM with Pope Paul VI, a meeting of subversive priests was organized under the auspices the priestly association ONIS (National Office for Social Information) led by Father Garatea. Sixty percent of the clergy present were Jesuits and foreign priests. The keynote presenter of ONIS was Gustavo Gutiérrez, a Peruvian priest who was not yet a Dominican (this was the same Gutiérrez who had participated in the 1964 meeting organized by Ivan Illich). During his conference, he shifted "from the language of development to that of liberation," which would crystallize all the revolutions on the continent.

He later recounted how he was "asked to speak at a national meeting of pastoral workers held in Chimbote in July 1968 on a topic that was then in vogue, the theology of development." "In preparing the conference, I came to the conclusion that rather than development theology, we should speak of liberation theology, that is, theology of salvation in Christ with all its historical consequences for today," he explained.

Gutiérrez became the darling of the ensuing CELAM Assembly in 1968 and was also official advisor to the Peruvian bishops. The publication of his book, *Teología de la Liberación*, in 1971, would establish him as the father of liberation theology.

1970

In a meeting in Buga, CELAM and the Departments of Education and University Pastoral Care of Colombia drew up a plan for the reform of the continent's universities in order to align them with the conciliar orientations. The Church, according to this plan, should not be absent from the great movement that was rocking the Latin American countries, and she needed to assert a strong spirit of integral and Christian humanism. The entire world of higher education switched over to progressivism, often choosing its most radical revolutionary form. The action of the Hispanic-American Student Council in Argentina tried in vain to alter the course of this tidal wave. Chile emerged as a pioneer of this kind of student revolution.

1976

In August, at the Foyer of the Holy Cross in Riobamba, Ecuador, under the leadership of Bishop Leonidas Proaño, some fifty people—bishops, clerics, and lay people—gathered to lay the foundations of a protest movement against authoritarian governments.

The Ecuadorian police had been following the affair since its inception and well knew the participants, all of whom were notorious activists. They stepped in and imprisoned them all; they were released the next day.

Among the "prisoners" were two archbishops and fifteen bishops, including a Venezuelan, three Americans, three Chileans, two Brazilians, three Mexicans, a Spaniard and a Paraguayan, and Bishop Sastre from Argentina.

Joseph Comblin, Dom Hélder Câmara's Belgian theologian, was among the priests.

As to the lay faithful, the presence of Adolfo Pérez Esquivel, an agitator who would go on to win the Nobel Peace Prize in 1980 after having developed the "Justice and Peace Service" throughout the continent, deserves a special mention. He was elected Man of the Day in the French communist daily *L'Humanité* on March 7, 2018.

On August 31, 1976, the Ecuadorian bishops signed the document known as the Evangelical Pact of Ecuador, or Riobamba Pact, under the leadership of the Pastoral Council of the Church of Ecuador. It condemned the minister behind this "imprisonment" and reaffirmed the bishops' commitment to the Ecuadorian people, demanding freedom of worship, religion, and assembly.

Meanwhile, Dom Hélder Câmara . . .

Dom Hélder Câmara left Rio de Janeiro in 1969, having been named archbishop of Olinda and Recife.

The following year was that of his famous European tour—especially in France, where since that day the progressive press has never ceased to sing his praises and weave crowns to his glory. Among his followers in France were Mgr. Riobé, bishop of Orleans, and José de Broucker, director of ICI (*Informations catholiques internationales*).

The entire official Catholic press offered its unwavering support to the Brazilian prelate for many years, from the now defunct *Informations Catholiques Internationales* to diocesan bulletins and the diocesan committees of the CCFD (Catholic Committees against hunger and for development). His works have been translated into French.

When Leonardo Boff published *La fe en la perifer\u00eda del mundo* (Faith in the periphery of the world) in 1985, he concluded his book with a poem to the Blessed Virgin: *Show Yourself to be a Liberating Mother* and the following poem by Dom Hélder Câmara to the Virgin of Liberation:

> Your thoughts were for all,
>> But you made a clear choice for the poor
> As later did your Son.
>> What is there in You, in Your words, in Your voice?
>
> In Your Magnificat You proclaim the overthrow of the mighty
>> and the exaltation of the lowly, the satisfying of the hungry,
> and the sending away of the rich.
>> What is it about you that no one dares call you subversive
> Or look at you with suspicion?[8]

Dom Hélder Câmara was awarded thirty-two honorary doctorates, from the Universities of Louvain, Paris, Chicago, Amsterdam, Uppsala, and many others. He received twenty-four prizes, including the Martin Luther King prize.

His country, Brazil, is undoubtedly the first country where liberation theology was openly set out.

---

[8]   Boff, *La Fe en la periferia del mundo,* p. 237.

Those who have experienced its manifestations in Brazil know that all the propaganda of the dioceses and organized movements was under the sign of the "Pôvo de Deus" (People of God). In 1975, the main theme of the first meeting of the base communities in Espirito Santo was: *A Church born of the people by the Holy Spirit*. Such a church claims to be directly guided by the Holy Spirit, without passing through the "juridical church," and the people in question are especially those who are poor and victims of cultural and economic oppression. At the time, it was customary to speak of a "new Church that is born in the midst of the people, mainly through the base communities."

In a Christian continent such as Latin America, the social, political, religious, and economic revolution cannot be carried out with the proletariat—a word unknown to the masses—but needs to be implemented in the name of the "people of God." The leaders of the Revolution are bishops, religious, and committed laymen. Since the higher clergy is assumed to be in league with the oppressors, the Church itself must also be changed.

Social, economic, and political life hardly changed with this Revolution. The Church, on the other hand, was caught up in a turmoil that continues to this day.

The word *people* became the rallying cry of all the oppressed. *Pueblo* or *Pôvo*: these are words everyone understands. In Argentina, the word *Pueblo* has a greater historical load than in other countries. For this "new" theology, all men, whomsoever they may be, are creatures, and therefore "sons of God," and they therefore belong to the People of God. This is what makes the birth of a more "universal" Church that is open to a new ecumenism possible.

For Cardinal Bergoglio, the preferential option for the poor did not consist in assisting them, which would be humiliating. It was about treating them as thinking people, with their own projects, including expressing their faith in their own way. They are considered to be active subjects, who are creative according to their own culture, and not objects of discussion, reflection, or pastoral action.

His friend, Archbishop Victor Manuel Fernandez, would later point out that "*the archbishop always insisted that parish priests be merciful and not defend rigid morality or strict ecclesial practices, and that they not complicate people's lives with complex norms authoritatively handed down from above."*

Cardinal Bergoglio embraced the positive appreciation of the popular faith, understood as a free and mysterious action of the Spirit. He talked with one and all and spent a lot of time conversing with non-Catholics. The aim of this pastoral principle was not to convert but to apply the principle of encounter. "Contribution to the common good implies being in conflict, suffering from it, resolving it and transforming it into a higher stage for a new process," he would say.

One category, however, is not included in these encounters: "*the self-referential*" with a "*closed identity*" who belong to the juridical Church—that is, the Church received from the apostles.

Pope Francis is opening up paths today that have already been opened. In 1976, the theme of the Brazilian base communities was: "*The Church, a people on its way*"; the following year, "*The Church, a liberated people*"; in 1981, "*The Church, an oppressed people organizing its own liberation.*"

Yves Congar, author of *True and False Reform in the Church*, and Karl Rahner (*Structural Change in the Church*) have long been committed to this change in the Church. The Dominicans of Salamanca have republished *Por una Iglesia Pobre y Servirodra* (For a Poor and Servant Church) by Father Congar in 2014.

And it goes on. A Congress of Liberation Theologians took place from October 7–11 in 2012, bringing together 733 participants, 533 of them from South America; they included fifteen Catholic bishops, all from Brazil but two—one Chilean and one Mexican—and three Anglican bishops. Among the bishops was Xavier de Maupeou, French bishop emeritus of Viana, Brazil. All these wonderful people were advised by Gustavo Gutiérrez; Leonardo Boff gave a brilliant conference on the theme: *Liberation theology and ecological concern*. Things have moved on from the revolutionary alphabetization of Paulo Freire in the 1960s to ecological alphabetization. But the objective is still the same. And it is the current program of Pope Francis.

The reception of the council in Argentina

Two main authors have best synthesized this liberationist impregnation: the above-mentioned Victor Manuel Fernandez and Rafael Luciani.

The former is an intimate of Cardinal Bergoglio, especially since the meeting of CELAM in Aparecida in 2007. He followed him to Rome before becoming one of the first archbishops to be appointed by the Argentinian pope in 2013. Archbishop Fernandez wrote the most controversial passages of *Amoris Laetitia*. Since then, he has received the office of rector of the Pontifical Catholic University of Argentina, which he left only to become archbishop of La Plata in June 2018 (and Prefect of the Congregation for the Doctrine of the Faith in 2023). He has summarized the pope's thought and action in several articles, as well as in a small book of interviews: *The Francis Project*. He had previously published an erotic book on the art of kissing.

The Venezuelan layman Rafael Luciani, a professor of theology at Boston College and other Jesuit universities, has written numerous articles and studies, including *Pope Francis and the theology of the people*. He is also a member of the theological commission of the Synod of Bishops.

Bishop Fernandez has provided an outstanding study in an article entitled "Pinceladas sobre el pensamiento pastoral del cardenal Bergoglio" (Sketches of Cardinal Bergoglio's pastoral thought) published in *La Revista Católica* in June 2013.

This article outlines the "perspectives" that were already held by Cardinal Bergoglio. Archbishop Fernandez explains: "The image he prefers when referring to the Church is that of People of God. The word 'people' is one he likes to use, because it values the people as a collective subject, which should be at the center of the Church's concerns, and the concerns of all authority."

Rafael Luciani, on the other hand, claims that Pope Francis wants to free the Church from Charlemagne's desire to create a "Christian cultural totalitarianism."[9]

---

9   In Luciani, *El papa Francisco y la teología del pueblo*.

Rafael Luciani, in order to show that we have entered a new era, quotes the profession of faith of the Jesuit Cardinal Robert Bellarmine in the face of the Protestants: "The one and true Church is the community of men brought together by the profession of the same Christian faith and conjoined in the communion of the same sacraments, under the government of the legitimate pastors and especially the one vicar of Christ on earth, the Roman pontiff."

It is this Church that the pope criticizes "as a *self-referential and self-centered* Church," of which Luciani specifies that it understood itself "on the basis of the visible elements that expressed its genetic and structural unity (profession of faith, sacraments, legitimate pastors)."

He continues:

> By reason of this it sustained its own credibility and proposed itself as the means by which believers could live out their faith (*medio de realización de la vida de la fe*). Grace was an unmerited and undeserved reality that could only be received by believing what the Church teaches, and by acting and the way it acts. Under this arrangement, believers are only objects, addressees who participate in ritual and go to church, but are not the agents of their own process of humanization nor do they have anything of their own to contribute as active subjects.
>
> For many Christians this is still the model for encountering God: through the mediation of an ecclesial culture, as opposed to the living out of a gospel life based on a relationship with the person of Jesus, and not on structures or disciplinary reforms. There needs to be a return to Christianity in which personal encounter with the Jesus of the Gospels is the axis around which Christian life evolves. Such an understanding would replace the prevailing clerical mindset with one that is more horizontal and familial. Francis understands that to attain this objective the Church must undergo a paradigm shift by which it ceases being self-referential, self-centered, or functionalized: by no longer reflecting its own light, but rather the light of Christ. And for this to happen, in order to decentralize, it must go to the peripheries, leave the center and the safe space and go to

those whom the world rejects, to those whom many consider should be discarded.

The better to convince the reader of the theological orientation of his remarks, Luciani then extensively quotes from the Jesuit Karl Rahner, who was also an expert at the council.

Rafael Luciani provides further insights collected in a long article he published in 2016 in the journal *Perspectiva Teológia* under the title "The theological-pastoral option of Pope Francis."[10]

"As a former professor of pastoral theology, the Pope realizes that precedence must be given to praxis, and then, as a second step, to theological reflection," he wrote:

> This vision—which is true to the impetus given by the Second Vatican Council—stems from a theology of historical redemption according to which the condition for salvation is found not in the fact of being Christian but in that of being human, because the Christian praxis is quintessentially that of *nearness* [italics in the text]. In it, "we rediscover the essence of Christianity, the way in which all men are saved, be they Christians or non-Christians". This is all about a mystical fraternity that requires our ethical connection with reality and contact with the people, "with the homes and lives of the people" so that theology, and hence the life of the Church, will not lead to "depersonalization" (cf. *Evangelii Gaudium*, 75).

According to Luciani, "this initial and necessary contact with reality is also set out in *Laudato si'* ": "Theological or philosophical reflections on the situation of humanity and of the world can come across as a repetitive and abstract message, if they are not presented anew following a confrontation with the present context, in what is new for the history of humanity."[11]

The said "present context" serves as an inspiration for Pope Francis "for his theological-pastoral option that is deeply influenced by some

---

[10]   Rafael Luciani, "The theological-pastoral option of Pope Francis," *Perspectiva Teológia*, pp. 81–115.

[11]   Luciani, pp. 81–115.

of the main categories of liberation theology and its methods. For the Pope, theological thought, pastoral praxis, the life of faith as well as the mission and the identity of the ecclesial institution cannot be conceived as isolated fragments: faith and socio-political life, academics and pastoral insertion, form pairs that cannot be considered separately without provoking a dysfunctional relationship between the thinking subject and the reality of the poor to whom they are morally obliged."[12]

It is difficult to understand these new categories which form the basis of the pope's thinking. The people, as such, embody Gospel values. This new paradigm is so integral to the discourse of the pope's followers that they actually copy each other. Thus, Luciani quotes Fernandez: "*We can observe in the poor a number of profoundly Christian values: a spontaneous attention to the other, an ability to devote time to others, to come to their aid without measuring time or sacrifice, while the well-to-do, who have a more organized life, hardly offer their time, attention, or self-denial to others in a spontaneous, obliging, and disinterested way.*"[13]

"The socio-economic reality of the greater part of humanity . . . , in Francis' eyes, is a social locus that decisively determines the theological 'what to do,' and is therefore a mode that allows one to understand reality as *theo*-logical, that is, as a primordial *locus theologicus*, a place where the presence of God is revealed and which expresses the historical-theological dimension of reality in the light of *Gaudium et Spes* (11)."[14]

We apologize for this convoluted language, but while it is abstruse for those are not familiar with liberation theology, it is illuminating for those who recognize the major inversion that it brings about.

For liberation theologies, the expression "*theological locus*" has a radically different meaning from the one received in the Catholic Church.

For the Catholic Church, theological *loci* are essentially the sources of the Catholic faith and the truths that flow from it, as listed by the

---

[12]   Luciani, pp. 81–115.
[13]   Luciani, pp. 81–115.
[14]   Luciani, p. 90.

Church's Magisterium: Tradition, the Magisterium, and Sacred Scripture, and the subsequent definitions. The *sensus fidelium*, the faith expressed by the faithful, cannot be anything other than the faith of the Church.

For liberation theology, by contrast, it is the place or *locus* where the word of God is elaborated. The poverty of the People of God makes them a new chosen people who receive directly from God the knowledge and interpretation of "the signs of the times," by way of the socio-economic reality. Salvation history thus becomes one with the history of humanity.

This *"historicization"* of theology was outlined and refuted by Cardinal Siri in *Gethsemane: The Origins and Rise of the Intellectual Revolution in the Church*.

If there is an initial unifying element among the various liberation theologies, this is the one. It has been used in various ways by all the tenors of the Latin American continent.

Their unchallenged leader is Jon Sobrino. In two books, *The True Church and the Poor* and *Jesus in Latin America,* he developed a new theology that would earn him a severe rebuke from Cardinal Ratzinger. An irate Sobrino fumed: "Ratzinger doesn't understand a thing," and appealed to the superior general of the Jesuits for support.

It is interesting at this point to note that Jon Sobrino's defense was led by Victor Manuel Fernandez and then by Jorge Costadoat, a Jesuit who was later banned from teaching at the Pontifical University of Santiago, Chile, for having called for the abolition of *Humanae Vitae*.

Jorge Costadoat defended Jon Sobrino in these terms: "In the Church of the poor, in a certain way, we have a new knowledge of Christ. This Church practices a following (*seguimiento*) of Christ from which it draws a deeper knowledge of Christ himself, a knowledge which in the end, has a decisive value. Praxis, in liberation theology, takes precedence over orthodoxy. . . . Praxis is the principle and the end. . . . Thence derives the full force of the precedence attributed by liberation theology to orthopraxis over orthodoxy."

This peculiar theologian wrote a study in 2015 entitled *¿Hacia un nuevo concepto de revelación? La historia como "lugar teológico" en la*

Teología de la liberación (Towards a new concept of revelation? History as a "theological locus" in liberation theology).

François Houtart offered the same analysis in 2006 in *L'état actuel de la théologie de la libération en Amérique Latine* (The present state of liberation theology in Latin America):

> In theology, this is a reversal of the logic of the usual approach. Traditionally, theology is deductive, that is to say, it starts from the divine revelation contained in the sacred texts, and then draws all the logical and practical implications at the level of reality. On the contrary, liberation theology follows an inductive approach, which leads it to construct a specifically religious thought starting from reality and social practice. Such an intellectual journey inevitably introduces an element of relativity into the theological discourse. It does not reduce the latter to the epistemological status of the human sciences, but is constructed using the latter as a starting point, thus implying that the quest for religious meaning can change its orientation depending on varying situations and the way in which they are analyzed. The discourse is therefore no longer dogmatic, but proceeds from an empirical necessity.

In the same article, the Marxist Canon from Belgium does not bother with subtleties: "Liberation theology takes as its starting point the situation of the oppressed. This is what we call a '*theological locus*', that is, the perspective from which the discourse about God is constructed."

All these changes that are taking place in the Catholic Church today appear to be borrowed from Hegelian Marxism. But what is modernism if not the "historicization" of all faith, all dogma, all morality and all discipline? For a long time, this ideological proximity led people to believe that it was all historical and dialectical materialism. Now that the Soviet Union has fallen, we can see that this is not the case.

It is not Marx and Lenin who have won, but the modernists.

CHAPTER 2

How the Church Moved from "Mystici Corporis" to Human Fraternity and the World Education Program

T he Mystical Body of Christ identifies with the Catholic Church, according to the 1943 encyclical *Mystici Corporis* by Pope Pius XII. With the council and its "The Church, People of God," this Catholic theology was left behind. It was Hans Küng who prepared Cardinal Suenens's speech on this theme. Father Congar, for his part, proposed the name "messianic people" for *Lumen Gentium* 9, with the result that the council retained both expressions.

This was truly a complete reversal, and the expression was described at the time as "dubious" by Fr. Joseph Ratzinger: "One had the impression that this 'people of God' was a sort of sociological group among others, seeking to enter into a relationship with other groups. The spiritual demands of the faith were thus projected onto a plane that did not suit it well."[15]

In 1985, the Jesuit magazine *Civiltá Cattolica* devoted an article to this subject under the title "From the theology of the 'Mystical Body' to the ecclesiology of the 'People of God.' " In the fifth part of this book, we will re-examine this important theme in the Bergoglian Church, using other sources.

---

[15]   Ratzinger, *Mon Concile Vatican II*, p. 225.

The council was intended to be pastoral, and the famous Schema XIII was its backbone. Joseph Ratzinger—who later became pope—was supportive of the great changes announced by the council: he indicated at the time that the intention was twofold; on the one hand, "to move away from scholasticism in order to open up to the Bible, and on the other hand, to adapt to the modern situation and its way of speaking."[16] One of the experts who drafted this schema was none other than François Houtart, the Marxist Canon of Louvain, who was later to teach "*Catholicism*" in Cuba and Hanoi (Vietnam) at the invitation of the Communist parties of both those countries.

In the new perspective lies a radical "change to the mission." Father Ratzinger went on to write, in his previously cited work: "To proclaim everywhere the message of salvation appeared . . . as the most pressing service of love of one's neighbor, because it did not merely address this or that distress to be relieved, but was concerned with the eternal destiny of others; it would determine an eternity of salvation or perdition."[17]

> Meanwhile, an idea was becoming prevalent that had previously been considered a rare exception: that God can save outside of the Church, even if ultimately not without it. The result was a new, optimistic understanding of pagan religions; it is difficult to find a biblical foundation for these ideas which are so dear to modern theology. . . . For if anything is foreign to Scripture, and can even be declared to be contrary to it, it is this present-day optimism about pagan religions which somehow conceives of them as factors of salvation. This, in fact, does not at all fit in with the biblical understanding of salvation.[18]

It was this reversal of perspective that opened the door to liberation theology.

According to Leonardo Boff, poverty, generosity, and suffering make the people an infallible interpreter of the divine will. All this is

---

16   Ratzinger, p. 219.
17   Ratzinger, p. 244.
18   Ratzinger, p. 245; emphasis added.

presented in his book *La Fe en la periferia del mundo: el caminar de la Iglesia con los oprimidos* (Faith in the Periphery of the World: The Church's Journey with the Oppressed).

According to Congar, as quoted by Boff on page 147, "Human 'nature' itself reveals an intrinsic catholicity, inasmuch as it is open to an unlimited and universal capacity for communion."

The natural goodness of the people to which is added the burden of the world's misery cannot leave God indifferent. That is why "the people," being poor, is not only the subject of *popular religiosity*, but is capable of reaching a higher degree of union with God in *popular piety*.

Of course, popular religiosity and popular piety based on the teaching of the Church, the ingrained grace received at Baptism, the reception of the sacraments, and pious and charitable works, do exist. But here, everything is different.

Fr. Juan Carlos Scannone has managed to drape this "theology" with all the theses of modernist theology and modern philosophy in order to pass it off as an elaborate, up-to-date way of thinking, quoting the likes of Lamennais and Maréchal, Blondel, Przywara, and Marion. However, his theology is in line with the praxis of the liberationists. Commenting on the 2007 CELAM meeting in Aparecida, Brazil, he wrote: "Aparecida took a step forward by speaking of 'popular spirituality and mysticism.' The expression 'popular mysticism' was introduced by another Argentinian Jesuit, Fr. Seibold. . . . It was ultimately included in the final draft, whose Editorial Committee was headed by Cardinal Bergoglio. In more recent days, the theme of 'Popular Mysticis' appeared twice in *Evangelii Gaudium*. This means that there is a true faith, a true practice of the theological virtues (even to the point of contemplative prayer in many cases in Latin America), whose collective subject is the People."

The Aparecida Document (n. 262) stated: "This is the way which will make it possible to draw on the rich potential of holiness and social justice encompassed in the people's mysticism" (emphasis added).

During a pilgrimage or a procession, according to Father Scannone, there is "a series of elements that lead us to live as the People of

God, as the Church, and produce an experience of communion that can reach a good contemplative and mystical level," no less.

But in this case, it is the community, the people, who save, not the institutional Church. It is the "experience of communion" on the occasion of a pilgrimage that imprints the theological virtues in the people as a whole, as well as a sense of social justice.

Rafael Luciani put it this way: "Christian praxis, both religious and socio-political, must be centered on fraternity in solidarity, social justice and the common good." So does the political-social praxis of pilgrimages take the place of divine grace!

This includes a transition from *sanctification* to *awareness-building*. The subject or the group abandons its fundamental reference points to enter into a new structure which can be described as follows: "We too are the Church," an expression that has blossomed in all corners of the world and in all languages. It is still the same word *Church*, but the content is different. The "*theological locus*" has changed.

This relationship between the new modernism and conscience was analyzed by Arnaud de Lassus in a very well documented study, *Un siècle de modernisme 1907-2007* (supplement to the *Action Familiale et Scolaire*, "A new century of modernism"). He quoted the Belgian cardinal Mercier: "The basis of modernism is this: that the religious soul draws from no source other than itself the object and the motive of its own faith." The theological, philosophical, and sociological discourse of modernism has but one objective: to make men believe, whoever they may be, that their conscience is the measure of all things, including divine things.

This experience of communion (*as first recognized by the council*) is proper to the people and constitutes an awareness-building experience which is in itself the source of union with God. "The people," by its very nature, is a vehicle for the supernatural. The personal consciousness of the subject, having become the supreme rule of all judgment, is in some way sublimated in the people. This transfer occurs thanks to a transmutation that is at once Teilhardian and prophetic.

Rafael Luciani took up this theme in a 2016 article titled "Francis and the Theology of the People: A New Way of 'Being Church.' "

The literature on the topic is overwhelming. One example is *Argentina, the Pope's **theological locus***, published on X.Pikaza's blog on the progressive web portal Religión Digital. For an understanding of what immigration means to the pope, we can turn to a dissertation by Morán Patiño: *The migrant as theological locus: a theological approach to the migrant as an expression of God's plan of salvation*. See also *Popular religiosity as a **theological locus** in the Apostolic Exhortation Evangelii Gaudium of His Holiness Francis* by Pablo Sudar, published by the Catholic University of Argentina. (All titles quoted are translated from the Spanish.)

The Pope and the Mystical People

Pope Francis himself has offered a very puzzling explanation of this peculiar novelty.

On November 13, 2015, he delivered a speech to the participants of the conference organized by the *Romano Guardini Stiftung*, the Romano Guardini Foundation.

The original German text has since been translated into at least five languages.

It is a masterpiece of sorts of the pontiff's art of dialectics: the art of turning to his own advantage and to that of his governance, an author whose writings have never had any bearing on his form of mind. This involves a manipulation of the meaning of a text, and at the same time a justification of that manipulation, which consists in ascribing to an author an explanation that he never formulated and that was never his own.

The pope's speech, which we quote from the Vatican edition, is based on a set of quotations.

In his book *The Religious World of Dostoyevsky*, Guardini takes up, among other things, an episode from the novel *The Brothers Karamazov*.[19] It is the passage where the people go to the *starec* Zosima to present their concerns and difficulties to him, asking for his prayers

---

[19]   Guardini, *The Religious World of Dostoyevsky* (Morcelliana, Brescia), p. 24ff.

and blessing. An emaciated peasant woman also approaches him to make her confession. In a soft whisper, she says she has killed her husband who in the past had greatly mistreated her. The *starec* sees that the woman, desperately aware of her guilt, is completely closed in on herself and that any reflection, consolation, or advice would hit a brick wall. The woman is convinced she will be condemned, but the priest shows her a way out: her existence has meaning because God receives her at the moment of her repentance. "Fear nothing and never be afraid; and don't fret," says the *starec*. "If only your penitence fail not, God will forgive all. There is no sin, and there can be no sin on all the earth, which the Lord will not forgive to the truly repentant! *Man cannot commit a sin so great as to exhaust the infinite love of God.*"[20] The woman is transformed by her confession and her hope is revitalized.

In fact, the simplest persons understand what this is about. They are taken by the grandeur that shines in the *starec's* wisdom and the strength of his love. They understand what holiness means—namely, a life lived in faith, capable of seeing that God is close to men, that He has their lives in His hands. In this regard, Guardini says that, by "humbly accepting existence from the hand of God, personal will transforms into divine will and in this way, without the creature ceasing to be only a creature and God truly God, their living unity is brought about."[21] This is Guardini's profound vision. Perhaps it is grounded in his first metaphysical book, *Der Gegensatz.*

For Guardini, this "living unity" with God consists in the concrete relationships of individuals with the world and with those around them. The individual feels interwoven within a people—namely, in an "original union of men that by species, country and historical evolution in life and in their destinies are a unique whole."[22] Guardini interprets the concept of "people" by distinguishing it clearly from an Enlightenment rationalism that considers real only what can be grasped through reason[23] and from what tends to isolate man, tearing him away from

---

20   Guardini, p. 25.
21   Guardini, p. 32.
22   Guardini, *Il sentiero della Chiesa* (Morcelliana, Brescia, 2007), pp. 21–22.
23   Cf. Guardini, *The Religious World of Dostoyevsky*, p. 321.

vital natural relationships. **Instead, "people" signifies "the compendium of what is genuine, profound, essential in man."**[24] We are able to recognize in the people, as in a mirror, the **"force field of divine action." The people**, Guardini continues, **"feel this operating in all places and perceive the mystery, the restless presence."**[25] Therefore, I prefer to say—I am certain of it—that "people" is not a logical category but a mystical category for the reason that Guardini offers.

Perhaps we can apply Guardini's reflections to our time, seeking to discover God's hand in present-day events.

The four quotations made by the pope, indicated in bold in the text above, are structured as follows:

The first is from the first chapter of *The Religious World of Dostoyevsky*: "The People on the Road to the Divine – The Pious Women."[26]

The second is from the second chapter, "The Silent Ones and the Great Acceptance – Community and Individual."[27]

The third and fourth are from the first chapter.[28]

Having quoted Guardini's words, "man cannot commit a sin so great as to exhaust the infinite love of God," the pope moves on to the second chapter and quotes the following sentence, "by humbly accepting existence from the hand of God, personal will transforms into divine will and in this way, without the creature ceasing to be only a creature and God truly God, their living unity is brought about."

This translation suggests that the mere recognition of God's existence turns the human will into the divine will. However, the original German text does not mention any such "transformation." Romano Guardini wrote: "*Vollzieht sich der Umbruch aus dem eigenen Willen in den Willen Gottes hinüber.*" Which translates as follows: "An upheaval is accomplished that causes one's self-will to move to the will of God." Umbruch is the upheaval, here the change of order.

---

[24]   Guardini, p. 12.

[25]   Guardini, p. 15.

[26]   Page 35 of the French version of Guardini's book published by Editions du Seuil.

[27]   Page 41 of the French version.

[28]   Guardini, *The Religious World of Dostoyevsky*, pp. 25 and 27.

In the paragraph that precedes the pope's quotation, Guardini had made the necessary distinction: "But God is not 'Nature,' the simple raw material of the present existence, the mere root of the world. Between the immediate natural given and God, there is a great gulf to be crossed. In everything that is, in all that happens, Christ has His place; in every event His will is law. It is in this spirit that the people confront that which is woven into every day of their existence: suffering."

The Italian, French, Spanish, and Portuguese translations by the Vatican follow the same erroneous version. This astonishing shift in meaning continues with a degree of contempt for Romano Guardini's actual text.

In giving the third citation, the pope stated, " 'people' signifies the compendium of what is genuine, profound, essential in man." This quote is from the first sentence of Guardini's first chapter. The German text reads, "*Das Volk hingegen ist, der Inbegriff alles menschlich Echten, Tiefen und Tragenden.*"

Notice that the quotation marks in the quote begin after "signifies," which is irrelevant since it is the translation of "*das Volk hingegen.*"

In his fourth quotation, the sentence cited by the pope is the conclusion of an untranslated sentence by Romano Guardini: the "force field of divine action." The quotation, as given by the pope, proceeds as follows: "The people'—Guardini continues—'feel this operating in all places and perceive the mystery, the restless presence.' "

Here again, the text is interpreted on the basis of the omission of the word that is to serve the final development of the pope's thoughts.

The German text of the pope's speech is more complete: "*Das Volk—fährt Guardini fort—fühlt, wie in allem von Gott her etwas vor sich geht. Es ahnt das Geheimnis dieses Geschehens, seine Nähe, seine Unruhe.*"

The phrase "*Geheimnis dieses Geschehens*" is not translated correctly. It should read, "The people sense the inner secret of events, its closeness, its disturbing character."

At the end of this demonstration, the pope makes the following essential statement: "Therefore, I prefer to say—I am certain of it—that 'people' is not a logical category, but a mystical category, for the reason that Guardini offers."

Yet nowhere does Romano Guardini suggest this interpretation. He analyzes Dostoyevsky's characters and the novelistic and realistic world in which they evolve. He does not dissert on the people *per se*. With dazzling mastery, at once fond and severe, he watches Russian society as it lives. I do believe that it has never been done more perfectly!

Here is what Guardini wrote in his first chapter, from which three quotes out of four are taken:

"Deep down, it (the people), for Dostoyevsky as for the Romantics, is a mythical being."[29]

> We just used the word "romanticism." Dostoyevsky was, without doubt, one of the greatest romantics; however, his people are by no means romantic creatures in the superficial sense of the word. Apart from the great Christian themes that are expressed in its life, this people is not idealized at all, but viewed instead from a very realistic angle—using this word in the sense of a bare, naked reality—a reality that Dostoyevsky would describe in the artist as dryness of heart and lack of imagination. This people is shown with all its filth, with all its vices, in its depravity and ignorance; thick, greedy, and above all devoted, in a frightful way, to drunkenness . . . but such as it is, it is 'people of God.' "[30]

But why this distortion of meaning, one might ask?

Romano Guardini wrote those words in 1932; he had been a doctor of theology since 1915. In 1943, he wrote *Prayer in Practice*, which includes a chapter on interior prayer and mystical prayer. It is totally implausible that he would have imagined the interpretation that the pope ascribes to him. It is a deliberate misappropriation of meaning and a misleading abuse of the text that deceives the reader.

This Francis-Guardini episode was to find an epilogue through one of the most distinguished thurifers of the pope, the Italian Massimo

---

[29]   Page 26 of the French version.
[30]   Guardini, The Religious World of Dostoyevsky, p. 40.

Borghesi, author of *Jorge Mario Bergoglio: An Intellectual Biography. Dialectics and Mysticism.*

This eminent professor gave an idea of his own intellectual smugness in an interview given to es.catholic.net, in which he proclaimed, "The critics of Francis are real quacks (*muy charlatanes*), they are a fierce minority whose real purpose is to delegitimize the Pontiff and with him, the entire movement of the Second Vatican Council."

We are therefore taking great risks, humbly conscious of our own inadequacy.

In his book, Massimo Borghesi presents the text of the above-mentioned speech of the pope to the audience of the Romano Guardini Foundation. On the face of it, Massimo is a very good connoisseur of this German author, since he devoted the third part of his book to the "Theory of the polar opposition. Bergoglio and Romano Guardini."

He accurately reproduced the papal speech, apart from the fact that the pope does not use the word *mythical* but *mystical*.

It can be verified that the five languages used on the Vatican website all use the same word: *mystische* in German, *mystical* in English, *mistica* in Italian and Portuguese, *mystique* in French. Borghesi also failed to notice that the pontifical dialectics were based on an association of unrelated sentences spread over more than forty pages and that the papal conclusions have nothing to do with those of the author Francis claimed to have cited.

The people, a "mythical" category

A quarrel of words over the concept of "people" had already played out a few years earlier between the pope and the *Osservatore Romano*: is it a "mythic" or "mystical" category?

To understand what this is all about, we need to go back to the meetings with anti-capitalist "popular movements" convened by the pope every year from 2014 to 2016. At the time, in the course of long-winded speeches, he referred to what he called the "mythical" character of the people. The word would reappear in his speeches thereafter, including during a symposium on the priesthood in 2022.

In February 2016, on returning from his trip to Mexico, Francis once again uttered those cherished words during his traditional in-flight press conference, claiming that the people of that country are mythical "because of Our Lady of Guadalupe!" But the report in *L'Osservatore Romano* replaced the words with "a mystical people."

The following summer, thanks to his friend Spadaro, director of the *Civiltá Cattolica*, the pope made a definitive correction:

> There is a very ill-treated word: we talk a lot about populism, populist politics, a populist agenda. But this is a mistake. "People" is not a logical category, nor is it a mystical category, if by that we mean that everything the people does is good, or that the people is an angelic reality. Rather, it is a mythical category, if there is one. I repeat: "mythical." The people is a historical and mythical category. The people builds itself through a process, with a purpose and a common project. History is built from this process of generations that follow one another within a people. You need a myth to understand the people. When I explain what the people are, I use logical categories because I need them to do so. But in this way, I cannot explain the meaning of belonging to the people. The word people has something more that cannot be explained in a logical way. To be part of a people is to be part of a common identity made of social and cultural bonds. And this is not an automatic thing, on the contrary: it is a slow, difficult process towards a common project.

A year later, in his book of interviews with Dominique Wolton, *The Path to Change: Thoughts on Politics and Society*, the pope again complained about this substitution, providing a revealing insight: "The word 'people,' as I think I said before, is not a logical concept, it's a mythical concept. Not mystical, mythical. . . . Once I said 'mythical' and, in *L'Osservatore Romano* they accidentally got the translation wrong, talking about the 'mystical people.' And you know why? Because they didn't understand the meaning of the mythical people. They said to themselves: 'No, it's the Pope who made a mistake, let's put mystical!'"

The point was made by Vatican expert Sandro Magister. In his review of Wolton's book, he noted: "In the middle of the first chapter, Jorge Mario Bergoglio also for the first time mentions the name of the anthropologist who inspired his conception of the '*people*.'" And he quotes:

> There is one thinker you should read: Rodolfo Kusch, a German who lived in north-west Argentina, a very good anthropological philosopher. He helped me to understand one thing: the word "people" is not a logical word. It's a mythical word. You can't talk about a people logically, because it would just be a description. To understand a people, understand the values of that people, you must enter the spirit, the heart, the work, the history and the myth of its tradition. That point is really at the root of the so-called theology "of the people". It means going with the people, seeing how they express themselves. The distinction is an important one. . . . The people is not a logical category; it's a mythical category.

But this was not the first incident to highlight the haphazard nature of the papal lexicon.

Gustav Mahler

Mrs. Ysabel de Andia, a doctor of theology and philosophy and a member of the Pontifical Academy of Theology, published an article on the *sensus fidei* in the *Nouvelle revue de théologie* (No. 142–2) in 2020. As a starting point for her lengthy study, under the title "Le flair du troupeau: *sensus Ecclesiae, sensus fideli* et *sentire cum ecclesia*" (The flock's sense of smell: *sensus Ecclesiae, sensus fideli* and *sentire cum ecclesia*), she used the *Letter of Pope Francis to the Pilgrim People of God in Germany* issued the previous year.

She wrote:

> Pope Francis, in his *Letter to the Pilgrim People of God in Germany* (June 29, 2019)—this title adopts a wording inspired by Ignatius of Antioch that emphasizes the "peregrinating" aspect

of the Church and therefore its "synodality"—develops the idea of a "*sensus Ecclesiae*": "It is a matter of living and feeling with the Church and in the Church, which, in many situations, will also lead us to suffer in the Church and with the Church." No one can have the "sense of the Church" if he or she does not live *in the Church*, in a living community, if he or she does not live *by the Church*, its sacraments and liturgy, if he or she does not live *with the Church* the events that make up its history.

"To do this," the Holy Father added, "we must immerse ourselves in the sources of the most living tradition": the sense of the Church presupposes immersion in tradition, which alone marks out the continuity from the apostles to the present day and opens up a future in continuity with the past and the present. Here the pope quoted Gustav Mahler: "Tradition is the safeguarding of the future and not the conservation of ashes."

Our first observation with regard to this introduction will deal with that last sentence, and the pope's quote which indeed appears in the second paragraph of Part 9 of the *Letter to the German People*.

There is no official English translation of the letter; we are following the Spanish translation: "*the mission of Tradition is to keep the fire alive rather than to preserve the ashes.*" A footnote refers to the author: Gustav Mahler. However, this footnote provides another text: "*Tradition is the safeguarding of the future and not the conservation of ashes.*" This formulation was used by the pope in another text.

The German version of the text of the letter is consistent with the Spanish version: "*Das Feuer am Leben zu erhalten statt, ledigliche die Asche zu bewahden.*"

But neither of these versions is correct. The Germans do not appear to have asked for a correction from the person responsible for the official text, who had probably never read Mahler and was content to retain the two phrases quoted in the pope's letter at their face value. The phrase chosen by Ysabel de Andia is the one in the footnote, and not the one included in the letter itself.

Fortunately, the French blogger Yves Daoudal, who found the phrase "cited" by the pope surprising, provided Mahler's authentic version in his November 19, 2019 blog: "*Tradition ist die Weitergabe des Feuers und nicht die Anbetung der Asche*," which translates as: "Tradition is the transmission of the fire, not the preservation of the ashes."

Immigration as a mystical practice

The lack of awareness of certain aspects of the pope's thinking leads to incomplete assessments among commentators.

When Laurent Dandrieu wrote his excellent book *Église et immigration—le grand malaise* (Church and immigration—the great disquiet), he reasoned as a Catholic and a Frenchman. He exposed the unexplained collusion between the pope's words and "immigration-invasion." As a citizen, he sensed the reality that "eluded" the pope, because the Catholic France that he loves is being culturally and religiously submerged by Islam. In the name of France's past, present, and future, Dandrieu stood up to the danger, using commonsense arguments and highlighting the essential truths that govern state politics. He emphasized that the distinction between the temporal and the spiritual has never been so necessary. The invasion policy advocated by the pope (in the name of spiritual power) endangers the existence of the temporal, the political reality: it endangers France.

Laurent Dandrieu presents a rigorous argument, except that the pope's theology is not that of his predecessors and that Francis has a conception of the "temporal-spiritual" relationship that has nothing to do with what has always been taught since Jesus Christ proclaimed: "Render unto Caesar the things which are Caesar's, and unto God the things that are God's."

We must always keep in mind that the "theology of the people" is just another form of liberation theology. The fundamentals remain the same.

Within this context, the liberation of the Jews crossing the Red Sea is the model and anticipation of all future migrations. Hence the migration of workers or of any other migrant must be considered as a paschal exodus.

Emilce Cuda is a theologian who knows Francis well. Along with Austen Ivereigh, she is part of the Pontifical Communication Network, and under the guidance of Father Scannone, she authored a sum in 2016 titled *Para leer a Francisco, teología, ética, política* (Reading Francis, theology, ethics, politics). In her study *The Exodus of the Worker as a Mystical Practice*, she wrote:

> What would happen if we began to see in the migrant a "being-in-exodus"—in search of better working conditions, in order to fulfill his hope of freedom for himself and his descendants—instead of seeing him as a threat?
>
> Could we recognize in the migrant worker the lineage of a new people like the one Melchisedec recognized in Abraham, Homer in the Achaeans, Evander in Aeneas? Could we consider that today's migrants can be the ferment of a better culture, as were the Achaeans who would produce the Greek civilization through seven centuries of aesthetic research?

Based on these thoughts, with the help of Plotinus, Hannah Arendt, Charles Tilly, Ernesto Laclau, and others, Emilce Cuda wonders whether migration should be seen as a Passover.

"In Latin America today, the exodus represents a migration of people in search of work; it frees them from oppressive conditions that do not allow them to leave their mark in the society where they live. That is why the exodus of the present day has taken the form of a migration of workers and a search for new conditions, that makes possible an exile from 'being poor' towards human dignity, which is not far from being a metaphysical exodus."

According to the Latin American Bishops' Conference, there is at present a flux of thirty million workers circulating throughout the South American continent.

The exiled, comments Cuda, are "beings in exodus," and "they raise a question that calls for political as well as theological reflection—because the question of being and its unity is akin to that of the Trinitarian relationship."

Here ends theologian Cuda's explanation. She reveals nothing of the mysticism that she describes as "being in exodus" with the Trinitarian relationship.

However, she proceeds to write: "When they start their reflexion from mysticism, theology and politics can make the migrant appear as he who generates spaces for new ways of speaking to erupt in public discourse, shifting words towards new common identifiers.... Mysticism is precisely that which joins theology to politics."

She concludes: "The theological category of 'exodus' should not only be considered as an equivalent of the category of 'migration,' although this would already provide the great benefit of changing symbolism.... It is one of the most important frontiers to be crossed, that of the public word, the social recognition of another path of access to justice."

This incongruous pathos of false philosophy and pseudo-theology makes it possible to understand the pope's discourse, of which she is one of the authorized interpreters.

For Pope Francis, the great migrations of history, including present-day ones, are transhumances that end up helping to understand mankind and the whole of humanity. In this view, the "primary host" is Melchizedek.

As bewildering as this conception of migration-immigration may be, it is the one implemented by the speeches of Pope Francis. Beyond his universalist ideology, he is only familiar with the great migrations of the American and Latin American continent, which have nothing to do with the one we are experiencing. The "American" migrations are similar to those that Europe experienced between the two World Wars. The immigrants of that time at any rate had knowledge of the Ten Commandments and natural law and even put them into practice, even when we consider the Spanish revolutionaries of 1939. When the pope's parents landed in Buenos Aires, they were no strangers to the Christian civilization that welcomed them.

This has nothing to do with conquering Muslims and African animists!

The pope is applying to this situation one of his famous "four principles" which, despite his claims, do not belong to the Corpus of the Social Doctrine of the Church.

"This requires acknowledging a principle indispensable to the building of friendship in society: namely, that *unity is greater than conflict*. Solidarity, in its deepest and most challenging sense, thus becomes a way of making history in a life setting where conflicts, tensions and oppositions can achieve a diversified and life-giving unity. This is not to opt for a kind of syncretism, or for the absorption of one into the other, but rather for a resolution which takes place on a higher plane and preserves what is valid and useful on both sides."[31]

The concept of "mystical people" mentioned above can be found in this setting.

One of the demands of liberation theology, be it Argentinian or not, is in fact to drop the essential notion of the "Mystical Body of Christ" and to replace it with the "People of God" and the "Mystical People."

Perfectly summarizing the modernist thesis adopted by the pope is what Fr. Maurice Vidal, PSS, has to say about it in *Cette Église que je cherche à comprendre* (This Church that I seek to understand).[32]

The majority of the Fathers shared the deliberate perspective of a greater commitment to ecumenical dialogue, which required the council to view belonging to the Church in a different way from that which Pope Pius XII had twice considered and taught: in 1943 in *Mystici Corporis* and in 1950 in *Humani generis*. If it is to be sincere, ecumenical dialogue must not be merely tactical, waiting for the other to move towards us and to join us where we are, in a place from which we have not moved. But Pius XII had, in a way, blocked the path because he had very clearly identified the Catholic Church with the Mystical Body of Christ: are part of the Mystical Body in this world, those who are part of the Roman Catholic Church, and who are subordinate to the pope, the visible head of the Body of which Christ is the invisible head.

---

[31]   Pope Francis, apostolic exhortation *Evangelii Gaudium* (November 24, 2013), no. 228.

[32]   Vidal, *Cette Église que je cherche à comprendre*, p. 109ff.

This ecclesiological vision of the Church was gradually imposed upon the Latin Church, in the Western Church, from the second millennium onwards, with the surprising consequence that the canonical point of view of submission to the Roman pontiff took precedence over the sacramental point of view of Baptism and the Eucharist! It is problematic to accept the theological consequences of this. To take the best case, that of a good Orthodox man, who is not only baptized but who participates in the Eucharist, who receives Communion and who, according to the Roman Catholic Church, really does receive sacramental communion in the Body of Christ: such a man is not a member of the Body of Christ! This is a blatant contradiction of both Saint Paul and the entire theological tradition of the Church Fathers and the Middle Ages. How on earth could this teaching have been arrived at? It continues to amaze me! How could a man like Pius XII, whose intelligence I so much admire, have perceived this in such a narrow way? It was therefore necessary to mark a break with Pius XII. This was done by refusing to identify, as he had done, the Roman Catholic Church and the Mystical Body of Christ.

Since Pius XII had defined membership in the Mystical Body, a clever way was found to avoid a head-on confrontation, one that was theologically elegant, by no longer speaking of membership in the Mystical Body but of the People of God. This concept had the advantage of not having been used by Pius XII.

The people of God, a polyhedral humanity

The people of God extends to the whole of humanity, or, according to the original expression coined by the pope, the "polyhedron," a concept he developed in *Evangelii Gaudium*. Two more recent statements by the pontiff, as well as the Amazon Synod, have led to the final stage of abandonment of the teaching of Pope Pius XII.

The entire program can be found in the exhortation *Evangelii Gaudium*:

> The whole is more than the part, and more also than the mere sum of these. Therefore, one should not be too obsessed with

limited and particular questions. We must always widen our gaze in order to recognize a greater good that will benefit all. But this must be done without escaping, without uprooting oneself. It is necessary to sink one's roots in the fertile soil and in the history of one's own place, which is a gift from God. One works on what is small, with what is close, but in a wider perspective. In the same way, when a person who keeps his or her personal particularity and does not hide his or her identity, integrates cordially into a community, he or she does not annihilate himself or herself, but always receives new stimuli for his or her own development. It is neither the global sphere, which annihilates, nor the isolated partiality, which makes sterile.

Here our model is not the sphere, which is no greater than its parts, where every point is equidistant from the center, and there are no differences between them. Instead, *it is the polyhedron*, which reflects the convergence of all its parts, each of which preserves its distinctiveness. Pastoral and political activity alike seek to gather in this polyhedron the best of each. There is a place for the poor and their culture, their aspirations and their potential. Even people who can be considered dubious on account of their errors have something to offer which must not be overlooked. *It is the convergence of peoples who, within the universal order, maintain their own individuality; it is the sum total of persons within a society which pursues the common good, which truly has a place for everyone.*

To Christians, this principle also evokes the totality or integrity of the Gospel which the Church passes down to us and sends us forth to proclaim. Its fullness and richness embrace scholars and workers, businessmen and artists, in a word, everyone. The genius of each people [in the original Italian, *"la mistica popolare"* and in Spanish, *"la mística popular"*] receives in its own way the entire Gospel and embodies it in expressions of prayer, fraternity, justice, struggle and celebration. The good news is the joy of the Father who desires that none of his little ones be lost, the joy of the Good Shepherd who finds the lost sheep and brings it back to the flock. The Gospel is the leaven which causes the dough to rise and the city on the hill whose light illumines all peoples. The Gospel has an intrinsic principle of totality: it will always remain good news until it has been proclaimed to all people, until it has healed and strengthened every aspect of humanity, until it has brought all men and women together at table in God's kingdom. The whole is greater than the part.[33]

On September 11, 2019, a meeting took place at Saint Martha's to discuss the *Document on Human Fraternity for World Peace and Living Together*. The date was chosen to display unfailing determination against all forms of terrorism.

On September 12, Pope Francis proclaimed the need for a global compact on education that must allow "fraternity to flourish" and "create a new humanism." Plans were immediately made for a great world assembly that was to take place on May 14, 2020, and due to COVID, was finally held in October 2021.

The fasting and the universal prayer addressed to God by all religions on May 14, 2020, were the logical outcome of this "people-humanity" viewed as one.

Thus did Francis become the world leader of humanity. No more Mystical Body of Christ, no more Prince of Peace. The UN and UNESCO will become redundant!

Leonardo Boff had made no mistake. In an interview he gave on January 2, 2017, he said of Francis: "He has made liberation theology the common good of the Church and he has spread it. Francis is one of us." He went on to describe how the pope had asked him for material for *Laudato si'*: "I gave him advice and sent him some of my writings. Some people, when they read it, told me: 'This stuff is by Boff.' "

Gustavo Gutiérrez, another prophet of this new theology, aired similar views at the time: "There will be no turning back."

But the question remains. For the pope, is the people "mystical" or "mythical"? If we are to understand his swing-wing thinking, we must consider the people of whom he speaks.

---

[33] Pope Francis, apostolic exhortation *Evangelii Gaudium* (November 24, 2013), nos. 235–37; emphasis added.

It is likely that Wolton, whom we mentioned above, has not widely read Rodolfo Kusch. Kusch, an anthropologist, journeyed throughout South America, and at every stage of his travels, he collected the mythical accounts of the populations he met, including those relating to the ancient gods and to the Pachamama. He explains that at the origin of peoples, there are myths—be they Greek or Hindu—which can be an explanation invented by the people themselves.

To the "myth," the pope adds the spirit, the heart, work, and history: all the values of the people. In his view, they are all supported by the unifying myth. "This point is truly the foundation of so-called 'people's theology,'" he insists.

According to Kusch, the original peoples of these lands have been deconstructed by successive colonizations. They have been cut off from their cosmological roots. This kind of analysis is in line with those of Dussel and Methol Ferré, at a moment when Argentinian liberation theology is searching for a new narrative.

What the pope did not tell Wolton was that Rodolfo Kusch was part of the interdisciplinary team headed by Father Scannone at the University of El Salvador from 1977 until his death in 1979. He was a member of the propaganda apparatus of the theology of the people.

Where Pope Francis calls Our Lady of Guadalupe a "mestiza"

Kusch's influence on Father Bergoglio was considerable. Discovering this proved a godsend that allowed us to understand the pope's famous words describing Our Lady of Guadalupe as a "mestiza," a woman of mixed blood. Pope Francis gave this example of the liberationist ideology during his homily for the feast of Our Lady of Guadalupe on December 12, 2019.

It should be noted that we are not dealing here with the doctrinal aspect of the "co-redemption" of Mary, which the first part of his sermon discussed. Rather, we are addressing the pope's communication, its method, and its meaning in the Latin American context.

To his official text, as often happens, he added a few elements of his own to push a point that was close to his heart without being constrained by a written text. He mainly improvised. His final tirade mocked the defenders of Mary Co-Redemptrix. He scoffed at them rudely: "When they come up with stories that this should be declared, or that another dogma should be made, let's not get lost in nonsense." Other translators wrote, "Let's not get lost in this foolishness." The Vatican website uses the word *chatter*.

These translators who were not familiar with the Argentine slang used by the pope thought they were dealing with the Spanish word *tonterías*, which they translated as "nonsense," which is possible in Spanish because the word has two values: one common, which can be translated as "nonsense," and another more aggressive: "stupidity" or "foolishness," depending on the speaker.

But the pope used the word *tonteras*, a frankly vulgar Argentinian expression that suggests that the speaker is not in full possession of his intellectual faculties. This is the obvious meaning: no time to lose with narrow-minded idiots (to choose a polite expression).

But what is the reason for this attack?

Like all politicians, the pope applies an infamous epithet to those who might oppose his argument. This has been his routine practice for a long time. Remember the reprimand issued to the cardinals under the form of derogatory labels. Remember also the taxing of Christians with *Pelagianism* and *Gnosticism*. It took an explanation from the Congregation for the Doctrine of the Faith, or what remains of it, to make the pope's vindictiveness intelligible.

There is nothing new here, just traditional Bergoglio-speak!

What is new, however, is the target. Until recently, it seems to me, one could be in favor of Mary Co-Redemptrix without being an imbecile or an idiot. Cardinal Charles Journet, for instance, is one of those "idiots." In his book *Entretiens sur l'Eucharistie* (Conversations on the Eucharist), he wrote on page 42: "No one has been as deeply involved in Christ's redemption as the Virgin Mary, who is the *Co-Redemptrix* par excellence." Pope Pius XI, speaking to pilgrims on November 30, 1933, declared: "The Redeemer had necessarily to associate his Mother with his work. That is why we invoke her under the title of Co-Redemptrix. She gave us the Savior. She led him towards his work of redemption, right up to the cross. She shared with him the sufferings of the agony and death in which Jesus consummated the redemption of all men."

But Pope Francis is not one for nuance. On the contrary, he spares no effort to eliminate the possibility of a "co-redemption" by the Virgin Mary: "Faithful to her Teacher who is her Son, the only Savior, she never wished to appropriate anything of her Son for herself. She never presented herself as a co-Savior. No, a disciple."

The level of his argument is mind-boggling!

Why should such a divide be established, dismissing to the outer world a whole class of men who are labeled as inept because they are unable to understand the theological elevations of the pope?

The method used is a typical message of liberation theology and the subversive discourse of Latin American revolutionary Catholicism. Thus, the great slogan which carried the cry of the people, first used in Brazil and later in the rest of the world, was summed up in the three "T's": *Tierra, trabajo, techo* (land, work, roof).

Similarly, the papal homily included the trilogy of the three "M's" related to Mary: *mujer, madre, mestiza* (woman, mother, mestiza). "The Church is feminine and our soul has this ability to receive grace from God, and in a certain sense, the Fathers saw the Church as a woman. We cannot think of the Church without this Marian principle. ... This Marian principle ... 'maternalizes' the Church and transforms it into Holy Mother Church."

The pope omitted the Catholic theology regarding this "feminization:" the Church is the Bride of Christ.

The pope then delivered a scathing attack on the litanies of Our Lady of Loreto, which he recognized as proceeding from filial love, but which he maintained "do not touch the essential nature of Mary's being: woman and mother."

All this is only a preamble. The teaching delivered in this homily was above all that of the "mixed race" of the Virgin of Guadalupe. It was in the last part of his improvisation that the pope explained the third title he had chosen: *mestiza*. "The third word that I would attribute to her as I gazed upon her: she wanted to be a mestiza (mixed race) for us, she chose to appear as a mestiza. And not only to Don Juan Dieguito but also to the people. She chose to appear as a mestiza in order to be the Mother of all. She made herself mixed for all of humanity. Why? Because she made a mestizo of God. And this is the great mystery: Mother Mary made a mestizo of God, true God and true man, in her Son," he said.

When the pope makes an incredible statement, he resorts to announcing a mystery.

On the following day, the French daily *La Croix* made this comment: "He [the pope] pointed out that the Virgin had 'mixed with God by bearing his Son'; she was *de facto* made a mestiza by her 'Yes'; she also 'chose' to 'mix with humanity' by adopting, through her son, all the human brothers of Jesus."

This is not the place to discuss the "theology of divine mestizaje" according to the theologian journalist of *La Croix*. Professor Roberto de Mattei considers it to be an old heresy. His response to these papal and journalistic ramblings can be read in Italian on the site corrispon-denzaromana.it (*La teologia meticcia di papa Francesco*).

Unless one is well-versed in the history of councils, which we are not, one has to believe that the message of the pope *who refuses the co-redemption* is to give an additional title to the Virgin, that of "*Mestiza of God.*"

This would be an astounding incongruity. What is this mestizaje compared to the perfection in which God has established the Virgin Mary?

Instead, let us listen to Saint Thomas Aquinas: "The humanity of Christ, from the fact that it is united to the Godhead; and created happiness from the fact that it is the fruition of God; and the Blessed Virgin from the fact that she is the mother of God; have all a certain infinite dignity from the infinite good, which is God. And on this account there cannot be anything better than these; just as there cannot be anything better than God."[34]

---

[34] *Summa Theologica* I, q. 25, a. 6.

Obviously, there is no need for people to get a theological explanation of this new "mystery"; that is not the point. The strength of the pope's declaration lies essentially in the *awareness* it creates. In other words, this is not knowledge taught by the magisterium but using *La Guadalupana* to allege the existence of "popular" knowledge of the Virgin that is superior to that taught by the Church.

But we should further assess these words of the pope: "Mary as a woman, Mary as a Mother, without any other essential title. The other titles—let us think of the Litanies of Loreto—are titles sung by children in love with their Mother, but they do not mention the essential nature of Mary's being: woman and mother."

This is the man who, forty-five years ago, was capable of saying against all truth that the people knew how to pray to Mary better than the Church. Now he has discovered that the little people of Loreto are incapable of formulating praises to the Blessed Virgin that are worthy of her dignity! He declared this on December 12, 2019 in St. Peter's Basilica. Then, on June 21, 2020, he added three new titles to the litany of Our Lady of Loreto: Mother of Mercy, Mother of Hope, and Comfort of Migrants.

This seems to have been done in a somewhat over-hasty manner: in the text of the litany on the Vatican website, "Mother of Mercy" was already listed in fifteenth place. But she has moved up and now comes just after "Mother of the Church."

"Mother of Hope" comes after "Mother of Divine Grace" and "Comfort of Migrants." In reality, this is a perfect example of *inculturation*, which we shall discuss in more detail later.

In the liberationist narrative, everything must align with "*the signs of the times*" that indicate the divine will. In this case, condescension toward "children in love" (*hijos enamorados*) gives way to the incorporation of contemporary problems involving migrants. Are we soon to invoke the "Mother of Ecology"?

Commentators of the pope's words simply mentioned whether they were pleasantly or unpleasantly surprised by them, but they did not trace them back to the Bergoglian system of awareness-raising of the pilgrims.

The "mestizaje" that came from afar

Sandro Magister's blog post on *Settimo Cielo* on December 30, 2019, published an accurate portrayal of this maneuver by Pietro de Marco: "The combative tone of the homily ('*no pretenden*,' '*no tocaba*,' '*tocaban para nada*,' '*jamás quiso*,' etc.) therefore appears ill-founded and poorly directed. There appears in it a sort of showy theological indifference, with contempt for the perennial Church, in order to have a free hand in practical arenas, even if this means alliances with progressive global public opinion."

These kinds of statements are the lifeblood of the pope's religion; they are also utterly absurd. All the great Marian shrines are at the heart of the Church, run by priests under the authority of the bishops. All the hymns sung there proclaim the faith of the Catholic Church. Czestochowa, Lourdes, Fatima, Mexico City, and other places in the world are impossible to imagine without the Church and its Magisterium.

On the other hand, in the cities and villages where there are fewer clergy, piety degenerates into superstition, paranormal phenomena, and other delusions.

The pope's words on "*mestizaje*" are in reality a political and ideological rant.

This is nothing new with regard to the Virgin of Guadalupe. The revolutionary Emilio Zapata and, in his time, the Movimiento Chicano had already hijacked the image of the *Guadalupana* to galvanize the people to fight for human rights and freedom.

We have found no trace of "*mestizaje*" in the history of Our Lady of Guadalupe, even among her secularist and atheist detractors. The Blessed Virgin is simply referred to as the "*Morenita*": having a matte or slightly tanned skin.

Instead, the word *mestiza* was spread in the United States starting in 1987 in an autobiographical novel, *Borderlands—La Frontera: the New Mestiza*. Its author, Gloria E. Anzaldúa, has received literary awards from lesbian movements. Her revolutionary work is considered to be a world-class model of the genre. Wikipedia depicts her work as follows: "Anzaldúa self-identifies in her writing as a feminist, and her major works are often associated with Chicana feminism [a mixed Mexican-White American background] and *queer* theory. . . . One of Anzaldúa's major contributions was her introduction to United States academic audiences of the term *mestizaje*, meaning a state of being beyond binary ('either-or') conception, into academic writing and discussion. In her theoretical works, Anzaldúa called for a 'new mestiza,' which she described as an individual aware of her conflicting and meshing identities. . . . The 'new mestiza' way of thinking is illustrated in postcolonial feminism."

In her work, presented in Spanish by *Analéctica*, there is an article entitled *Eurocentrismo y ontología indígena: la Pachamama* (Eurocentrism and Indigenous Ontology: Pachamama). It appeared two years before the Synod on Amazonia.

Even more disturbing is her shared view with Pope Francis on the future and on the indeterminate nature of the future world: "Traveler, there is no path. The path is made by walking."

The *mestizaje* highlighted by the pope is an ideological exploitation that aims to renew and reinforce the theme of the poor and of the migrants who become impoverished in the long run. The term can be found in the immigrationist political discourse in France. France's High Council for Integration spoke of the process of integrating young people from the suburbs as early as 1980: "The development of a 'mixed-race' republican elite ought to be our government's roadmap. This elite would be made up of whites, blacks, Arabs, Muslims, South Americans and Asians, without distinction of religion, gender, sexual orientation, political or union convictions, or race. Plural identity is not a divisive factor if it is wisely used."

On Francis's lips, such words also represent a politicization of Marian devotion, for even if the archbishop of Buenos Aires (and later the pope) was not aware of French politician Bernard Stasi's remark in 1984—"The future of the world therefore lies in cultural cross-breeding"—it is easy to identify the presence of an invention that has nothing to do with Marian piety or theology. The formulation was borrowed from leftist-globalist political sociology. The true message of this man who would establish a popular form of piety toward Mary is to present the faithful with a pathetic and insulting title for the Queen of Heaven. This makes it easier to understand why for liberationists, pilgrimages function as awareness-raising events and are a far cry from the traditional devotion of Our Lady of Loreto.

In Peru, the term *nación mestiza* is used to designate various kinds of mixtures, such as *mestizo de la sierra* (half breed of the mountains) and *mestizo de la costa* (half breed of the coast). The examples are endless.

Perhaps the pope's inspiration can ultimately be found in one of Father Bergoglio's early readings, which we discovered thanks to Wolton's previously mentioned book.

The pope's certified biographers, Massimo Borghesi and Austen Ivereigh, do not mention Rodolfo Kusch. Yet, he can be seen as the inspiration behind the pope's claim of Our Lady of Guadalupe's "mestizaje." Three of Kusch's early books and articles deal with "mestizaje": *Paisaje y mestizaje en America*, 1951; *La ciudad mestiza*, 1952; and *La seducción de la barbarie: análisis herético de un continente mestizo*, 1953.

Will we have to wait for another "confession" from the pope to hear where he got his inspiration for inventing a theology of miscegenation that no Father of the Church has ever heard of?

In 1973, Kusch gave a conference for a symposium of the faculty of El Salvador: *Towards a philosophy of the Latin American liberation*. Speaking alongside leading figures such as Assmann, Dussel, Roig, and Scannone, he offered an "original" reflection entitled *A logic of negation to understand America*. Drawing largely on abstractions and anecdotes collected from the Aymara tribes, he "demonstrated" that the human being cannot understand him or herself outside of his or her cultural environment. Need we comment?

To conclude, here is a much more accurate account provided for this book by Jacques Camredon, a great connoisseur of Latin America and liberation theology and a regular columnist on the diocesan radio station in Bayonne, France:

Surely, Our Lady of Guadalupe's face has the features of the Mexican Indians; is she not the Mother of all men? But above all, when she gave her name, "*coatlaxopeuh*", which is pronounced "*quatlasupe*" in the Aztec language, Nahuatl, she knew in advance that this name would be understood by the bishop of Mexico City at that time, the Franciscan Bishop Zumárraga, as "Guadalupe", the name of a famous Spanish Madonna. In this way, the conquest of Mexico by the Conquistadors was approved and blessed by Heaven through the use of a Spanish name for the Mother of God.

This is nothing less than an inclusion, but an inclusion that is the opposite of the kind promoted by the followers of the Argentinian pseudo-theory of the people.

I have been thinking about this point since the first of my many visits to the Basilica of Guadalupe, where the Indian face of our Mother and her future maternity (the Virgin is clearly pregnant) made an immediate impression on me. Since her name, "Guadalupe" was the result of a misunderstanding by Bishop Zumárraga, who was of Basque origin, it was obvious that the Blessed Virgin had intended this misunderstanding, for being in eternity, where time is a perpetual present without flow or duration, she knows everything about the future.

Because the Blessed Virgin ratified in advance the Spanish name, she created a synthesis between the Catholic conquest and the Aztecs, whose symbol had always been the eagle devouring the serpent. The Aztecs had seen a snake on an island in the middle of a lake when they were looking for a place to settle permanently. Seeing it as a sign, they decided to found Mexico City on Lake Texcoco under the name Tenochtitlan.

Our Lady chose to call herself in Nahuatl "the one who crushes the serpent", and in Spanish "Guadalupe". This was a simultaneous reference to Genesis, to the Aztecs, and to the ongoing Catholic iconographic tradition which represents the Virgin crushing the serpent. It is a perfect example of the admirable supernatural synthesis that only Heaven can invent and pass on to men.

February 18, 1974, a key date for an understanding of Bergoglio's views on the Virgin Mary

On February 18, 1974, Jorge Mario Bergoglio gave a talk to his Jesuit confreres at the opening of the fourteenth provincial assembly. This is the day when the Catholic religion plunged into the nothingness of the theology of the people; it represents a decisive milestone in the expression of Bergoglian ideology. After quoting a text from Denziger without providing a reference, he concluded: "If you want to know what Mother Church believes, go to the Magisterium, because it is the Magisterium that is responsible for teaching infallibly; but if you want to know how the Church believes, go to the faithful people. The Magisterium will teach you who Mary is, but our faithful people will teach you how to love Mary."[35]

When separating the veneration and love of Mary from the Magisterium, Pope Bergoglio is true to his own way of thinking. He also contradicts the *Catechism of the Catholic Church* by creating a false divide.

> The Church's faith precedes the faith of the believer who is invited to adhere to it. When the Church celebrates the sacraments, she confesses the faith received from the apostles. . . .
>
> For this reason no sacramental rite may be modified or manipulated at the will of the minister or the community. Even the supreme authority in the Church may not change the liturgy arbitrarily, but only in the obedience of faith and with religious respect for the mystery of the liturgy.[36]

The rest of Father Bergoglio's text confirms that he was going even further astray.

> Our people have a soul, therefore we can speak of the soul of a people; we can indeed say it possesses a hermeneutic, a way of seeing reality and *a conscience.*

---

[35]   Papa Francisco, "*como se la quiere a Maria,*" *Meditaciones para religiosos*, p. 47.
[36]   CCC 1124–25.

I feel in our Argentine people a strong consciousness of its
dignity. It is a historical consciousness, with a personality that
is not derived from an economic system.

This is just pseudo-reasoning and pseudo-logic designed to "historicize" religion and make the "people" bear the responsibility for the
religious, economic, and political changes that the new clerics learned
from modernism and liberation theology.

All liberationist frameworks are built on the same model. They
will be discussed in the seventh part of this book because this ideology
was to become that of the Society of Jesus itself, which embraced in
full the theories of Father Bergoglio in *Boletín de Espiritualidad* n.°
55 of April 1978, with an introduction by the Father General Pedro
Arrupe himself.

At that time, General Perón had just been elected president of
Argentina, but he was in poor health.

Bergoglio's relations with General Peron's followers were excellent,
and thanks to the team of priests around him, the Jesuit provincial
understood that there was a way to loosen the ideological shackles of
liberationism by turning to a people who had just brought its idol to
power. For Father Bergoglio, 1978 was the year in which he drew up
his ultimate *forma mentis* (see chapter 8).

It marked his commitment to a new and radical conception of
the Church, as set out in his previous presentation to his confreres. It
marked a radical and surprisingly impudent change in the veneration
of the Blessed Virgin: it was not just a form of expression but a hijack
of the Catholic faith!

On this occasion, Father Bergoglio claimed before his fellow Jesuits to have arrived at a "formulation of the Christian tradition." It was
so important to him that he was unable to provide an exact reference.
"The believing people is infallible *in credendo*," he stated, adding:
"From this, moreover, I have derived my own formulation, which is
probably not very accurate." In what sense was his formulation "not
very accurate"? It had at any rate "helped him a lot": "*pero que me
ayuda mucho*," he said.

"If you want to know what Mother Church believes, you go to the Magisterium, because it is the Magisterium that is responsible for teaching infallibly; but if you want to know how the Church believes, you go to the faithful people" (*pero cuando quieras saber como cree la Iglesia andá al pueblo fiel*).

What the young provincial of Argentina had invented regarding the veneration of the Blessed Virgin, he went on to apply to the Church.

Faced with these obvious facts that leave no room for ambiguity, Austen Ivereigh has crafted an explanation pointing to a pseudo-conciliar source that destroys Bergoglio's words, "my own formulation": "The Vatican II document, *Lumen Gentium*, had recast the Church not as an institution so much as a people, the 'People of God'; from Denzinger, he [Fr. Bergoglio] had grasped that the 'people' was also a depository of the faith. As Bergoglio later wrote: 'When you want to know *what* the Church teaches, you go to the Magisterium . . . but when you want to know *how* the Church teaches, you go to the faithful people.'"[37]

We have here translated the English text, but it is not a translation of the Spanish text of 1974. It is an interpretation based on a false reference to the council that lends credence to all subsequent fabrications.

What did the council say in *Lumen Gentium*, which deals with "the people of God" in chapter II?

Paragraph 12 speaks of the meaning of "faith" and "the charisms" in the faithful people:

> The holy people of God shares also in Christ's prophetic office; it spreads abroad a living witness to Him, especially by means of a life of faith and charity and by offering to God a sacrifice of praise, the tribute of lips which give praise to His name (cf. Heb 13:15). The entire body of the faithful, anointed as they are by the Holy One (cf. 1 Jn 2:20, 27), cannot err in matters of belief. They manifest this special property by means of the whole peoples' supernatural discernment in matters of faith when "from the Bishops down to the last of the lay faithful", they show universal agreement in matters of faith and morals. That discernment in matters of faith is aroused and sustained

---

[37] Ivereigh, *The Great Reformer*, p. 111.

by the Spirit of truth. It is exercised *under the guidance of the sacred teaching authority, in faithful and respectful obedience* to which the people of God accepts that which is not just the word of men but truly the word of God (cf. 1 Thess 2:13). Through it, the people of God adheres unwaveringly to the faith given once and for all to the saints (cf. Jude 3), penetrates it more deeply with right thinking, and applies it more fully in its life."[38]

Benedict XVI, who often spoke out against deceptive interpretations of the council, understood what was afoot. In 2011, on this subject, and more specifically on the fabrications that were rampant in the theology of the people, he called on the International Theological Commission under the authority of Cardinal Müller to conduct a complete study. The latter reported and published the conclusions of the commission in December 2014.

It was already in the apostolic exhortation *Evangelii Gaudium* of November 24, 2013, that Pope Bergoglio proclaimed this transition from the one, holy, catholic, and apostolic Church to the "Church of the People."

Paragraph 111 of *Evangelii Gaudium* provides decisive proof of this:

The entire people of God proclaims the Gospel.

Evangelization is the task of the Church. The Church, as the agent of evangelization, is more than an organic and hierarchical institution; she is first and foremost a people advancing on its pilgrim way towards God. She is certainly a mystery [similar to the mystery of "mestizaje"?] rooted in the Trinity, yet she exists concretely in history as a people of pilgrims and evangelizers, transcending any institutional expression, however necessary.[39]

This deserves a closer examination:

1. Evangelization is a people walking toward God. This people is something beyond the Church, which is an organic and hierarchical institution. Therefore, this people conquers in the face of a

---

[38]   Vatican Council II, Dogmatic Constitution on the Church *Lumen Gentium* (November 21, 1964), no. 12; emphasis added.

[39]   Pope Francis, apostolic exhortation *Evangelii Gaudium*, no. 111.

static Church. This is actually a cliché of the liberation and people's theologies.

2. *Evangelii Gaudium* speaks of the Church as "a mystery rooted in the Trinity, yet she exists concretely in history . . . transcending any institutional expression, however necessary." "A mystery . . . in the Trinity." The pope remarks, "It is certainly a mystery," which is not very helpful.

The expression "exists concretely in history" is a throw-off from Maritain's expression "a concrete historical ideal" in his book *Integral Humanism*. Maritain created it to ensure that his system would avoid socialist-oriented utopia. As he explained: "What we call a concrete historical ideal is not an *ens rationis*, but an ideal essence which is realizable . . . an essence capable of existence and calling for existence in a given historical climate, and as a result corresponding to a *relative* maximum of social and political perfection." So it has nothing to do with mystery, nor more than the Holy Trinity.

"Transcending": the rejection of the institution, that is to say, of the Church, is here reiterated. Note the qualifier: "however necessary"!

Here verbiage is at its peak, and the text's hollow emphasis defeats its own purpose.

But the following paragraph holds a different kind of surprise, in the course of article 112: "The Church is sent by Jesus Christ as the sacrament of the salvation offered by God. Through her evangelizing activity, she cooperates as an instrument of that divine grace which works unceasingly and inscrutably."[40]

So the Church, the bride of Christ, "*cooperates*"? This is a far cry from what Joan of Arc said at her trial: "About Jesus Christ and the Church, I simply know they are just one thing," or from Bossuet's words: "The Church is Jesus Christ spread abroad and communicated." These days, divine grace will not suffer to be submitted to scrutiny.

But the biggest surprise comes when the pope quotes Benedict XVI in support of his "*mystery people*" theory.

The exhortation *Evangelii Gaudium* is full of quotations that add body to an intellectually quite meager text, but not always to good

---

40   Pope Francis, apostolic exhortation *Evangelii Gaudium*, no. 112.

effect. For example, Benedict XVI is quoted in paragraph 14 in a misleading way that suggests that he opposes and condemns proselytism in the Church.

This alleged endorsement is taken from a meditation by Benedict XVI at the Assembly of the Synod of Bishops on October 8, 2012, in which he explained that evangelization originated in the prayer of the apostles awaiting the Holy Spirit. At Pentecost, God created the Church: "They prayed and in prayer they waited, because they knew that only God himself can create his Church, that God is the first agent. . . Pentecost is the condition of the birth of the Church. . . It was only on God's initiative that the Church could be born. . . In the same way today only God can begin, we can only cooperate, but the beginning must come from God."

In no way does this suggest that there is an action of Church which is beyond God's control. The sentence that immediately follows the words of Benedict XVI quoted by Francis sets the rule: "God is always the beginning, and it is always only he who can make Pentecost, who can create the Church, who can show the reality of his being with us."

Francis's drift continues in paragraph 113: "This people which God has chosen and called is the Church. Jesus did not tell the apostles to form an exclusive and *elite* group."[41]

Next comes: "Being Church means being God's people, in accordance with the great plan of his fatherly love."[42]

"The People of God is incarnate in the peoples of the earth, each of which has its own culture."[43]

"To Christians, this principle also evokes the totality or integrity of the Gospel which the Church passes down to us and sends us forth to proclaim. Its fullness and richness embrace scholars and workers, businessmen and artists, in a word, everyone. The genius of each people receives in its own way the entire Gospel and embodies it in expressions of prayer, fraternity, justice, struggle and celebration."[44]

---

[41]   Pope Francis, no. 113.
[42]   Pope Francis, no. 114.
[43]   Pope Francis, no. 115.
[44]   Pope Francis, no. 237.

The words "popular mysticism"[45] here refer to the people that is the only one that welcomes the Gospel in its entirety, in a way that surpasses that of the Church.

Yet there is no such thing as an infallible people, either *in creden-dum* or in any other respect, except if that people includes priests, bishops, and the pope! Neither the people of the time of Noah, nor the people who came out of Egypt, nor the people of Jerusalem on Palm Sunday, nor the people instructed by Peter after the Resurrection are as such infallible. And what about the people who applauded the French king at the revolutionary Feast of the Federation in 1790?

On October 26, 2012, the Synod of Bishops addressed a "message to the People of God." This people is described as "often distracted and confused" and compared to the Samaritan woman in Saint John's Gospel, who is "beside a well with an empty bucket."

When Ecclesiasticus praised the Fathers, it was thus: "Such as have borne rule in their dominions, ... And ruling over the present people, and by the strength of wisdom instructing the people in most holy words" (Sirach 44:3–4).

The pope who canonized John XXIII has clearly forgotten that the Church is *Mater et Magistra*.[46]

The invention of a People of God outside of the Mystical Body hides an irrepressible desire for power and "social justice" under the cover of religion; it is the desire of a clergy that has gone astray like the one that condemned Christ to death. That clergy proclaimed: "We have no King but Caesar." This is the modern-day version: "We have no king but the people!"

At the time of the council, the episcopate—barring a few exceptions—was incapable of understanding what was going on. Today's episcopate lacks a solid understanding of the history of the Church in

---

[45] Translator's note: The words *mistica populare* in the original Italian are rendered in the official English translation by "the genius of each people," but § 87 speaks of a shared "'mystique' of living together" and § 124 evokes "the people's mysticism." *Mistica populare*, or *mystique populaire* in French, suggest an entity of its own.

[46] Mother and Teacher.

the first half of the twentieth century, and it is even more ignorant of what happened in Latin America in the 1960s and after the council. So how could it recognize the poison that comes from the South?

The pope has repeatedly referred to the *infallible people,* for example, at the Assembly of the Pontifical Mission Societies on May 21, 2020. When outlining the "distinctive features" of the mission, he dwelt on "the '*sensus fidei*' of the People of God":

> There is one reality in the world that has a kind of "feel" for the Holy Spirit and his workings. It is the People of God, called and loved by Jesus, who for their part continue to seek him amid the difficulties of their lives. The People of God beg for the gift of his Spirit: entrusting their expectation to the simple words of their prayers and never entertaining the presumption of their own self-sufficiency. The holy People of God are gathered together and anointed by the Lord, and in virtue of this anointing are made *infallible "in credendo",* as the Tradition of the Church teaches. The working of the Holy Spirit equips the faithful People with an *"instinct" of faith,* the *sensus fidei,* which helps them not to err when believing the things of God, even if they do not know the theological arguments and formulas that define the gifts they experience. The mystery of the pilgrim people, who with their popular piety travel to shrines and entrust themselves to Jesus, Mary and the saints, draws from this and shows that it is connatural to the free and gratuitous initiative of God, apart from our pastoral planning. (*This is to be understood as being outside the hierarchical context.*)

One last remark will help understand Pope Bergoglio and his "teaching." His major writings are always accompanied by reassuring, if somewhat puzzling, quotes. The ones we point out here are not alone. As with the countless photos that accompany his actions, he knows how to market himself. One of his truthful biographers coined a word to define this practice, which was already his in Buenos Aires. He called him "*un papa marketinero.*" The suffix *ero* designates a professional activity: *zapatero*, a shoemaker; *cartonero*, a cardboard collector in the streets of the Argentinian capital.

The pope is an expert at commercial advertising. In some respects, he could even be mistaken for an illusionist.

CHAPTER 3

The Role of the Jesuits

Pope Francis is a product of three factors: Fr. Pedro Arrupe, superior general of the Jesuits from 1965 to 1981; Fr. Lucio Gera (1924–2012), a revolutionary theologian from Argentina; and General Juan Perón (1895–1974).

Our brief overview of what we saw being set up in the years following the council will show only the tip of the iceberg. To be complete, it would be necessary to add a host of symposiums and congresses, both national and international.

But we would venture to say that, in spite of the very real subversive power of all these movements, the most important aspect is to be found elsewhere.

Arrupe's reform of the Society of Jesus surpassed in scope, effectiveness, and subversion all that was occurring in the Latin American continent and in the rest of the Catholic Church. As Ricardo de la Cierva has observed, "the Society of Jesus was a key element for the promotion and coordination of the liberationist movements, thanks to the deep internal crisis that shook it during the generalate of Fr. Arrupe, coinciding with the post-conciliar era in the Church."[47]

In order to realize how long this revolution in the Church has been ongoing, we must consider its actors, and among these, the largest and most active group. This huge panorama reveals a hydra with a

---

[47]   Cierva, *Jesuitas, Iglesia y Marxismo, 1965-1985, La teología de la liberación desenmascarada*, p. 26.

thousand heads, manifesting itself at different times and in different places under different appearances.

First of all, there was the innumerable cohort of Jesuits who were devoted body and soul to Father Arrupe and to the transformation of the society and of the Church.

Fr. Vincent O'Keefe—who made a thunderous statement following the death of Pope Paul VI, calling for a more liberal Church—assisted Arrupe for eighteen years. He served as his assistant from 1965 onwards and was assistant general and general councilor from 1975 to 1981. In 1981, he was appointed vicar general of the Society of Jesus by Arrupe, and when Arrupe suffered a cerebral thrombosis that prevented him from continuing to exercise the generalate, O'Keefe moved to the first rank of succession. Pope John Paul II did everything to prevent this election. In 1983, Fr. Peter-Hans Kolvenbach was elected to lead the society.

When Father O'Keefe died in 2012, it was the pro-LGBT American Jesuit James Martin who delivered his eulogy. Father Martin was received at length by Francis on October 2, 2019, and later presented the audience as an endorsement of his "LGBT pastoral care."

The second Jesuit who led the transformation of the society alongside Father Arrupe was Fr. Jean-Yves Calvez. He is the definitive and virtually universal reference on Marxism thanks to his book *Karl Marx's Thought*. His expertise led him to travel all over the world, including the Soviet Union. He spoke English, German, Italian, Spanish, and Russian. He taught in Argentina, where he addressed the Argentinian Freemasons at a white dress event in Buenos Aires. During his many visits, he had the opportunity to meet Father, and then Archbishop, Bergoglio. He was appointed vice-president of the 31st General Congregation in 1966. He was councilor and moderator at the 32nd General Congregation in 1974–1975.[48] In 1974, he also became assistant general. He was the final contributor to Father Arrupe's letter on Marxism. He was one of the four temporary vicars appointed when Father Arrupe ceased his activity in 1981 and remained in that position until Father Arrupe's death on February 5, 1991.

---

[48]   See La Bella, *Pedro Arrupe, Superior General of the Society of Jesus.*

In addition to these masters, there were the German Karl Rahner; Fr. Hugo Assmann, who led the Latin American revolution in Chile and at CELAM; the Jesuits of El Salvador, Ignacio Ellacuría and Jon Sobrino; the Spaniards from *Fe y Secularidad;* the Italian Bartolomeo Sorge (who recently declared that Matteo Salvini was like the mafia); the Belgian Jacques Dupuis; and the incredible Juan Carlos Scannone from Argentina, who succeeded for over fifty years in making people believe that liberation theology is the crowning achievement of modern thought, from Maurice Blondel to Jean-Luc Marion. Scannone has written more than 150 books and thousands of articles. As a philosopher and theologian, he has tried in every way to give intellectual consistency to liberation theology by linking it to Blondel's philosophy, which was the subject of his doctoral thesis.

Blondel belonged to the French modernist school of the end of the nineteenth century, and despite the condemnation of his theses in 1924, he remained one of the masters of modernist thought until his death. In his letter "on the demands of contemporary thought," he foretold the great battles to come. As early as 1906, Father Garrigou-Lagrange condemned Blondel's claim to change the definition of truth, *adequatio rei et intellectus* (the agreement of things and of our thoughts, i.e., the conformity of judgment to the extra-mental reality and to its immutable laws) into *conformitas mentis et vitae* (conformity of the mind with life, i.e., the conformity of the judgment with the demands of human action or of life which are always changing).

The last of his propositions was condemned in 1924. It is a summary of the current religion disseminated by all the media sympathetic to Pope Francis: "Nulla propositio abstracta potest haberi ut immutabiliter vera.... Etiam post fidem conceptam, homo non debet quiescere in dogmatibus religionis, eisque fixe et immobiliter adhaerere, sed semper anxius manere progrediendi ad ulteriorem veritatem, nempe evolvendo in novo sensus, immo et corrigendo id quod credit." (No abstract proposition can be held as immutably true.... Even after having arrived at the possession of faith, man must not rest in a fixed and immovable adherence to the dogmas of religion; but remain ever anxious to reach a deeper truth, giving new meanings to his belief and even modifying it.)

In 2004, *Cristiandad* published the first Spanish translation of Blondel's *History and Dogma, On the Historical Value of Dogma*. It came with a lengthy and admiring preface that did not even contain a passing mention to the 1924 ruling.

But the story does not end there.

Maurice Blondel's prestige was on the wane, but his star rose anew with the condemnation of the Action Française, and when he died in 1949, his friends seriously considered launching his canonization process. In 1950, the family received a warm letter from the substitute for the Secretariat of State, Giovanni Battista Montini—the future Pope Paul VI—thanking them for Blondel's posthumous book, *Philosophical Exigencies of Christian Religion*. In 1974, Cardinal Villot added his own voice to the praise: "Famous as a philosopher for the breadth and rigor of his thought, Maurice Blondel can also be presented as a model Christian philosopher." John Paul II quoted Blondel at his general audience on November 9, 1983. Ten years later, in a letter to Bishop Bernard Panafieu on February 12, 1993, he would once again express his peculiar appreciation of Blondel: "In a world where relativism and scientism are on the rise, Blondel's thesis is of great value because of its search for the unification of being and its attention to intellectual peace."

One of his many eulogists, too numerous to mention here, Fr. Peter Henrici, SJ, considered that Blondel helped Lubac, Congar, Chenu, Balthasar, and Rahner to rediscover and reinterpret the authentic tradition of the Church.

Father Ladaria, SJ, himself joined the chorus of praise in his capacity as prefect of the Congregation for the Doctrine of the Faith. In a letter to the archbishop of Aix-en-Provence dated February 27, 2016, he stated that "from the point of view of the Congregation for the Doctrine of the Faith, there is no obstacle to a possible introduction of the cause of beatification of Maurice Blondel."

The most recent meeting of the "Friends of Blondel" took place on November 15 and 16, 2019, and was graced with a message of encouragement from Pope Francis.

This is a long-term issue. To date, the formidable network of intellectual, moral, and spiritual entrapment that has been built up over such a long period of time, and whose meshes continue to spread, has not been properly identified.

Arturo Sosa, the current general of the Jesuits, deserves a special mention. He considers hell to be symbolic. He claims that the indissolubility of marriage has no basis in the Gospel, because we don't know what Christ really said about it since "there was no tape recorder at the time." He was himself the successor of César Jerez as head of the province of Central America, where he was known for his unwavering support of the Jesuit liberationists in Central America.

As circumstances dictated, they all met and supported each other. If to the sheer number of these players who have been working to demolish the Church since 1964, you add the tens of thousands of books, the tens of thousands of national and international meetings, and the hundreds of thousands of articles produced; if you add the hundreds of thousands of radio and television broadcasts, connected to all the networks on the planet; if to all this you add the active or silent betrayal of cardinals, bishops, clerics, religious men and women, it is easy to understand how the present dereliction of our two-thousand-year-old Church has come about.

There is no smoke without fire. The effect must be proportionate to the cause. We are not claiming to explain and reveal everything. But one of the features, and not the least, of this gigantic revolution is the concealment of its motives behind words, expressions, and Catholic discourses that have been diverted from their meaning. For proof of this, it is sufficient to reread the first letter on liberation theology written in 1984 by Cardinal Ratzinger. It had no real effect. Even at that time, a letter was no longer sufficient to stop the tidal wave that was sweeping through the Church that was sheltering behind the imposing stature of Saint John Paul II. Words could not stop it, and the steamroller has remained intact.

On October 5, 2019, Francis officially received in Rome all those who brought him to power: Scannone, Gutiérrez, Sobrino, Ivereigh, Carriquiry, Galli, and Gianni La Bella, a counsellor of Sant'Egidio.

The prominent role of the Society of Jesus in the spreading and implementation of the conciliar revolution

The leading role of the Society of Jesus in the implementation of the Second Vatican Council is little known to French Catholics because the sources of information available to them were largely dominated by pro-conciliar and progressive currents within the Church. It was mainly a publication named DIAL (*Diffusion de l'Information sur l'Amérique latine*), directed by Charles Antoine from 1971 to 1995, that provided information to the entire episcopate and to diocesan organizations, as well as a host of third world magazines that were dedicated to the liberation of the peoples. In addition, there were all the newsletters of charitable works related to third world aid, at the forefront of which was the CCFD (Catholic Committee Against Hunger and for Development), which provided continuous funding to further the aims of the liberationists.

In France, the publications that were aware of the revolution that was rocking the Society of Jesus—*Itinéraires*, *La Pensée Catholique*, and *Le Monde et la Vie*—confined their study to Teilhard de Chardin.

As early as September 1965, *Le Monde et la Vie* published a special issue on "The Council: the great transformation of the Jesuits," in which Prof. Henri Rambaud crushed Father Rideau and his defense of Teilhard de Chardin. Rambaud highlighted the tactics of the Society of Jesus in the face of the *Monitum* of John XXIII condemning the works of the Jesuit evolutionist.

In the same issue, Michel de Saint-Pierre tried to reassure his readers, quoting Father Daniélou in order to give a Catholic interpretation of the council that was drawing to its close.

Yet this was a world away from Latin America.

Fr. Malachi Martin, a former Jesuit who left the society in 1965, published an analysis of the origins of its reversal in 1987 under the title *The Jesuits*.

"Not that this is the first time that one or another group in the Church has broken ranks and declared war on the papacy. But it is the first time that the Society of Jesus has turned on the papacy with the clear intent of undoing the papacy's prerogatives, to dilute the hierarchical government of the Catholic Church, and to create a novel Church structure, and it is the first time that the Society of Jesus both corporately and in its individual members, has undertaken a sociopolitical mission," he wrote. We are not unaware of the slander campaign that was waged against him at the time. But despite a number of factual errors, his study remains a rich source of information and insights.

The entire history of the society is indeed summed up in this judgment. Those Jesuits who did not fit into the new mold were silenced, with the result that their protests were rarely heard. The matter of this upheaval is so plentiful that we can only offer glimpses of it here.

Paul VI, John Paul I, and John Paul II tried to fight against the society's drift. They failed in the face of Father Arrupe's phenomenal skill and the power of the modernist revolution carried by Jesuit theologians since the mid-nineteenth century—not to mention their covert opposition to Saint Pius X's rejoinder.

The time between World Wars I and II was the era of the maturation of the most radical progressive theses. The process of development was kept discrete and even, at times, hidden and secret. The Teilhardian theses were disseminated behind closed doors. Following World War II, Pope Pius XII's censures were of no avail, and his encyclical *Humani Generis* went unheeded.

The Second Vatican Council became the catalyst for all these modernist forces when Father Janssens died on October 5, 1964. Father Arrupe succeeded him on May 22, 1965.

It is no exaggeration to say that it was the council of the Jesuits. Not only were all their leaders up front—de Lubac, Rahner, Daniélou, and so on—but there were also many Jesuits present in various capacities: fifty-eight Council Fathers (bishops), the fifty-eight expert-writers in the preparatory commissions that produced the constitutions and the council decrees, and forty-eight members of the council commissions.

Gianni La Bella describes Arrupe as "a man who understood his personal service at the head of the Society as being about a single mission: the impregnation of the Jesuits and the whole Society with the spirit of the Second Vatican Council. Between the Council and the generalate of Fr. Arrupe there existed a profound interplay. While his election was in part the fruit of the new climate created by the Council, it was the Society that in turn provided it with a powerful impulse."[49]

You don't need to have read the complete works of Teilhard to realize that the openness to the world and the boundless optimism displayed at the council against a background of science, outlined for mankind a new future taken directly from the works of the evolutionary scholar. The most amazing part, besides the power of the modernist current within the society, was the speed with which the reforms were implemented.

To fully understand this, it is necessary to look at the statistics. The Society of Jesus was at the height of its power in 1965. The number of Jesuits, regardless of status, was 36,038. Over the previous five years, their numbers had increased by one thousand. They had four thousand teaching centers, with fifty thousand non-Jesuit teachers and 1.25 million students. In the United States alone, there were fifty-two educational centers, media outlets, ten university colleges, and eighteen universities. They owned thousands of newsletters and journals. Their alumni association included 500,000 registered members and 2 million non-registered members. They ran Marian Congregations throughout the world. They were all over Rome, in the universities and in the dicasteries. Their missionary presence was considerable. No one could rival them.

As for Hispanic America and the presence of the Jesuits on that continent, the dates of the creation of the society's universities speak for themselves: Santo Domingo, 1538; Lima, 1552; Argentina, 1622; Quito, 1622; Bogotá, 1623; Chile 1625; Cuzco, 1648; Guatemala, 1675.

Others were established more recently. In Brazil, the University of Rio was founded in 1941; that of Santo Leopoldo in 1969. In Venezuela, the founding took place in Caracas between 1953 and 1962. In San Salvador, the UCA was founded in 1965. As of 2018, the Association of Jesuit Universities of Latin America (AUSJAL) comprised twenty-nine institutions.

---

49   La Bella, *Pedro Arrupe*.

It is easy to imagine the power of such an organization with regard to the reception of the council itself and to the post-conciliar period.

In the words of Father Arrupe's official biographer, Fr. Gianni La Bella:

> Starting in 1967, he was elected for five successive terms to head the Union of Superiors General. For about 15 years, he was recognized as an authority by all the religious families. More than 250 Superiors General belonged to the Union and felt represented by him, with all his prestige and popularity, and this was also true in the world of female religious.
>
> During these years he set up an intense and open collaboration with Bishop Eduardo Pironio, one of the leaders of the Latin American Catholic renewal. A former president of CELAM, Pironio had been called in by Paul VI, who wanted to internationalize the Curia and appointed him as head of the Congregation for Religious and Secular Institutes. The two men successfully collaborated in helping hundreds of congregations to promote the renewal of religious life by adapting their respective constitutions to the spirit of the requests made by the decree *Perfectae Caritatis*. In 1986, Cardinal Pironio was the special envoy of John Paul II to Cuba for the first assembly of the Catholic Church, after a ban that had lasted twenty-five years!
>
> Arrupe was involved in monitoring the follow-up of the Council. He attended all the synods convened in Rome by the Holy See. He was also a consultant for various dicasteries of the Roman Curia: from the Congregation of Religious to that of *Propaganda Fide*. He participated in the Second and Third General Conferences of the Latin American Episcopate, in 1968 in Medellin, Colombia, and in 1979 in Puebla, Mexico.
>
> Lastly, he took part in several pan-African symposiums organized by the episcopates of that continent.
>
> His interviews were broadcast by specialized agencies and magazines, to the extent that he became a leading figure in the post-conciliar Church. Renowned weeklies such as the American magazine *Time* and *Der Spiegel* in Germany featured him

on their covers as "man of the year." His fame extended beyond
Catholic and ecclesiastical circles. He was a man and a priest
who appealed to the general public and even, as people used to
say at the time, to non-believers.

We made a point of quoting this praise from Arrupe's society-
approved biographer. It spares us a lengthy exposition that could have
been construed as a biased overstatement.

César Jerez, who was the provincial of Central America from 1976
to 1982, summed up Arrupe's power in one phrase at a Jesuit meeting
in Boston: "The mission of Jesuits in the Third World is to create conflict. We are the only powerful group in the world that can do that."[50]

Father Arrupe, the true inventor of the Bergoglian Church

This is the key to what we are going through today: Pope Francis is
implementing within the Church the reformist agenda of the Society of Jesus instituted by Pedro Arrupe, general of the society and
twenty-eighth successor of Saint Ignatius. This agenda was set up by
Father Arrupe himself to obtain the transformation of the Catholic Church received from the apostles. Arrupe has been called the
"re-founder" of the Society of Jesus, and Pope Francis's biographer has
called the latter the "Great Reformer."

One can hardly be more precise.

This agenda has been set forth in thousands of books and arti-
cles written by thousands of authors who all support this reform.
Some may object that it was about the reform of the society, not of the
Church. That would be to forget the one hundred writings of Father
Arrupe that were published in 1982 under the title *La Iglesia de Hoy y
del Futuro* (The Church of Today and Tomorrow).

In his preface to the book, Cardinal Tarancón, archbishop
of Madrid, wrote: "[This book's] title perfectly summarizes and

---

[50]   Quoted by Ricardo de la Cierva in *Oscura Rebelión en la Iglesia*, p. 11; see
also *New England Jesuit News*, April 1973.

synthesizes the great objective to which Fr. Arrupe committed his mission as head of the Society of Jesus: effectively to help the Church of today to adapt to the demands of a future that is almost already present, and that strongly challenges those who have the duty to proclaim the Gospel message in all its authenticity and integrity in order to make it accessible to the mentality and psychology of the people of the year 2000."

For his part, Manuel Alcalá noted that the title of the book "did not please some of the Pope's collaborators, who thought that the topic was a matter for the Pontiff's own competence."[51]

Arrupe's own speech, "*El futuro de la Iglesia*" (The Future of the Church), delivered in Trier at the *Katolikengtag* on September 10, 1970, is also relevant.[52]

We suggest that the takeover of Roman power by the Society of Jesus is a realization of the third temptation: "*Haec omnia tibi dabo, si cadens adoraveris me.*" (Then the devil took him up to a very high mountain, and showed him all the kingdoms of the world in their magnificence, and he said to him, "All these I shall give to you, if you will prostrate yourself and worship me.") Obviously, Father Arrupe did not bow to Satan. But he was aiming to bow down the Church before the world, of which Satan is the prince. The Tempter used the same "future tense" as in the temptation in the Garden of Eden.

When Pope Paul VI declared on the feast of Saint Peter, on June 29, 1972, "Through some crack, the smoke of Satan has entered the Church of God," one might think that he had in mind the admonition (written by the pope's own hand, according to Father Arrupe), which he addressed to the society on November 16, 1966, and which had no effect at all on the reformers: "Do you, sons of St. Ignatius, soldiers of the Society of Jesus, want even today and tomorrow and always to be what you were from your beginnings right up to today, for the service of the Catholic Church and of this Apostolic See? There would be no reason for asking this question had not certain reports and rumors come to our attention about your Society, just as about other religious

---

[51]   La Bella, *Pedro Arrupe, Superior General de los Jesuitas 1965-1983*, p. 410.
[52]   Arrupe, *La Iglesia de Hoy y del future*, pp. 35–49.

families as well, which—and We cannot remain silent on this—have caused us amazement and in some cases, sorrow."

This was exactly one year after Dom Hélder Câmara's Pact of the Catacombs.

The selection of the one hundred texts collected in Father Arrupe's "sum" spans from 1965 to 1981 (including two interventions at the council), prior to the stroke that would lead to his death in 1991. His many biographers have emphasized the prophetic and visionary character of his work.

One of these, Father Calvez, later stressed that Arrupe was an avid reader of Teilhard de Chardin: "His devotion to the Sacred Heart and his references to Teilhard as a basis for his suggestion that the Church could be revitalized, in any case offer further proof of the importance of this source of all life." This extraordinary rapprochement can help measure the depths of the abyss in which we find ourselves today.

Pedro Arrupe was born in the Basque Country, like Saint Ignatius. For reasons related to the Spanish Republic, he studied in Belgium with his countrymen, but also with confreres from Germany. In 1936, he completed his studies in the United States, first in Kansas, then in Cleveland. He sailed from Seattle to Japan, where he set foot on October 15, 1938; his crossing of the Pacific Ocean had taken a month and a half.

In 1942, he was appointed master of novices in Nagatsuka near Hiroshima. In 1943, he took his vows in the Society of Jesus. He was there when the first atomic bomb exploded. He recalled this event on the occasion of the twenty-fifth anniversary of the explosion for the Italian daily *Avvenire*, remembering how he had stood up amidst the rubble and seen the clock fixed to the wall, motionless: "It was ten minutes past eight. For me that silent and motionless clock has been a symbol. The explosion of the first atomic bomb has become a para-historical phenomenon. It is not a memory, it is a perpetual experience, outside history, which does not pass with the ticking of the clock. The pendulum stopped and Hiroshima has remained engraved on my mind. It has no relation with time. It belongs to motionless eternity. A sad eternity."[53]

Contrary to what may have been written, Father Arrupe was by no means isolated from the world in Japan, where he lived for more than twenty-seven years. Although he became its first provincial in 1958, he traveled the world to raise funds and recruit new Jesuits for his mission: "These trips provided him with the opportunity to make himself known to his confreres in Europe, the United States, Canada, and Latin America. Between the end of 1949 and the end of 1950, he made a trip around the world. He was away from Japan for extended periods of time: in 1954, in 1957, and again in 1961," wrote Gianni La Bella.[54]

At the time of his election as the general of the Society of Jesus, Pedro Arrupe was fifty-one years old. He spoke seven languages, including Japanese. As Father La Bella writes, he was no outsider: "He was, however, known and valued by many of his confreres, especially in Spanish, Latin American and Anglo-Saxon circles."[55] He was also well-known to the French Jesuits, whose Teilhardism he appreciated. He was elected in the third ballot, on May 22, 1965.

Arrupe was not the object of any specific disapproval, but at the General Congregation that elected him, some delegates from Japan expressed "unflattering judgments about him: excessive idealism, a dreamy character, lack of planning and organizational skills, insufficient capacity for government."

• "His election constituted a powerful sign of discontinuity, and a break from the expectations and desires of the Roman Curia, also within the order itself."

• "His way of living and acting was characterized by robust optimism and unconditional confidence in the beneficial effects which, at that time, were deemed likely to flow from the myth of progress."

---

[53] Arrupe, p. 20.
[54] La Bella, *Pedro Arrupe, Superior General de los Jesuitas*, p. 12.
[55] This and the following quotes; La Bella, pp. 13 ff.

• "For myself, as one who knows the heart of the man well—and the rest of his life proved me right—I always greatly appreciated his qualities as a chief, as a leader, and his ability to carry out unprecedented reform without faltering. During his eighteen years as General, he set out the *aggiornamento* of the Society a hundred times without any deviation, at each stage specifying the reasons for adaptation to the world."

At no time did he express sadness at the sharp decline in the number of novices.

• "Fr. Arrupe felt called to carry out this reform in obedience to the Council and the decrees of the 31st General Congregation. It was in no way a cosmetic exercise, but a real and genuine *re-foundation* [emphasis added]. It was not merely a matter of adapting structures, methods and apostolic activities, nor of bringing about an *aggiornamento* of the specific approaches of the various apostolic fields. Even less was it a matter of modernizing the internal organization and governing procedures. Rather, he sought the re-orienting the journey of the order in the light of a renewed spirituality, which was the fruit of the indications of the Council and of the reading of the signs of the times."

With unwavering determination, he pushed the society and the Church into the most frenzied kind of modernism inspired by Teilhard de Chardin, of whom he was an admirer: "In a letter dated June 13, 1981 to the Centre Sèvres in Paris, which was about to celebrate the hundredth anniversary of the birth of the famous Jesuit, he wrote, after having set out several other aspects: 'A third trait of Fr. Teilhard's personality and work is even more precious to us: his burning love for Christ was at the core of his passion for the world transformed and fulfilled in Christianity.' "[56]

The council had been prepared and set on its path by his confreres. It was to serve his purposes and ambitions wonderfully, as well as those of the modernist Jesuits who were chomping at the bit. "The Council

---

56   Calvez, *Le P. Arrupe – L'Église après le Concile*, pp. 216–17.

has brought about a historic splitting of the waters, and has become the origin and source of renewal in the Society. The acceptance of the teachings of Vatican II and the adherence to its spirit summed up the orientation of the entire Generalate," Gianni La Bella explained.

This maneuver is very reminiscent of the fall of the French monarchy: when the Estates General opened in Versailles on May 5, 1789, the Revolution had already been completed. We have observed a similarly organized power grab in the CELAM Assemblies in Medellín, Puebla, and Aparecida.

Obviously, the simpleminded will say that this was a conspiracy.

But there was nothing secret about it. Everything was published in broad daylight. Arrupe's two communications in the Second Vatican Council hall contained all the principles that would set in motion the changes in the society and in the Church. Remember that he has been called the "re-founder" of the society, and it has even been written that there were three societies: that of Saint Ignatius, approved in 1540, that of the refoundation of 1814 with Saint Joseph Pignatelli, and that of Father Arrupe.

Father Arrupe addresses the council

We have selected some significant texts in order to trace the components of this re-foundation, the better to follow Father Arrupe's process in chronological order.

Just four months after his election, Father Arrupe made a conspicuous entry among the Council Fathers. They were in full debate about the famous schema XIII that would develop into *Gaudium et Spes*. In the final text, *The Church in the Modern World*, atheism is the topic of numbers 19, 20, and 21.

Father Arrupe commented on the text that was to be approved definitively by Pope Paul VI on December 7, 1965.

From the outset, he attacked the wording of paragraph 19. "Without doubt against the intention of the drafters," he said, it remained in his opinion "on an excessively intellectual level." "The Church has the truth, the principles, the arguments. But does it transmit all this to the world in a truly effective way? That is where the problem lies."

He followed this up by describing a mismatch between the world and the Church: "To create this [favorable] atmosphere it will be necessary to establish the concrete bases and the method of work. We have an obligation to examine our pastoral methods, especially with regard to the serious problem of atheism."

Facing the Council Fathers who were not used to receiving orders, he outlined a concrete plan of action in four numbered points, summarized below:

1. We need to bring together the best specialists, truly experienced men, in order to draw up a scientific and exact portrait of the current situation, without allowing ourselves to be guided by immediate emergencies.

2. We must define the broad outlines of a coordinated worldwide action, in a way that is sufficiently comprehensive for it to be adaptable to the specific circumstances of each region, and submit them to the supreme pontiff.

3. The pope will then assign to each section of the People of God, under the guidance of the pastors established by the Holy Spirit to govern the Church of God, various fields of action, in which they will work with a spirit of obedience and charity "as wide as the world." This will require sacrifices to overcome individual and collective egoism, by means of a "kind of collective mystical death": the sacrifice of the particularities of dioceses, religious institutes, and even social rank. "All this must die so that Christ may triumph in the world, just as the grain of wheat must die in order to bear fruit."

4. Let us invite all men who believe in God to this common task, so that God may be the Lord of human society.

Father Arrupe concluded his speech by describing the "bridge that will allow us to go from truth to life" in three additional points: "scientific investigation illuminated by faith and thus clothed with the strength of prayer, absolute obedience to the Supreme Pontiff, and fraternal charity that encompasses all."

Arrupe's talent can only be admired. He dictated an idea, provided the means to carry it out, and confirmed it with a mnemonic so that the listener would not forget any of it. The new Jesuit general made a successful debut: he had embodied the future of the People of God, and his didactic style made it easy to memorize what he said.

His key ideas were simple: the Church was no longer in tune with the modern world, now dominated by social communication media: television, cinema, radio, the press. The world had been internationalized, its elites were scientific and technical. It was now necessary to reform the social structures that generate practical, structural, and vital atheism.

Arrupe was to create a communications service for the Society of Jesus that would be comparable to that of a state. For him, this was a battle of ideas, a societal challenge. This is exactly what Pope Francis would later do.

This speech on atheism was a response to the pope's express appeal to all provincials and vice-provincials on the previous May 7. In a solemn and serious tone, the pope addressed the Jesuits, recalling both their status and their obligations toward the supreme pontiff: "It is the special characteristic of the Society of Jesus to be champion of the Church and holy religion in adversity. To it We give the charge of making a stout, united stand against atheism, under the leadership, and with the help of St. Michael, prince of the heavenly host. His very name is the thunder-peal or token of victory."

In Paul VI's mind and expression, this was the philosophical atheism of the Enlightenment and especially the atheism of modern, mainly Hegelian-Marxist, philosophy and all its offshoots.

Clearly, this intellectual struggle was not and would not become that of the society. Arrupe's words were not flatly opposed to this, but they already suggested the direction the society intended to take: social justice first and foremost!

Arrupe's second contribution to the council, on October 12, 1965, was on the situation of the mission in the world today. His method of presentation was identical: "*The work of the commission sets out very well the theological foundations of missionary work in the Church. But . . .*" But, according to Arrupe, what was needed in our time was a renewed understanding of this task. The common idea (*idea vulgar*) that prevailed, according to Arrupe, was partly due to the image that the missionaries themselves presented when returning to their homeland.

In order to be efficient, said Arrupe, the following three points must be observed. First, the world had changed: on the one hand, there were underdeveloped countries, and on the other, hyper-developed countries. It was therefore necessary to take into account the stages of evolution. Secondly, missionary work was complex and difficult because of the ancient cultures of religions, and these ought to be integrated into the City of God. A spiritual influx was also needed because without it, the fusion of cultures would have no soul and would sink into materialism. Finally, dialectical-materialist ideology could not bring peace: peace is everyone's business.

This panorama, which did not contain any idea other than that change was essential, was completed by a list of the obstacles to renewal, which we also summarize here below:

1. The "childishness" of those who see missionaries only as taking care of children and needy people, and who do not understand the intellectual and material needs of the missions.

2. The sentimentalism of those who want to help children and the sick first and foremost, while neglecting higher education and scientific publications on the history and the cultures of foreign religions.

3. A feeling of superiority that is not really Christian, and that does not recognize the genius of the different peoples.

4. Shortsightedness, which leads one to see as bigger that which one sees from closer up, and to seek to satisfy whatever emergency is nearest to one's home.

5. The superficiality of those who have paid a quick visit to the missions and have opinions on everything.

6. The erroneous criteria guiding the choice of missionaries: we are sending out the mediocre.

7. Begging. Missionaries are forced to spend their time looking for money.

At the end of this inventory, Father Arrupe retained the following four points: men must be chosen in line with the mission, and the acquisition of knowledge must be put in place in view of suppressing feelings of superiority; an excellent formation must be provided locally so as to ensure that the next generation of missionaries will be recruited from among the indigenous people; all must consider the development of the missions as being their own responsibility; missionaries are waiting for the council to recognize the superior importance of the mission.

What is striking in the list of obstacles mentioned above is that Arrupe was in fact referring to categories of people. His list is an accusatory enumeration of the "enemies" of the missions. It consists in a deliberate stigmatization of a section of the faithful, presented as "out of their depth" in the face of increasing urgency and new practices. Within the people of God, there are two categories of faithful. And because the world is changing, one of them can no longer serve.

Arrupe's inventory reminds us of Pope Francis's famous list of the cardinals' ailments, as well as the splitting of the Catholic world in two: on the one hand, the righteous, and on the other, the "Pelagians" and the "Gnostics" whose numerous masses had no idea that they belonged to these heretical categories!

Designating adversaries or alleged incompetents has more to do with ideology than with fraternal charity.

When in the following December, Arrupe presented these criteria for the development of the mission in the French magazine *Réalités*, he added a new category to the list: the paternalists.

This was already a sign of a certain departure from the traditional teaching of the Jesuits. According to this logic, the theology of Saint Thomas is all very well, but it is necessary to adjust our cultures and abandon our Western ways. When asked if Fr. Teilhard de Chardin might be helpful in bringing about this change, Father Arrupe referred to what he had already said: there is more good than bad in Teilhard. The important thing, he said, was to create bridges—to work without rest so as to build many solid bridges that connect Catholic thought to the various branches of human intellectual activity: scientific, philosophical, and social.

During the general audience on July 27, 2018, addressing the *Catholic Theological Ethics in the World Church* network's Sarajevo Congress on the theme "A Critical Moment for Bridge-Building: Catholic Theological Ethics Today," Pope Francis echoed Arrupe's leitmotif: "The theme of your meeting is one to which I myself have often called attention: the need to build bridges, not walls."

This theme of "the mission" was repeatedly taken up by the superior general, in particular during a conference in Rome on April 2, 1968, under the title "Christian Faith and Missionary Action Today."

Having pointed out the collapse of missionary recruitment and its sociological causes, the end of colonialism, and the birth of nationalism, Father Arrupe addressed two crucial issues: the conciliar interpretation of the maxim "No salvation outside the Church" and that of religious freedom.

"Religious pluralism is a fact that we must accept," and "religious freedom, as we have already said, is a fact that is no longer open to discussion," he asserted.

And again: "It is a general principle of pastoral theology that the truth, by the very fact of being the truth, does not offer of itself the capacity to be understood": "preparation" is needed.

But what preparation? For him, it was in fact a question of seeing a "portion of truth" in the recognition that "other religions have a salvific value because they form a more general providential plan than that of the Judeo-Christian religion for its faithful." Here he referred to Karl Rahner, who taught that non-Christian religions contain "supernatural elements" in themselves.

This is precisely what would later be called the "theology of the people."

Lastly, Arrupe asserted, this suffering world expects something other than an incomprehensible catechism. The conciliar decree *Ad Gentes* and *Populorum Progressio* changed the picture for missionaries, he said: "the action of the missionary Church in favor of the progress of peoples is above all a requirement that is internal to the Church itself."

He mentioned new sins that demand a new apostolate: those that were already being called "structural sins" which prevent conversion. His words regarding these sound like a statement made by a worker-priest in the 1950s.

We must never forget that the Second Vatican Council was intended to be above all pastoral. This "pastoral" claim was prompted by the following observation: the modern world no longer understands the Catholic religion because of its failure to adapt its language and communication to this world.

Father Arrupe and the synods

Arrupe's statements at the council and throughout his term of office would later spread throughout the Christian world. Here we will focus on three aspects, regrouping the interventions of the superior general according to their audience. This seems to us to be the best way to follow the phases and the progression of Father Arrupe's pastoral theses. The texts below are all taken from the previously cited book, *La Iglesia de hoy y del futuro*.

With great generosity and practical wisdom, Father Arrupe offered his collaboration to all the religious. He invented expressions demonstrating a desire for change that he would convey to all religious congregations. In our view, the most radical and complete presentation of this idea is to be found in his address to the General Chapter of the Sisters of the Institute of the Slaves of the Sacred Heart in March 1969.

His remarks at the Synod of Bishops on cooperation between the Holy See and the Episcopal Conferences on October 24, 1969, dealt precisely with the desire of the Union of Superiors General to cooperate with the ecclesiastical hierarchy.

> In order to achieve greater elasticity and adaptability in these post-conciliar times, and following the decree *Perfectae Caritatis*, all Congregations are assessing in their special Chapters the greatest possible adaptation of their own charism to present-day circumstances, including by means of profound changes not only in their structures but also in their Constitutions themselves, always respecting and leaving intact their fundamental charism.
>
> We are entering a new age, profoundly rooted in a theology of religious life and in a sense of the apostolate that should foster a close collaboration of the religious so greatly desired by the episcopate . . . because it will renew or do away with past rigidity . . . thanks to a deep commitment to inserting oneself into the overall pastoral scene by means of new forms and structures based on healthy pluralism.

We all know the devastation produced by such reforms. Nuns have abandoned their convents or institutes to live in the world, turning into a kind of female worker-priests. We now have diocesan virgins living at home under the authority of the bishop.

On October 4, 1971, Father Arrupe addressed the Synod of Bishops with a talk named "The Vital Problem of the Priest in his Ministry."

Arrupe basically said that with the crisis of the priesthood, it is the voice of God that is calling us to something great, and giving us the opportunity, today as never before in history, for a greater understanding, a renewal and an adaptation of the priesthood to our modern times. God is with us: "*Dios está con nosotros.*"

"When speaking of the ministerial priesthood, our analytical mind divides it into doctrine and praxis . . . but life is one and cannot be 'divided.' . . . We are facing a total and vital problem," he said. He added that a global answer including praxis and doctrine should be sought for, based on four "aspects" which we summarize below:

1. A doctrinal aspect

The doctrinal aspect must be "the foundational stone," but while it should be affirmed clearly and firmly, it must also be "a doctrine of *healthy openness* [emphasis added] in order to confront problems through serious investigation and without taboos: today there can be no taboos if we do not want our priests to be taboo for us."

2. An institutional aspect

"There exists a break in trust between the priest and the institution, and the people who represent them. Even if bishops are very fine people, they do not cease to represent the institution, and to embody it with all its weight of structure, tradition, and even immobility. . . . The presbyteral body is sound and full of good will. . . . We are experiencing a dynamic cultural change that is very different to the more static one in which we grew up and were raised. . . . We need to develop a favorable openness to initiatives that are born of the action of the Spirit."

3. An apostolic aspect

"We need to create apostolic enthusiasm. . . . To make priests feel useful . . . We must constantly choose ministries which correspond to the concrete needs of the People of God. . . . It is vital for us to have an inexhaustible capacity for adaptation and inventiveness in order to face new situations, new challenges, and growing apostolic prospects."

4. A personal aspect

Let the priest feel "immediately responsible for the building up of the Church . . . and for the concrete manifestation of this charism in a concrete service of the People of God." Arrupe added: "This is about a life given to Christ. . . . The true solution to priests' problems is found in the priest himself, in his intimate contact with the person of the High Priest."

In conclusion, Father Arrupe called for "discovering the action of the Spirit, the plans of God, the signs of these times of light and grace in which it has been given to us to live, in order to incorporate ourselves into the impulse that the Spirit today gives to his Church and to the world."

As we shall see, Father Arrupe's self-assurance was unshakeable at all times. To the bishops who were struggling with the terrible difficulties of the aftermath of the council, he indicated the sure paths to the future, "the future of the Church."

In September 1965, Paul VI published an encyclical "on the Holy Eucharist," *Mysterium Fidei*, and in June 1967 came another encyclical on priestly celibacy, *Sacerdotalis Caelibatus*. In 1971, were these topics still relevant to Father Arrupe's eyes? That year, the synod dealt with two topics: "The ministerial priesthood" and "Justice in the world." Fr. Jean-Yves Calvez, reporting for CERAS (Center for Research and Social Justice) summed it all up in a few words: *Justice and World Society.*

Did Father Arrupe speak on this subject? We do not know; however, for the Society of Jesus, it was the hottest topic at the time. In reading this synodal document, forty-seven years later, the depths of abyss into which the Church was sinking are plain to see. It was pompously presented as "an organic body of doctrine," from *Rerum Novarum* to *Octogesima Adveniens* and *Mater et Magistra*, *Pacem in Terris*, *Gaudium et Spes*, and *Populorum Progressio*, but it was in fact a compilation of all the socio-political demands of the third world Leftists, not least those of all the Catholic NGOs.

On the occasion of the Synod of Bishops held from September 27 to October 26, 1974, on the theme "Evangelization in the Modern World," Father Arrupe spoke three times, including twice during the synod itself. His talks were on "The Global Experience of Evangelization" and "Evangelization and Human Promotion."

Prior to the event, he had written extensively in the *Omnis Terra* preparatory documents, covering fifteen very concentrated pages. The principle of his discourse never changed: *priority must be given to praxis.*

"Discernment is a gift of the Spirit that fills the universe as a principle of life, development and renovation in our history," he wrote. He went on to describe four other "explosions" in the history of the Church: "the entry of the Church into the world of Mediterranean civilization"; the barbarian invasions, by which the Church became "European"; the great discoveries of the sixteenth century, where the Church became "truly Western"; and lastly, evangelization in the colonial era, which brought the Church "squarely into the world community."

Today, the Church has once again become "like a small flock scattered throughout the world, which can be described as a 'diaspora.' . . . It is like the leaven that must ferment all humanity," wrote Arrupe.

Here he quoted Paul VI: "This new and providential situation of the Church in the world makes us aware of the great obligations and enormous advantages that are open to us in the field of missionary cooperation in order to spread the missionary ideal on a worldwide scale, and in view of a large-scale contribution to all the missions of the Church."[57]

Father Arrupe then discussed the theme of "evangelization – growth towards catholicity" in a number of points.

1. "We are seeing a dynamic force that affects both the Church and humanity as distinct from the Church. . . . [The] double dimension of growth, of the Church in the world and of the world in the Church, are two aspects of the same process," he wrote. Here it is difficult not to notice a Teilhardian touch!

2. "This progressive presence of the Gospel in human history, through the word and life of the Church, is what we here refer to as 'the growth of catholicity.' "

3. "This phenomenon of growth, like all organic development processes, presents a number of contradictions and gives rise to a process that we can describe as dialectical.

"As in all growth, there is a transition from one stage to another. This transition includes a time of death and a time of birth to a new life. The opposition between these two moments is real, and it is the condition for making possible the growth that consists in overcoming this opposition. . . .

"The present stage of salvation history is an intermediate period between the irrevocable establishment of salvation through the advent of Christ and its consummation in the fullness of the

---

[57]   From a speech given on May 21, 1972.

Kingdom to come; each stage of this development has a double moment: that of the 'already' and that of the 'not yet', and no historical achievement can ever be presented as complete in the field of salvation, since the eschatological perspective transcends each historical moment."

The whole policy of initiating processes dear to Pope Francis perfectly obeys the dictates of this dialectical philosophy of history.

Having laid the foundations, Father Arrupe examined the methods to be used—namely, study and dialogue. This is a transcendent dialogue that goes from the Trinity to the Incarnation of the Word, completed by the action of the Holy Spirit.

But there is another side to this dialogue.

From Father Arrupe's point of view, the vocation of Christians in this world, which they share with atheists and non-believers, is to establish a dialogue and to join with them in building a better world. "Pluralism" requires a "new development of Catholicity." Other cultures are indeed bearers of a religious tradition. Therefore, local churches must practice cultural identification and adaptation.

He explained it like this:

> This "incarnation" or particularization in a culture is the path by which the development of catholicity and universality must take place. Since the universe of men *de facto* finds itself in the dispersion of cultural pluralism, it is only by entering into this pluralism that the Church will be universal—universally present and universally understandable—the sign and promise of salvation. . . .

> We are convinced that the Church is at the dawn of a new era of development, a development towards a real, authentic and universal presence. . . . At the same time, she will respond to the profoundly religious aspirations of the peoples, complementing and sanctifying their cultural aspirations and enlivening them with the abundant outpouring of the Holy Spirit.

According to Father Arrupe, such evangelization is meant for a youth that is indifferent to traditional forms: "We do not think it is too romantic to say that youth can be the best power of purification, renovation and creativity in the world."

This can be compared with the "youthism" of Pope Francis: "We need you, young people . . . you challenge us to emerge from the logic that says, 'but it's always been like that,' " he said on March 19, 2018, speaking to three hundred young people. At the Youth Synod, six months later, young French people were nonetheless rejected as being too "traditional"!

Father Arrupe continued: "One of the most important fruits of the rejuvenation of the Church through active contact with youth will be the forming of a new Christian humanism."

By 1974, the great transformation of the Society of Jesus, whose full expression would be revealed at the 32nd Congregation in the following December, had already taken place. Arrupe could not conceive of speaking of the new evangelization without associating it with social development. Social progress, understood as the liberation of man and the humanization of the universe, has three aspects: political, economic, and cultural. This aspect was further developed during the third intervention of Father Arrupe at the Synod of Bishops: "*Evangelization and Human Promotion.*"

At the heart of his talk, he stated that "achieving fraternal union among men requires an effort on the part of all today in order to promote" the following:

1. "Equality: the elimination of the exploitation of the weak; the suppression of unnecessary inequalities in the economic, social and political order." (It reads like something by Auguste Comte, who inspired the constitution and motto of Brazil: *Ordem e Progresso.*)

2. "Solidarity: responsibility with respect to the common good, channels of cooperation, dialogue, participation and development of the associative life."

3. "Freedom: as a norm and not as an exception; acceptance of pluralism; rejection of authoritarianism and violence."

4. "The subordination of the economy to the integral good of the people and the rejection of quantitative economic growth."

5. "The authenticity of human relationships: truthfulness, information, communication among persons, fraternal dialogue."

Next came a series of characteristic expressions: we must strive to "obtain the full liberation of man"; the sciences may develop but "at the service of the human person"; we must suppress "all forms of exploitation in order to establish fraternal equality at all levels of human coexistence." To conclude, it is necessary to "suppress egoisms themselves, to which all men are subject because of sin." The list could have been longer.

The nature of Father Arrupe's demands, his illuminism, not to say his propheticism regarding future society, may seem surprising. However, it is important not to let this catalog be the end of the story. What is important, and what remains today, is a conception and philosophy of history, the dialectic of progress that is deemed to generate universal brotherhood, and the specific role of the Holy Spirit who watches over the proper unfolding of eschatological progress, since He is its master. Going even further, all of this could be described as a superficial froth; the final aim is to change the Church. The social revolution, even when mitigated by quotes from the Gospel, irrevocably leads to the ruin of the Catholic Church—and that is now what is happening before our eyes. To understand what is going on, we must consider the current outcome of such thought and of the universal action that Father Arrupe led from 1965 to 1983.

Arrupe concluded his third intervention at the 1974 Synod of Bishops with these words: "Evangelization cannot reduce the proclamation of the Gospel to a mere intellectual presentation of the Christian message, nor can it reduce the reception of faith to a ritual or sacramental response. The Church, when she evangelizes, proposes with the help of the grace of the Holy Spirit, to obtain a conversion that transforms ways of thinking and personal and community attitudes.

Evangelization tends to make Christ the integrating principle of personal life and community relationships in historical reality."

The better to understand the nature and origins of this "evangelization," it is necessary to turn to a long text from January 2008 in which Cardinal Bergoglio presented his vision of "inculturation" following the CELAM Assembly in Aparecida the previous year: "Medellín was of such importance for Latin America and even for the universal Church, that when in 1974 the president of CELAM, Eduardo Pironio, went to Rome for the Synod on Evangelization, he took with him three pastoral suggestions that would later have a significant influence on Pope Paul VI's famous apostolic exhortation, *Evangelii Nuntiandi*. The three suggestions were: base ecclesial communities, the liberation theme and popular religiosity."

Archbishop Pironio was created a cardinal by Pope Paul VI in 1976 at age fifty-six. He remained an active agent of the revolution in the Church until his death in 1998.

During the 1977 Synod on "Catechesis and Inculturation" (the synodal council had proposed several topics, but Paul VI chose this one), Father Arrupe made two presentations.

The first was aimed at interrogating Marxism and at teaching young Christians to discern beyond political programs, how they are also the expression and assertion of values. We already know what this type of practice has produced. But in 1977, Father Arrupe stated that he had perceived "a certain kind of evolution in the Marxist world."

The second presentation is much more relevant to the trajectory we are dealing with here. It was entitled *Catechesis and inculturation*, and it allows us to join the dots between all that we have already discovered about this thinking and the tools of its implementation. The term *inculturation* is after all a key word in the theology of the people.

"Imposing foreign cultural forms on people who have their own culture as the only way to express the faith and the way to live it is a strong obstacle to catechesis," said Father Arrupe.

According to him, "faith and culture call out to each other: faith purifies and vivifies culture, and cultures enrich and bring to light the inexhaustible potential of faith . . . , clothed in the unchanging and unchangeable deposit of the splendor of the gifts that man has received from God.

"Not to have taken these principles into account may be one of the causes of the current de-Christianization of our cultures, and a strong and obvious obstacle to evangelization," he insisted.

Father Arrupe therefore set out in four points what inculturation is in relation to catechesis.

1. "It is the practical corollary of the theological principle that Christ is the only savior and that he saves only what he assumes. Hence, he must take up all cultures in his body, which is the Church. Naturally, he must purify them of everything that is contrary to his Spirit, and thus save them without destroying them."

2. "It is the penetration of faith into the deepest levels of man's life, thus affecting his way of thinking, feeling and acting according to the animating action of the Spirit."

3. "It offers the possibility of the equality of the service of the Gospel to all cultural values."

4. "It is an ongoing dialogue between the Word of God and the many ways in which people express themselves."

"This is how inculturation makes us capable of speaking with (and not just speaking to) the men and women of today about their problems and needs, their hopes and values."

At the end of his talk, Father Arrupe quoted Father de Lubac to reinforce his position.

He returned to the subject in a conference at the Lateran University on March 15, 1978: "Aspects and tensions of inculturation." This capital topic was truly one of the intellectual keys to current modernism.

I can well understand that the reader may have doubts regarding the intellectual and filial relationship that exists between Arrupe and Bergoglio. However, on this particular issue, Austen Ivereigh reports the following:

In September 1985 Bergoglio hosted at the Colegio Máximo a major conference with 120 theologians from twenty-three countries on the topic of "the evangelization of culture and the inculturation of the Gospel," in order to mark the four hundredth anniversary of the arrival of the Jesuits in Argentina. His opening address was pure Puebla, identifying both faith and culture as "privileged places where divine wisdom is manifested." The first was the Gospel, which reveals God's saving plan through His visible image, Jesus Christ; the second was "the different cultures, fruit of the wisdom of the peoples" that reflected "the creative and perfecting Wisdom of God." At the end of his address he paid "filial homage" to Father Arrupe "who in the Synod on Evangelization of 1974 had pronounced what was then the novel word "inculturation."

To convince oneself of the folly of the thesis of inculturation, it is well worth reading the chapter on catechesis in *Iota Unum* by Prof. Romano Amerio: "Arrupe does not want catechisms to have 'complete, strict and orthodox definitions, because these could lead to an aristocratic and involutionary form.' He speaks as if the truth consisted in confused approximations, as if orthodoxy were a nonvalue and as if authentic catechesis were born of the 'ochlocracy' or power of the mob."

Cardinal Benelli made similar comments at the synod and the majority of the bishops rejected the idea of a "question and answer" catechism.

Technical note on the functioning of the synod

Fr. Giovanni Caprile, a Jesuit who reported on the synod, gave a very interesting account of its workings: "In the course of 1975, the first meeting of the newly created Council of the General Secretariat was tasked with drafting all of the documentation on evangelization that was to be submitted to the Pope as the basis for the document that would become the Apostolic Exhortation *Evangelii Nuntiandi* of December 8, 1975."

It was therefore the synod that provided the material, with all that this implies. It was common knowledge that Father Lebret had inspired *Populorum Progressio*, but in this synod's case, there was a real system of dependence. The Jesuits, ever the largest group in all the Vatican bodies, were at work in all areas. Pope Francis's synods have shown that they are well-versed in all kinds of operations. The Curia of the Church has become the Curia of the Jesuits, or if you will, the Curia of the Jesuits has become that of the Church.

The synods of the Church of Pope Francis have demonstrated the formidable capacity of the Jesuit apparatus and its allies. Nothing and no one surpasses them in the art of obtaining a desired end. The Church has become a "*mater jesuitica*."

Pastoral care and religious life

This analysis would be very incomplete if it did not take into account the following two major concerns of Father Arrupe. He described them in several conferences included in *La Iglesia de Hoy y del Futuro*: "Evangelization and Religious Life," 1974; "The Future of Religious Life," 1974; "New Challenges and Opportunities for the Experience of God in Religious Life Today," 1977; "Religious Life and Insertion in the World," 1977.

To fully understand Father Arrupe's radical demands for change, we must remember what the council said about itself: it was a pastoral council. This was its defining feature, before which all things must surrender. The council's pastoral approach was warranted by the modern world that could no longer understand the old ways of evangelization. Hence the desire to draw up a catechism without "fixed" questions or answers, as these were not considered appropriate for a world that was constantly changing. The key word, therefore, was *adaptation*.

Discovering the demands of the modern world and *adjusting* to them are the two pillars of all the superior general's addresses on pastoral ministry. They are the two things requiring that the religious, both men and women, should give up a number of their ways and even modify their Constitutions.

There are plenty of formulations of this kind, and the message they convey is perfectly coherent:

- "We cannot betray the charism of our foundation, but we must do our utmost in order the better to understand it and apply it to the present historical circumstances."

- "A fundamental concern is that modern thought and mentality are evolving, and it is not clear how they will define themselves in the future; on the other hand, this uncertainty compels us to try an experiment that will sometimes involve great risk and claim victims who, under normal circumstances, would not exist and would have been able to survive."

- "The Church and Religious Life today are living in a situation of *gigantic exodus* (and in some way they have always lived and will always live so): an exodus from a culture, from concepts, from securities, from ideologies, from a social order; this exodus implies ruptures and uprooting that are sometimes violent and extremely painful, or at times unconscious, in order to begin something new, something unknown."

- "Ultimately, the challenge of *doing*, of Praxis, is the primary value."

- "It is certain that the authentic experience of God to which we have just referred, produces commitment. The faith of the Christians is a historical faith."

The eight hundred pages of Father Arrupe's collected works are no more than a dramatization of the need to adapt to history. In every development of his thought, he is never far away from Teilhardian evolution: "The authentic experience of God will never turn inward. It opens up in an endless spiral. The poor (I give this word a very broad meaning, that includes all types of poverties) become a genuine '*locus theologicus*' for discovering the inexhaustible newness (or news) that is God in Jesus."

When the poor become *loci theologici*, sources of theological cognition, the core of the theology of the people has been reached.

To support his point, Father Arrupe quotes a religious from the slums: "The oppressed understand the language of the oppressed and the message of the Gospel is written in the language of the oppressed, those who are marginalized in society, minority groups who are constantly under threat. Can we possibly understand the Gospel if we read it from our privileged position in the system, from a position of power or security, from the institution?"

The comment of this anonymous priest provides a conclusive explanation. It is final. "The poor" is a socio-political category. The "very broad meaning" mentioned by Father Arrupe is an illusion. There is no "*locus theologicus*"; it is a purely ideological contraption!

The Jewish people were oppressed by the Egyptians and liberated by Moses, but they did not immediately enter the Promised Land because of their persistent unfaithfulness.

The question arises: Wherever did this strange experience of God come from?

Father Arrupe's references include Karl Rahner and Jean Mouroux. Their names recall antagonistic positions in the Society of Jesus at the height of modernism in 1910.

At the time, Fr. Pierre Rousselot, SJ, supported the doctrine of the illumination of the signs of credibility by grace. Another Jesuit, Father de Broglie, made a decisive clarification, according to Father Faux, SJ, who wrote: "It mainly refuted the idea that a faith based on external signs would thereby cease to rest on the grounds of divine authority." Rousselot's thinking is similar to that of Blondel: "In Blondel as in Rousselot, the act of faith is born in the universe of signs." In his lecture, Father Arrupe quoted Jean Mouroux's thesis: "The whole Christian experience must be embedded in these constitutive relationships (with Christ); it is there that faith constitutes the affirmation of our ontological and spiritual immanence in Christ, it is the awareness of our rootedness and our initial foundation (*fundamentación*) in the love of Christ."

This is not a theology book. We are merely pointing out that behind all of Father Arrupe's reforms, there was not only a necessary *aggiornamento* sought after by the council, and a response to the modern world for a Church of the future, but more importantly, a revival of the modernist theses that had been circulating in the society for a long time. They are the new and conciliar apparel of a theology that is completely alien to the Catholic tradition.

This supports our contention that neither the council nor its implementation are the primary causes of the situation in the Church today, but rather a revival of ancient heresies.

Father Arrupe's 1977 lecture, quoted above, was echoed in 2011 by Fr. Antonio M. Pernia, superior general of the Society of the Divine Word, under a very similar title: "Challenges and Opportunities for Consecrated Life in the Context of the World and the Church Today."

It deserves mention because it offers a good view of the radicalization of the discourse and the new orientations that were already present in Father Arrupe's talks.

It was during the seminar of the International Union of Superiors General in Rome, on February 11, 2011, that Father Pernia disclosed his updated version of "openness to the world," as presented thirty-four years previously by the superior general of the Jesuits.

He described the advent of a global world: "Life in the world is now like life in a village." The globalization of the economy leads to the "relentless pursuit of profit" and to the disregard of moral and ethical considerations, he stressed, but also to international migration. Among the casualties of globalization, he named "Mother Earth." He also explained that globalization is the source of secularization, which leads to a decline in vocations.

What, then, is the place of the religious life in this globalized world?

"The present crisis of the relevance of religious life is just one aspect of the more fundamental crisis of religion as such; or to be more precise, of religion in its present socio-cultural form ... hence the need for a new socio-cultural form of religion, or even of a 'post-religion religion', that can satisfy the religiosity of humanity in the post-modern world of our cybernetic age," was Father Pernia's response.

What follows is entirely logical: the rise of a global Church. Again, there can be no question as to the origins of this process as described by Father Pernia:

- "At Vatican II, the Church was really felt to be a global Church, even if this was true only at its start, with a universal episcopate acting in harmony with the Pontiff."

- "This development implies that the Catholic Church has become a polycentric Church."

- "The rise of a global Church therefore implies the disintegration of Christianity's identification with the West."

- "Things changed with Vatican II and its positive appraisal of the cultures of the peoples. Theology began to discuss inculturation [a word coined by Father Arrupe] and the building of the local Church. There is no longer just one way of being Church or of being Christian in the world. There are as many different ways as there are cultures."

- "The mission has become multidirectional."

In a lecture he gave in 2014 in Tagaytay, Father Pernia elaborated extensively on Father Arrupe's understanding of the experience of God. In his talk, he fully incorporated both Father Arrupe's plan and his own into Pope Francis's strategy.

A little-known scandal: the banned Jesuits

To complete the picture, the point of view of the Jesuits who did not comply with Father Arrupe's reforms needs to be heard. As far as official history is concerned, they never existed. And when, by chance, they are mentioned, their insights are overlooked. They asked Rome for permission to create a "new Society of Jesus" in vain.

The key elements of their struggle were gathered in the book *La Verdad sobre la Compañía de Jesús* (The Truth about the Society of Jesus) by Ignacio Javier Pignatelli—a pseudonym that used the names of three prominent figures of the society. The book accurately reflected the thinking of European and American Jesuits faithful to the Church, to Saint Ignatius, to the Ignatian spiritual exercises, and to the Constitutions of the Society of Jesus.

According to these anonymous witnesses, the demolition of the society first took place from 1967 to 1970, and then from 1971 to 1974. The preparation of the 1974 Congregation was entrusted to one of the most radical Jesuits, the well-known Jean-Yves Calvez. In Italy,

Fr. Bartolomeo Sorge joined the Frenchman's efforts by pushing for a new Catholic cultural identity and the re-foundation of Christian democracy. In those days, there were two societies: one faithful, the other progressive.

The book described ten errors of the society as Arrupe was promoting it: putting the emphasis on human sciences, idealism, relativism, existentialism, historicism, progressivism, and futurism and abandoning that which existed in the past: the treasures of Christianity and Saint Ignatius himself. The book also includes a doctrinal assessment of these errors.

Under Arrupe, the society used various forms of violence to eliminate its opponents: maintaining power with the appearance of legality, corrupting youth, spreading false information, seducing the naive, intimidating the fearful, and reducing the resistance of faithful Jesuits.

If ever the hidden documents of this so-far unsuccessful attempt to restore the Society of Jesus to its authentic form should be brought to the light, then the present pontificate will appear in all its truth!

The Jesuits and social justice

One last tableau will reveal the transformation of the Society of Jesus and its politico-religious action in Latin America.

From July 25 to 29, 1966, the first meeting of the Latin American Centers of Investigation and Social Action (CIAS) took place in Lima, Peru. Fourteen months had passed since Father Arrupe's election, and preparations for the 31st General Congregation were in full swing. On December 12 of that same year, in a letter to the major superiors of Latin America, the general set forth the vital importance of this meeting which he himself had been unable to attend:

> The importance that I attached to this congress was such that I insisted that it be held at all costs, in spite of obstacles and difficulties of which there was no shortage, and I did not hesitate to have the two assistant fathers from Latin America represent me. I also decided that the assistant father from Germany and

one or the other father from the Institute of Social Sciences of the Gregorian would be present, in order to give a broader base and perspectives to its proceedings. The objective of the meeting was for the fathers to get to know each other, to analyze together what has been done so far, together to create a common awareness of the issued at hand and viable solutions in the social field, and to present to me the fruit of their work, their conclusions and their responses.

Arrupe noted that the fathers had in fact focused on developing a common definition of the CIAS, whose nature and function would be summed up in its being described as "a specialized body of the Society exclusively dedicated to the apostolate of social justice."

"The majority realized that the lack of a common consciousness within this definition had been largely responsible for misunderstandings and disagreements both within the CIAS as such and in their relations with superiors," he continued.

The conclusions of this congress led to the creation of the Latin American Council of CIAS (CLACIAS). The final document was approved, and a petition entitled "An official position of the Company on the social conflict in Latin America" was added for internal use only.

This was all promulgated on December 12, 1966.

At this point, the strength and determination of Father Arrupe must be emphasized once again. The commitment to social justice was already in place when he lined up his troops for battle. Until then, each CIAS had its own methods and its own more or less specialized members. Those days were gone. The CIAS were to recognize that they had one leader and that they had to follow a common policy in an integrated manner.

References to the council led to stressing the need for a reform of mindsets and structures in order to correct "scandal and exaggerated inequalities in economic and social matters." These conditions had already been identified by Father Arrupe's predecessor, Father Janssens, and described by the council as "contrary to social justice, equity and human dignity and to social and international peace."

Father Arrupe put forward this conclusive argument:

> The Church possesses the know-how, lights and energy which
> derive from its primary, religious mission; these make it suited
> to the temporal structuring of society. It is certainly true that the
> changing of temporal structures as such belongs to the laity, while
> our task has more to do with the changing of mindsets. But we
> cannot forget that these same secular activities are not the exclu-
> sive competence of the laity. I therefore urge the provincial fathers
> once again to reflect on this duty—humanizing and personaliz-
> ing society—and to see to it that it is properly understood, even
> by those who are not part of the CIAS, so that no one will stand
> in the way of this seemingly less priestly commitment, but that,
> instead, all shall cooperate, each according to their own forces.

Here precisely can be found the origins of the creation of the
Jesuit ideology, that essential part of the conquest of power, whatever
that power may be. By a clever trick of language, Father Arrupe abolished the distinction between temporal and spiritual power, which
is the foundation of the Church's social doctrine. Worker priests had
embraced the class struggle; the revolutionary clergy of Latin America was launching liberation struggles. As to Father Arrupe, he had
invented a new trilogy: "*humanization – personalization – changing
the mindset.*"

Beyond doubt, more than fifty years later, this is the driving force
behind the political and religious thought of Pope Francis.

The scope of Father Arrupe's vision is impossible to gauge if one
does not perceive what he imagined what would follow, beyond the
organization of the CIAS, from obedience to the council. He saw international peace as the outcome of action for social justice: "It is my
desire," he said, "to be able to establish close to me a Center for the
Promotion of World Social Justice, one of whose functions would be
to cooperate in the financing of the CIAS."

From that moment on, the society changed. The Jesuits hired
competent personnel. They were more active than ever on the Latin
American continent.

The great transformation of the Society of Jesus and its redeployment into social and political struggles followed on the heels of the council. Father Arrupe, a high-flying strategist, fully grasped the new direction that would be taken at this assembly of all the Latin American bishops. He already knew its key players. He was the most well informed because the company was present everywhere.

Before anyone else, he had realized what the 1968 CELAM meeting would be like. Therein lies his genius. Like a military general, he rallied the troops and confirmed the strategy.

Father Arrupe called a meeting of all the provincials of the continent from May 6 to 14, 1968, in Itapoan.

He visited poverty-stricken Brazil, where he was deeply moved:

> I was invited to celebrate Mass in one of the poorest places in the middle of a suburban slum, a favela where about a hundred thousand people lived. They lived there in the mud, because this suburb had been built in a valley that was flooded every time it rained. The faithful sang a hymn accompanied by a wretched guitar, *"To love is to give oneself."* As the song unfolded, I felt a lump in my throat. I had to make a great effort to continue saying Mass. . . . The consecration took place in tremendous silence. . . . When I gave Communion I saw their dry, hard, sunburned faces, some with tears that flowed like pearls. . . . My hands were shaking.

At the end of this visit, followed by a process of synthesis, the provincials published a letter known as the Letter from Rio. This manifesto set out once and for all—if such a thing were needed—the Jesuits' plan for the continent and the world as a whole.

This five-page letter consisted of eleven paragraphs.

Its ideological references were the council, *Populorum Progressio*, the desires of the bishops, and Father Arrupe's December 22, 1966 letter, which we have already discussed.

Here are the main points of the *Letter from Rio*, as summarized by us:

• Urban and rural society are in a state of appalling misery.
The values of traditional society and culture are incapable of

responding to a new reality. The dynamism of the people and their conscientization can open up new horizons.

• We are living in a particular moment of salvation history, and these problems are a top priority for our apostolic strategy. The Society of Jesus is present in the entire temporal existence of man today. It does not exercise power, but it inspires personal and collective consciousness. This implies a number of ruptures. Our goal is the liberation of man from all forms of servitude: the right to equality and freedom, not only political but economic, cultural, and religious. We reject all aristocratic and bourgeois attitudes.

• Our universal apostolate will elicit unavoidable reactions, but we will continue to preach the gospel of the poor regardless. The society will summon Christians to this reflection and to this love in order to stimulate them to fulfill their earthly commitments.

• There can be no separation between religious life and professional or public life. The teaching of philosophy and theology is that of a global vision of man and humanity, and it requires an introduction to human sciences.

• That is why we are moving our apostolic forces to the innumerable masses of the abandoned. Jesuits are working in social centers to train rural and working-class leaders so that they may become the authors of their own liberation. We will resort in particular to the education of the popular masses and to the animation of base communities. For us, this will mean a change of lifestyle.

• All the members of the communities must work together. The situation in Latin America demands radical change in all aspects of education. The families who entrust their children to us must commit themselves to be sincere collaborators of this, our social concern. Our universities, as they become more democratic, will need to excel in human and educational sciences in order to plan for change in our society. We will work for and with the laity.

- The media, through their power and scope, will become agents for the formation of a collective cultural and social togetherness.

- We will never succeed in building a more humane society without the divine input that the world expects from us priests and religious. Can the society keep in its midst those who do not want to pray? The fulfillment of the commitment expressed in this letter ultimately depends on the answer to that question.

- This will lead to new standards of decision-making. We are under no illusions: this total and far-reaching change will take time. We hope that with the help of divine grace, the Society of Jesus in Latin America will be able to accomplish this necessary conversion in order responsibly to carry out that which this historical era demands of us, for the greater glory of God.

This manifesto was both a declaration of war against the continent's society and a commitment to class struggle; it displayed unwavering determination and proclaimed the continuation of the permanent reform of the society. In Mexico, this letter was published full-length in the Jesuit magazine *Pulga* in August 1968, and it had a devastating effect, especially on educational institutions. This was a year and a half before Jorge Bergoglio was ordained to the priesthood.

Father Arrupe's grand design in response to Paul VI's appeal

The appeal Paul VI made to the Society of Jesus in May 1965 was crystal clear: to fight atheism, and especially communist atheism which was overwhelming the world.

According to Father Arrupe's interpretation, it is not only communism that leads to atheism but social injustice, and the Church had lost the working class by not taking a firm stand against poverty and ruin caused by liberal capitalism in the third world.

The history of the social apostolate of the Society of Jesus has been thoroughly reviewed for the years 1950 to 2000. Ricardo Antoncich, SJ, compiled all its key events in seventy pages under the title *Historia del Sector Social.*

When reading the individual episodes of this great adventure, one is struck by the sheer number of operations carried out over fifty years, and which continue today under the pontificate of Pope Francis.

Father Antoncich's work highlights an aspect that a fragmented reading would not have allowed us to discover. At the risk of irritating the reader, we can but admire the perseverance and the determination shown in the pursuit of the objective set by Father Arrupe. Undoubtedly, the permanent adjustments and changes of tactics used to stay the course also deserve appreciation. Apart from the Communist Party, we know of no other organization that practices self-criticism as does the Society of Jesus.

When considering the upheavals in the Church today, it can be said that the Jesuits were and are to the Church what the Communist Party was to the Soviet Union. To re-found the society was certainly a superhuman project, but to transform it to the point where it succeeded in replacing the millenary Church is nothing short of superb!

The tone is that of the most straightforward liberation theology. "In times of a crisis of fundamental values, in cases of flagrant injustice, the service of the Word demands that the priest adopt prophetic attitudes. The service of the Gospel demands that evil be denounced and the Kingdom be announced, but he must do so as an envoy of the Christian community," noted Father Antoncich.

Welcome back to the Old Testament! Well, almost. "By virtue of the eschatological vocation of his ministry, the priest is a 'protestor par excellence,'" he wrote. The fall of the USSR would not curb this denunciation of injustice; it would only lead to changing the factors of consciousness-raising. After promoting development as a source of peace, followed by the fight against dictatorial regimes and unbridled capitalism, the "Apostolic Project" would go on to denounce neoliberalism, discrimination against indigenous people, and the loss of popular culture and its supplanting by liberal consumerist culture.

Ecology, ecumenism, globalization, and human rights are now part and parcel of the agenda of the announcement of the kingdom.

The Jesuit University of Córdoba in Argentina states in its promotional material that "the University should be capable of lucid criticism of all types of power: political, economic and religious. . . . The ultimate goal of university activity is to change structures. That is to say, we do not work with the power of the word within the culture, in a critical way, to transform only the people. We are certainly seeking to transform consciences from a more human and Christian point of view; but the University must have as its ultimate horizon the intent to transform society in its structures."

Since the 32nd General Congregation (1974–1975) that endorsed a "Faith and Justice" approach for the society, modeled in part on the French Jesuits' *Action Populaire*, and following the "preferential option for the poor" that was emphasized in this context at the 33rd Congregation in 1983, the focus has now shifted to overcoming racial and gender discrimination. James Martin, a Jesuit, now champions the LGBT cause in the United States: the globalized world opens its borders to all and "compels us to have a unified vision with a sense of the interdependence of all people," he said following a meeting with Pope Francis. This is at the heart of post-conciliar Jesuit ideology.

During all these years, the Jesuits have unceasingly created a variety of institutions: Support for Development, IBRADES (Brazil), Social Studies, ILADES (Chile), Popular Education, CINEP (Colombia), Research and Social Action, Centro Gumillas (Venezuela), Welcoming and Social Assistance, CRAS (Mexico). They have consistently exerted pressure on all the populations of the continent to meet the requirements of the injunction of decree 4 of the 32nd General Congregation, which permanently reformed the Society of Jesus. That text is the foundational document of the new orientation that Father Arrupe imposed on all Jesuits. It can be said that all that had been done to that end was here brought to completion. Father Antoncich's *History of the social sector*, of which we have just described some key elements, constantly and reverently refers to this new founding document.

This crucial episode was chronicled by two authors with radically opposed viewpoints: the first report, by Fr. Alfonso Álvarez Bolado, who was one of its main actors along with Father Calvez, can be found in *Pedro Arrupe, Superior General de los Jesuitas* (1965–1983).[58] The second is by Ricardo de la Cierva, in *Jesuitas, Iglesia y Marxismo.*[59]

The former described the new vocation of the Jesuits and the new-found power of the society; the latter, a well-documented historian, confirmed that Paul VI's intentions and the apostolic traditions of the society had been deliberately abandoned.

Obviously, at the time, neither of them could have imagined that the newly appointed provincial in Argentina would become pope and that he would canonize Paul VI, who had been aware of the appalling drift but had never succeeded in stopping it.

The 32nd General Congregation opened on December 2, 1974. It was the future Cardinal Carlo Maria Martini who selected its topics and priorities. There were 236 Jesuits from all over the world assembled at the General Curia in Rome; among them was Father Bergoglio, who there met Carlo Maria Martini for the second time, having first made his acquaintance in Jerusalem the previous year during a trip to the Holy Land, when Martini was the rector of the Pontifical Biblical Institute in Jerusalem.

An unnamed delegate asked a preliminary question that would set the course for the entire meeting. As in any revolutionary assembly, be it in 1789 or in the Second Vatican Council, there is always an initial question that changes the agenda. But on this occasion, everything had been planned in advance:

> Before we can decide on priorities in the plural, we need to choose one: the apostolic mission of the Society in today's world, where atheism and injustice are rampant. This priority of priorities, so to speak, must be presented first of all as a subject of communication and dialogue to be promoted among all the members of the Congregation, and through all the minor circles, be they linguistic or supporting. In such a way can we hope to arrive at a profound unity of all the delegates, starting from what we believe defines our vocation in the deepest sense.

---

58   La Bella, *Pedro Arrupe, Superior General de los Jesuitas*, pp. 189–97.
59   Cierva, *Jesuitas, Iglesia y Marxismo*, pp. 433–92.

The other priorities and the commissions' works could thus receive fresh light, based on a wide-ranging debate inspired by this fundamental question.

This proposition was accepted by the assembly.

The die was cast; the Holy See validated the decrees. The observations that the pope added to them were negligible in view of what was at stake. Arrupe could conclude on March 7: "Thus our Congregation will be a new step, a new chain, a new chapter in the history of our company, certainly not the last, but the one we had to make, or at least the one we were able to offer at this concrete moment in history."[60]

Where were the liberation theologians at that time? The Gutiérrezes, the Boffs, the Sobrinos, the Segundos, the Dussels, the Nolans, the Frei Bettos, the Casaldaligas? All of them together hardly carried any weight in the face of the steamroller that was the society!

By now, they have all rallied around Francis. Their works survive only as a punishment for their readers. Their religious creed has become irrelevant, and liberation has freed them all from dogma, discipline, and hierarchy. Boff is able to write that liberation theology owes nothing to Marxism while Father Bigo publishes a book to insist that liberation theology is not necessarily Marxist. The truth is that they all have a modernist, Hegelian, or Teilhardian mentality. And the great midwife of utopia is history. "In the light of the history of the Society, we ought to have a special sensitivity for a new humanism that is essential to the 21st century," Father Antoncich argued.[61]

All of this may seem like an exaggeration. However, a priest from Le Havre, Fr. Marcel Maurin, described in *Pedro Arrupe et l'engagement pour la justice* (Pedro Arrupe and the Commitment to Justice) what he saw as an epic adventure for the society on par with those it had undertaken in the past. In this book, he recalled the central role of Father Arrupe: "After the Synod of 1971, the Pontifical Commission for Justice and Peace called on Fr. Arrupe to write a booklet aimed at highlighting the actions that Christians can undertake in the cause of

---

60   Arrupe, *La Iglesia de hoy y del futuro*, p. 235.
61   Antoncich, *Historia del sector social*, no. 147-e.

justice: *Witnessing for Justice* was circulated widely. The reservations of Paul VI and Cardinal Villot were put aside for a long time, and then forgotten. This was a worldwide campaign!"

Fr. Martin Maier confirmed this testimony in *Pedro Arrupe, Witness and Prophet*: "It was not just about the saving of souls, but about embracing the totality of the human person, body, soul and being, and also taking into account the material conditions of life." He added that Father Arrupe even "went so far as to say that Vatican II had made it possible for the Society of Jesus to be more Ignatian today than it was in the time of St. Ignatius."[62]

The past relationship with "politics," which was based on distinguishing between temporal and spiritual power, was cancelled out by the broad vision of the council and the Jesuits. They give two reasons for this: first, that such a distinction was the source of centuries of subservience to the monarchies, including that of the Church, and that these times were over; second, that we are living, as they saw it, in a new era in which temporal power is embodied in the poor, who know their own needs better than anyone. The poor are first in the order of faith and also in knowledge of the demands of the true social, economic, and political order.

What has remained of this, fifty years after this worldview was adopted, is easy to assess: spiritual power has been in search of an ever-elusive temporal power, which has been dubbed democracy. Its goal has been reached in our day, and the globalization of struggles has given rise to the alliance of a spiritual power that is entirely linked to and associated with the globalized governments and their continental intermediaries and penetrated by them. We shall mention only two very visible examples: ecological power and the Marrakech Pact. It is beyond doubt that the beatification process of Father Arrupe will provide an opportunity to re-launch the globalist machinery. He had himself stated after his election: "Our universalism does not consist in the fact that our people, here and there in all parts of the world, should take care of everything, but that all of us should collaborate in a universal work that requires perfect unity."

---

[62]   Maier, *Pedro Arrupe, Witness and Prophet*, p. 11.

Socialism and revolution

The General Congregation of 1974 represented the completion and the climax of the definitive orientation of the new society. It earned Father Arrupe his title of "third founder."

Once the reform of the CIAS was underway, the Latin American continent clearly became the playing field for the development of the new strategy. The great speeches that made their way throughout the Catholic universe calling for a third world pope were born from this crucible. This is not to say, though, that the modernist cardinals and bishops were not involved.

Father Arrupe, contrary to what one might imagine, did not restrain the most revolutionary tendencies that had emerged, especially in Chile and Uruguay.

In Chile, the Jesuit Gonzalo Arroyo was the organizer and main "developer" of "Christians for Socialism," CdS. This was all described in detail by Ricardo de la Cierva.[63]

The case of the Belgian Jesuit Roger Vekemans, founder of the Bellarmine Center and creator of the Christian Democracy movement in Santiago, is more intriguing. Christian Democracy's lack of substance made it an easy prey to the influence of the Marxified Christians of the CdS. In 1967, the Catholic University and the cathedral were taken by storm. "Volodia Teitelboim, a member of the Central Committee of the Communist Party of Chile, described the conversations he had with his group and various priests, especially Jesuits, welcoming the new attitude of the Church towards communism."[64] Another Jesuit, Arturo Gaete, wrote an article in the Society of Jesus' magazine *Mensaje* under the title "Eucharist and Class Struggle" to celebrate the historical encounter of the coming of Christ and of the revolutionary utopia. The French Jesuit and former worker-priest Pierre Bigo, who was passionate about politics, was sent to Chile to develop social doctrine studies with Bishop Manuel Larraín, Hélder Câmara's accomplice at the council. He

---

63   Cierva, *Jesuitas, Iglesia y Marxismo, 1965-1985*, pp. 106–16.
64   Donoso, *Los Cristianos por el Socialismo*, pp. 121ff.

went on to wreak havoc in Brazil and at the CELAM. In 1990, he wrote that the foundation of "Christians for Socialism" had raised great hopes.

The Jesuits who chose the side of the Marxist revolution were in fact never challenged.

The book *Autopsia del mito Vekemans* (Vekeman, Autopsy of a Myth), written by himself, states that in 1973, Father Arrupe defended both his own "democratism" and the radical Marxist Jesuit Arroyo's thinking. Likewise, the society's superior general gave free rein to liberationist theologians such as Rahner, Dirks, Greinacher, and Metz in their attacks against Bishops Castrillón and López Trujillo, who opposed liberation theology.

In 1977, the Jesuit Fernando Cardenal was one of the "Group of Twelve" who planned the overthrow of Somoza in Nicaragua. In 1980, he was put in charge of the revolutionary consciousness-raising of the population, and later became Minister of Education of the Sandinista government from 1984 to 1996.

In a book published by the Ministry of Culture of "Free Nicaragua," he was asked if he had been sanctioned or warned by his community, his superiors, or the bishops with regard to his political activities from 1973 to 1979, the year Daniel Ortega took power. "On the part of my Order I had no problems. None at all. They always considered my work, my commitment, my struggle, to be an exceptional service, one that was necessary and urgent for a people that was being slaughtered. . . . I was in contact with the provincials [of the society], who were close to me at that time, and I always consulted them about fundamental decisions," he explained. After being sanctioned by Saint John Paul II, he would resume his place in the society and all the penalties imposed by the saintly pope were rescinded by Pope Francis.

At that time, the Jesuit Central American University was the stronghold of the Revolution. Among its rectors were Fr. Cesar Xerez, provincial, and Fr. Xabier Gorostiaga, who later became Ortega's director of planification.

Marcel Maurin, mentioned above, uncritically referred to this type of behavior.[65] Father Arrupe never interfered with the blatant revolutionary involvement of the Jesuits in Nicaragua or El Salvador.

When in 1986 Leonardo Boff and his brother Clodovis explained that liberation theology is not Marxist, even though it uses Marxist methods of analysis, they used Arrupe's well-known letter on the subject, dated December 8, 1980, in order to vindicate themselves.

It is important to understand that this kind of "freedom" given to the Jesuits did not come about because of an error in government. Father Arrupe had chosen four assistants as *missi dominici* precisely with the intent to *change the society*.

Should this situation be considered in relation to the unprecedented choice of Father Bergoglio as provincial at the age of thirty-six, it is easy to understand that he was only given this position in order to enter into the new system where, in a sense, anything goes!

"Fe y secularidad"

With the founding in Madrid, in 1972, of the Jesuit Institute *Fe y Secularidad*—which can be translated as "faith and the secular state"—all this exuberance gained substance. The name of the institute refers to the separation between the clerical state and the political commitment of clerics, with a view to abolishing it.

Its founders were two prominent Jesuits, Alfonso Álvarez Bolado and José Gómez Caffarena.

The former was a sociologist, philosopher, and theologian. His eulogy praised him as "an undisputed master of a Church that was open to all social and political postures, always in the name of freedom and commitment to the underdogs and the poor of society." He had personally selected his main enemy: everything related to General Franco and "national Catholicism." His obituary, posted on a progressive Spanish website (*Comunidad de Vida Cristiana en España*), pointed out: "As vice-rector of the Pontifical University Comillas of

---

65   See also Cierva, *Jesuitas, Iglesia y Marxismo, 1965-1985*, pp. 115–16.

the Jesuits of Madrid, and president of 'Justice and Peace,' he studied the modern process of secularization and worked in favor of effective dialogue and for a platform for collaboration between the Christian faith and non-Christian interpretations of existence. He was also the head of the *Cristianismo y Democracia* Forum, which emerged from the *Instituto Fe y Desarrollo* (Faith and Development Institute)."

The second key figure of this Institute was Prof. Caffarena. He had been the president of a Jesuit commission for the study of non-belief in 1967. It should be remembered that at that time, the society's differences with Paul VI were already notorious: the pope wanted to fight against communist-based atheism, as indicated in his letter of May 1965, whereas the society pointed to social injustice as the main cause of that same atheism.

Caffarena participated in the founding of *Fe y Secularidad* and was its director from 1972 to 1986. One of his biographers noted: "How is it possible to be faithful to faith and modernity at the same time? He began to ask himself questions out of fidelity to his Christian humanist entrails, as he used to say, up to the point of opening up hope to other humanisms, be they religious or irreligious." And again: with him "we have reinterpreted Thomas Aquinas."

Fe y Secularidad was one of the ideological crucibles of the new Society of Jesus.

It is not surprising, therefore, that the institute, with its close ties to Europe and America, should have organized an event that was later known as "The Escorial Meeting" from July 8 to 15, 1972. Its proceedings were published under the title *Fe cristiana y cambio social en América latina* (Christian faith and social change in Latin America). Ricardo de la Cierva gave a very complete account of the meeting, but he missed its core issue; he could not possibly have identified it because his analysis was entirely focused on fighting Marxization.

All the leading figures of liberation theology were present. In the midst of this learned assembly, Gustavo Gutiérrez was the unchallenged master. Those Jesuits who were present did not mention that they belonged to the society. Among them were Álvarez Bolado, Rolando Ames Cobián, Enrique Dussel, Joseph Comblin, Aldo J. Büntig, Segundo

Galilea, Renato Poblete, José Miguel Bonino, Juan Luis Segundo, Gonzalo Arroyo, and Juan Carlos Scannone. De la Cierva mentioned the
latter, reporting a remark of his that was of no interest regarding the
other participants but still constituted a stunning acknowledgement:
*"The political analysis from which the language of liberation in Latin
America emerged is strongly influenced by the use of the socio-analytical
instrument of Marxism."* De la Cierva's analysis was content with this
statement, but Father Scannone's paper was actually proclaiming the
Jesuit ideology that is still prevalent in the Vatican today.

Father Scannone was a doctor of philosophy. It is difficult to associate him with a particular philosophical trend: he was not a Thomist,
and his thought encompassed all the nuances of contemporary phe-
nomenology. He was a kind of nominalist who bounces on words.
His flexibility was akin to that of one of his masters, Blondel, and
he had an infatuation for the forms of German philosophy which he
eagerly copied.

His conference summarized here below is certainly somewhat
boring; however, it will allow us better to grasp the absolute novelty
of a kind of liberation theology that retains all the characteristics of
the revolutionary dialectic, save its terminology.

Faced with a squadron of liberation theology preachers,
Father Scannone embarked on a complex journey toward finding a
fresh approach to the relationship between Church and politics. His
aim was to maintain the revolutionary dynamic while using language
inspired by Catholicism.

His speech at the Escurial was not just an ideological statement: it
was designed to set up a network of the liberation theology's human
and propaganda resources. After the meeting, its participants would
spread throughout the continent with a novel message that was less
influenced by Marxism. His lecture was entitled "Theology and politics. The current challenge to the language of liberation theology in
Latin America."

Here below is our summary.

The contents of liberation theology are both dynamic and dialectical. It is connected to a socio-political model that is fixed, one-sided,

and predetermined: Marxism. Theology can easily absorb the language of liberation into a biblical language that refers to total liberation (Moses and the liberation from Egypt come to mind). But the abstract formulations of Marxist ideology cannot account for dialectics and for concrete, historical realities. A theological language of liberation tailored to new situations must therefore be found, but without losing political commitment or historical realization.

While the goal of a future classless society remains unachievable, salvation history is essentially open to the unforeseeable. Eschatological tension (the end of the world and the last judgment) reveals a definitive, transcendent reality; this tension guards against closing ourselves off to the gratuity and unpredictability of God's liberating historical action. Perón's populist nationalism evolved into a non-Marxist socialism that was both national and humanist in form.

This is consistent with the language used by Argentinian prelates such as Bishops Angelelli, Devoto, and Nevares, who were implementing the resolutions of Medellín in their dioceses.

How do we ensure that the language of liberation does not become "depoliticized," thereby losing the dialectical and practical force inherent to Marxist-inspired liberation theology, yet not remain one-sided?

To achieve this, theological language must leave its own sphere and not remain in an ethereal or abstract transcendence, but it must not empty itself of the "*theos*" or merge with socio-analytical or political language. It must become incarnate, without giving up on socio-analytical and political mediation; it must define itself as a concrete and effective practical response to the very real oppression and suffering of the Latin American man.

The basis for this change lies in a new understanding of what the Council of Chalcedon expressed about the Word made flesh: the divine ("*theos*") is united with the human without confusion or division. Latin American theology must respond to the ecclesiological challenge posed by history in the light of this Christological faith.

Scannone rejected the "dualist theology" which holds that the only moral principles that can be deduced from faith are those that serve to judge and shed light on a political situation generically and whose positive transposition into concrete circumstances belongs to Christians, not as Christians but as citizens, within the range of political alternatives that are deemed of equal value as long as they do not include elements that run counter to the said principles. This position tends to view things abstractly, in themselves, rather than historically.

On the contrary, we need to look for a dialectical way of thinking, such as that reflected in the Christological formula "without confusion or division," not a Hegelian or Marxist dialectic that does not respect the mutual interplay of their freedom. This could be described as a "historical union" between a given political option and the theological charity that is embodied in it, even if the latter criticizes, liberates, and transcends it. There could even be a "necessary link" between them if we are talking about the necessity of love that seeks and discerns "the most effective way," here and now, to serve the liberation of our brethren.

There is, therefore, a historical-salvific unity between faith and politics.

Following this line of thought, theology becomes a critical reflection of the Church's faith. According to Fr. Hugo Assmann, theology must reach a strategic-tactical level and become incarnated theology at the practical level.

This last consideration can help to understand why a dualistic theology, which separates the sphere of universal principles from their contingent application, is unsuited to theological reflection on history as the history of integral salvation. God's salvific will cannot be understood by simply deducing from or applying universal principles but through discernment. This discernment of God's signs in history is a hermeneutic of faith, not a deduction, not even a dialectic deduction: it is a hermeneutic that moves in a free environment and accepts historical risk. Christians who make a political choice on the basis of faith do so as "church," as members of the people of God, and not just as citizens.

Consequently, the prophetic word of the Church comes from the bishop, from the presbyteral college; it is liberating and does not inflict a yoke and is expressed within the framework of time and place. It fosters the free discernment of a prophetic community. The Church's prophetic function must be distinguished from its legislative function. Prophetic discernment is not a law that imposes itself on the conscience.

The language of liberation has abandoned the univocal nature of Marxism in favor of an openness to the gratuitous novelty of the historical-salvific. This departure from one-sidedness is not the consequence of a dualistic separation or the anti-dialectical solidification of the theological and political levels of language and commitment. History, like the hypostatic union, is seen as being "without division or confusion": it is both political and salvation history. This is why the Christian's concrete historical option is always "undivided and indivisible"—that is, both political and faith based.

For this reason, theology, like the Church whose life it critically reflects, is a "pilgrim" in history. The Church (i.e., each of its members, the people of God, and the Church as an institution) is not the "mistress" or *Magistra* of truth; it lives in and of the truth that is Christ. This is the Church that discerns the historic call of the Father's love in the signs of the times and commits herself to His side. Together, the call and commitment are situated within a single history, of which Christ is the alpha and omega.

From this point of view, the Church is no longer "*Jesus Christ spread abroad and communicated*"; it is instead a party that chooses the events in history from which to wage the struggle for justice on behalf of the poor. This aspect of liberation theology was described by Cardinal Ratzinger in a lecture given in Rome in December 1983 under the title *Liberation theology against the Faith*. Its text was published in Italy, Mexico, Spain, Chile, Peru, and in France, by *L'Homme nouveau* and *Diffusion de l'Information sur l'Amérique latine* (DIAL). This liberationist mouthpiece—a favorite of the French episcopate as mentioned above—scathingly reviewed the document with the following comment: "Faced with such a damning indictment, we can only deplore its total lack of understanding of the concrete realities and the faith of the humble folk of the 'base ecclesial communities.'"

This startling comment was reiterated in 2016 by theologian Emilce Cuda under the authority of Father Scannone in her book

Para leer a Francisco (Reading Pope Francis).[66] This recent book clarifies that such is indeed the pope's thinking and his guiding light for action. It also points out that, according to Father Scannone, the culture of poor Latin Americans is not the same as that of poor Europeans. In his view, the vital synthesis of poor Latin American believers is "salvationist" and not "*creationist*" and "*moralist*" like that of the Europeans.

Behind the relentless verbiage of liberation theology surrounding the Council of Chalcedon—one that Father Scannone did not dare adopt in *La théologie du peuple* that was published in French in 2017—lies a gross error that Saint John Paul II denounced at the 1979 CELAM meeting in his famous Puebla speech:

> In the abundant documentation with which you have prepared this Conference, especially in the contributions of many Churches, a certain uneasiness is at times noticed with regard to the very interpretation of the nature and mission of the Church. Allusion is made, for instance, to the separation that some set up between the Church and the Kingdom of God. The Kingdom of God is emptied of its full content and is understood in a rather secularist sense: it is interpreted as being reached not by faith and membership in the Church but by the mere changing of structures and social and political involvement, and as being present wherever there is a certain type of involvement and activity for justice. This is to forget that "the Church receives the mission to proclaim and to establish among all peoples the Kingdom of Christ and of God. She becomes on earth the seed and beginning of that Kingdom" (*Lumen Gentium*, 5).

At this point, John Paul II cited his predecessor, John Paul I who, "in one of his beautiful catechetical instructions, . . . speaking of the virtue of hope, warned that 'it is wrong to state that political, economic and social liberation coincides with salvation in Jesus Christ, that the Regnum Dei is identified with the Regnum hominis.' " John Paul II added: "In some cases an attitude of mistrust is produced with regard

---

66 Cuda, *Para leer a Francisco*, pp. 195–208.

to the 'institutional' or 'official' Church, which is considered as alienating, as opposed to another Church of the people, one 'springing from the people' and taking concrete form in the poor."

Never once did the proponents of the Latin American pseudo-theology correct any of their ravings.

In 1984, Cardinal Ratzinger was equally blunt in his instruction *Libertatis Nuntius*. He not only targeted Father Scannone but also his fellow Jesuit, Fr. Jon Sobrino: "Of course the creeds of the faith are literally preserved, especially the Chalcedonian creed, but a new meaning is given to them which is a negation of the faith of the Church. On one hand, the Christological doctrine of Tradition is rejected in the name of class; on the other hand, one claims to meet again the 'Jesus of history' coming from the revolutionary experience of the struggle of the poor for their liberation."[67]

Fr. Roberto Oliveros Maqueo, SJ, a liberation theology historian, has carefully recorded the main encounters that shaped the development of this revolution which has spread to all the continents. His account illustrates the Church's inability to defend herself against the worst of all the heresies that have affected her history. This was only made possible by the funding of Catholic NGOs such as Misereor, Adveniat, CCFD, Paix et Développement, CRS (Catholic Relief Services), and so on.

For further background, the synthesis by P. Josep-Ignasi Saranyana, *Teología en América Latina*, vol. III is also very useful.

Surprisingly, all this research has been to no avail, and the massive tsunami now sweeping through the Church, though long predicted, has not been met with an appropriate response. And this is true not only of doctrine and discipline but also of government; among the cardinals created on February 21, 2001, there is a surprising array of prelates in favor of this trend: Bergoglio, Maradiaga, Kasper, Murphy-O'Connor, Lehmann, and the ex-cardinal McCarrick.

All Joseph Ratzinger's attempts, whether as a cardinal or later as Pope Benedict XVI, were powerless to stem the tide.

---

[67]　Ratzinger, *Libertatis Nuntius*, X, 9.

The milestones of a relentless indoctrination: 1972–2017

The Escorial meeting in 1972 was just the beginning. It was followed, right up to the present day, by a very large number of national and international events during which all the themes that form the basis of the present pontiff's action emerged: all this has been brewing for a long time, and this book only offers a glimpse of it. While Fr. Oliveros Maqueo's work provides a good overview of these realities, it only goes as far as 1990 and omits cases relating directly to the Society of Jesus. He also misinterprets John Paul II's assertion that "liberation theology is useful and necessary." We refuted this misinterpretation in our book *Terrorisme pastoral*.[68]

The guidelines for social and political combat given by Father Arrupe in 1966 were constantly updated until 1992. Father Antoncich's synthesis, *Historia del Sector Social*, remains an essential tool for tracking this development.

Already in the days of Superior General Janssens, every country organized a CIAS (Center for Investigation and Social Action) to counter the spread of communism and liberal capitalism. By 1966, there were twenty-three such centers, staffed by 165 Jesuits, including eleven in Latin America—one per Jesuit province—run by 87 Jesuits. Oddly enough, the specific orientations of the CIAS were entrusted to two individuals whose origins were diametrically opposed: Fr. Manuel Foyaca, a Spanish nobleman with Francoist origins, and Father Bigo, who in 1932 had been drawn to the *Action Populaire*, the Jesuits' social combat organization founded in France in 1903. "This mission filled me with joy, because I was always interested in politics," Bigo would later say. In 1952, he became superior and director of the *Action Populaire*. He was then sent to Colombia and Chile. In Brazil, he founded IBRADES (Brazilian Institute for Economic and Social Development). He was assisted by Fr. Michel de Certeau, who made two trips to Brazil (and also Venezuela, Chile, and Argentina) in 1966 and 1967.

---

[68]   Moreau, *Terrorisme pastoral*, pp. 82–88.

Father de Certeau was an admirer of Che Guevara and of Hélder Câmara, whose entire paternal family was Masonic. On March 23 and 24, 1968, he took part in a symposium organized by the Catholic Left and third world liberation movements, *"Christianisme et Révolution."* Paul Chopelin titled his well-documented account of this episode "A Christian understanding of Che Guevara? Michel de Certeau and the ethics of revolutionary violence."

The CIAS took the *Action Populaire* as their model. Father Bigo was a leading figure in Medellín, and together with the Chilean group ILADES, he prepared and backed the advent of Salvador Allende.

As mentioned above, the Latin American Council of CIAS, CLA-CIAS, was founded in 1966. Its headquarters was in Chile. Father Bigo was its general secretary and Alberto Sily, from Argentina, its coordinator.

The CIAS's situation reached a boiling point in 1970. It was then that the CLACIAS organized a general meeting to express itself on two controversial themes, which had led some of the Catholic hierarchy to oppose it: protest within the Church and the foundations and reasons for the Jesuits' presence in the socio-political and socio-economic field.

The first theme was the product of a cultural revolution affecting the social and political order: for the Church, it was a question of the co-responsibility established by the council between laity and priests and therefore of the involvement of clerics in a pastoral approach toward political and economic-social reality. The conflict was severe, and the art of dialogue proved useless. The poor were designated as some kind of oracle: "All power in the Church, whether formal or informal, must faithfully reflect the thinking of the poor, in the biblical sense of the word as understood by the Church." It was also decided that "the formation of base communities appears to be the best way of exercising ecclesial co-responsibility."

The second theme complemented the first: how to justify the role of Jesuits in the development of the political dimension of their work?

Their answer was telling: "Because of the eschatological vocation of his ministry, the priest is 'a protester par excellence.' " Remember that utopia breeds impatience and that politics is the art of the possible.

In short, the Jesuits were looking for a common response to the Catholic hierarchy. It can be summed up as follows: all things must be ordered to Christ. Christ succeeded in subordinating the legitimacy of worship to respect for humankind and in identifying love of neighbor with love of God. He was thus the liberator of oppressed humanity from iniquity. Therefore, theological concepts must be renewed.

Their project was to become the main theme of countless national meetings, and it underwent many changes. Father Bigo was replaced by Fr. José Luis Alemán, and CLACIAS moved its headquarters to Santo Domingo.

In Latin America, the CIAS were divided into two geographical groups: the northern group, known as ALN, and the southern group (ALS).

We will focus here on the seminar for the southern group, which took place from July 15 to 21, 1974 in Buenos Aires under the title "Faith – People – Power."

This title implies that the Faith has a political dimension. The three words were indeed unequivocally defined as follows:

> By "faith" we do not mean dogmatic content, but the fundamental attitudes of human beings insofar as they evaluate their existence in history in order to build a future based on the message of Jesus. But this deep-going, radical attitude must be assessed within the framework of mediators such as the ecclesial institution and its action in a given society, the attitudes of believers and their religious expression, and within the framework of human relations as a whole, etc.

> The word "people" is understood by the participants as designating the large majorities who can obscurely perceive and read a historical design in their own history, because of the oppression of social groups whose interests do not coincide with those of the large majorities.

The word "power" does not mean political power in the narrow sense, but should be understood as a pivotal point in social life and as the fulcrum of decisions that affect the whole community and shape many types of relationships. But we must bear in mind that there are other powers beyond that of politics, such as economic, ideological, scientific and technical power, as well as the power to persuade the masses, all of which have an impact on political power and should therefore be of interest to us.

In our view, these three objectives are part of a sociologically oriented analysis that we summarize here below:

1. It assesses the relationship between political parties and the people and their culture, the relationship between pastoral work and popular culture, and the attitudes of pastoral workers with regard to popular religiosity. What interests the participants is to know to what extent the Church acts as an institution that is critical of power, and in which ways it demands the desacralization of powers seeking religious sanction for their actions—that is, the "ideologization" of faith.

2. It is an attempt to define the relationship between the social sciences and theology, with particular attention being paid to the historical forms of expression of faith, together with the Magisterium of the Church, which is seen as an expression of the critical function of the Faith and of the "ideologizations" of the Faith.

3. The objectives of the CIAS need to be redefined in the light of current events in Latin America. The social concern that gave rise to the CIAS must now be refocused on a global historical process.

It is obvious that the Society of Jesus decided to "historicize" the whole of Revelation so as to make the world a fairer place. It was a massive undertaking, and one that the Jesuits would implement throughout the world.

The leading figures in this new religion—several of whom we have already encountered—were many: Ricardo Antoncich (Peru), Alberto

Sily (Argentina), Fernando Boasso, Vicente Pellegrini, Juan Carlos Scannone (Argentina), Orlando Yorio (Argentina), Ignacio Ellacuría (El Salvador), Juan Hernández Pico (Central America), Guillermo Corte (Mexico), Juan Luis Segundo (Uruguay), and Emilio Veza Iglesias (Paraguay) to name but the best-known of these Jesuits. This is one of the essential components of the revolution that developed in Latin America, the consequences of which continue to unfold daily before our very eyes.

It is impossible to mention here the countless symposia, congresses, seminars, and other meetings that have been held since that date.

The Mexico City meeting that took place from July 11 to 15, 1975, featured contributions from more than fifty theologians and "pastoralists" on the occasion of the anniversary of the arrival of the Spaniards on the continent. The proceedings of this meeting were compiled into an enormous, 648-page volume.

From February 6 to 10, 2017, the "First Ibero-American Theological Meeting" was held at Boston College, Massachusetts. It produced the "Boston Declaration," which was presented to Pope Francis, and whose first paragraphs read as follows:

> For several days, Catholic theologians from Ibero-America met in the city of Boston, United States, guided by a spirit of interculturality, ecumenism, and solidarity. Our ecclesial vocation inspired us to examine, learn, teach, and communicate the richness of the Christian faith in the church and society. We shared our experiences, reflections, prayers, and the Eucharist to commonly discern the signs of the times in this new global era. In this declaration, we share some of the fruits of our work with both the church community and the public in general.
>
> We recognize, with happiness and joy, that we live at an auspicious time for the development of theology and in the life of the church. We live in an ecclesial *kairos* moment, evident in the new processes initiated by Francis, the bishop of Rome and the first Latin-American pope. His efforts towards evangelical renewal, expressed in the need for a reform of both our limited

ways of thinking and our ecclesial structures, encourage us to consider the presence of God in history and to examine the realities that reject God therein. Our deliberations uncovered shared features and signs of a common history, and it is from them that we want to examine the present and future challenges of this global era. Hence, we stress the importance of examining, from the perspective of the Word of God proclaimed in the church, the socio-political and economic situation of our nations, which is an essential *locus theologicus* for the church. It is in this situation, in this place, that the church is called to incarnate itself in order to accompany, as the people of God, the peoples of this world.

We want to discern our experience as believers from the perspective of the key social questions of this time. Socioeconomically, this experience is characterized by the presence of social systems and relationships of exclusion and inequality. The socio-cultural sphere points to the need to move from the pluri-cultural to the intercultural. The socio-political calls for the urgent need to consolidate representative democratic systems and foster those expressions of civil society that propose a more humane vision of the world. In this context, we confirm our preferential option for those who are poor and excluded.

Latin America and the Caribbean are not the poorest region in economic terms, but continue to be the most unequal.

The six-page document covers forty years of demands made by liberation theology, but this time under papal cover.

Excerpts:

- "We insist on the urgent need to collaborate with the theology and pastoral plan of Pope Francis."

- "As Ibero-Latin-American theologians, we support with great hope the process of reform that the current Bishop of Rome has called for in the mentalities and structures of the church."

- "We believe that the peripheries are theological places that force theology to ask: When is a people authentically Christian? When it has many churches, or when it rejects poverty?"

- "The reality of migration invites us to build processes of interculturality as a key element in our theological reflection."

- "Our practices cannot continue producing forms of domination, like those marked by the clericalism that disrespects lay people" [men and women].

With its mentions of "inculturated prophetic theology," "mestizaje," "the value of the new contextual theologies," "creative fidelity to the spirit of the Second Vatican Council," and "synodical reform" as "an inescapable presupposition," the declaration is a mishmash in five languages of the prevailing phraseology in the Church today.

Its authors were hardly a bunch of halfwits. They didn't just cluelessly repeat those magic words. They all belonged to the conquering elite serving the pope. Among their ranks were the two Argentinian icons, Virginia Raquel Azcuy and Emilce Cuda. Their leading quartet—Rafael Luciani, Carlos Maria Galli, Juan Carlos Scannone, and Felix Palazzi—acted as "coordinators." Among the thirty or so signatories were Agenor Brighenti, Victor Codina, Harvey Cox, José Ignacio González Faus, Gustavo Gutiérrez, Jon Sobrino, Pedro Trigo, Carlos Schickendantz, and Gonzalo Zarazaga.

At this point, we need to focus on Emilce Cuda, whom Pope Francis appointed on July 26, 2021 as head of office of the Pontifical Commission for Latin America, before entrusting her with its executive direction as co-secretary. She is praised unreservedly by all those who introduce her, and she herself attracts attention to her person by interspersing her texts with her individual opinions and judgments. She is the archetypal female theologian, and she is always eager to describe the difficulties she met when entering the clerical world of theology. She is a pure product of the network of theologians gathered in Boston, and one of the most active agents of that movement; she has the confidence of all its key players, not least Juan Carlos Scannone, whom we meet at every juncture.

Cuda joined the bandwagon of the "Great Reformer" (Pope Francis) in 1985. After attending the Catholic University of Argentina, where she studied Latin, Greek, Italian, German, French, and English, she avidly studied the views of another Argentinian, Ernesto Laclau, a former progressive Peronist living in England. He is a Gramscian who, like his inspirer, seeks to lift the class struggle out of its rut; he believes that, beyond the Hegelian dialectic, the people are the source of power. For Laclau, the people themselves are the historical force that changes the world, hence his theory of "new populism." He inspired Podemos and Syriza. He has been praised by the French left-wing media, Mediapart and *Le Monde*.

All Emilce Cuda's studies and assessments are shaped by this ideology. She is also a member of all the liberationist movements; initially, this was in Argentina, but she then joined them throughout Latin and North America. She has spoken on democracy and Catholicism in the United States and has attended countless congresses, including the First Congress of German and Latin American Women Theologians in 2008. She took part in the Continental Congress of Theology in Brazil, entitled "The Exodus of the Worker as a Mystical Practice," which was one of the sources of inspiration of Pope Francis.

It is hardly possible to underestimate the significance of the "Boston Declaration," of which Emilce Cuda was one of the most prominent signatories.

In our opinion, following the Pact of the Catacombs in 1965 and the Declaration of the Bishops of the Third World in 1967, the Boston Declaration is nothing less than the charter of the new church called for by Pope Francis. It is a pity that Catholic reporters should not have mentioned this crucial milestone in the huge battle raging in the Catholic Church today.

It should be recalled that Boston is the hub of the "committed" American Jesuits of the day: of Fr. Jim Keenan and of the Catholic Theological Ethics in the World Church (CTEWC) group, which is part of Pope Francis's networks of governance. We must also remember that the 2017 meeting in Boston was encouraged and supported by the current general of the Jesuits, Fr. Arturo Sosa Abascal.

The significance of the Boston Declaration cannot be fully grasped if we overlook the Argentinian, Latin American, and Jesuit claim to provide the world with the new Church it supposedly needs.

CHAPTER 4

People and Events in Father Bergoglio's Life from 1958 to 1973

I t is impossible to understand who the pope really is if you are not familiar with the history of the Society of Jesus. But beyond that, it is absolutely essential to be aware of the historical, political, and religious context in which he received his formation.

Father Jorge Mario Bergoglio is the product of the Cuban Revolution, the Second Vatican Council, Father Arrupe's reform of the Society of Jesus, and the corresponding revolutions throughout Latin America.

Jorge Mario Bergoglio entered the Jesuit novitiate in Buenos Aires on March 11, 1958; at the end of that year, in December, Che Guevara would win the decisive battle of Santa Clara. On January 1, 1959, Fidel Castro proclaimed his own victory in Santiago de Cuba; on January 8, he made his triumphant entry into Havana. It was the first conquest, and one that would serve as a mythical model for all those that would follow.

Two revolutionary models served as beacons for revolutionary action in Latin America: the Vietnam War and the conquest of Cuba. Admittedly, the young Bergoglio did not read the newspaper every day, but the world around him was full of the portraits, declarations, and hopes of an ill-defined and confusing political liberation that was capturing the imagination of the peoples of the world.

One year later, on January 25, 1959, Pope John XXIII announced the opening of a new council in the following terms: "Venerable brothers and our beloved sons! We announce to you, indeed trembling a little with emotion, but at the same time with humble resolution of intention, the name and the proposal of a twofold celebration: a diocesan synod for the city, and an ecumenical council for the Universal Church."

All the structures of the progressive Catholic world promptly embarked upon methodical preparations to revolutionize the Church. The council became the catalyst for all subversive powers, mainly the Jesuits and Dominicans, but also the bishops' conferences of Germany, the Netherlands, Belgium, and France, not to forget all those in Latin America who were following in the footsteps of their European counterparts.

Pope John XXIII inaugurated the council on October 11, 1962. At the time, Bergoglio had been sent to Chile as a young novice to complete his classical studies. In 1963, he returned to Argentina, where he taught literature and psychology at the Jesuit College in Santa Fe from 1964 to 1965, and that was where he was at the time of the closing of the council by Paul VI on October 8, 1965; the following year, he was a professor in Buenos Aires. The new general of the Jesuits, Pedro Arrupe, had already been elected head of the society in August 1965, and in that capacity was able to deliver two communications to the Conciliar Assembly (see chapter 3).

Father Arrupe's letter of December 1966, also mentioned above, set the Jesuits on the path of the continent's social struggles and created a violent upheaval not only within the society but also in all clerical and Catholic Action groups; this was true at all levels. Six months later, the first Catholic student rebellion broke out in Santiago de Chile. Political convulsions in Argentina were causing unrest throughout the land.

This was the time (1966–1968) when the first guerrillas made their appearance. In Colombia, a group of priests involved in the "Golconda" guerrilla movement was founded in 1968; prior to this, Fr. Camilo Torres, who had joined the "national liberation army," had been killed in 1966 during clashes with the Colombian army. Chile saw the creation of "Sacerdotes por el Socialismo," while in Mexico, the "Sacerdotes por el Pueblo" were set up. In Peru, the ONIS group (*Oficina Nacional de Información Sacerdotal*) was formed. Other groups appeared in Bolivia (where Che Guevara was killed in 1967) and Uruguay.

It was during this period that several key protagonists of the revolution in the Latin American Church emerged on the scene.

Bishop Manuel Larraín Errázuriz

Fr. François Houtart reports that as early as 1960, CELAM was working on an in-depth reform of the Church. The Chilean bishop of Talca, Manuel Larraín, was the driving force behind this enterprise.

He had been a pupil of the Jesuits from an early age (and also a companion of Alberto Hurtado, SJ, who was canonized in 2005). He studied at the Gregorian University in Rome. Ordained a bishop in 1938, he became active in CELAM at the 1955 meeting in Rio. He was named as its first vice-president in 1958 and remained in that position until 1963, with Bishop Hélder Câmara as his second.

At the 1960 CELAM meeting, it was Larraín who called for the input of sociology and psychology, which he felt were essential to prevent a purely theoretical pastoral approach from ignoring reality. His request was backed by Bishop Alfredo Rubio Diaz of Colombia, who used data from FERES (the International Federation of Socio-religious Research Institutes created by the same Father Houtart) to break with pastoral centralization and replace it with sociological categories based on scientific studies. The FERES documents were distributed to the council in summarized versions with a view to making the pre-eminence of the new sociology the norm for the apostolate.

The two comrades, Larraín and Hélder Câmara, made their presence felt at the council, where the Latin American Council Fathers represented a third of the bishops present. The former was one of the handful of bishops who took action radically to alter procedures as soon as the assembly was opened. The latter regularly organized informal meetings between the bishops and the experts, who had a significant influence on the drafting of the texts. Naturally, Bishop Larraín signed the Pact of the Catacombs that was launched by Dom Hélder Câmara at the end of the council.

The Chilean bishop was one of the best-known figures of the time. He was a personal friend of Paul VI, but also of the Stalinist poet Pablo Neruda and the feminist poetess Gabriela Mistral, Jacques Maritain—who championed Christian democracy in Latin America—and Pastor Roger Schütz of Taizé.

Together with Fr. Alberto Hurtado, he made up the most progressive tandem in Chile. He was heavily and efficiently involved in the Chilean "Agrarian Reform" alongside the archbishop of Santiago de Chile, Cardinal Silva Henríquez.

In 1962, two weeks before the opening of the council, he had already invited Fr. Gustavo Gutiérrez to a meeting in Buenos Aires to discuss the Latin American situation and the global role that the Church should play there. At the time, Gutiérrez was still virtually unknown in his native Peru.

Gustavo Gutiérrez

Gustavo Gutiérrez is one of a tiny and select group of great revolutionaries who subverted Latin American Christianity, and subsequently Christianity throughout the world.

He was born in Peru on July 8, 1928. A sickly child, he began studying medicine in 1947, hoping to become a psychiatrist, but at twenty-four, he entered the seminary. His personal qualities led his superiors to send him to study philosophy and psychology at Louvain from 1951 to 1955. From 1955 to 1959, he studied theology in Lyon, specializing in pastoral ministry. He was awarded a doctorate in theology.

As did Hélder Câmara and Bishop Larraín, Gutiérrez had ties with modernist Europe. He had frequent contact with Fathers de Lubac, Congar, Chenu, Ducoq, and Schillebeeckx. He was a regular visitor to both Le Saulchoir, the Dominican convent in Paris, and Fourvière, the Jesuit centre in Lyon. "Belief in God is grounded in a specific historical situation; the believer is part of a cultural and social fabric. . . . The first task is not how to talk about God in an adult world, but how to tell the poor and oppressed that God loves them," he would later write.

Gutiérrez was attracted by the Dominicans, but he was also familiar with the thinking of Karl Rahner, Jean-Baptiste Metz, and Hans Küng. He was in touch with the Protestant theologians Karl Barth, Jürgen Moltmann, and Dietrich Bonhoeffer and scientists such as François Perroux, and he held many discussions with them. His ideas on development were those of Father Lebret, who was one of the authors of *Gaudium et Spes* and who inspired *Populorum Progressio*.

At Louvain, he chanced upon Camilo Torres, a pupil and friend of François Houtart. He also made the acquaintance of François Houtart, himself one of the aforementioned masters of subversion, less than ten in number. This other revolutionary figure would later teach historical and dialectical Christianity in Cuba.

Gutiérrez returned to Lima in 1960, where he was appointed professor of theology at the Pontifical University of Peru. He was in charge of the Catholic students and took part in various movements, including the World Social Forum, created in 2001 and financed among others by the French "anti-hunger and pro-development" organization, CCFD. It became the regular meeting place for all the revolutionary socialist leftists. These included the Uruguayan-born adviser to the French episcopate, Elena Lasida.

From then on, Gutiérrez attended every meeting, including those in Petropolis in 1964, Montevideo in 1967, and Chimbote (Peru) from July 21 to 26, 1968. It was there, during a meeting of ONIS (the National Office for Priestly Information), that he first used the expression "liberation theology." As mentioned in chapter 1, Peru had already for some years been home to a group of dissenting priests, including the notorious Fr. Gastón Garatea, founder of ONIS. This priest was later to be banned by the cardinal archbishop of Lima in 2012 for having advocated the marriage of priests and homosexual unions. He was reinstated in 2018 under pressure from Rome.

He was an expert for the Peruvian bishops at the CELAM Assembly in Medellín in 1968.

Father Gutiérrez's work was only just beginning. In 1971, he published *A Theology of Liberation: History, Politics, Salvation*, a book that earned him the reputation of being the father of liberation theology. His followers abound. In an attempt to "reintegrate" himself into a less radical school of thought, especially under the pontificate of Benedict XVI, he tried to tone down his decidedly Marxist positions, to the extent that some have gone so far as to say and write that these more recent texts are not his own.

Unlike Boff and Sobrino, Gutiérrez did not rebel against Roman authority. When on October 27, 1995, the Congregation for the Doctrine of the Faith, then under the orders of Cardinal Ratzinger, asked him for clarification and correction of his writings, he replied almost three years later, on October 3, 1998, with an article entitled *La Koinonía Eclesial*.

In the meantime, in September 1996, the same Cardinal Ratzinger had congratulated Gutiérrez for a "Christo-centric" presentation he had given at a conference on the theology of the third millennium in Latin America.

After some back and forth with the Peruvian Episcopal Commission, his reply reached Rome on January 15, 1999. In May of the following year, the Roman Congregation asked for a further response, as Gutiérrez had not taken sufficient account of its observations. It was only in 2004 that he sent a new draft of his 1998 article to the Peruvian Episcopal Commission, which notified it to Rome on August 18, 2004.

On September 15, 2004, the Congregation for the Doctrine of the Faith accepted his corrections and recommended their publication.

Although Gutiérrez had genuinely capitulated, he still parades around in liberationist circles. This reflects his character; besides, he understands that his own revolution is past and that others have taken over.

When Francis was elected, Gutiérrez declared that with the new pope, there would be no turning back. Gutiérrez himself was welcomed into the Vatican through the front door. He received a letter of congratulations from the pope on his ninetieth birthday in May 2018: "With you I give thanks to God, and I also thank you for all that you have contributed to the Church and to humanity through your theological service and your preferential love for the poor and those rejected by society."

Since Pope Francis was elected, we have entered the era of reintegration. But there is no longer a need for liberation theologians, because liberation has risen to power in the Church.

1967–1968:
Bishop Hélder Câmara lights a fire in Argentina

From 1967 to 1970, the novice Jorge Bergoglio studied theology in Buenos Aires; he was ordained to the priesthood before completing his studies on December 13, 1969.

1967 was the year in which the revolutionary Brazilian educationist Paulo Freire published *Pedagogy of the Oppressed* and created the Church's Basic Education Movement in Brazil, a foundation that was to have a worldwide influence. At the same time, he was developing his revolutionary literacy-critical consciousness method.

In 1967, Dom Hélder Câmara's appeal to the bishops of the third world, also known as the "Manifesto of the Eighteen," led to the creation of the Movement of Priests for the Third World in Argentina. One of its first members was the young Bergoglio's theology teacher, Fr. Lucio Gera, whom we will discuss in more detail in chapter 5. All the progressive priests in Argentina joined the movement.

It was on August 15, 1967, that seventeen bishops (eight Brazilians, including Hélder Câmara, an Algerian, a Wallisian, an Egyptian, a Colombian, a Yugoslav, a Lebanese, a Singaporean (expelled from China), a Laotian, and an Indonesian) published this document known as the "Manifesto of the Bishops of the Third World."

The name of the eighteenth signatory is nowhere to be found.

Part of this nine-page document was published on September 2, 1967, by the Madrid newspaper *A.B.C.* (pp. 37 and 38), under the headline: "Message from some bishops of the Third World." In France, *Témoignage chrétien* also published the text.

The signing bishops had no juridical connection with each other. However, they had worked together during the sessions of the council. According to *A.B.C.*, this was a unique document in the history of the Church: never before, it said, had an ecclesiastical text used such radical and daring language. We translate *tajante* as "radical." Perhaps we should have preferred "bloody," because the word also means "trenchant"!

Here is the most significant passage of this radical text:

> Not all revolutions are necessarily good. Some are merely palace coups: they only lead to new forms of oppression of the people. Others do more harm than good, they "engender new injustices" (*Populorum Progressio*). Atheism and collectivism, with which some have seen fit to associate themselves, constitute grave dangers for humanity. But history shows that some revolutions were necessary, and that they abandoned their temporary anti-religiousness and produced good fruit. There is no better proof of this than the French Revolution of 1789, which led to the proclamation of human rights (cf. *Pacem in Terris*). Many of our nations have had to, or are having to, live with these profound changes. What should the attitude of Christians and the Church be in this situation? Pope Paul VI has already shown us the way in his encyclical on the progress of peoples.

Such is the ideological basis of the Movement of Priests for the Third World—we will use the Spanish acronym, MSTM—about which thousands of articles and hundreds of books have been written.

Father Bergoglio and the violence in Argentina

Some highly politicized Argentinian priests later signed a document derived from this letter. Among the signatories was a Jesuit Fr. Carlos Mugica.

He was a figurehead of the revolution in Argentina and was always quoting the great revolutionary writers. He went to Bolivia to recover the mortal remains of Che Guevara. Together with Fr. Jorge Vernazza of the MSTM, he was on the flight that brought Perón back to Argentina after his exile in Madrid.

Carlos Mugica's tendency to romantic exaltation does not fully account for his blind acceptance of the folly of Latin American, Guevarist, and Cuban Marxism. Born to a wealthy family, he devoted his whole life to leading the poor into the struggle for justice, but he had nothing in common with the Mexican Cristeros. He and his confreres weaponized the Word of God. They were activists for a political cause to which they were radically committed.

Here are two conclusive pieces of evidence of this. The first hails from Carlos Mugica's friends, the second from an opponent who was murdered for having exposed the MSTM's revolutionary activities with surgical precision.

This is public evidence. It is something that should be known to all those who presume to assess this movement and the men who were its members. Disregarding this evidence, or pretending that it does not exist, amounts to pathetic disinformation and constitutes a serious breach of the truth.

The Manifesto of the Eighteen was received in Argentina toward the end of 1967. Miguel Ramondetti, a worker-priest, helped to found the MSTM. In an interview he gave toward the end of his life, he clarified the causal relationship that existed between the MSTM and this manifesto, created by way of Dom Hélder Câmara's parallel magisterium, in the wake of the Pact of the Catacombs that the same Câmara had launched in 1965 in order to guide "the spirit of the Council":

> This is how it went: I was in Paternal [*a district of Buenos Aires*], but I wanted to go and work in the interior of the country. It was towards the end of '67. A member of the group we were working with in Buenos Aires had been appointed Bishop of Goya. A group of parish priests wanted to settle there, so I spoke to him and went to see him. During our conversation in his office at the curia he said to me: "Hey look, I just received this, it might interest you," and he tossed me a brochure. Its title was "Manifesto of 18 Bishops from the Third World." . . . I leafed through

it and I got really excited, because I thought it was the sort of thing that would move things forward, and moreover from an angle that would help us a lot, because these were bishops, they weren't a bunch of lone, slightly unhinged priests, as we used to say, and they spoke with a different language, from a different position, about the situation of the poor in the world. As far as I know, it was the first time that an ecclesiastical document of this magnitude included some kind of option for socialism. . . .

We simply decided to spread the document and ask for people to join. That's when things started to take shape, without much effort. There were three or four of us, all parish priests; we made a list and sent out the text. We were surprised when we began to receive an impressive number of subscriptions, we were swamped with letters, nearly everyone replied. There was one common denominator: they all stressed the need to organize a meeting. So, from Buenos Aires, we organized the first meeting in Córdoba. The letter was sent in November 1967. The meetings started at the beginning of 1968.

The bishop of Goya mentioned by Father Ramondetti was Bishop Alberto Devoto, the "bishop of the poor" in a diocese of estate owners. He was a defender of those imprisoned during the military dictatorship and also set up base ecclesial communities in his diocese; he was a modernist inspired by Maritain and Teilhard de Chardin. He is now considered as having inspired the MSTM and as one of its key members.

Miguel Ramondetti gave further details in a separate interview, in which he stated that the document he had indeed been given by Archbishop Devoto was in French. Back in Buenos Aires, he got together with two confreres engaged in the same struggles as he was, Rodolfo Ricciardelli and André Lanzon. The latter, a perfectly bilingual Frenchman, translated the document into Spanish. The text was then duplicated on the old Paternal parish roneograph.

The presence of this Frenchman at this point may come as a surprise to the reader. Another, just as subversive as he was, will appear later on. It is worth noting that the French, be it in Argentina, Brazil, or elsewhere in Latin America—and this is still true today!—were at the heart of the revolution in the Church, along with Spaniards, Belgians, and Germans; the Americans were not to arrive until later.

The fact that the document was written in French clearly demonstrates Bishop Devoto's links with Marxist Christians in Europe. It is reasonable to assume that this text came from the entourage of Canon Houtard of Louvain, since at the time he was much more responsive and had more international connections than the French.

The growth of the MSTM

The number of members rose from 50 at the end of 1967 to 270 in February 1968 (including 47 from the diocese of Buenos Aires), and then to 400. The MSTM would eventually have a maximum of 524 members—that is, 9 percent of the Argentinian clergy.

On December 31, 1967, Miguel Ramondetti sent Hélder Câmara the following letter, which was later published by CEME (Centro de Estudios "Miguel Enriquez," a left-wing research center in Chile):

Dear Bishop,

As 1967 draws to a close, our group of priests in Argentina has made public this declaration of support for the message you signed with seventeen other bishops from the Third World. [There is always the same error concerning the number of signatories. This suggests that there were originally eighteen signatory bishops, and that one of them withdrew.]

We fully support the text of the Message of the 18 Bishops of the Third World. We pledge to work with all our strength to put into practice, here in our country, the evangelical and prophetic content of this document.

We earnestly desire that our bishops should also publicly endorse the insights of this message, which is no less than a clarification and an application of the Council and the encyclical *Populorum Progressio* to the reality of the Third World, and consequently to that of Latin America. Especially "at this time when poor peoples and races are becoming increasingly conscious of themselves and of the exploitation of which they are victims, this message will give courage to all those who suffer and fight for justice, an imperative condition for peace".

We are well aware that our numbers are still very small at present, representing only 10 percent of the diocesan priests in this country. [This was not true at the time.]

Your testimony, and the way you released this document even though you represent only a tiny minority of the bishops of the Third World, also help us in this respect. However, we know that there are bishops in our country who support your document, even if they have not made this public for the time being. Hopefully they will do so soon. In the same way, we hope that over the next few weeks new signatures from priests will continue to arrive, as we have not yet received responses to our invitation from several dioceses.

It heartens us to see that positions such as those you are publicly taking are helping to resolve the conflict between Christianity and socialism, and to raise awareness about the fact that the Church cannot identify with any social system, least of all with capitalism and the international imperialism of money. *With positions such as these, Christianity is reconciled once again with the upward march of history* [emphasis added], and the Church is making a move towards putting into practice the Conciliar Constitution *Gaudium et Spes*. [Remember that Canon Houtart was one of the drafters of *Gaudium et Spes*.]

We are convinced that our Church in Latin America is facing an urgent and decisive choice in the face of current events. By endorsing the document you have published, we are aware that, as priests, we have taken the first step in committing ourselves to the process of transformation in Latin America.

We thank you for having inspired us and helped us to take this step.

We will remain united with you in every future step we take.

With all our affection in the Lord,

Miguel Ramondetti
(for the organizing committee).

In February 1968, the signatories called themselves "The Parish Priests of the Third World." It was under this name that they appeared in the media. In March of the same year, an office was set up with a general manager, a secretary, and coordinators, as well as a branch in each diocese. Miguel Ramondetti was to remain in office until 1973.

We cannot go into all the details of MSTM's revolutionary activity in this book. Not only did the movement operate underground but it also produced a highly political newsletter, *Enlace*, which was connected with *Christians for Socialism* in Allende's Chile. It had ties with Cuba and with the progressive French movement, *Echange et Dialogue*. It opened its pages to Garaudy, Schillebeeckx, and the like.

On the occasion of the CELAM Assembly in Medellín in 1968, MSTM published a letter to the bishops intended to guide their discussions in a certain direction; it was signed by 431 Argentines, 200 Brazilians, 100 Uruguayans, 50 Bolivians, and a number of others. A similar move would be made in 2007 in view of the Aparecida Assembly.

Argentina's MSTM was at the forefront of the revolution. Its exemplary attitude prompted Gustavo Gutiérrez to dedicate one of the chapters of his first book in 1971, *A Theology of Liberation: History, Politics, Salvation*, mentioned above, to Miguel Ramondetti.

At the time, Miguel Ramondetti also wrote for another Argentinian firebrand publication, *Cristianismo y Revolución*.

On the subject of Fr. Carlos Mugica's involvement with the MSTM, here is a definitive testimony about this priest who supposedly "listened to the people." It was a report on a meeting led by Mugica, published on June 19, 1970, by *La Razón*, a publication that supported him: "Fr. Mugica described the assimilation of the Marxist school of thought as a more Christian way of fulfilling the Church's demands. . . . He extended his condemnation of capitalism to the Soviet regime, in which the Marxist system had been distorted, in his opinion, and was unable to express authentic socialism's 'demanding' and egalitarian essence." The report specified that the meeting had ended with the Peronist anthem.

Apart from a very small number of exceptions, the ecclesiastical authorities remained silent or powerless, despite appeals for help from laypeople and priests in the face of what was undoubtedly the most subversive and dangerous movement in Argentina.

Pope Francis has said of the members of the MSTM: "Some claim they were communist priests. No, they were eminent priests fighting for justice. They were men of prayer, men who listened to the people of God, men who taught the catechism and fought for justice."[69]

These comments are totally out of place in the light of the history of the movement. The revolutionary romanticism, the loss of the Catholic sense of justice, and the political commitment of its members are all proof of the clerical subversion that swept across not just Argentina but the whole of Latin America.

The MSTM was not in the least a group of priests who "listened to the people," nor did they love justice in the Catholic sense of the term. Their model was a mixture of Cuba and Perón.

It is truly unfortunate that Pope Francis should have indulged in a declaration in their favor—a declaration, moreover, that bears no relation at all with the truth of the matter. He was in Argentina at the time of the tragic confrontation; he was at its heart. He well knows that behind the appearance of a fight for justice, there was a political and ideological agenda and that their Christian rhetoric was no more than a cover.

Carlos Sacheri

Nor did Prof. Carlos Sacheri's evidence catch the pope's attention. He was a witness to the truth, and he was murdered by the Montoneros in front of his wife and seven children as they were leaving Mass on December 22, 1974, for having exposed the MSTM deception.

Yet the history of liberationist Argentina cannot be told without his testimony.

Carlos Sacheri was no ordinary individual. He was still a young man, with a doctorate in philosophy, who taught at the Catholic University of Laval in Quebec. As a traditional Catholic, he professed an

---

[69]　*La Nación*, March 14, 2014.

interpretation of the Second Vatican Council in keeping with Tradition and did so right from the start of the post-conciliar period.

Carlos Sacheri took part in the Lausanne Congress in 1968.

Two years later—he was thirty-six at the time—Carlos Sacheri published a book that told the exact truth about the MSTM and also included a ninety-page account of the causes of the revolutionary deviations that led to the creation of the movement. His book, *La Iglesia Clandestina*, was never translated into French or English but was reprinted at least four times in Spanish.

His 183-page book kicked off with more than ten quotations from Pope Paul VI demonstrating the requirements of the Catholic faith in terms of dogmatic, moral, and historical knowledge.

The titles of its first chapters provide a good overview of Sacheri's approach: "Crisis of unity, crisis of faith"; "Psychological warfare in the Church"; "From modernism to progressive neo-modernism"; "The clandestine organization of modernist groups"; "Immanent heresy and progressivism"; "A typical example: Teilhard de Chardin"; "The formation of the post-conciliar underground Church"; "Prophetic groups and the charismatic Church"; "The IDO-C"; "Inverted clericalism"; "A 'third-worldist' preamble: The manifesto"; "The movement of Third World priests in Argentina."

Prof. Sacheri was no hotheaded political activist. He was a thinker who sought to know things by their cause. He focused on real facts, not on emotions or words that his listeners wanted to hear. In such a painful and novel situation for the Church in Argentina, he offered the best of what he knew to be the truth.

It was in his chapter "The 'third-worldist' preamble" that he analyzed the flagship text of the so-called "third-worldist" bishops, which was drafted at the initiative of Dom Hélder Câmara.

The recurrent ideological theme of this manifesto can be summarized as follows: countries were prey to a multitude of misfortunes caused by capitalist structures. It was therefore necessary to change the structures, to establish socialism and to suggest the use of organized violence against unjust structures. (A few years later, the term "sinful structures" was coined; what was not said at the time was that, since the Church was linked to these structures, it too had to change its own governance.)

Carlos Sacheri first questioned the legality of this kind of clerical movement. In canon law, there is no ban *per se* on such a movement, which was at any rate exceptional. But by its very nature, it entailed the creation of a parallel authority that was potentially detrimental to the Church, both because its aims were not specifically priestly and because its methods were open to criticism. In any case, it was up to the competent episcopal authority to decide whether or not to grant permission for it to exist. In support of this, Sacheri quoted Cardinal Daniélou on the errors of post-conciliar progressivism.

Carlos Sacheri also noted that in Argentina, the movement was anonymous. Only one name appeared in the open: that of Fr. Miguel Ramondetti, the movement's secretary general. When asked, the Argentinian bishops and archbishops admitted that they did not know who was in charge; one of them, however, saw Father Ramondetti as "the real leader" of the MSTM. But as is the case with all clandestine organizations, be they the Freemasonry or the Communist Party, it is not those who are visible who are in charge.

It is nevertheless essential to know who this secretary general really was, and Sacheri went into great detail in this respect. And here's a surprise: at the beginning of 1960, the parish of All Saints in Chacarita, which was also Father Ramondetti's, welcomed a French worker-priest from the Mission de France, Gilbert Ruffenach. He had fled France after helping the FLN in Algeria.

Ruffenach, who was born in 1926 and ordained in 1951 for the diocese of Paris, had gone to the Mission de France seminary in Lisieux, where he was incardinated in 1955. He lived in Gennevilliers. In 1958, five priests from the Mission de France were called to serve in Algeria. They refused. Two were finally sent there on August 30, 1958: Nicolas Obermayer and Gilbert Ruffenach. The latter had the rank of lieutenant and attended psychological warfare training courses in Constantine. He kept a diary, which he smuggled back to France to expose army abuses. He returned to France in January 1959 and joined the FLN[70]

---

[70]   Translator's note: the Soviet-backed liberation movement in Algeria.

support networks, which he had already helped locally during his stay in Algeria. We have identified at least twelve members of the Mission de France who were simultaneously working in FLN aid networks. It was the most revolutionary and politicized institute of the day.

It was this expert on underground activities who turned up in Buenos Aires. There, he trained Ramondetti, as well as another parish vicar, García Morro, who was later to leave the priesthood and who had set up a kind of workers' apostolate in 1956. As the parish priest, Father Trusso, was unlikely to welcome the "subversive ideas and methods" of his two disciples, Father Ruffenach, remembering the advantage that the priests of the Mission de France enjoyed by living among themselves, convinced Ramondetti to ask Father Trusso to split the parish into two so as to have more freedom of action. On March 5, 1961, the parish of the Incarnation of the Lord was created with the approval of the curia: Ruffenach and Morro used the opportunity to carry out large-scale subversive action thanks to an institute linked to the parish. Ruffenach established widespread and frequent contacts with the communists in the Villa Crespo cell. Meetings were held in the new parish. The names of their members are well-known: among them was a member in charge of the support campaign for Cuba, and another, a personal friend of Fidel Castro, Perelman, known as "Chiche," later took Ruffenach under his wing when the latter was suddenly forced to leave Argentina in 1961 via Mexico. There, Ruffenach met Ivan Illich and Archbishop Mendez Arceo (the latter having stayed in Argentina clandestinely in order to meet the progressive Church). He then slipped off to Cuba.

Returning to France in 1962, Ruffenach resumed his activities, in particular by supporting his fellow "bag-carrier" for the Algerian rebels against France, Father Davezies, during the latter's trial. Reliable sources indicate that he gave shelter to Saâd Abssi, the FLN's fundraising agent. By 1971, he was a delivery driver; he died in 1995.

Back to Ramondetti. Sacheri noted that he had extensive contacts with the Communist Party. When he was appointed to head the new parish, he set up a building cooperative and welcomed priests from all over the country for month-long sessions. As a professor at the Villa

Devoto seminary, he was able to indoctrinate the seminarians. One of them complained about this to the superior, but it was the seminarian who was expelled!

Esther Borzani acted as liaison between the parish and the Communist Party. In 1962, she was invited to the World Congress for General Disarmament and Peace; she became Ramondetti's right-hand woman.

In 1964, Ramondetti travelled to France and Algeria and took part in a Communist Party congress. This was reported in Argentine newspapers.

In 1967, he left his parish to work directly for Bishop Devoto, one of the pillars of clerical subversion in Argentina. His career history speaks for itself when it comes to understanding the true activities of the MSTM.

Two other figures stand out as active supporters of the MSTM.

Fr. Milán Viscovich and Fr. Arturo Paoli

Milán Viscovich was an Argentinian priest and a crypto-Marxist activist. Officially, he studied at Louvain to complete his training. In reality, much like the guerrilla priest Camilo Torres, he there became a follower of the Marxified Catholic religion taught by Canon Houtart. When he returned home in 1954, he was already denying that the indissolubility of marriage was a matter of natural law. Ten years later, he coined a slogan that was to become a powerful catalyst for dialectics in the Argentine Church: "I stand with the Church of the General Workers' Union and against the Church of the Stock Exchange." Other stances he took forced him to leave the Catholic University of Córdoba, of which he was dean, no less! In 1969, he played an active role in the student revolt in Córdoba and in the press campaign that forced the archbishop of Rosario to leave his diocese. He associated with Marxist intellectuals and was finally arrested. At that point, he made a declaration of social Catholicism worthy of the most orthodox writers in order to obtain his release. Called to order by his new bishop, he became an "expert in economic relations in the context of a socialist state."

Arturo Paoli was Italian. Born in 1912, he had a doctorate in philosophy from the University of Padua. He was a teacher and took part in the Resistance in Italy, saving Jews and winning the gold medal for civil merit. In 1954, he joined the Little Brothers of Jesus. He then embarked on politico-religious work and actively took part in the FLN's operations in Algeria. He arrived in Buenos Aires at the same time as Father Ruffenach and ran the "Fortin Olmos" Mutual Aid Center. Using the Center's van, he distributed Communist Party tracts and leaflets. In 1967, he published a book that foreshadowed the theories of the MSTM, *Persona, mundo y Dios*. He was an active participant in MSTM meetings. In 1974, he made a hasty escape to Venezuela before moving to Brazil, where he was involved in all the activities of liberation theology from 1985 onward.

He stayed with the Jesuits in Buenos Aires for a time in 1969 and there met Bergoglio. Bergoglio later welcomed him to the Vatican as pope on January 18, 2014. Father Paoli had previously been declared "Righteous Among the Nations."

In Argentina, all these clerics who had gone over to the revolution were acting in secret. We have already mentioned the existence of *Enlace*. Among other things, this publication passed on information from Fr. Jorge Vernazza, the MSTM's diocesan priest in Buenos Aires.

In 1969, the daily *La Prensa* published a document from the *Revolutionary Castrocomunist-Maoist Central Committee* referring to the situation in Argentina. The committee's instructions were notably implemented during a bloody confrontation in Córdoba in 1969 called the "Cordobazo," a popular protest featuring workers' and students' strikes, and a sort of Argentinian May '68. The committee's approval could not have been greater: "The union of students, workers and peasants will constitute the most powerful force for the liberation of America," it stated.

The MSTM was one of the driving forces behind this struggle.

One of the instructions of the committee was that "the image of Christ must preside over all major acts of transformation in order to ensure the cooperation of the revolutionary Church."

These instructions appear in part in the conclusions of the National Meeting of the MSTM at Colonia Coroya.

Anyone who still dares argue that the MSTM priests were innocent and that they were not communists is forgetting Father Ramondetti's own statement on June 27, 1969: "We consider it necessary to eradicate private ownership of the means of production, totally and once and for all."

Carlos Sacheri cites these words in his book, which is a must-read for anyone wishing to understand the true nature of the MSTM's ideology.

1968:
Year 1 of the final revolutionary offensive against the Latin American Church

The CELAM Assembly

The revolutionary onslaught against the Church in Latin America had been prepared well in advance by a series of meetings of conciliar Church bodies. It came to fruition at the CELAM meeting in Medellín, Colombia, from August 24 to September 6, 1968.

According to Germán Doig Klinge, all the CELAM meetings were continental instruments for the spreading of the most firmly established conciliar doctrines. The same was true of the Aparecida meeting in 2007, which the said author, who died in 2001, obviously did not mention. Here are his words:

> The General Conferences of the Latin American Episcopate are fundamental stages in the pilgrimage of the People of God in Latin America. They are important milestones in the process of the Church's developing consciousness of her mission in the history of peoples from the Rio Grande to Tierra del Fuego. There is no doubt that they had a profound impact on the life of the Church in the second half of the twentieth century, which is now drawing to a close. As part of the great current of renewal

expressed by the Second Vatican Council, they need to be considered as moments of grace and responsibility, as moments of
a conscious effort to discern God's plan with an eye and a heart
that are attentive to the signs of these times, which are so intense
and dramatic, so contradictory and at the same time so laden
with the seeds of hope.

Tens of thousands of pages of this kind of gushing praise have
already been written, as if a new incarnation had taken place! The
truth, however, is light years away from such enthusiasm.

In the same way that the French Revolution was prepared by the
"*sociétés de pensée*" of the intellectuals and by lists of grievances, the
council and all the assemblies of CELAM were well and truly "set up."

All those who have analyzed this period agree that it first began
with the Pact of the Catacombs, but the meeting in Petrópolis
(Brazil) in March 1964, mentioned several times above, should not
be forgotten.

Since then, but also during the run-up to the council itself, continental meetings never ceased to take place.

An initial meeting was held from June 5 to 11, 1966 in Baños,
Ecuador, followed by another in Argentina at Mar del Plata, where
Bishop Pironio was auxiliary bishop at the time. The Marxist Canon
Houtart points out in his history of CELAM: "The most signifi-
cant of these meetings was probably the one in Mar del Plata. It was
devoted to the problems of justice and development and drew up
the orientations to be taken in Medellín. The final declaration was
called: *The presence of the Church in the development and integration
of Latin America.* Interestingly, it was presented by a delegation of
Latin American bishops to the UN Secretary General, Mr. U Thant."
Bishop Hélder Câmara was present, as was the Belgian liberationist
José Comblin. Hélder Câmara signed another document along these
lines; it was published by *Témoignage Chrétien* on August 31, 1966.
It declared that "the peoples of the Third World constitute the proletariat of today's world."

Pope Paul VI in Medellín

Pope Paul VI travelled to Medellín in 1968 for the CELAM assembly. It was the first time a pope had set foot in Latin America. The success of his visit surpassed all expectations: the Colombian people turned out *en masse*, not to mention those who came from neighboring countries. The pope was deeply moved. He greeted the bishops, priests, and all the faithful of the Holy Catholic Church of this great continent on several occasions. When he recalled the great apostolic work of almost five centuries that had led to the evangelization of Latin America, he exclaimed: "God bless this great work! God bless those who dedicated their lives to it! God bless you, beloved Brothers, who have dedicated yourselves to this gigantic task!"

On August 22, he presided over the ordination of two hundred deacons and priests. He dedicated his homily to the praise of God Our Lord, calling Him to witness and invoking Him with passion: "Look, Lord, at these new priests, these new deacons; may they be proud to be your ambassadors, your heralds, your ministers for this blessed land of Colombia and throughout the Christian continent of Latin America."

His homily for the assembly's bishops was equally masterful. He addressed them as "successors of the Apostles, guardians and teachers of the faith, and shepherds of the people of God." "We cannot do without the practice of an intense interior life," he said, exhorting all to adopt a modest appearance. "The angels see us in the transparent purity of our single love for Christ, which is so shiningly manifest in the firm and joyful observance of our priestly celibacy," Paul VI added, recalling that faith is "the foundation and the source of all things." This is why he referred at that point to his own solemn profession of faith. He recalled that the obligation to remain faithful to the "*philosophia perennis*" had lost none of its relevance, as opposed to the works of "fashionable thinkers." "We are tempted by historicism, relativism, subjectivism and neo-positivism, which are at the root of a subversive spirit of criticism in the realm of the faith. . . . Unfortunately, there are also among us theologians who do not always follow the right path. . . . Some . . . thus fall into the self-examination that destroyed the unity of the Church itself."

Paul VI also corrected the errors and practices of the charismatic Church, clarifying the content of the Church's social doctrine. Finally, he reiterated what he had just published in the encyclical *Humanae Vitae*: the Christian attitude it describes, he said, "is an apologia for life, which is the gift of God, the glory of the family and the strength of the people." He stated that he had reaffirmed this "in homage to the law of God."

All this was said with unusual force, yet it was all deliberately ignored. Of the pope's words, the conclusions of the assembly would include only those on liturgical reform, a reference to *Populorum Progressio*, and the episcopal texts on the subject—not forgetting the Jesuit provincial fathers' firebrand letter from Rio mentioned earlier. The pope's declared intention to recall principles was never taken into account. Social justice on the continent was to be based solely on the theology of liberation and the theology of the people.

The conclusions of the CELAM Assembly in Medellín

The assembly brought together 130 bishops and representatives of the Conference of Religious with voting rights, as well as several hundred experts, advisers, religious, and lay people. It resulted in a document of over sevety-three pages, under the title *Message to the Peoples of Latin America*. It is beyond our scope to analyze all the chapters and their recommendations. We simply mention here its sixteenth chapter, which deals with the means of social communication. Paragraph 21 encapsulates the ideological flavor of the whole document: "This attitude of openness encourages the necessary freedom of expression that is indispensable in the Church, in accordance with the spirit of the Second Vatican Council."

The document was in fact calling for radical reform of the Catholic Church on the Latin American continent.

CELAM was its politburo. The reform was based on the evolution of the world and aimed at the necessary adaptation to this new and future world. Almost all of its references were inspired by *Gaudium et Spes*, which was written by Canon Houtart and Monsignor Pierre Haubtmann, former rector of the Institut Catholique de Paris. Talk of "liberation" and poverty was everywhere. The text planned for the transfer of power to CELAM on the grounds that the reform would require sociological studies to reflect the realities experienced by the poor. At times, it reads more like a skit in favor of the class struggle than a document intended for evangelization.

From that moment on, base ecclesial communities began to flourish. Participants at the CELAM Assembly and its analysts agree that it set a "continental Church" in motion. According to Virginia Azcuy, a feminist theologian whom we have already met in previous chapters, "the Medellín Conference clearly took on the liberationist theme and language. . . . The consciousness of this situation of underdevelopment triggered attitudes of protest and of aspiration to liberation in vast sectors."

Jon Sobrino, a Salvadoran Jesuit, gave a lecture on the Pact of the Catacombs in Rome on November 14, 2015. In his view, Medellín was its logical extension. Taking stock of these years of struggle and martyrdom, he said: "Let us go further: we should not be surprised that Francis is under attack. He has taken up the themes mentioned in the wake of Medellín."

The seven bishops who gave the most important speeches at Medellín were all staunch "conciliarists."

Virginia Azcuy is of the opinion that the progressive bishops were not the majority, but they were the more enthusiastic, and they gave the event a significant impetus with the help of expert theologians and guest intellectuals.

Gustavo Gutiérrez and Pierre Bigo, SJ, had written the preparatory texts on peace; Gutiérrez, the one on poverty; Hélder Câmara, Renato Poblete, SJ, and Samuel Ruiz, the one on justice. Chapter 12 on the religious was written by Father Arrupe himself. Of the six drafters, three were Jesuits. They had learned the lesson of the council well.

Later, Archbishop López Trujillo was to make a courageous attempt to interpret the Medellín texts in a Catholic way, but almost no one listened to him.

It was here that, according to commentators who support him, Gustavo Gutiérrez found the inspiration for his book on liberation theology which he published four years later in 1972. In Medellín, he was already advisor to the Peruvian episcopate.

Fifty years on, the verdict is in. Latin American Christianity has collapsed.

We should never lose sight of the fact that behind ideas, there are people. It was these people who waged the formidable ideological battle that was to rock Latin America.

The limited strictly revolutionary agitation instigated by Cuba and the Soviets was nothing compared to what CELAM was to achieve. The only country where Cuba imposed itself for a time was Nicaragua. The Cuban presence there was so strong that those who went there for training came back with a Cuban accent! Cuban aid to Chile was a disaster, and a US intervention brought General Pinochet to power.

The real conquering machinery was made up of cardinals, bishops, priests, religious men and women, lay people, and all the movements modeled on European Catholic Action.

This revolution, the real revolution, provided itself with a powerful apparatus that spanned all human activities on the continent, directly or indirectly.

The secretary of CELAM, the Argentinian bishop Eduardo Pironio, was to play a decisive role over the following twenty-five years. He became the linchpin of the whole process of conquering the spaces and hierarchical powers of Latin America.

In his capacity as bishop of La Plata in Argentina, Pironio encouraged the development of subversion in his diocese. He chaired CELAM from 1968 to 1972, from 1972 to 1974, and again from 1974 to 1975. His subversive action within the Assembly of Latin American Bishops was exposed, but to no avail. He surrounded himself with a host of revolutionary priests: Fr. Joaquín Alliende, the French Jesuit Pierre Bigo (one of the worst), the Belgian Joseph Comblin (Dom Hélder Câmara's theologian), the Marxist Jesuit Arturo Gaete, Fr. Lucio Gera, Fr. Gustavo Gutiérrez, Fr. Alvaro Mejía, Fr. Renato Poblete, a Jesuit who collaborated with the Allende regime, and so on. There were also lay people such as the Marxist historian Enrique Dussel, and Alberto

Methol Ferré, a writer, journalist, and historian from Uruguay who was the editor of the Uruguayan Catholic-Marxist magazine *Víspera*.

Bishop Pironio was declared a Servant of God by Benedict XVI on June 23, 2006, and his beatification process is currently underway.

When we talk about long-established networks, readers can see for themselves that we are not making things up.

All the CELAM Assemblies that followed—Puebla, Santo Domingo, and Aparecida—did nothing other than extend the most disastrous theses put in place at the Second Vatican Council and in Medellín toward their logical conclusion.

It was in 1985 that Cardinal Alfonso López Trujillo, then archbishop of Medellín, launched his aforementioned attempt to put a check on this deluge of errors, the consequences of which are so visible in our time. From January 11 to 13, in Arequipa, Peru, an International Congress for Reconciliation was held, in line with the thinking of John Paul II as set out in his post-synodal apostolic exhortation *Reconciliation and Penance*. This remarkable synthesis of the Catholic faith was to remain without effect. The Mexican movement *Cristianismo Sí* was almost the only group that published it in Spanish and English. None of the speakers were Argentinian.

One year later, in Cuba, in January 1986, on the occasion of the first national meeting of the Catholic Church to be authorized there after twenty-five years of dictatorship, the official launching of a theology of reconciliation took place, which was devised by Fr. René David Rosset, a French priest who had been living on the island since August 26, 1970. This priest was to remain in the service of the Castro regime until April 25, 2004. Devoted to the Cuban communist regime, Father David advocated the "reconciliation" of Fidel Castro's Marxist-Leninist socialism with Catholicism.

The pope's representative at the meeting was none other than Bishop Eduardo Pironio, whose role in Latin America was well-known to all Cubans. Visits by Pope John Paul II in 1998, Pope Benedict XVI in 2012, and now Pope Francis have done nothing to bring change to this forgotten dictatorship, where faithful Christians remain under constant police surveillance to this day.

CHAPTER 5

Pope Francis and Juan Perón

F ather Bergoglio received what you could call his philosophical-theological anointing from his Jesuit mentor, Father Scannone, but before that, he had been permanently shaped by Juan Perón. This imprint is so profound that those who wish to understand it, especially if they are not from Argentina, will need to immerse themselves in a somewhat fantastical world.

Juan Perón was the quintessential charismatic man. With his words, his presence, his eloquence, and his generosity, he metamorphosed the hardships of the Argentinian people into a beacon of justice. He caught imaginations by the power of his actions and of his beliefs, and this power was so intense that it suggested that his art was somehow divine, supernatural, and superhuman. Both he and his second wife, Eva, appealed to Divine Providence, and the difficulties he experienced with the Argentine Church did nothing to undermine the "mystical" relationship (the expression was his own) that existed between the people and their Guide.

He was neither a Duce, nor a Führer, nor a Conducator. He sought to be the humble servant of the people and bring them happiness.

Such an absolute bond had no parallel in Argentina's history. When Perón was already close to the apex of power, he was imprisoned on October 12, 1945 by the "conservative military regime" because he had formed close ties with the trade unions. It was the people who set him free on October 17, 1945, and it was through a workers' strike that he was brought to power without a coup d'état. This unique event would henceforth be called "Fidelity Day." Perón had silenced the oligarchy. He lived by the people and for the people.

Juan Perón became Bergoglio's political role model. Indeed, it was the only one the young man would ever have. Dictatorships were to mark the political life of Argentina during the period of Bergoglio's maturity and his episcopate in Buenos Aires, but they would never be anything other than military dictatorships or oligarchic regimes.

Juan Perón was born in 1895 and was baptized a Catholic in 1898; his parents were officially married in 1901. He would later claim Indian ancestry. What is known for certain is that he had a French paternal great-grandfather from Baïgorry in the Basque country. His parents settled in Buenos Aires in 1905. In 1913, he graduated from military college as a second lieutenant; by 1915, he was a lieutenant.

During the first democratic elections in Argentina in 1916, he voted for the Radical Civic Union; he was a "legalistic nationalist."

The British had grabbed the country's economic activity and controlled its industrial, agricultural, and forestry sectors. Besides being badly underpaid, the workers of "La Forestal" in the north-east of the country were harshly treated: these slave-like conditions led to frequent revolts. The army was often sent in to crush strikes and uprisings. Lieutenant Perón himself was sent there in 1917, and on that occasion, he was able to demonstrate his skill in restoring order and negotiating with the British for decent working conditions and time for rest.

This initial encounter with the exploited laborers played a decisive role in Perón's understanding of future social struggles.

In 1919, Perón witnessed the workers' riots in Buenos Aires. What is now remembered as the "Tragic Week" left seven hundred people dead. There was even talk of a pogrom, as the victims included a large number of European Jews. Perón's role in this upheaval was to supply the police and army with arms and ammunition.

In 1924, he was promoted to the rank of captain. Two years later, he joined the War Academy (Escuela Superior de Guerra), and by 1929, he was a member of the General Staff. During this period, he wrote a number of short treatises on strategic and tactical training and familiarized himself with all the great captains of history, with

Napoleon as his personal favorite. In 1930, he was appointed a professor at the War Academy, initially as a substitute, then as a full professor at the end of the year.

Perón's political commitment was still quite hazy at the time, although he did take part in General Uriburu's coup d'état on September 6, 1930. After consenting to the putsch and taking part in secret preparatory meetings, he provided security for the 1,500 or so military personnel involved. In this role, he defended the presidential buildings which had been stormed by rioters.

Perón described this adventure in detail in the first part of his book, *Tres Revoluciones Militares*, in which he voiced his deep contempt for the organizers and the disgraceful lack of preparation for their "maneuvers." He was pitiless toward those involved: in his view, they were only looking out for their own interests. "I was an officer who, from the first days when an armed movement was considered, put himself at the service of the cause, and not of the men who led it. I cooperated honorably, with no personal interest. . . . But I cannot accept that we should have been the toys of the incompetence and lack of knowledge of those who gave us missions like the one I personally received, and which can only have been assigned by irresponsible or unbalanced people," he wrote.

The coup was a disaster on the military front, and it was the people who saved it, Perón observed: "We owe this miracle to the people of Buenos Aires, who poured into the streets like an avalanche, shouting 'Long live the revolution'; it was they who seized the presidency, it was they who made the troops decide to support the movement . . . , it was they who made possible a victory that would otherwise have been too costly, if not unattainable. That is why today I believe, with deep satisfaction, that our people have lost nothing of the 'sacred fire' that has made them great throughout one hundred and twenty years of history."

On September 7, 1930, just when he was preparing to join the General Staff, he was informed that he had been appointed private secretary to the Minister of War, Major General Francisco Medina.

His diplomatic career in Chile began in 1936, when he was appointed military attaché with the rank of lieutenant-colonel.

In 1939, Perón joined a study mission to Europe. In Italy, he took courses in economics, philosophy, and general culture. He also enjoyed skiing and mountaineering and received military training with the Alpine troops.

He traveled to Germany, France, Spain, Hungary, Yugoslavia, and Albania. Returning to Argentina on January 8, 1941, he was promoted to the rank of colonel and took command of a mountain unit.

From one coup to the next

The fascination that Juan Perón was to exert on Argentine political life for more than thirty years had nothing to do with any kind of exceptional military aura. He won no wars. He was not a putschist. His role in 1930 was a minor one, and he received no reward for it.

The essential quality that he constantly perfected was that of an organizer. He conceived social and political life from the point of view of a staff officer. He acquired a considerable amount of knowledge in all areas of state management: history, economics, community life, and international politics.

His one and only desire was to serve the Argentine people. He wanted to lead the people in order to settle it firmly in justice and happiness. This aspiration to greatness was perfectly in tune with "*el gran pueblo Argentino*," the great Argentine people, the self-image of the Argentine people as expressed in their national anthem.

General Iruburu died after two years in government. He had tampered with the voting rules to ensure that he would remain in power, but it was his successor who was to benefit from the scheme.

Augusto Pedro Justo held power from 1932 to 1938. The Argentines refer to this period as the "infamous decade." At the time, capital equipment and manufactured goods were sold to the British at knock-down prices.

From 1938 to 1946, Argentina had five presidents, some of them *de facto*, because they didn't even have time to take their oath of office pledge. Ministers came and went even more often.

In 1938, widespread anarchy and the hardships of the people led to elections that were rigged in favor of Roberto Marcelino Ortiz. He remained in power until 1942. He was embroiled in a scandal involving the sale of military land and at the same time fell victim to diabetes, which left him blind. Vice-president Ramón Castillo took over in 1940. At this point, the political trend changed. There was a shift from the Radical Civic Union to National Democracy. Fraud continued unabated. Argentina fell prey to all kinds of internal and external profiteers. Castillo was overthrown by Pedro Ramírez, his Minister of War, on June 4, 1943.

The June 4, 1943 revolution was organized by a group of officers known as the GOU (United Officers Group). Juan Perón remained in the background even though he was a member. The GOU was not a Masonic organization but rather an association of conspiratorial officers from different backgrounds who were simply waiting for the right moment.

According to one commentator, the ideology that brought them together was very mixed, which partly explains why the group disintegrated so quickly: it was similar to those developed in Europe at the time by men like Maurras in France, Ernst von Salomon in Germany, and Ramiro de Maeztu and Primo de Rivera in Spain.

The GOU's demands were published in various documents. The military government of Pedro Ramírez was directly inspired by this text: "Schools without religion are anti-democratic and anti-constitutional and do not prepare children for the supreme honor to which every Argentine can aspire, that of being President of the Nation." Several members of the GOU affirmed the Catholic nature of the revolution, and they wanted to express this in the media. An anonymous author with links to the GOU wrote in the Catholic periodical *El Pueblo*: "Secular and agnostic liberalism are guilty of depriving the nation of a moral doctrine." When you add to this the belief in *Hispandad* ("Hispanicity"), the disapproval of English influence in Argentina and the rejection of Marxism and Anglo-Saxon imperialism, it is easy to understand why these colonels were so opposed to one another. The Second World War was at its height: some were pro-German, others were pro-American, and still others in favor of complete neutrality toward the warring powers.

In the end, Argentina maintained the neutral position it had adopted for fifty years, much to the dismay of some officers.

Juan Perón did not appear in the cabinet structure until October 1943. At his own request, he was then put in charge of the National Labour Department—an obscure position in a toothless administration which consisted of maintaining contact with the trade unions, or what was left of them, and listening to their grievances.

It was from this position that Juan Perón began his conquest of power, working in a junior post that held no interest for anyone, but which his political genius and experience of the people would transform.

The country was in total disarray. Its new rulers introduced a program of social, economic, and political reform. The army grew from 30,000 to 100,000 men, and the country developed its own arms industry, but Colonel Perón had other things to do.

In the aforementioned book, he described his actions at the time in the following terms: "I shall sow these seeds in the fertile earth of the workers of my land whom I know understand and share my truth, through that extraordinary intuition which the masses possess when they are led with loyalty and honor. . . . By defending those who suffer and work in order to build and shape the greatness of the Nation, I stand for the fatherland, in fulfilment of the oath by which I pledged my life. And life is but a trifle when comes the time for it to be offered on the altar of the fatherland."

He converted his government tip-up seat into a "Secretariat of Labor and Forecasts," which ushered in the era of social policy in Argentina with the restoration of workers' rights, employment laws, the organization of trade unions, labor-management agreements, and so on.

Within eight months, Perón had acquired a name and an authority that no one could challenge.

The government of which he was a member was openly conservative and Catholic and took measures to ensure that religion was taught in schools.

On January 26, 1944, Argentina broke off diplomatic relations with Germany and Japan. It had chosen its side.

The vice-president and Minister of War, Edelmiro Farrell, at this point disbanded the GOU, as a result of which Pedro Ramírez resigned on February 24, 1944. Farrell stepped in as president of the nation.

On March 27, 1945, Argentina declared war on Germany and Japan and won a seat at the UN despite Stalin's objections.

A coup d'état minus the army

On March 11, 1944, Juan Perón became Minister of War; he was also appointed vice president and kept his post at the Secretariat of Labor.

This allowed him to pursue his program of social reform, introducing a special status for rural workers and paid holidays for industrial workers. He also created a National Labor Court of Justice.

Perón faced increasing opposition from the military in the Farrell government, some of whom were allied with the radicals: they had realized the scope of his ambitions.

On October 8, 1945, General Ávalos, who was in command of the Campo de Mayo, demanded Perón's resignation from the government.

On the next day, Perón resigned from all his posts, just when an initial workers' campaign in his favor was getting underway. On the 10th, the Minister of the Interior announced general elections in a bid to restore calm.

On the 11th, Perón applied for retirement. General Ávalos became Minister of War.

Strikes and demonstrations erupted on the 12th. The CGT (General Workers' Council), that favored Perón, violently opposed the communists.

On the 13th, the chief of police, Colonel Mittelbach, arrested him under the pretense that his life was in danger. Perón was taken away on the gunboat *Independencia* and was held prisoner on the island of Martin García.

On the 14th, there were fears that the prisoner's health would "deteriorate," so it was decided to transfer him to the Belgrano military hospital in the capital. The people were given assurances that their social gains would be preserved.

On the 15th and 16th, demonstrations were held throughout the country in support of Perón. A military opposition to Perón was formed in the capital's Military Circle, but it was totally unsuccessful. Faced with the human flood that had swept into the streets of Buenos Aires, General Ávalos announced that the troops would not open fire.

On the morning of the 17th, Perón was transferred as planned, but because the decision had not been made public, a general strike was scheduled for the 18th. The government and President Farrell were no longer in control of the situation. At 11:00 p.m., Perón appeared on the balcony of the government palace alongside President Farrell.

On the 20th, Perón was reinstated. He simultaneously withdrew from all military functions. On October 21, 1945, he married Eva.

The peronisation of
Pope Francis and how it happened

When he graduated from high school at age sixteen or seventeen, one of Jorge Bergoglio's teachers gave him Evita Perón's book, *La Razón de mi vida*, published in 1951, in which she told the story of her life and love for Juan Perón. The president's wife was dying of cancer and had only a few months to live (she died on July 25 of the following year). "Her" book was distributed for free throughout Argentina. It was meant to be read by all. Evita's popularity was unparalleled. She was devoted to the people, and the people were devoted to her. In the 155 pages of her book, the word *people* appears 226 times.

These people were the poor, the *descamisados* (the shirtless) who had freed her husband, and it was the poor, the workers, and the humble who would continue to be the source of his power until his death.

"Evita" became the mother of the humble. She imitated her husband. She used to proclaim to the crowds: "*Solamente los humildes salvarán a los humildes*" (only the humble will save the humble). She told the women's Peronist party: "I believe that only women will save women." This kind of language was a perfect echo to that of the first principle of the International Workers' Association, the future First International: "Considering that the emancipation of the working classes must be conquered by the working classes themselves . . ." The expression had thrived, with a few variations, throughout the nineteenth century, in particular in Bakunin's work.

Evita even declared herself to be the "spiritual leader of the nation," the protector of the humble!

Four years after Perón granted women the vote, Evita wrote:

> We [women] are neither in the Vatican nor the Kremlin. Nor are we in the headquarters of the imperialists. We are not on "atomic energy commissions", nor in the big consortiums, in the Freemasonry, or in secret societies. We are not in any of the great hubs of world power.
>
> And yet we have always been there when death throes set in, we were there in all humanity's bitter hours. . . . Our symbol should be that of the mother of Christ at the foot of the cross.[71]

The preface to the 2009 edition still carries the fervor of Loyalty Day (October 17, 1945): "We faithfully honor her memory with the true Peronist sentiment that our Santa Evita deserves."

Anyone familiar with the Argentinian people knows for a fact that this legendary couple permeated the political and social ideals of many generations to their very core and will continue to do so for a long time to come.

Did the young Jorge Bergoglio attend Eva Perón's spectacular funeral? It seems reasonable to think so. Nobody appears to have asked him about this. But we can safely say that his readings at that young age, in a context that lent itself to the sublime, must have anchored Peronism permanently in the mind of the future pope. When Juan Perón was ousted from power in 1955, Jorge was nineteen.

The "Liberating Revolution" allowed General Aramburu to grab power on November 13, 1955. All the social laws and apparatus put in

---

[71]   Perón, *La Razón de mi vida*, p. 139.

place by Perón were abolished, and all the trade unions were outlawed. The decree 4161 of March 5, 1956 prohibited the use of images, symbols, signs and expressions, doctrines, and works of art by individuals or organizations representing Peronism. The ban extended to flags, insignia, and even to Perón's name. The words *Peronism, Peronist, Justicialism, Justicialist,* and *Third Position* were also banned, as were any songs associated with them, as well as speeches or parts of speeches by the general.

On June 9, General Valle, who was sympathetic to Peronism, attempted a coup against Aramburu. It failed, and he was charged with civil and military rebellion. On June 12, he was shot along with some thirty other people. He accused his murderers in a protracted letter: "I shed my blood for the cause of the humble people, for justice and freedom for all, and not for a privileged few. . . . I pray to God that my blood may serve to unite the people of Argentina."

This bloody page of Argentina's history triggered a violent reaction from Perón's supporters, and it was to have a lasting effect. Aramburu was defeated in the following elections by the radical Frondizi, who was allied to the Peronists and lifted all restrictions. General Illia was to succeed him in 1963 for three years; meanwhile, in 1964, the young novice Bergoglio returned from Chile. Peronism was legalized and the Peronist Youth Movement formed anew. The Communist Party was also legalized. Illia adopted many of the social provisions of Peron's program. The Peronists won the 1965 elections.

However, Perón's military enemies were preparing another coup. General Onganía seized power on July 26, 1966. It is fair to say that he had no political acumen whatsoever. He wanted to build a true-blue, Catholic, and counter-revolutionary Argentina; he called his attempt the "Argentinian revolution." Violence took hold of the country on a permanent basis. In 1969, a full-scale civil war broke out in Córdoba, the army deployed, and there were many casualties: this was the Cordobazo student revolt mentioned in the previous chapter.

Part of the clergy was driven by the post-conciliar atmosphere: the Jesuits' activity on the continent in favor of social justice and the success of the Third World priests' movement were gaining ground. The revival of the young Peronists in 1970 led to the fall of Onganía. Between 1970 and 1973, Argentina would have four presidents: Roberto Levingston, Alejandro Lanusse, Héctor José Campora, and Raúl Alberto Lastiri, the latter of whom called early elections that effectively handed power to Perón, who was preparing his comeback in Spain. On October 11, 1973, Perón was once more at the helm of the Argentinian state.

Perón and the Catholic Church

It is not always easy to keep track of the currents that swept through Argentina's political landscape with each passing *pronunciamento*. Some say that Peronism, especially after Perón, was an example of the implementation of Catholic social doctrine. The reality is quite different.

Argentina, like all Latin American countries, is a Catholic country under Masonic domination. Ecuador, whose President García Moreno was murdered by order of the Lodges, had tried to escape this new form of racist colonization, whose main protagonists were the Spanish, Portuguese, and above all, the English Masons.

But the last strongholds of Christendom resisted with great bloodshed, especially in Mexico and Argentina, thanks to the Italian immigrants. As a result, the first International Eucharistic Congress on the South American continent was held in Buenos Aires from October 10 to 14, 1934.

It was a triumph—a Catholic triumph as evidenced by the photos taken at the time. More than 1.2 million people attended, including the cardinal archbishops of Madrid, Paris, and Warsaw. Pope Pius XI sent his Secretary of State, Cardinal Eugenio Pacelli, as his legate. Argentina had never seen a gathering of this size (and would only see the likes of it when Eva Perón and her husband rallied the crowds, giving rise to a sense of belonging to a national community with modern political parties).

The congress was interpreted as the revenge of Catholicism. The archbishop of Toledo praised Hispanic identity, which he associated with "Argentinian identity," saying: "*America es obra de España*"

(America is the work of Spain). The evangelization that had led to the birth of this new Christianity was the theme of one of Legate Pacelli's speeches. He recalled the martyrdom of the first "criollo" Jesuit (a European born on the American continent), Saint Roque González de Santa Cruz, who wrote the first catechism in Guarani. He emphasized the Eucharistic tradition of the Argentine people.

The future archbishop of Buenos Aires, Bishop Quarracino, wrote in 1977: "The Eucharistic Congress had a before and an after." The story goes that the president of the Republic, Augustin Justo, showed too much consideration for the Church and for the pope's envoy and was struck off the list of members of his Lodge.

At the time, Jesuits were everywhere, especially in education: 153 in Buenos Aires and 116 in Cordoba.

Although the Argentine population was still predominantly Catholic at the time, governments were directly inspired by the Freemasons and their business cronies ever since independence and the British takeover of the economy. The political class fluctuated in line with the successive *pronunciamientos*. The people, on the other hand, had no major political interests: immigrants fought first and foremost for their own survival, because life was hard. Massacres of the natives and workers' uprisings were put down by the army. The workers did not really organize as a movement until the arrival of Perón, who would never be a Catholic.

Church structures, meanwhile, remained fragmented.

Men who did not practice a religion were known as "radicals"— as was the case with the pope's uncle. His father, on the other hand, remained attached to religious practice.

From the end of the First World War, imitation of Europe began to develop, together with an embryonic Christian democracy. Later, Spaniards fleeing Franco's regime would embrace Perón's "justicialism."

But it is fair to say that the greater part of Argentinian Catholic society was still faithful to the spirit of the Eucharistic Congress at the time of Jacques Maritain's visit to Argentina from August 15 to September 14, 1936, during the year that saw the publication of

Humanisme intégral, in which Maritain expressed his decisive break with his Thomistic work. It was also the year in which the Spanish Civil War broke out.

It was Tomás Casares, director of the Cursos de Cultura Catolica (CCC) and the Centro de Estudios Religiosos (CES), who invited Maritain. But the latter was also a guest of the Buenos Aires PEN Club as part of the International Committee on Intellectual Cooperation, which campaigned against fascism.

At the time, the good and unsuspecting Argentinian Catholics only knew the Thomistic Maritain. "Two months in Argentina was long enough for Maritain to become an object of attack for most of those who, just a few months before, still worshipped him," wrote Olivier Compagnon in his book *Jacques Maritain et l'Amérique du Sud: le modèle malgré lui* (Jacques Maritain and South America: the unwilling paragon).

It was a fierce controversy, and the new Maritain left his mark on "advanced" minds for many a year to come.

While these religious ups and downs were taking place, Perón acted as an enlightened opportunist and not as a "social Catholic." However, he was taken for one, because he constructed Argentina's first social system, created trade unions, introduced paid vacations, pensions, welfare services, and so on. They read like a catalogue of practically all the things social Catholics would set up.

When Perón came to power in 1943, after the "Infamous Decade," he had the support of the Catholic Church. He immediately confirmed a decree establishing religious education in schools; he increased the salaries of staff paid by the state from 50 to 100 percent; he handed out subsidies for pilgrimages and trips abroad; he also funded the upkeep and construction of churches. These were all vote-catching measures that gave him an aura of authentic Catholicism.

Perón had been a military attaché in Italy since 1939. At the time, Mussolini was at the height of his power, and his cultural, educational, and political approach left a lasting mark on the future "Conductor." Perón's liberal opponents accused him of "Francoism," even though it was fascism that had won him over. The difficulties that Perón experienced with the Church were precisely the same as those the Duce had faced in Italy.

The enrollment of the Church in the Peronist project was prepared by Eva Perón's trip to the Vatican

Juan Perón was elected president of Argentina in February 1946, four months after his marriage to Eva Duarte. The Peróns shared out the conquest of power. While her husband was bullying the clergy, Eva declared that "the doctrine of Christ inspired Perón's doctrine." Argentina was covered with Peronist charities that competed with those of the religious institutes so that the attempts to gain control over the population did not seem all that obvious at first sight. Besides establishing free education, public assistance, and labor laws, Perón also undertook an act of international scope that left no doubt as to the Catholic nature of Argentina and his own desire to "secure" the practicing electorate.

During a trip to Europe from June 6 to August 3, 1947, Eva Perón became the grand ambassador of Peronism.

First stop: Spain. General Franco personally presented her with the Grand Cross of the Order of Isabel the Catholic at the Palacio de Oriente. Argentina, for its part, offered assistance to Spain, which had been bled dry by the civil war and excluded from the American aid plan for Europe.

In Paris, Eva Perón contacted the CGT (the communist workers' union) on behalf of Argentinian workers, and at the same time became the muse of Jacques Fath, Pierre Balmain, and Christian Dior, who declared in 1953: "She is the only queen I ever dressed." In 2014, the Madrid daily *A.B.C.* lampooned this "queen" with a rare sense of humor: "Eva Perón, the leader of the 'sans-chemises' (the *descamisados* or "shirtless") who only ever dressed in Christian Dior." Even her funeral dress was signed by the great couturier.

During this trip in 1947, President Vincent Auriol received Evita amidst the glitz and glamour of the Republic: there was a lunch at the Élysée Palace, a lunch at the Château de Rambouillet, and so on.

Her trip climaxed in Rome, where she was treated as a head of state. The whole of Italy thanked her for the help Argentina had given to war-torn Italy and for the unforgettable welcome the Latin American nation had given to Italians forced to leave the country. The head of state, Enrico de Nicola, welcomed her to the Quirinal. The mayor of Rome presented her with a bronze "Lupa," the Roman she-wolf. She socialized with the aristocracy, particularly with Princess Pallavicini. She travelled to all of Italy's major cities, despite her exhaustion and the sweltering heat.

She addressed the following speech to the Italian people:

> I have come to age-old Italy as a messenger of peace and hope on behalf of the workers of Argentina. The leader of the Argentine workers, General Perón, has raised the banner of social justice to lay the foundations of a better society, in which happiness will be possible and permanent, under the Christian sign of the divine Master and Redeemer. . . . I am happy to have come to Italy, because I have been able to see that, as in the past and as always, the hearts of Italians are filled with cordial feelings for Argentina, which, through me, sends the Italians an embrace [*abrazo*] of love and fidelity, together with the hope of a rapid and complete resurrection of Italy, in peace and Christendom.

Her speech and Christian references provided a framework for utopian declarations about well-being and happiness for all. Touched by the charm and the sincere warmth of her words, the people acclaimed her, but the Roman Curia had little sympathy for her political rhetoric.

She hoped that the pope would make her a Marchioness and that she would receive some kind of distinction. When she met Pope Pius XII, she wore the Grand Cross given her by Franco. Witness accounts indicate that her meeting with the pope lasted between twenty and thirty minutes. She received a medal commemorating the papal election, as well as a black rosary mounted on gold, which she kept with her on her deathbed.

The pope expressed his fervent desire for the continuation of the Catholic laws enacted in Argentina. He saw Perón's action as a means of ensuring that the working class would escape Communist machinations.

On the occasion of a reception at the Spanish embassy, an official of the Holy See presented Eva Perón with the insignia of the Grand Cross of Gregory the Great, which was intended for her husband.

But this did not mean that the Catholic vote had been won over by Juan Perón. On the other hand, he was determined to make the Catholic Church submit to the Social Pact, which he saw not just as a sharing of charity but as the construction of a new society. He nationalized the railways and the telephone company and socialized assistance for the poor: this was the socialist welfare state for which he coined a new name "*justicialism*" (justice and socialism).

On December 8, 1948, following an initiative of the Congress of the Franciscans in which members of his cabinet had taken part, Perón addressed a letter to Pope Pius XII in which he asked that 1950 be declared a "Marian Year." It would be hard to imagine such an exploitation of the faith anywhere else.

But as Perón gradually ditched measures favorable to the Catholics, the radicals rallied to his side. The Communists ceased to oppose him when Argentina established diplomatic relations with Moscow on August 31, 1946 and July 26, 1952.

At the end of the day, was there ever a Christian Perón? We must proceed with caution before answering this question. What the pope had to say about him, especially when his words were filtered through journalists' reports and the comments on these journalists' reports, can easily become meaningless.

Javier Cámara and Sebastián Pfaffen, in their biography *Aquel Francisco* (That Francis) published in 2014, mention a curious remark made to them by Pope Francis, which echoes and completes what his confreres have said about him: "I have always been passionate about politics, always."

Even more surprising is his assessment of the Peronist doctrine as expressed to Cámara and Pfaffen: "In the formulation of the Peronist doctrine there is a link with the social doctrine of the Church. We mustn't forget that Perón sent his speeches to Bishop Nicolas De Carlo, who was at the time Bishop of Resistencia, in the Chaco, so that he could read them and tell Perón whether they were in line with the Church's social doctrine."

Pope Francis added: "Bishop De Carlo was a Peronist sympathizer, but he was also an excellent pastor, although the first point has nothing to do with the second. In April 1948, Perón, speaking from the balcony of the seminary overlooking the central square of Resistencia, came to the end of his speech and said he wanted to clarify something. He explained that Bishop De Carlo had been accused of being a Peronist and said: 'That's a lie. In reality it is Perón who is a Decarlista.' De Carlo was the man who helped Perón with the Church's social doctrine."[72]

In 2017, the first quote was repeated by a French journalist who was ignorant of Argentinian reality, Nicolas Senèze, who then commented: "For the young Bergoglio, Perón undoubtedly embodied the best political avenue for applying the Church's social doctrine." In 1948, the young Bergoglio was twelve years old, and while later, he would become an attentive follower of Perón, it would be for other reasons. Moreover, we have found no trace of this intervention by Perón on the date indicated.

But this episode enables us to enter an area of the Perón-Bergoglio relationship that has been totally ignored until now.

The words used by the pope caught our attention because they contain two major restrictions that considerably tone down any compliance of Peronist doctrine with that of the Church: "*formulation*" and "*link*." The pope is always very attentive to words and uses them with care. He is also skilled at conveying what he has not said, but which his audience will hear. In the present case, the pope used this art by telling an unverifiable anecdote, which, on the face of it, does not seem belong to Pérón's *modus operandi*, especially at that date: April 10, 1948.

---

[72] All of Francis's words above are from Sandro Magister's blog, where they were quoted on August 26, 2015.

The true story of
Bishop De Carlo and President Perón

Numerous works have been written on the ties between Bishop De Carlo and Juan Perón. This section draws on the analyses of Jorge Torres Roggero, Roberto Bosca, Susana Bianchi, and above all on the study by Maria del Mar Solís Carnicer and Mayra Maggio. These two researchers offer the added advantage of not neglecting alternative analyses to their own.

Their paper, *Monseñor Nicolás De Carlo y la Iglesia Católica en la construcción del peronismo chaqueño* (Bishop Nicolás De Carlo and the Catholic Church and the construction of Peronism in the Chaco), is mainly based on their research using local documents, including the magazine *Acción Chaqueña*, which was founded by Bishop De Carlo himself.

The province of Chaco is located in the north of Argentina, separated from Paraguay by the province of Formosa. It was evangelized, but only with difficulty, from 1750 onward. In the 1870s, however, the province saw a large influx of Italian immigrants, which led to the creation of the "Resistencia" colony. The new arrivals were almost all Catholics, and by 1940, 90 percent of the population professed Catholicism.

The first parish in the region was founded in Resistencia in 1900. A general ecclesiastical vicariate for the Chaco and Formosa was created in the 1930s. The diocese of Resistencia was erected in 1940.

Bishop De Carlo arrived as apostolic administrator of the vicariate before being appointed first bishop of Resistencia by Pius XII in 1940, a position he was to hold until his death in 1951. This admirable bishop received from the pope the titles of Assistant to the Papal Throne and Count of Rome.

Together with his main collaborator, José Alumni, he turned his diocese into a model of evangelization that encompassed all aspects of life, from parish life and Catholic Action to the creation of a college and seminary, as well as a home for orphans. But his most spectacular achievement was the creation of the Catholic Welfare Organization.

The bishop set up manual training workshops for mothers and children in a large number of neighborhoods. The aim was not only to provide for the family's internal needs but also to teach the rudiments of a trade such as sewing, embroidery, weaving, cooking, hairdressing, typing, bookkeeping, or radio telegraphy to help earn a little extra money.

In the same spirit, he also set up carpentry, ironwork, typography, and similar workshops for the men. By 1943, there were forty-three family workshops.

In Resistencia, people used to keep abreast of political events. Catholics were urged to shoulder their responsibilities in line with their faith. Anti-clerical parties were strongly criticized. *Acción Chaqueña* of November 16, 1945, put it like this: "We must give ourselves to the people in word and deed, with our human understanding and Christian affection, because justice is the cement of social harmony and love is the essence of our doctrine."

Perón's triumph was well received, thanks to the women's vote and the law on religious education in schools. A solemn *Te Deum* was celebrated on this occasion. In 1947, the bishop lent out his car for the official census.

Meanwhile, Perón was a politician who wanted to consolidate his power by basing it on the people to whom he belonged. To achieve this, he observed and identified anything in the country that could help his cause.

The Peronists of the Chaco were in touch both with the bishop and the national authorities to such an extent that on October 26, 1947, the president and his wife, Eva, went to Resistencia for the "National Cotton Festival." They visited the workshops. Perón laid the foundation stone for the diocesan seminary and pledged his full support. Funding was given for two additional workshops that were to bear his and his wife's names.

On his return to Buenos Aires, the president signed decree no. 34 442, officially and publicly recognizing the social and Christian work of Bishop De Carlo. As a sign of his gratitude, he decided to present the bishop with a gold pectoral cross bearing an amethyst.

It is easy to imagine, therefore, how the bishop's zeal came to be identified with the government's policies and endeavors.

The following year, on April 10, 1948, the president returned with his wife for the presentation of the pectoral cross, and the magnificent ensemble took on a political meaning that the Catholics had somewhat forgotten. In the presence of ministers, members of the Supreme Court, the governors of Chaco and Formosa, archbishops and bishops, all the priests and religious, and of course the laity, Perón delivered a historic speech.

Jorge Torres Roggero has written a comprehensive analysis of the speech, describing Perón's art of oratory, his ecclesiastical and religious knowledge, and his persuasive dialectics. Perón quoted from the Gospel and also from Saint John Chrysostom and Saint Ambrose. He understood perfectly the distinction between temporal and spiritual power. His vast culture and personal talent were such that he did not require the assistance of any clergyman.

An important detail is that the seminary was not inaugurated until 1954, and it is obvious that Perón could not have addressed the crowd from a problematical balcony that could scarcely have existed in 1948—and which one might assume was a fruit of Pope Francis's imagination. On the other hand, it is also easy to imagine such an anecdote circulating within the Peronist party.

Perón's manipulation at Resistencia was a masterpiece. What did he say to the assembled clergy—with the exception of the cardinal archbishop of Buenos Aires? He accused them of not following Bishop De Carlo's example!

De Carlo, who had been given the speech beforehand, had suggested modifications, but to no avail; obviously, Perón ignored them. So, when thanking the president for his eulogy, the bishop proceeded to explain to his peers that his "action in this heterogeneous milieu" had demanded a great deal of sacrifices and self-denial, but "it did not exceed the limits of the obligations imposed on any bishop, as a minister of the Church who loves the citizens of the fatherland."

But what could Bishop De Carlo do against the Peronist machine? In July 1948, he donated two city blocks in Resistencia to the Ministry of Public Affairs for the construction of working-class housing for the Eva Perón Foundation. In May of the following year, Eva Perón returned to inaugurate a chapel and to visit the workshops she had previously sponsored. The bishop concluded: "Christian love and social justice are equally the foundation and ideal of Social Aid."

By special decree, Fr. José Alumni was named a member of Argentina's commission to attend Pope Pius XII's Jubilee in Rome.

When on October 13, 1951, the bishop suffered a heart attack, the presidential plane was dispatched to take him to Buenos Aires for the best possible care. Bishop De Carlo was to die in the Argentinian capital on October 19. Perón issued the necessary decrees for him to receive the honors that are usually paid to brigadier generals.

The only surviving opposition party was the Socialist Party. Its program, which was focused on democracy, social justice, and socialism, was no longer popular, and it was swept out of any kind of representation in the local elections. Perón had literally siphoned off its electorate.

The socialists still had enough power to criticize Perón's regime through their newspaper, La Vanguardia. They were the only ones to criticize the Conductor's regime, which they described as Nazi-fascist. Press laws were enforced against the journal, which was put under various forms of intimidation: its directors were imprisoned for a time, printing paper was withheld, issues were seized, and on August 27, 1947, the printing plant was even shut down because of complaints about noise. The socialists reacted by publishing an underground edition. According to reliable studies, the last edition dates back to 1950. The party did not publish a yearbook that year; the last one was to appear in 1951. Subsequently, two attempts were made to launch a new newspaper: El Socialista and Nuevas Bases. The Buenos Aires socialist fortnightly El Sol agreed to publish a page entitled "La Vanguardia" on the last page of each of its editions. The last director of La Vanguardia, Américo Ghioldi, left Argentina in secret in 1952 after a failed coup against Perón.

Why is it so important at this point to focus on the history of the socialist newspaper?

Pope Francis, who made up the balcony story in Cámara and Pfaffen's book, told another equally fanciful anecdote to the same journalists who, once again, were not very inquisitive.

"In those days, political culture was very much alive. I liked to sneak in everywhere. In 1951 and 1952, I used to look forward three times a week to the visits of the socialist activists who sold the newspaper *La Vanguardia*." The trouble is this newspaper no longer existed at those dates. In 1952, it was printed in Montevideo on bible paper to facilitate its underground circulation. All this is described by Norberto Galasso in *Perón: Formación, ascenso y caída, 1893-1955*.[73]

This pontifical practice of telling little stories that "rang true" could be ascribed to a faulty memory were it not for the fact that, as we shall see, his relationship with Peronism was packaged in a way that actually went much further.

All the pope's thurifers emphasize his Peronism and at the same time surrender unsuspectingly to his charm. In the first place, Perón is his country's political idol, and they absolve Francis of his erring ways because of the *second-style Perón* of 1972–1974. Be that as it may, Pope Francis feels the need to make his audience understand that Perón had a true Catholic background and that he himself also had "left-wing" associations. However, the example of *La Vanguardia* is particularly ill-chosen, as this newspaper had sided with the Republicans who, during the Spanish Civil War, massacred five bishops, hundreds of priests and nuns, and thousands of good Catholics.

But it's time to get back to what Juan Perón's relations with the Catholic Church were really like in the years of his first presidency.

The Argentinian Five-Year Education Plan, the first of its kind launched by Perón in 1947, was driven by a philosophy of education based on the "balance between materialism and idealism." Its pedagogical principle was the education of the mind; instruction was geared toward the acquisition of a trade, connection with society, and integration into the nation. "We spoke of the masses until we took control of the government; then we spoke of the people, because our

---

[73]   Galasso, *Perón: Formación, ascenso y caída, 1893-1955*, pp. 554 ff.

aspiration is to transform the masses . . . into an organization with a social conscience and a social personality," Perón was to explain during his third lesson at the Superior Peronist School in 1951.

In practical terms, Perón opened over two thousand free elementary schools for the poor. Secondary education also became free for the most destitute. The illiteracy rate dropped from 15 percent to 3 percent in ten years.

All state structures were also established at that time, starting with a Ministry of Education and a Ministry of Agriculture.

Technical and agricultural education were introduced everywhere; 295 vocational schools were also created. University tuition fees were abolished, while across the board, scholarships were introduced which were also open to foreign students. Over one thousand kindergartens were created.

In all, more than eight thousand establishments were created, more than in the entire interval between 1810 and 1946. In 1955, the number of students was 2.87 million for a population of 18.79 million. The number of college students rose from 47,000 in 1945 to 138,249 in 1955.

This was the fruit of state planning that took control of all educational matters; this situation was soon to provide the occasion for a major conflict with the Church. The compulsory teaching of the Catholic religion in primary and secondary schools, decreed in 1943, was replaced by the teaching of religious and moral values in 1947; this, in turn, was abolished in 1954, along with the relevant department in the Ministry of Education.

The dream of the very secularist President Sarmiento, who had promoted state and secular education in the Argentine constitution of 1853, had come true a century later.

That same year, in 1954, the Chamber of Representatives amended the Civil Code and authorized divorce with the right to remarry. The final blow came with decree no. 4.633/55 ratifying law no. 12912: it legalized prostitution, which had been banned nationwide since 1937. Henceforth, the town halls would manage brothels. At the same time, the municipality of Buenos Aires prohibited the display of religious figurines at Christmas time.

When Evita died in 1952, a genuine icon-worship sprang up in her honor. As we have already seen, several million copies of her autobiography, *La Razón de mi vida*, were distributed in support of the Peronist culture. But she was also declared Head of the Nation and Protector of the Poor. This devotion continues to this day: "Don't cry Argentina, my soul will always be with you."

Gradually, religious festivals, pilgrimages, and public processions were abolished. Steps were taken to encourage Protestant and Jewish worship. Roberto Bosca speaks bluntly of the desire to create a Peronist national church subservient to political power, along the lines of the Anglican model, since even before his return to Argentina in 1972, Perón was maneuvering to create groups of Catholics who would be loyal to him. An "Argentinian Apostolic Catholic Church" was even founded in 1970.

Although the 1949 constitution recognized the Roman Catholic and Apostolic faith, tensions remained high; for example, Perón refused to receive the papal legate for the Rosario Eucharistic Congress in 1950. The same year saw the creation of the *Humanist Student League*, which was made up of "Catholics for a pluralist and democratic society" opposed to Peronism. Perón's "organized society" faced competition from Catholic associations. Conflicts proliferated, particularly with the influential Basilio Scientific School Spiritist movement, whose slogan was "Jesus is not God." Having been opposed by the government at first, it received its support when Peronism turned against the Church in 1950.

On May 25, 1954, Perón refused to attend the *Te Deum* for the National Holiday.

In July 1954, the Christian Democratic Party was founded without the support of the hierarchy. In December, the traditional grand celebration that was to close the Marian Year was banned in the Plaza de Mayo, in the heart of the capital.

In February 1955, Cardinal Copello, archbishop of Buenos Aires, met Perón, but to no avail. In March, the Argentinian Church was declared subject to taxation. In May, a bill called for the separation of Church and State, as well as a radical change to the Constitution. For months, the clergy had been speaking out against the government in their homilies, and several priests were arrested.

On May 24, Cardinal Plá y Deniel, archbishop of Toledo and primate of Spain, published a letter of support for the Argentinian Church.

The Corpus Christi procession was due to take place on June 9, 1955, but the episcopate postponed it until June 11. This change of date made the procession illegal. The procession went ahead anyway; part of it went to the square in front of the assembly, and an Argentinian flag was burned. On the 14th, Perón ordered the expulsion from Argentina, without trial, of the auxiliary bishop of Buenos Aires, Bishop Manuel Tato, and a priest, Fr. Ramón Novoa. They were told they could go to Chile or Uruguay but were forcibly taken to Rome.

On June 15, a Peronist demonstration was bombed by the air force, as a prelude to a coup by the air force and navy: more than two hundred people were killed and eight hundred wounded.

On June 16, the Holy See excommunicated all those who had been involved in the expulsion of the bishop and priest. The Peronists argued that the excommunication was invalid, as it had not been signed by the pope; another interpretation stressed that, out of consideration for the Head of State, the latter's name had not been included in the act. In reality, these arguments were totally worthless. It was an excommunication *latae sententiae* in the special form reserved for the Apostolic See. Perón later acknowledged his condemnation in Madrid, repenting in the hands of the cardinal-archbishop before leaving for Argentina to regain power and to try to rally the Catholics.

On the night of June 16–17, fourteen of the oldest churches in Buenos Aires were burnt down, along with the archbishop's chancery. Several uprisings took place throughout the country. On August 31, Perón announced his resignation from the CGT, the majority trade union that was his main supporter. He left Argentina on September 16, 1955.

At this point, a comment is in order.

There is a clear link between Mussolini's doctrine of fascism and Juan Perón's policies. This has been disputed, but the texts speak for themselves (see chapters 8, 9, and 10 of *The Doctrine of Fascism*).

On March 10, 1929, the Duce declared: "A people rise inasmuch as they are numerous, hard-working and well regulated." This is Perón's "organized community" to a tee. For Mussolini, the state "safeguards and transmits the spirit of the people, elaborated down the ages in its language, its customs, its faith." And again: "Fascism respects the God of ascetics, saints, and heroes, and it also respects God as conceived by the ingenuous and primitive heart of the people"; "The State does not have a theology, but it has a moral code."

Mussolini was opposed to liberalism and historical materialism, class struggle, and the like. "The State stands for the immanent conscience of the nation," he proclaimed.

The "organized community" would be the model adopted by all Peronist organizations, including the "Iron Guard" (which had nothing to do with Codreanu) in the years 1969–1974.

If we look at "culture," this is even more obvious. Perón was deeply impressed by the Duce's references to Italy's glorious cultural past. He himself worked hard to enhance Argentina's popular and political culture, and he claimed to have an "Indian" among his ancestors.

At the close of this chapter, some may still object that Perón abandoned his war against the Church from 1966 to 1974. This is true. But, as he often said, doctrine changes in line with historical circumstances. On February 24, 1974, four months before his death, Perón renewed his ties with Cuba and Fidel Castro. "Better to do than to say; better to achieve than to promise. Cuba and Argentina are demonstrating this through practice," he said at the time. Those were the days of "socialist nationalism."

CHAPTER 6

From Liberation Theology to the Theology of the People

The years of revolutionary effervescence that we are about to discuss in this section are those of Father Bergoglio's formative years, his contacts with the Peronist movement upon its return to power, and his appointment as provincial of the Jesuits (1973). At that time, he had frequent dealings with many of the priests, theologians, and lay historians listed here.

Fr. Roger Vekemans, mentioned above, catalogued some 1,700 works on the subject of liberation theology. Fr. François Malley, in his succinct bibliography of liberation theologies, already identified a thousand writings in 1974.

This revolutionary effervescence was comparable to that which preceded the French Revolution. All the key protagonists were preparing for the fray. When Pope Francis was elected, everything was in place.

We have already come across the names of four theologians: Lucio Gera, Rafael Tello, Carlos Maria Galli, and Juan Carlos Scannone on several occasions. These four leading agents of Argentina's political and social clerical subversion deserve to be known in greater detail.

Among them, only one survives today: Father Galli (born in 1957). Suffice it to say that this Argentinian theologian, who is a member of the Theological Commission and a renowned specialist on the thinking of Pope Francis, is one of the masterminds behind the theology of the people. He presented his doctoral thesis on Lucio Gera from September 7 to 9, 1973, marking the anniversary of the 1968 Medellín meeting.

In addition to our in-depth presentation of Fathers Gera, Tello, and Scannone, we will also focus on Félicité de Lamennais, a forerunner of the theology of the people who could even be considered as its founding father.

Lucio Gera (1924–2012), the pioneer

Surprisingly, there is little information available in French about Fr. Lucio Gera, apart from the very succinct article published by Denis Chautard, a priest belonging to the "Mission de France" and a retiree of the French Ministry of Education, on his personal blog. His concise review is of no interest whatsoever. It merely repeats what foreign "informants" have been saying everywhere.

The second surprise is that Wikipedia's most comprehensive entry on Gera is in German. Fortunately, there is a lot of documentation in Spanish and English, but it is very dispersed. Ironically, this abundance is also a source of great difficulty, as our research has revealed that Gera's admirers systematically "forgot" important facts. Fortunately, friends on the ground in Argentina undertook a most interesting quest to provide us with the best sources. This original documentation has enabled us to correct the universal hagiography and to report here indisputable facts.

Lucio Gera was born in Italy, in the province of Udine, on January 16, 1924, and was baptized at birth. His parents moved to Argentina in 1929: that year, he was confirmed, and he made his First Holy Communion in 1930. The first signs of his vocation became apparent at the 1934 Eucharistic Congress in Buenos Aires. He entered the Metropolitan Seminary of Buenos Aires on March 5, 1936, and was ordained on September 20, 1947, by Bishop Antonio Rocca. Until 1952, he held various posts as vicar both in the poor suburbs and in Recoleta, an affluent neighborhood. He was entrusted with the chaplaincy of the

JOC, the Young Christian Workers. His first article appeared in *Notas de pastoral Jocista*.

He would never forget his roots: "My immigrant background meant a lot to me: it was an experience of solidarity and struggle. What is an immigrant? A mixture of solidarity, distrust and fear. . . . The immigrant is forced to question his or her identity ('ultimately, who am I?'), and to find out how to choose an identity. We have chosen an identity among the people, not in the oligarchy."[74]

The information below is taken from studies by Maria Mercédes Amuchástegui, who is much closer to our subject than any of his thurifers, despite some startling omissions.

She quotes an interview with Lucio Gera in which he describes how, during his theology studies, he had no access to any books from Europe. It was not theologians who drew him to theology but literary works and poetry: Dostoyevsky, Claudel, Bloy, Papini. He also studied existentialism with Heidegger before leaving for Europe in 1952 to continue his studies at the Angelicum.

At the time, the brightest students from Latin America were routinely sent to Europe to study in Germany, France, Spain, and Belgium, where the University of Louvain had a special section for Latin Americans, the CEPAL (Centre pour l'Amérique Latine), founded in 1953.

Father Gera obtained his licentiate in theology in Rome in 1953. Thanks to the support of Bishop Enrique Rau, he received a scholarship to study in Germany.

The said Argentinian bishop had also been a chaplain with the YCW, and it was in this capacity that he came to know Gera.

Like his brother bishop Antonio di Pasquo, he belonged to the reformist wing of the Church in Argentina. Even before the Vatican Council, both prelates promoted the use of the Spanish language in the liturgy. In 1951, he became auxiliary of Buenos Aires before being appointed to Resistencia in 1954 and Mar del Plata in 1957. He is an acknowledged authority among Argentinian intellectuals.

---

[74] See *Escritos Teológicos Pastorales de Lucio Gera, del preconcilio a la Conferencia de Puebla, 1956-1984*, by Virginia Azcuy, Carlos María Galli, Marcelo González (Buenos Aires: Ágape-Universidad Católica Argentina, 2006), p. 25.

On his return from the council, he was one of the very first bishops to revolutionize his diocese.

It was a pivotal time for Lucio Gera. As a young priest, he read Congar and Teilhard de Chardin. Of the latter, he would say: "He had no influence on my formation, but later I embraced him with a certain enthusiasm. He had a way of thinking that fecundates theological thought in its entirety; from the point of view of modern science, of course. What's more, he's a deeply religious, pious man. . . . His theology is permeated by his religious leanings and is in no way atheistic." Gera also read some of the works of Maritain.

Lucio Gera received his doctorate in dogmatic theology under the direction of Johann Auer in Bonn in 1956. His doctoral thesis dealt with a classic subject: *Die Geschichtliche Entwicklung der Transubstantiationslehre von Thomas von Aquin bis zu Johannes Skotus* (The Historical Development of the Doctrine of Transubstantiation from Thomas Aquinas to John Duns Scott).

In Germany, he read the works of Max Scheler and discovered Henri de Lubac. He received a visit from the future Argentinian Cardinal Eduardo Pironio, who was to promote liberation theology at CELAM and whom we have already met in previous chapters. It was he who persuaded Lucio Gera to return to Argentina.

On his return in 1957, among other occupations, Gera was appointed a professor at the major seminary attached to the Villa Devoto Faculty of Theology. He continued to publish articles in *Notas de pastoral Jocista*, in which he lamented the absence of the Church among the working classes.

In this vein, Gera wrote in his article *Reflexión sobre Iglesia, Burguesía y clase obrera* (Reflections on the Church, the Bourgeoisie and the Working Class, 1957):

> The Church must neither become gentrified nor proletarianized, but rather be effectively Catholic in the concrete history of this century, as it is in its own structures. To be Catholic does not mean to withdraw from this world or to be absent from its temporal structures, but to create one's own history in all that

this world is, and not just in a small part of it. . . . It means committing oneself fully as a Catholic, which means committing oneself to everything that is this world, to take up the human interests of whatever social class there may be, and in this way to be present to all classes without identifying with any.

In 1958, he became prefect of Theological Studies and assumed the position of dean of the faculty. He was reunited with Eduardo Pironio, who was appointed rector of the Metropolitan Seminary.

In 1962, Lucio Gera founded the theology review of the Catholic University of Buenos Aires, *Teología*.

It was the year when the Second Vatican Council opened in Rome and the start of the great changeover.

It is impossible to understand what was about to happen on the Latin American continent without taking into account how the council was prepared in Latin America and how the council itself unfolded there.

Its three main protagonists, Lucio Gera, Rafael Tello, and Juan Carlos Scannone, all graduates of German theology faculties, worked systematically and squarely to drag the Latin American Church and the whole Catholic Church into the most radical progressivism.

In 1965, Father Jorge Mejía (the future cardinal) summed up the council, in which he had participated as an expert, with these words: "The theology of the conciliar documents . . . is the theology of the periphery. The great architects of these documents were men who, until recently, were regarded with suspicion in Rome."

Lucio Gera was the first to realize that overly visible Marxist analyses would always be frowned upon in a continent shaped by five hundred years of Catholicism.

He is widely regarded as the pioneer of the pseudo "theology of the people." Cardinal Bergoglio named him Argentina's greatest theologian and ordered that he be buried in Buenos Aires Cathedral with this epitaph: "*Lucio Gera. Sacerdote. Maestro en Teología. Iluminó a la Iglesia en América Latina y Argentina en el espíritu del Concilio Vaticano II.*" (Priest. Master of Theology. He enlightened the

Church in Latin America and Argentina with the spirit of the Second Vatican Council.)

Curiously enough, Lucio Gera's thurifers never quote his three initial declarations. These were firebrand presentations of the revolutionary ideology that would sweep across Argentina and the entire South American continent. His active membership of the MSTM is only very seldom mentioned.

First Declaration

Lucio Gera published his first major indictment of the Argentinian episcopate in the Argentinian magazine *Cristianismo y Revolución* (No. 25, September 1970), a revolutionary Peronist journal sympathetic to Cuba and Che Guevara, under the title *Apuntes para una interpretación de la Iglesia Argentina* (Notes for an interpretation of the Argentinian church).

A few months later, the text was taken up by the Documentation Center of the International Movement of Catholic Students (IMCS), which published the complete edition in December 1970 in Montevideo, Uruguay. The last section, "Towards Unity," had been modified in this later edition to give it a more Catholic orientation.

The text had been written between December 1969 and April 1970 by Lucio Gera and the Argentinian priest (and future bishop) Guillermo Rodríguez-Melgarejo.

By this time, the main author's revolutionary commitment was beyond dispute. As we have seen, even before the end of the council, in 1964, he took part in the Rio meeting that launched the conciliar revolution throughout the continent and later joined the Third World Priests' Movement. We should also bear in mind that according to Cardinal Bergoglio, Lucio Gera is the man who "illuminated" the entire Latin American continent.

In *Cristianismo y Revolución*, Lucio Gera was introduced with all his titles:

> Doctor of Theology, Dean of the Faculty of Theology at the Argentine Catholic University from 1965 to 1969, expert to

CELAM, expert at the two Synods and member of the International Theological Commission; he was assisted in his work by the newly ordained priest Rodríguez-Melgarejo [*who was ordained on May 24, 1970*]. He has selected the significant facts from national reality that shape the features of the current face of the Argentine Church, as they manifest themselves from a theological perspective.

But the ultimate question posed by theologian Gera is this: "How can a Church that lives according to the imperatives of the Second Vatican Council, and which owes it to itself to belong to the concrete history of each people, clearly and courageously recognize the sectors within it that have taken up the cause of the working people who are fighting from below against the powerful interests that oppress them?"

This presentation perfectly reflects the article's contents. The preface by the Uruguayan revolutionary academic Héctor Borrat was also clear:

From Medellín onwards the famous "institutional church"—so thoroughly thrashed by the avant-garde sectors—acquired a novel prestige. For the first time, and at the highest continental level, it spoke the language of the political left. . . . The institutional Church has thus become a potential ally for many on the left, be they Catholic or not: it is seen as a useful instrument insofar as it can serve left-wing politics.

Medellín has made this irreversibly clear: the Church must serve liberation, and this leads it to confront neo-colonialism and internal colonialism. . . .

By adopting parts of the leftist political lexicon, the Latin American episcopate has gone one step further, ideologically, than the conciliar texts and encyclicals. . . .

The typology has been enriched by immediate contact with a fundamental opposition between the elite and the people. . . . In this way, that which is "popular" takes hold of history and, on the basis of this, defines its own path: that of a popular Catholicism.

Reading these lines, you might think that this is an umpteenth version of liberation theology, featuring an unspoken class struggle, institutional subversion of the Church, and an appeal to the direction of history. This is true: all the ingredients were there; they had simply been remodeled. Héctor Borrat continues:

> It is a given of our history that the people have blended their Catholic faith with a national current—ever since Facundo's cry, "Religion or Death", and more recently through Peronism—reaching far beyond all the edicts of the official Church and the elites as a whole. Today, it is even more accurate to say that a large proportion of the population identifies politically with Peronism. This is a mainstream movement, albeit without fully developed theoretical formulations. The People is defined by the land, the fatherland, religion, indigenous traditions and folklore. The Movement of Priests for the Third World, which was originally part of the social protest movement, would today be much more in line with the popular nationalist movement as a prophetic and liberating presence within Argentinian and Latin American problematics. Popular Catholicism would thus appear to have the virtue of purifying the Europeanized left-wing movements, stripping them of their Marxist-Leninist character and nationalizing them, thus rediscovering the traditions of leaders such as Facundo Quiroga, "Chacho" Peñaloza, Artigas, Ramírez, López, Yrigoyen and the Peronist phenomenon.

"Consciousness-raising is the order of the day," added Héctor Borrat. This is a phrase that Lucio Gera used time and again.

It is he, the doctor of theology, who was tasked with putting together an indictment of the Catholic Church in Argentina. He was a professor to Father Bergoglio, who was ordained at the same time as the document was being drafted. Its references to Perón are crystal clear, although the latter would not return to Argentina until 1972–1973.

The seven chapters of the document form an indictment in which the Argentinian Church was reduced to the state of a political party favoring the rich and refusing any kind of review or self-criticism out of fear, sluggishness, and skepticism. It was incapable, Lucio Gera claimed, of opening up a path that could have built organic unity between conflicting groups. Fortunately, he said, the '35–'45 generation was trying to "build bridges." You will have recognized the expression so often used by Father Arrupe and Pope Francis. It is a magic formula that the whole world has come to repeat.

It should also be remembered that the project presented was one of global reform of society, where the Church would also have to reform herself in order to be attuned with the change. Her structure, her codes, and her laws must be in harmony with the great universal upheaval. Gera wrote: "The Church moves forward with difficulty in a course of history that is moving faster than she is, so that she appears as an advocate of the status quo who is at the same time nostalgic for renewal."

The major "contradiction" existed in his view between "the elite and the people." Lucio Gera drew some surprising arguments from Marxist historian Enrique Dussel. From this perspective, the Argentinian Church is presented as Constantinian, the product of Spanish colonization—which in turn would have been influenced by the doctrine of the Caliphate that dominated Spain!

As a true revolutionary, Lucio Gera managed to camouflage the destructive nature of liberation theology. He and Enrique Dussel formed a truly exceptional pair.

A closer look at Dussel's book, *History and Theology of Liberation*, will give you a clearer picture. The historian noted that the suppression of the Jesuits and the collapse of the Spanish monarchy were a catastrophe without saying a word about the Masonic tidal wave that swept across Europe. He overlooked the English Masonic invasion, focusing only on England's merchant conquest, and claimed that England was not interested in the religious dimension. He paid lip service to Colombia's first constitution, which separated Church and State as early as 1849 (Perón implemented a similar separation in 1954, as noted earlier). He then observed that "power belongs to an elite that is fundamentally anti-Catholic."

Fortunately, from his point of view, Maritain's book on *New Christendom* appeared on the scene, as did Congar and Teilhard, not to mention the Second Vatican Council and its Latin American aftermath, together with the calling into question of any kind of religious-political order.

This Marxist reading of history served as a standard for Lucio Gera and other South American ideologists. They saw no reason to dispute their master's claims: "Marx was born in Europe, and although he was secularized and apparently anti-Christian, he created the conditions for a form of humanism whose full flowering and true completion can only be found in Christianity."

On the subject of Islam, he wrote: "Islam faces major problems in our time. The Islamic state is theological; according to the Koran, it is theocratic. But modern states are secular, like Turkey. This is a serious theological-political dilemma that puts the Islamic faith itself in crisis. The Islamic state is dissolving in the face of modern states." Several decades later, Enrique Dussel must have seen how actual history has inflicted a rebuttal on one of his delusions based on historical and dialectical materialism.

This world-famous professor met Paul Gauthier in Palestine: this was the priest who distributed a liberationist pamphlet at the council before leaving the priesthood (see the introduction). Some biographers present Dussel as a theologian but can give no references to support this claim; on the other hand, he holds a licentiate in the history of religions from the Institut Catholique de Paris (1967). He taught at the Pastoral Institute of CELAM, the main center for the propagation of Catholic-revolutionary ideology on the Latin American continent.

Three years later, Enrique Dussel and Lucio Gera again joined forces. At the time, they were in a strong position at the heart of the Faculty of Philosophy and Theology at the Universidad del Salvador in Buenos Aires.

Lucio Gera's 1969–1970 work was a comprehensive indictment of the Argentinian episcopate, including a ranking of the good and the bad. He contended that the majority of bishops and part of the Argentinian Church clung to the established system, maintaining a "liberal capitalist mentality." Their pastoral care failed to incorporate the dynamics of a genuine encounter with the entire ecclesial community and the destiny of the Argentinian people, Gera deplored: for him, faith is a historical encounter within a people.

Chapter IV, *Behaviors of the Official Church*, forms the nucleus of the accusation. Already it comes with a demand for a constitutional church subject to the power of the people, who—again according to Gera—clamor for "communion" rather than "institution" in order to overcome "contradictions." By this logic, the Church's distinction between the temporal and the spiritual changes hands to the benefit of the poor, who gain control of their own historical destiny, liberated at last from all forms of domination.

The final chapter is about unity. This, it says, can only be conceived as being pluralistic, in line with a "Church of the World" that conforms to the historical situation, rather than a "Church of Bishops-Priests-Laity."

Over the next few years, Lucio Gera was to articulate this new concept of the Church-as-people, whose dialectics borrowed both from the class struggle that was in vogue across the continent, and from the people as saviors of their own cause, derived from Peronism.

Second Declaration

Lucio Gera's second Declaration is a 1974 reprint by *Colección Justicia y Paz*, the mouthpiece of a Madrid-based Catholic body for popular propaganda, of lectures given by Lucio Gera at the Buenos Aires Justice and Peace Commission study center in 1972.

We initially approached it, as we did with the indictment of the Argentinian episcopate, without knowing that it was not among the texts selected by Carlos Maria Galli, who collected Lucio Gera's works in view of their publication.

We owe this discovery to a radicalized priest whom we quoted in our book *Terrorisme pastoral* in connection with the CELAM Assembly in Aparecida in 2007. We shall turn to him again when we discuss Pope Francis's relationship with liberation theology. He is Fr. Eduardo de la Serna, from the diocese of Quilmès, who knew Lucio Gera well.

The Good Lord will judge his religion, but in the light of the truth that he has restored, he is likely to be saved! Not only did he reveal the biographers' omission regarding Lucio Gera's participation in the subversive MSTM organization, but he also provided the source of the "forgotten" text that we are dealing with here.

The text we are assessing was taken from a book written by François Houtart, Ivan Illich, Lucio Gera, and Alex Morelli. Under the title *Del Subdesarrollo à la liberación* (From underdevelopment to liberation), the four authors embarked on a spree of subversive thoughts and propositions. Pope Paul VI's 1967 letter *Populorum Progressio*, inspired by Father Lebret, offered a new dimension to all Christian ideologues: integral development turned into integral liberation.

The names of Gera's co-authors have already been mentioned several times: Canon Houtart, president of the "doctrinal" commission of Justice and Peace in Belgium, who worked hand in hand with Fidel Castro; Ivan Illich, who drew up the reform of the priesthood that is now coming into the open; Alex Morelli, the Frenchman of the team. The latter positions development within an anti-capitalist trend: "Socialism, when it is democratic and humanist, tries to reconcile freedom and justice; in the socialist project, social injustice does not disappear, but at least it diminishes. According to Teilhard de Chardin, since socialism is a process of personalization, it is oriented toward the communion of people within love."

Eduardo de la Serna provides details and titles of the lectures given by Lucio Gera at the Center for Justice and Peace Studies in Buenos Aires in 1972. They were photocopied the same year under the title *Teología de la Liberación* by MIEC-JECI in Lima, then published in *Perspectivas de Diálogo* in 1973 in Montevideo and Lima. These were the same texts as those published in Madrid in 1974, with identical subtitles. Uruguay and MEIC-JECI once again proved to be a hub for revolutionary publishing, which was difficult to organize in Argentina at the time.

Eduardo de la Serna undertakes a complete analysis of the documents to show that Lucio Gera's choices were totally liberationist and radical. He restores the truth: Lucio Gera was never a learned theologian, he was a utopian who wound up in mysticism. He was a conscious revolutionary who wanted to change the Church and the world.

On the occasion of Lucio Gera's death, Eduardo de la Serna published a tribute in August 2012 entitled *Una alegría. Una preocupación* (A joy and a concern: a reflection based on the fitting tribute to Lucio Gera). He was to take up this text in a later work as follows: "I write with the freedom that comes from expecting nothing. I have no expectation of gaining recognition from what I write. I imagine that some people hope to be recognized as Lucio's 'true heirs.' I do not, for the simple reason that I am not one of them. I never received the slightest recognition nor even a handshake from him, I simply knew him."

De la Serna then recalls vivid memories of his seminary days, and later as a participant in the Third World Priest Movement and a developer of liberation theology. He reports that Father Gera was banned from many Argentine dioceses but still preached his ordination retreat.

He goes on to talk about the way Gera referred to liberation theology:

> There was a conflict—a perceived conflict: it was that of liberation theology being supposedly pitted against culture theology. Culture theology, of which Gera was the main advocate, had apparently arisen as a counter-proposal to liberation theology. So three of us, all parish priests, went to see him to talk about it. We wanted to listen to him, question him, hear his suggestions and opinions—and to talk about culture theology. I remember a few of these ideas [expressed by Gera]:
>
> "When I was the dean, we were under a dictatorship and we couldn't talk about liberation theology, that's why we talked about culture theology."
>
> "There is no theology I feel closer to than Gustavo Gutiérrez's."
>
> When we told him that some people were saying that culture theology appeared to oppose liberation theology ... "Which theologian supports that?" he said. So we told him it was Antonio Quarracino, and he replied: "I asked: which theologian?"

On this point, Eduardo de la Serna obtained the opinion of Gutiérrez himself, with whom he had spoken about the issue: "Not only is it
the same, but I feel closer to no theology than that of Gera." He knew,
moreover, that in Puebla, Gera had explicitly said: "It is Gutiérrez who
should be here!"

"In a later conversation, Leonardo Boff asked me about Lucio's
health, which was beginning to fail; he told me: 'What a great character! A wise man!' Alluding to tense moments during the Puebla era,
he added: 'That's all a thing of the past,'" wrote De la Serna.

The latter notes that on the occasion of Lucio Gera's fiftieth anniversary of his priesthood, this obfuscation of his past was already
underway. He adds, with a touch of irony, that a "Gerian left" and a
"Gerian right" are fighting over his legacy.

But to be clear: anything that might recall Lucio Gera's revolutionary past has been erased, weaponized, or blithely set aside.

———————

At this point, it is worth considering Gera's relationship with liberation
theology (of which Gustavo Gutiérrez is the "father") and the theology
of the people that is referred to in connection with him.

Liberation theology, which emerged in Latin America, claims to
go beyond the obvious dualism between God and man. It leads us to
think about theology in a different way. The concept of "religion," presented as dominating and oppressive, takes on a new dimension with
liberation theology, by including the social and the political: such is
the "integral liberation" advocated by this new theology. In the Lord's
Prayer, we collectively ask for daily bread. Therefore, in a just society,
decisions must be taken in common and not left to an "enlightened
group," says liberation theology, which also amounts to the socializa-
tion of politics.

It says that Latin America has the historical experience of the *other*
as an aggressor, by way of the experience of (Spanish) imperialism
and dependence (capitalism). But it stresses that the experience of the

other as a human being in this culture also exists and then starts talking about "the people," "culture," and "popular religiosity."

"If there is only one God, Father and Creator of all, then all men without exception are sons of the same God, all brothers, and they must make manifest a human, fraternal and not an 'imperial' conviviality."[75]

Pope Francis merely echoed this vision when, on February 4, 2019, he signed the Document on Human Fraternity with the grand imam of the Al-Azhar University: "The pluralism and the diversity of religions, color, sex, race and language are willed by God in His wisdom, through which He created human beings. This divine wisdom is the source from which the right to freedom of belief and the freedom to be different derives."

Lucio Gera has been deliberately passed off as something he is not and never has been. The texts in which he expresses himself freely and publicly date from 1969, 1970, 1971, 1972, and 1973. They never mention a "theology of the people."

Having reached this point in our investigation, we need to look more closely at this intriguing fact.

Bernadette Sauvaget, who specializes in religious issues for *Libération*, *Témoignage chrétien* and *Esprit*, interviewed Father Scannone in *Le pape du people—Bergoglio raconté par son confrère théologien, jésuite et argentin* (The People's Pope: Bergoglio presented by a fellow Jesuit and Argentinian theologian). When asked, "Why did the topic of the people take such a leading place in this theological current in Buenos Aires, even to the point of giving it its name?" he replied:

> The members of COEPAL (Episcopal Commission for Pastoral Care) did not want to use the categories of liberal sociology, nor those of Marxist sociology. That's why they were looking for their own way of talking about and categorizing Latin American history and culture. In the course of their reflections, they came up with the category of the "people." Throughout Latin America, there is a strong tradition regarding this theme, which was very prominent in the Mexican revolution, for example.

---

[75]　Gera, *Del Subdesarrollo a la Liberación*, p. 95.

In Argentina, it predated Peronism. It was important at the
beginning of the 20th century in the "yrigogenist" movement,
as a current of radicalism. From a theological point of view, the
Second Vatican Council renewed the importance of the theme
of the people of God.

Mrs. Sauvaget, who clearly has scant knowledge of both Mexican
and Argentinian history, took Father Scannone's remarks at face value.

Which Mexican revolution is he talking about? Was it the revolution of independence in 1813, waged to the cries of Our Lady of
Guadalupe? Or was he speaking of those that followed over more than
a century, led by Mexican and American Freemasons? Was he thinking of the *Guerra Cristera*, which claimed 200,000 lives in the wake of
the secularist Constitution of 1917, and in which the Cristeros were
fighting for their faith? Of the 4,300 priests in Mexico at the time, only
350 were left after the massacres and expulsions. Moreover, when the
Freemason Calles spoke of "the people" in Mexico at that time, he was
referring to the 1793 "Terreur" in France!

Nor is Mrs. Sauvaget familiar with the history of Argentina. President Yrigoyen, also a Freemason, was a bourgeois radical. His inspiration came from Spanish Freemasonry, that of Cuba's "liberator,"
José Martí.

Why, then, this miserable attempt by Father Scannone? For two
reasons: to make people believe that the process is inherent to the
politics of the continent and to downplay the Peronist connection.

Mrs. Sauvaget insisted: "What does this category, 'people,' mean?"
Scannone replied: "It's a category that can indeed be considered to be
ambiguous. It's not an *a priori* category like class or class struggle. It
depends on historical circumstances. Gera preferred the concept of
people to that of culture."

Father Scannone did his best to break "the theology of the people"
away from its implications: "The people are thought of in terms of the
nation, not of social class." But he finally conceded: "The theology of
the people accepts the fact of oppression and dependence. That's why
it too speaks of liberation. But I repeat, it thinks of the notion of the
people in terms of the nation."

We shall see later how Father Scannone rearranges history to suit his own purposes. The wars of the Latin American peoples were waged by military conquerors for whom culture and people counted for little—the latest example being the attempt to carve up tiny Paraguay for the benefit of its neighbors.

As for the nation, it is understood in its most revolutionary sense, inherited from the French Revolution. It is to Dom Hélder Câmara's approach that Lucio Gera adheres! Cardinal Bergoglio, in his homilies for Argentina's national holiday, spoke of the people and the fatherland, never of the nation, even though he used the adjective *national*.

But the most important element of Father Scannone's reply is the reference, which Mrs. Sauvaget overlooked, to COEPAL: we will come back to this later.

Third Declaration

An August 1973 lecture, published in 1974, constitutes Lucio Gera's third declaration. We shall see that the man who "illuminated" Latin America actually ignited it with the fire of revolution, enabling flammable spirits to spread destruction and desolation across the world.

The Faculty of Philosophy and Theology at the Universidad del Salvador of Buenos Aires had been organizing an "Academic Week" for some years. In 1973, the theme and speakers were once again focusing on the economic, social, and religious revolution.

Five speakers shared the challenge. Juan José Llach, (*Dependencia cultural y creación de cultura en América Latina*) dealt with the capitalist system that imposes its culture; Bartomeu Meliá, SJ, described how Spanish colonization wiped out indigenous languages and eliminated the culture of native populations; Augusto Roa Bastos concentrated on the people as victims of the "non culture" imposed on them by large industrial groups. The two main speakers were Enrique Dussel and Lucio Gera.

Dussel, in a lengthy presentation illustrated with graphs on variations in cultural dependence, developed the theme of imperial culture, Enlightenment culture, and the liberation of popular culture. His conference presented a vast fresco, spanning time and space, of the dialectical relationship between situations of economic and political domination (including a startling passage on liturgical "oppression"). He also highlighted the "return to roots" brought about by Kemal Atatürk, Gandhi, and Mao.

Oddly enough, it was not Lucio Gera who tackled "the concept of the people," nor the question of "the creation and liberation of popular culture," but Enrique Dussel.

Reading these two authors who were used to working together reveals that they shared the same tool for dialectical analysis.

They arrived at the same conclusions about the overthrow of the established order. Both distanced themselves from incipient armed violence and from subordination to the Soviet Union. They were convinced that Latin America had everything it needed to make its own revolution. This did not stop them from honoring Camilo Torres and Che Guevara. They celebrated the fall of Saigon as a victory over "dependency." The Cuban model was omnipresent.

They all had contacts abroad—and Dussel had more than most. As early as July–August 1965, Dussel was published by the Paris-based magazine *Esprit*. In his presentation, *Chemins de libération latino-américains* (Paths of liberation in Latin-America), Dussel himself described how he had lectured on the subject at the CELAM Institute in Quito, at the Catholic Theology Institute in Valparaíso, Chile, at the Faculty of Theology in Louvain, to a group of fifty-two bishops in Medellín in 1971, to another twenty in Guatemala, and so on.

Lucio Gera also traveled; the hubs of his activity were Argentina and Medellín in Colombia. He prepared the Puebla meeting in January 1979: it would see his triumph.

His thinking may be summed up as follows: theology must be re-founded and return to its biblical sources; salvation is for the poor, the oppressed, the exploited who have been delivered into the hands of oppressors and exploiters. His new hermeneutics were aimed at reinterpreting the exegetical instrument in the light of a faith that takes historical time and the future seriously; the signs of the times must be read in the *continuum* of biblical revelation.

In an essential chapter of his book, *El Pensamiento cristiano revolucionario en América latina y el Caraíbe* (ediciones huracán, 1989), Puerto Rican sociologist Samuel Silva Gotay described what he presented as a rediscovery of the political dimension of faith at the time. "Religion," he contended, "distorted knowledge of true faith by imposing codifications and constraints. Thanks to liberation theologians, Christians recovered the concept of faith as a historical and political practice. Faith in God, therefore, is a faith that liberates for the sake of justice, providing hope with a historical foundation."

Samuel Gotay quoted Lucio Gera from the mimeographed collection of his three founding lectures, *Teología de la Liberación*: "Hope is the attitude with which we look at history, feel it and experience it as terribly harsh, difficult, almost impossible to realize as a history that is not domination of one group over another. . . . However, this very hope allows man to adopt an attitude of daring and to make the attempt (to hope), despite the harshness and resistance opposed by history. . . . In the very rigid carapace of this history of domination, he encounters a crack that opens up the possibility of 'the new man.' "

In his contribution to *América latina en sus ideas*, published by Leopolda Zea with the support of UNESCO, Gotay quoted Gera's conclusion: "Christian faith, which is faith in salvation understood as liberation from sin, implies in itself an attitude of commitment with man in his historical-temporal (*histórico-secular*) liberation, meaning economic and political liberation."

This is the thinking of one of the main inspirers of Pope Francis, whose faith is entirely contained in this statement; the papacy is now at the pinnacle of history.

Behind this language lies a desperate attempt to rebuild a new Christendom—that is, a "temporal and spiritual" entity unified in the work of salvation.

It involves a comprehensive restructuring, which Gotay described as follows: "Liberation theology rejects an abstract, metaphysical conception of God and affirms the historical, temporal conception of God that emerges from the Bible. . . . Tangible justice and love are received directly from the historical, human Christian community, through which God's love is perfected."

Rafael Tello (1917–2002)

The Argentinian priest Rafael Tello was a member of Father Scannone's team; arguably, the previously mentioned "culture theology," and all that relates to the theme of religion and language, was his work. He was exploited, and his name is rarely cited, even though it was he who provided the sociological matrix for the "religion of the people."

He played an active role in shaping a "popular pastoral ministry," reviving pilgrimages to Our Lady of Luján, which he saw as an ideal vehicle for directing the devotion of the faithful toward political awareness. This activism was to be his undoing.

His zeal for the people and his definitive verdict on the hierarchy led him to conceive and plan the creation of a seminary to train priests according to popular pastoral practice. Following a dispute with the cardinal archbishop of Buenos Aires, the latter sanctioned him and, in 1979, forced him to resign from his position as professor at the Faculty of Theology. He had to withdraw from all public life in the Church, living from then on in a form of reclusion, which he made the most of to produce a large part of his written work.

On November 18, 2017, on the eve of the World Day of the Poor instituted by Pope Francis, his ashes were transferred to the Basilica of Our Lady of Luján by decision of the local archbishop. As archbishop of Buenos Aires, Jorge Bergoglio had said of him: "He invites us to transform the Church into the home of the poor. . . . Fr. Tello's life was a gift from the Spirit to our Church."

Juan Carlos Scannone (1931–2019)

The Jesuit Juan Carlos Scannone was the driving force behind the gigantic philosophical and theological upheaval that was to establish liberation theology as the "theology of the people." He wrote hundreds of articles and dozens of books on the subject.

The most important book that helps to understand this revolution of the mind is Emilce Cuda's *Para leer a Francisco* (Reading Francis – Theology, ethics and politics). It was never translated into French or

English. It is a comprehensive resource for interpreting Francis's papal thought and understanding its main components.

It is incredible that no one should have commented on or exploited this study, despite the fact that it is, in our opinion, the most complete and well-documented in existence.

It would not be exaggerated to the prologue to this book a king of "*imprimatur.*" This certificate of compliance was signed by Juan Carlos Scannone, one of the pope's most eminent theology professors. The third part of Mrs. Cuda's book is devoted to the specific contribution of the said Jesuit to the "theological" construction of the pope's thought.

In her work, Emilce Cuda constantly refers to her master, Scannone. She is active in all the networks that disseminate the theology of the people.

A single word summarizes the intellectual approach of both mentor and pupil: *recategorization*. According to Carlos Maria Galli's analysis, the unity of Scannone's work derives from three *speculative keys*:

> These "keys" enable us to understand the philosophical matrix of his thought—in which themes such as the Chalcedonian model, which unites and distinguishes levels of reality, the Blondelian interpretation of action, and the character of the people considered as a subject in its own right as an ethico-historical "we", the use of an analectic in which analogy assumes and surpasses dialectic, the theory of the Lonergan method, an anthropological and historical understanding of culture, the value of the symbol in the light of Ricœur, etc., are all, much like an instrument, placed by the author at the service of theological, pastoral and social reflection. This factor undoubtedly plays a part in achieving "the unity of thought that runs through the whole work."[76]

As is the case in all the literature of liberation theology, but even more so in that of the theology of the *people*, the reader is swamped with a multitude of references taken from all the modern philosophers.

---

[76] Galli, *Evangelización, cultura y teología. El aporte de JC Scannone a una teología inculturada.*

It needs to be said over and over again: the theology of the people has nothing Argentinian or Latin American about it, let alone anything popular!

In a 2008 lecture on *Transcendence as intrinsically constitutive of ethics and politics*, after focusing on Jean-Luc Marion's *"saturated phenomenon,"* Father Scannone cited no less than ten philosophers to support his thinking: Paul Ricœur, Claude Romano, Edmund Husserl, Michel Henry, Jacques Derrida, Merleau-Ponty, Levinas, Hans-Urs von Balthasar, Kendall Walton, and Dominique Janicaud, starting on page two.

This overabundant eclecticism renders all efforts to achieve a synthesis of his thought highly unpredictable, depending on which author is given priority.

Emilce Cuda's book, *Para leer a Francisco*, turns this abstract universe of philosophy, method, sociology, and anthropology into something even more profuse, with theological outbursts that quickly abort, thus further complicating efforts toward a synthesis. To the three authors selected by Galli, she adds dozens of others, including Ernesto Laclau, without realizing that this profusion is destructive of her own purpose, since "reading the Pope" would require having read a mountain of documents, books, articles, theses, and testimonies.

In an attempt at simplification to help us poor mortals, however, Emilce Cuda delivered the mystery of Pope Francis in a handful of clichés.

"In my opinion, the election of a pope like Francis is a sign of the times, not only because he is the first Latin American and the first Jesuit Pope, but because he is the prophet of the people at a time of scientific, political and cultural crisis—and I do not say economic, because according to Francis, this is a consequence, not a cause," she wrote on page 48.

Consequently, as she added on the same page, the Catholic Church seems to be "the first historical institution to have been able to read the signs of the times on time": "Francis today represents a deterritorialized *auctoritas*, a 'decisive' voice." The pope is no longer the pastor of the universal Church; he aims to be the voice of all mankind, as we can so often verify.

Mrs. Cuda had already opined on page 39: "*En Francisco, el pastor es un profeta*" (In Francis, the pastor is a prophet, and this comes closer to the political function as a vocation, a long way away from a conception of politics as the administration of particular interests). Scannone even goes so far as to say that "Pope Francis is himself the sign of the times, 'in person.' "[77]

Father Scannone's introduction to *Para leer a Francisco* sheds light (but not very successfully) on chapter 6:

> It addresses the starting point and theological foundation of the theology of the people, drawing on the two key mysteries of the Christian faith: the Trinity and the Incarnation. On the one hand, the Trinitarian circumincession between the three divine persons provides the theological basis for social communion and political participation (but also for a participatory conception of democracy), founded on interpersonal relationships. And on the other, the Chalcedonian Definition of the Incarnation (union without confusion or division of two natures in Christ) is—similarly to circumincession—the model of *polyhedral unity* [emphasis added] both in differences and from differences as a starting-point. From this stem the ethical and political priority of interpersonal relations, the culture of encounter and dialogue, the resolution of conflicts in a superior synthesis that values different contributions, the model of the polyhedron and the need for conversion, in order to break out of the closed, self-referential cultural paradigm and move towards another that is open and relational.[78]

Understanding "the theology of the people" is utterly impossible for rank-and-file Catholics on the basis of Scannone's writings. This is why we shall endeavor to break down the contents of this "theological foundation," which is completely unintelligible to average Catholics,

---

[77]   Cuda, *Para leer a Francisco, Teología, ética y política*, p. 49.
[78]   Cuda, p. 20.

be they in Latin America, Europe, or anywhere else. The theology of the people is an intellectual construct that has nothing to do with the people, nor with theology.

Father Scannone does confirm that this paradigm shift (renewing words and their meaning) is Pope Francis's practice. When the pope opposes the culture of life to the culture of death, it has nothing to do with the fight against abortion or euthanasia. It is about the rebirth of the interpersonal relationship between man and God: an openness to the infinite that opposes "self-referentiality and self-sufficiency that exclude the other" and "produce death." These words refer to the pre-conciliar Church and express that which is most opposed to liberation theologies.

There is a before and an after to Pope Francis. The foundations of the Church have changed.

What does Father Scannone have to say about this? Essentially, this: relations between the persons of the Holy Trinity, which are models of interpersonal relationships, abide in man who was created in the likeness and image of God, whatever his religion or lack of religion, and constitute the principles of democracy.

This feels like a return to the past, to the 1863 Malines Congress with Montalembert. Or back to the time when Abbé Naudet and his journal *La Justice Sociale* were making their demands. The speeches of Marc Sangnier also come to mind.

But Father Scannone is more knowledgeable and cleverer than his predecessors. He is smarter because he has read everything there was to read; as a longtime Blondelian immanentist, he has a genius for hiding behind all kinds of ideas that make you think that the world of philosophers and theologians agrees with him. In reality, though, the claim that "circumincession" is the foundation of democracy makes no sense at all.

In his book *La Trinité et l'histoire*, Father de Margerie, SJ, cited Saint Fulgence: "Saint Fulgence had already stressed that the natural unity of three men (and *a fortiori* their reciprocal presence) is not . . . an image of the circumincession of the three divine Persons: neither the soul nor the body of any of the three is common to the other two. Circumincession, on the other hand, is a mutual comprehension of Persons whose original relations are immanent to the one divine nature and who are truly distinct; mutual understanding due to the identification of each with the numerically one divine nature."[79]

It is truly amazing that not a single Catholic theologian has ever read and refuted Father Scannone's delusions. The idea that circum-incession, or even the Chalcedonian Definition (one person and two natures), could be the model for the polyhedral unity of peoples has more to do with mental aberration than with theology. According to Scannone's logic, man in his humanity is no longer simply a created being in the image of God but a creature that "partakes" in the Trinitarian substance and the divine act. As for the definition of the Council of Chalcedon, as revised by the "theology of the people," he sees it as demonstrating both the "divine" superiority of the people (in the same way as Christ is God) and its ability to insert itself into human history (in the same way as Christ is man).

Words cannot describe this gigantic theological-philosophical deception.

In his introduction, Father Scannone applies his paradigms to the pope's actions: "Pope Francis experiments with this as a prophet, by denouncing injustice and iniquity, and as a pastor, by encouraging conversion towards others, and other peoples, especially the poor, those who suffer and the excluded."

Where does this "theology" lead?

An article by the American journalist John Allen, "For Pope Francis wisdom comes from the poor," written at the time of the papal visit to Kenya in 2015, provides a partial response. He quoted Francis: "The path of Jesus began on the peripheries, it goes from the poor and with the poor, towards others."

John Allen wittily concluded: "If you want to understand Francis' agenda, in other words, you don't need to Google the Catechism of the Catholic Church or the Code of Canon Law. You'd be better off heading to some place like Kangemi" (a Nairobi slum where the pope made his remarks).

---

[79]   De Margerie, *La Trinité et l'histoire*, p. 253.

Quoting priests from the shantytowns of Argentina, the pope had gone on to say:

> The culture of poor neighborhoods, steeped in this particular wisdom, "has very positive traits, which can offer something to these times in which we live; it is expressed in values such as solidarity, giving one's life for others, preferring birth to death, providing Christian burial to one's dead; finding a place for the sick in one's home, sharing bread with the hungry, showing patience and strength when faced with great adversity. . . ." These values are not quoted in the stock exchange, are not subject to speculation, and have no market price. I congratulate you, I accompany you and I want you to know that the Lord never forgets you.

Sandro Magister's analysis of this speech was even more incisive: he titled his November 27 article in *L'Espresso*: *L'innata "saggezza" dei poveri, terza fonte della Rivelazione* (The innate wisdom of the poor, third source of the Revelation).

This adulation of the people is an ancient error that has already been condemned. Seeking to reform the Catholic Church by injecting it with an age-old error dating back to the millenarian heresies and the fragmentation of Protestantism, with the hope of enabling it to face our era of modernity, is simply absurd. The bishops' ignorance and their innate fear of progressive pressure groups have made them blind.

Lamennais, founding father of the "theology of the people"

The fire has been smoldering under the ashes for a long time: for 184 years, to be precise. It is only our own lack of awareness, our failure to reflect on the deeper causes of the events we are living through, and our obsession with immediate affairs (we are not saying that these are unimportant) that have prevented us—to borrow from the conciliar jargon—from "reading the signs of the times."

Some essential reference points may even have been intentionally suppressed. For example, in the *Compendium of the Social Doctrine of the Church*, quotations from pontifical texts starts with Pope Leo XIII (only one text is cited) and omit Saint Pius X entirely. This strikes us as a serious shortcoming, for the evils with which we are plagued made their appearance following the Revolution and the Empire, and were perfectly identified and condemned with all due precision from the outset by Popes Gregory XVI, Blessed Pius IX, Leo XIII, and Saint Pius X.

At least four authors have linked liberation theology to Félicité de Lamennais: Julio Loredo, in *Teologia della Liberazione*; Jean-Pierre Rissoan, in *Traditionalisme et révolution*, vol. I; Philippe André-Vincent, OP; Jean de Saint-Chamas, in his *Commentaire sur la théologie de la libération* (*AFS* n°54, August 1984), which is extensively quoted here below.

> 1. Lamennais's intellectual approach was based on the unstoppable progression of history, of which the French Revolution was a milestone. It was rooted in a global vision of the past, present, and future, as evidenced by the title of the journal he founded: *L'Avenir*.

Lamennais considered himself to be at once the heir to a world in collapse, the birthing father of a new society, and the prophet of a world to come. His rantings and his mimicries of the Old Testament prophets leave no room for doubt in this regard.

This *direction of history* is common to nineteenth-century utopians and writers such as Chateaubriand, Michelet, and Victor Hugo, who was dubbed "Jocrisse in Patmos" by Louis Veuillot—Jocrisse being a famous French literary buffoon.

> 2. According to Lamennais, the major characteristic of the past is the corruption of both temporal and spiritual powers; the spiritual power was subservient to the temporal, and the pope was not a head of a state. Because of this, his word and his government were in serfdom and were tied in with the corruption of the civil power of princes (this is exactly what all liberationists say). Lamennais was to defend the pope against temporal power.

3. In the face of this injustice, only *the people* remains. The second edition of *Paroles d'un croyant* (*Words of a Believer*) directly addressed the people. In 1838, Lamennais wrote a short opuscule called *Le livre du Peuple* (*The People's own Book*). The following quotation defines its general tone: "I hoped, and had faith in the future prospects of the human race. Its destinies will change whenever it shall will them to change; and it shall so will, whenever the consciousness of its malady shall be combined with a clear perception of the true remedy."

Lamennais's entire work is a call for the mobilization of the people, seen as future history's driving force.

4. The people in question are the poor.

At a time when Marx's cry, "Proletarians of all countries, unite!" had yet to ring out, Lamennais wrote in the aforementioned booklet: "The *rabble*, as the common people are contemptuously called, . . . have generally been the property of those who regulate the relations between the members of society, the operations of industry, the conditions of labor, its price and the division of its fruits. What it has pleased them to ordain, they have named law, and laws have been for the most part only measures of private interest, means of augmenting and perpetuating the domination and the abuse of the domination of the few over the many."

He added: "With the exception of a privileged few who are buried in mere enjoyment, the people are the human race."

5. Lamennais was no armchair philosopher. He had disciples. He published constantly, and his writings spread throughout Europe, in Belgium, Poland, Ireland, and even as far afield as the United States. His books, pamphlets, and leaflets flooded every level of society and entered the seminaries with the *Aphorismata ad juniores Theologos*. *Words of a Believer* had a print run of 400,000 copies. His style was often hailed, and rightly so, as rivaling that of Châteaubriand. His classical prose was brilliant. He beguiled his readers and feared nothing. Because he had defended the pope's rights against the Gallicanism of Louis XVIII and Charles X, no

one dared attack him. He had Lacordaire as an ally. He won over most of the young clerics, while the bishops generally remained silent or tolerant. It would take the courage of a few to rouse the majority.

6. Where did this man, this priest on the verge of apostasy, come from?

As a young man, he read Voltaire, who inspired him with his violence, invectives, and revolutionary spirit. It was from Voltaire, the insulter of Joan of Arc, that Lamennais borrowed the motto of his newspaper: "*Dieu et liberté*" (God and freedom). Rousseau, the reformer, provided it with its granite foundation: "*Man is born free!*" Lamennais's philosophy was that of Malebranche. He associated with the liberal French establishment and was a frequent visitor to Lamartine and Victor Hugo. He was elected to parliament, where he sat among the "Montagnards" (the most radical of the revolutionaries).

He was liberal in all things: the press, education. But he went further, demanding absolute freedom of conscience, free trade, freedom in everything and for everyone.

One of the experts who examined his ideas on the origin of power has shown that Lamennais did not in fact invent anything: his doctrine is that of Edmond Richer, a convicted master of the Sorbonne who later recanted his doctrine "*quatenus multa continens falsa, erronea, scandalosa, schismatica et prout sonant heretica*" ("insofar as it contains many false, erroneous, scandalous schismatic things, and insofar as they give the impression of heresy").

7. Why, then, was he able so successfully to upset Europe, which was still Christian at the time?

The answer is tragically straightforward. The backbone of his discourse was the French Revolution. The Revolution revealed to him the original power of the people, who alone can change the course of history and overthrow the tyranny of princes and popes in their irresistible march forward. The people's power would benefit not only society and humanity as a whole but also the Church, which Lamennais was determined to regenerate. This central demand of the Revolution was decisively elucidated by the academic Philippe Pichot-Bravard in the chapter *"La dictature régénératrice"* ("The Regenerating Dictatorship"), from his book *La Révolution Française* (The French Revolution). It was the idea that inspired Lamennais's entire work. And when he abandoned all hope of changing the Church, he decided to invent a new one.

Such had been the shattering effect of Europe's political, social, and religious turmoil that the evil genius of Lamennais found its way into the breach, offering the world a new redemption and a new salvation.

With this observation in mind, it cannot be argued that liberation theology and the "theology of the people" could only have developed, in Latin America and elsewhere, in the wake of the world revolution initially led by the Soviet Union. Indeed, in the 1967 *Message from Dom Hélder Câmara and the bishops of the Third World*, it is the French Revolution of 1789 that is cited as the revolutionary model for the people and for the Church.

> 8. The eighth point of convergence with Lamennais relates specifically to the Argentinian-style *theology of the people*.

Under its airs of originality and science, the theology of the people actually revives the theory of the three ages or three manifestations of Revelation.

This theory was addressed in the fourth item of the censure issued by the Holy See against Lamennais's *Essay on indifference in matters of religion*.

The censure stated the following:

> These propositions, which set forth a doctrine found throughout the work, and which the author understands in this sense, namely that before Jesus Christ, the universality or at least the plurality of men had always distinctly believed in the existence of a unique, immaterial, eternal, infinite, all-powerful God, creator of the universe, father of all that is, the true God, are false, contrary to the word of God and to the constant tradition of the Holy Fathers; they obliterate one of the greatest and

most indisputable benefits of the Incarnation, which consisted in reviving on earth the fundamental dogma of one God, the true God.

Lamennais's theses were developed as early as 1826, in Abbé Gerbet's *Catéchisme du sens commun* (The Catechism of Common Sense); Gerbet was his collaborator at *L'Avenir*. (The latter was condemned; he submitted, became vicar-general of Paris and Amiens, and finally bishop of Perpignan in 1853.)

Developments in theology of the people extended to all the world's religions this capacity to attain an innate universal religion, as well as its propagation; this resulted in a globalized ecumenism.

The discovery of the true theological origins of the theology of the people offers proof of the archaic nature of the theology and philosophy built up by the Jesuit Scannone and his followers; these origins were swept under the carpet.

A basic knowledge of history should have enlightened their confused minds. All of biblical history, from the Flood to the Tower of Babel, is there to teach that peoples left to their own devices will sink into the most terrifying paganism. The Jews, whom Moses freed from Egyptian slavery, fell back into the vilest idolatry. The unfaithfulness of the Jewish people, who had been liberated and showered with divine care and miracles, was such that none of those who had been freed from Egypt entered the Promised Land. At the time of the prophets, the Jewish people were reduced to slavery in Babylon, and only a small faithful remnant remained.

When missionaries returned to Japan three centuries after its initial evangelization, they found only a handful of believers.

Père Emmanuel, who evangelized the Champagne region after the French Revolution, once observed that without evangelization, the people there would end up worshipping beasts.

The 3 or 4 percent of churchgoers in France today are living proof that this great Catholic nation of Christendom has collapsed. No amount of rantings of the theology of the people will restore the *Pax Christiana*!

CHAPTER 7

"Theology of the People": An Intellectual Scam

How the modernist wolf donned the sheep's fleece of the theology of the people

The only French-language book on the theology of the people to date was published by Father Scannone in 2017 with Lessius, the publishing house of the Belgian Jesuits. Its footnotes are mostly in Spanish and sometimes in English and German; a few are in French. It was translated into English and published under the title: *Theology of the People: The Pastoral and Theological Roots of Pope Francis* (Paulist Press, 2021).

In his book, Scannone emphasized the Argentinian origins of the theology of the people: "Because it is the theology of the poor, it contributes to the professional theologian and to academic theology as a discipline and institution, a privileged hermeneutical locus in order to come to know the God of Jesus through an evangelical, ethical, and historical conversion to the poor. Thus, respecting the autonomy of theology as science and hermeneutics, it gives them a new horizon and perspective that is more evangelical, more human, and more historical. ... Popular theology could raise a 'methodological suspicion' in an academic theology too far removed from spiritual life, human life, or historical reality."

Traditional theology, it would seem, lacks bite. But the Jesuit father's dialectics got over that difficulty. He put it like this:

> First, due to epistemological rupture—or better still, the methodological one—between both knowledges in interchange, the subject of this are professional theologians or the community of the same. However, we can also affirm that, due to the unity of the formal object (and perhaps even of the inculturated hermeneutical horizon) there is a true unity of subject (communitarian and organic) between both theologies.
>
> Such unity is derived above all from the ecclesiality, both of faith and theology, since this is a charism and task given to the Church, in which there is an organic diversity of charisms and functions. However, if the professional theologian as such has brought his conversion of faith to the preferential option for the poor and to the evangelical, ethical, and historical consequences of it, and even its cultural ones, his academic theology will share with popular theology the fact that he has made the same journey not only the light of faith and faithfulness to the doctrine of the Church (which are based in the intrinsic analogy between them as theologies), but also a hermeneutical horizon, cultural roots and pastoral and historical relevance. Thus, the organic and internally differentiated unity of the subject is demonstrated in and despite the epistemological or methodological rupture and the irreducible specificity of both theologies.

It would appear that to date, not one "professional theologian" has given any thought to this demonstration.

Francis's first document as pope, *Evangelii Gaudium*, unequivocally articulated this theology (No. 154):

> The preacher also needs to keep his ear to the people and to discover what it is that the faithful need to hear. *A preacher has to contemplate the word, but he also has to contemplate his people.* In this way he learns "of the aspirations, of riches and limitations, of ways of praying, of loving, of looking at life and the world, which distinguish this or that human gathering," while

paying attention "to actual people, to using their language, their signs and symbols, to answering the questions they ask." He needs to be able to link the message of a biblical text to a human situation, to an experience which cries out for the light of God's word. This interest has nothing to do with shrewdness or calculation; it is profoundly religious and pastoral. *Fundamentally it is a "spiritual sensitivity for reading God's message in events,"* and this is much more than simply finding something interesting to say. What we are looking for is "what the Lord has to say in this or that particular circumstance." Preparation for preaching thus becomes an exercise in evangelical discernment, wherein we strive to recognize—in the light of the Spirit—*"a call which God causes to resound in the historical situation itself. In this situation, and also through it, God calls the believer."*[80]

According to this rationale, God's call resounds in a given historical situation. The preacher, listening to the people, then translates this call and connects the message of the biblical text to a current human situation. But if that is so, it is no longer the Church that is the depositary of the teaching received from the apostles; rather, it is the history experienced by the people, who thanks to the light of the Spirit (this is a quintessentially Protestant and modernist expression), receive a religious meaning tailored to particular circumstances.

In the same papal document, the word *people* is repeated 164 times, making it the most frequent noun used. This makes it easier to understand Cardinal Müller's statement that "Pope Francis is not a professional theologian."

In his report on the synod, *The Family's Vocation and Mission,*[81] the Jesuit Antonio Spadaro gave a theological-olfactive interpretation of the theology of the people: "The fact that the synodal process began with a questionnaire reveals a fundamental value in its content. Indeed, as the Pope himself has said: 'The *sensus fidei* prevents a rigid

---

[80]   Passages in italics were highlighted by us; the last two are quotes from Pope Paul VI in *Evangelii Gaudium.*

[81]   Spadaro, *The Family's Vocation and Mission* (*Civiltà Cattolica*, 2015), pp. 372–91.

separation between an *Ecclesia docens* and an *Ecclesia discens*, since the flock likewise has an instinctive ability to discern [in French, "an instinctive flair for discerning"] the new ways that the Lord is revealing to the Church.' "

Depending on the author and particular circumstances, the flock changes names: people of God, periphery, popular religion, the Church of the poor, the Church of the oppressed, and so on. The learned, together with Antonio Spadaro, would say it like this: "*Episcopal collegiality must live within a wholly synodal Church.*"

Therefore, two theologies coexist: one for the learned and another that is naturally embodied in the poor—that is, the people or its synodal representation. This theology of the poor is chiefly linked to history and to the signs of the times.

In a 2013 article entitled *Teología y política en el discurso del Papa Francisco. Dónde está el Pueblo?* (Theology and politics in the Pope's discourse. Where is the people?), Emilce Cuda took up similar topics. She reasserted the European origins of this new theology, mentioning the "resignification of certain theological categories": thus, pastoral action is here understood as political action, in accordance "with the constitution *Gaudium et Spes*," while justice is given the new meaning of "the development of peoples," as in *Populorum Progressio*:

> These new categorizations were taken up in Europe under the name of Political Theology by Jean Baptiste Metz and Hans Küng, starting from a progressive position. In Latin America, they were taken up under the name of liberation theology by Gustavo Gutiérrez, Ignacio Ellacuría and Jon Sobrino, who, in contrast to European currents, were striving for a total change in political, economic, legal and social structures. In Argentina, it emerged as the Theology of the People with Lucio Gera, Rafael Tello and Alberto Sily, with a form of its own that sees the working people as an eschatological category on the margins of class struggle. Theology of the People had forerunners in other settings, such as the French "worker-priests" movement in the 1950s, or the "shantytown priests" who received the support

of a section of Argentina's bishops, such as Jerónimo Podestá, Antonio Quarracino, Alberto Devoto, Enrique Angelelli and Eduardo Pironio.

Remember that Quarracino summoned Bergoglio as auxiliary bishop, that Devoto supported the Third Worldists, and that Angelelli was murdered.

Argentina's theological model thus consists in developing a new Church model based on that part of the people identified as the poor, with the aim of wiping out memories of an archaic Catholic Argentina.

The better to highlight the distinctive nature of theology of the people in relation to other liberation theologies, Emilce Cuda took up the pseudo-distinction established by Father Scannone, who divided it into four currents: that of Bishop Pironio, that of the Brazilian Hugo Assmann, that of Gustavo Gutiérrez, and that of the theology "of the people" or "of culture."

In Pironio, the subject of this theological current is "*the whole people*," guided by an "agent": "lay people engaged in evangelization and politics."

In Assmann's view, the subject is the working class as a whole, also led by an "agent": Christian groups engaged in revolutionary actions.

For Gutiérrez, it requires "using the sociological knowledge of Marxist analysis to interpret reality in a theological way"; the subject of this current "is the poor people as an embodied class, and the people which embody the proletarian class, while the agent consists of the base communities as a conscientized Christian sector."

For the Argentines, the subject is the people, not as a class but as the poor ("*el sujeto es el pobre, pero no como clase sino como pobre*"). It has its own structure, its own lifestyle, which determines its culture— that is, its unity. "The agent is the people as an organized community."

To put it in a nutshell: the theology of the people substitutes class struggle with an eschatological future, the Kingdom of God, which the poor are already experiencing by anticipation. From this, the people derive a dignity that surpasses all others. The people are superior to "the class."

In 1973, the Jesuits and their Peronist affiliates set out to conquer power. Argentinian liberationists invented the theology of the people, which did not seek confrontation but divided the field of politics between the people and those who opposed the people. According to Emilce Cuda, this constitutes a third way in the face of Marxism and liberalism: "This path is aligned with Peronism, but with differing internal axes. In my opinion, this is the theological-political context in which Bergoglio was formed and lived for 45 years, and which has shaped the theology of the reigning Pope Francis."[82]

Further details provided by Emilce Cuda under the heading "From the secularization of theology to the theologization of culture" are key to understanding Pope Francis:

> The fact that the "theology of the people" is also called the "theology of the culture" both by Scannone and by other contemporary theologians, is due to the idea that culture refers to ways of doing and dynamics, to a *movement that always leaves open the possibility of new interpretations and reinterpretations of reality and of the Gospel.*
>
> It is a cultural dynamism whose founding event is the incarnation of the Logos. Latin American liberation theology, in all its components, identifies with the culture of the poor, and seeks to transform the Church so that it ceases to be the Church of the upper spheres of society, and becomes the Church of the poor. This is why, in the 1960s, a group of Latin American theologians—Gera, Gustavo Gutiérrez, Juan Luis Segundo—decided to "implant" the Latin American Church among the poor. Today, Pope Francis, a Latin American pastor, has decided to implant the entire Catholic Church among the poor, by articulating theological categories within political discourse in a new way, as a result of the enormous mass media impact of his public words. Is this a secularized theology? In my view, it is a theologized culture.[83]

---

[82]   Cuda, *Para leer a Francisco, Teología, ética y política*, p. 17.
[83]   Cuda, p. 21.

Liberation theology . . . sees a historical determinism . . . in the social and economic reality of the region. The theology of the people, on the other hand, sees this same reality of poverty as an eschatological moment, but one in which hope is already present in this life. This trend considers that rising from nothingness to being is achievable here and now, by alleviating the suffering of the poor. Making social contradictions more acute in order to hasten the Parousia is a Marxist position that the theology of the people rejects; instead, it holds that working on reality in order to promote social justice is a politically popular position that fosters the hope of man's total development, on both eschatological and earthly levels. *We could choose this last proposition as exemplifying a theologized concept of Peronist political culture.*"[84]

Emilce Cuda developed her analysis in an article published in London in 2015: *The theology of Francis. Difference between Liberation theology and theology of the people.*

This article makes it clear that we are gradually entering a thought system that no longer has anything in common with the traditional theology used by the Catholic Church. Its intellectual, metaphysical, and theological categories belong to another, familiar world: that of the age-old errors that have marred the history of the Church, along with a kind of mental delirium that is typical of utopias, both ancient and modern.

When Pope Francis was elevated to the pontificate, everyone was struck by the fact that he presented himself in the loggia without having donned the insignia of his office. While he passed through the "Room of Tears" on his way out of the Sistine Chapel, he refused to don the red mozzetta trimmed with white ermine, the golden cross, and the traditional red shoes worn by popes. He refused; according to Professor Hubert Windisch, he even declared, "The carnival is over." The symbols of his office are alien to him. Perhaps he remembers the Pact of the Catacombs, which forbids wearing rich ornaments for the sake of the poor?

---

[84]   Cuda, p. 23, emphasis added.

The red mozzetta recalls the Passion and the Blood of Christ shed for redemption; the cross is the sign of the office that the pope holds from Christ and its dignity; the red shoes echo the ancient custom of Byzantine bishops and the suffering that comes with the office.

On the balcony, Francis did not bless the crowd but instead asked the crowd to bless him. This request, which is totally alien to tradition, has a meaning that can be traced back to the conventions of the "theology of the people," but it is also profoundly Peronist. When Perón would appear on the balcony of the presidential palace to address the people, he always conveyed with a few words the "mystical union" between himself and his people. This resemblance has never been mentioned, as far as we know.

Theologies of the people

If we are to avoid common misconceptions, we must first point out that all liberation theologies have a shared addiction to the "direction of history," by which they vindicate all political, social, and religious changes. These transformations are specific to each country or group of countries and their own historical features. In other words, liberation theologies do not march in step with one another, but they are all in line with the direction of history.

Ever since these theologies made their appearance, they have been referred to by the English expression "*contextual theology*." Thus, there are a variety of liberation theologies, in South Korea, South Africa, India, and elsewhere. There is even a Jewish liberation theology, presented by Marc H. Ellis in *Toward a Jewish theology of Liberation*, and *An Asian Theology of Liberation*, described in a book by Aloysius Pieris, SJ.

Their core concept lies in a historical analysis on which all societal changes and variations in the churches are based. In South Africa, for example, the new Catholic movement of the Lumko Institute brought this trend to the English-speaking world. But these movements are not exclusively Catholic. Many Protestants have published on this subject in Latin America, and they can be found alongside Catholics:

their books include *Teología de la Liberación, una perspectiva evangélica* (Liberation theology: an evangelical perspective) by Emilio A. Nuñez. In the United States, among the many existing books, Gayraud S. Wilmore and James H. Cone's *Black Theology* deserves a mention.

In 1983, the Commission for the Participation of Churches in Development of the World Council of Churches in Geneva published *Poor, Yet Making Many Rich: The Poor as Agents of Creative Justice*. In its own way, this book expands on the economic-political themes of liberation theology, with an appendix pointing out that both Ghana and Indonesia are involved.

Leonardo Boff, in Brazil, first focused on the struggle of the "landless," before switching to the ecological sphere and inventing the "eco-theology of liberation," almost forty years before the Amazon synod. These theologians gorge themselves on catchphrases, running after an inventiveness of expression that they believe to be quite new.

Pope Bergoglio's links with liberation theology were well-known at the time of his election. The propaganda machine that surrounded his arrival in Rome did all it could to rub out this unfortunate relationship by giving the impression that he stood behind a "Catholic" theology of liberation: the theology of the people. Yet never once in the writings of either Cardinal Bergoglio or Pope Francis is the expression *"theology of the people"* to be found.

In 2012, the Argentinian priest Enrique Ciro Bianchi published *Pobres en este mundo, ricos en la fe* (Poor in this world, rich in faith). Three years later, the work was translated to the Italian under the title *Introduzione alla teologia del popolo* (Introduction to the theology of the people). Both versions feature the same preface by Cardinal Bergoglio. The cardinal graced his readers with all the subtleties of "popular religiosity," "popular piety," and "popular spirituality" to be found in this book that was written in memory of Father Tello of Argentina. He added that the articulation between faith and different cultures leads to a cultural way of learning and expressing one's faith: "All this has penetrated to the very marrow of our people, even though they are unable to express it conceptually." This is a far cry from a "theology" of the people!

But that was not enough to deter the commentators from making a large number of comments.

As early as January 28, 2014, Estéban Pittaro, who had already observed that the word *people* was used 164 times in *Evangelii Gaudium*, headed one of the passages in his commentary for *Aleteia* on Pope Francis's theology with the phrase: "*A school that is neither liberal nor Marxist.*" Referring to Scannone, he pointed out that this wording probably originated in the National Chairs of Sociology at the University of Buenos Aires, where academics were striving to identify categories that were neither liberal nor Marxist in order to understand and explain Latin American and Argentinian history.

On March 13, 2015, Zenit.it offered a reflection on Cardinal Kasper's fresh explanation of the theological foundations of Francis's pontificate: "He is not 'a Franciscan in disguise'; he is a Jesuit in every respect." It quoted the cardinal's explanation that Francis, in the spirit of Saint Ignatius, does not set out from doctrine but from the concrete situation and then applies the rules of spiritual discernment to arrive at concrete decisions.

"Francis does theology based on a given context, and in his contextual theology, his intention is 'to shed light on the situation of the church and of the Christian in today's world from the perspective of the Gospel. Here, the Christian faith is not an ideology that tries to explain everything; it cannot be likened to an artificial light illuminating the entire course of our lives; it's more like a lantern that lights up the path of life insofar as we ourselves are moving forward,'" observed Zenit, quoting the cardinal.

The implications of the above are obvious: doctrine = ideology = artificial light.

On April 27, 2015, the same news agency featured an "Introduction to the Theology of the People" as a way of discovering Bergoglio's theological roots. On May 5, 2015, *Aleteia* headlined: *Papa Francisco ha abrazado la Teología del Pueblo, no de la Liberación* (Pope Francis has embraced the Theology of the People, not Liberation theology).

Again on *Aleteia*, Rafael Luciani published an article on July 30, 2015 under the title *La teología del pueblo, según el Papa Francisco* (The theology of the people, according to Pope Francis). He immediately clarified: "Unlike liberation theology, it does not seek to change social and political structures for their own sake, but to discern the mission of the Church." On August 10, 2015, the same theologian addressed a similar topic: *Francisco y la Teología del Pueblo: un nuevo modo de "ser Iglesia"* (Francis and the theology of the people: a new way of "being Church"). "It's about a new way of being Church, based on the preferential option for that part of the people that is constituted by the poor," he wrote.

There is no shortage of articles on the subject. Juan Carlos Scannone, a specialist if ever there was one, summed up the history of this intriguing theology, whose author and founding date nobody seems to be able to pin down, in *Perspectivas eclesiológicas de la "teología del pueblo" en la Argentina* (Ecclesiological Perspectives on "People's Theology" in Argentina) published by nuevaevangelizacion.com.co on October 8, 2014.

Father Scannone believes that the theology of the people had a variety of origins since the time of the council: in his opinion, Lucio Gera was "the most important figure" of the one that developed in Argentina, with its emphasis on popular culture and religiosity. "Specifically, it involves a theological reflection on the relationship of the People of God with peoples (especially the Latin American and Argentinian peoples), their culture and their religion. This was the source of important Argentinian contributions to post-conciliar ecclesiology."

According to Scannone, this is a separate form of liberation theology: "a theology based on the praxis of Latin American peoples." His statement clearly indicates a total departure from the strictly religious and Catholic sphere in order to embrace a historicist ideology based on sociological data.

This has been confirmed by Gustavo Gutiérrez and Karl Lehmann. The latter, quoted by Scannone, considered it "an independent and very valid form of liberation theology." The classification was adopted by a number of authorities, including the archbishop of Buenos Aires, Antonio Quarracino, when he was president of CELAM, as Scannone points out. Others gave it different names, such as "populist theology" or "a national and popular approach." Father Scannone has also called it a "popular pastoral theology."

He went on to describe the role of the COEPAL (Episcopal Pastoral Commission) in shaping a theology of the people that emerged in the political context of Peronization. According to Scannone, it is easy to understand that the ecclesial and political contexts were closely intertwined during the years of General Perón's return in 1972–1973.

Scannone discussed in greater detail "the general characteristics of the theology of the people," because, he said, the expression had not yet become generally used.

1. Latin American theology, he argued, rejects the meaning of people as a class oppressed by capitalism. It refers to an understanding of a "people" as both rooted and secular, but also considered analogically with a theological reference to the People of God. The Argentinian model is that of a People's Church that does not ignore dependency and structural injustices but in which "the people is above all understood from a historical-cultural perspective." It is the subject of a common history and culture. It understands itself as a nation but only on the basis of a "specific culture," a set of "shared values."

Scannone then returned to the Peronist discourse: "The 'people' is a category that presupposes unity prior to conflict," without remaining indifferent to injustice: facing the *people* is the *anti-people*—these are explicit categories of the Peronist system. The Church is *de facto* on the side of the poor. The poor are the "heart of the People"; they can be sinful, or even have "a rich man's heart," hence the need for "ethical-historical and theological discernment in order theologically to interpret the people and their relationship with the People of God."

2. What method should be used to manage this system? Scannone set aside theology in favor of the "analytical-structural contribution" of the social sciences and "scientific mediation," but beyond this, he stated that the theology of the people would "have to privilege the sapiential knowledge both of the people and, theologically, of the People of God insofar as it knows the people and recognizes in them the signs of the times, in a sapiential way, in the light of faith and of the 'unction of the Most Holy.' " Meanwhile, "scientific mediation"

encompassed all aspects of research from the historical sciences, culture, the social sciences, and religion. Scannone continued: "This is why it employs ethical-anthropological and historic-cultural analysis, without forgetting the socio-structural." As we have already pointed out, all this is completely foreign to the people, and even more so to the poor.

The fifteen general principles of popular pastoral care

A rarely quoted document does exist that synthesizes the relationship between the people and liberation theology through the themes presented at the Popular Pastoral seminar held from September 7 to September 9, 1973 at the Higher Institute of Religious Culture in Buenos Aires, on the occasion of the fifth anniversary of Medellín. It took place five weeks after the election of Father Bergoglio as head of the Argentinian province of the Society of Jesus. The list of participants is significant. Alongside the Argentinian priests Lucio Gera, Rafael Tello, Gerardo Farrell (a sociologist), Juan Filipuzzi, Fernando Boasso, and Guillermo Rodríguez-Melgarejo, there was the third-worldist nun Aída López (who was later forced to resign as provincial of the Society of the Divine Master for having spoken out in favor of the ordination of women) and the laywoman Chela Bassa, a regular member of these groups as secretary; also present was the layman Ignacio Palacios Videla, a Peronist political leader and a close associate of Lucio Gera. This executive team was joined by the liberationist bishops Angelelli and Pironio (remember that Pope Paul VI would later make the latter a cardinal), fifteen priests, fifteen nuns, and twenty-one lay people from all parts of the country.

The first two—Fathers Gera and Tello—were responsible for presenting the themes selected, which can be described as fifteen general principles of popular pastoral care.

We translated and quoted them in full here below; in our opinion, they are a key feature of the new direction taken by liberation theology in Argentina, both in terms of content and authorship. They were handed out to the participants at the start of the meeting as a basis for discussion and were then distributed throughout the country.

1. Latin American peoples are the collective subjects and agents of our continent's history.

2. Our peoples are a historical, cultural, and above all, political reality. They are the great majorities, generally oppressed and marginalized, who have historically been confronted with successive imperialist projects of dependence.

3. Our peoples have always rejected the economic, political, and cultural dependence imposed on them by centers of power. These centers have always harnessed to their own ends the literate minorities who have self-marginalized themselves with regard to the reality of the people.

4. The people—which is a historical and cultural reality—includes the oppressed and those who do not oppress, insofar as they are part of its dynamics and identify with its project.

5. Popular culture expresses itself in a shared attitude toward nature, toward other human beings and other peoples; toward oneself and towards God; a shared attitude toward the end of life and death.

6. The popular project is the historical ideal of liberation that the people sets for itself, based on its own contents and ways of life—that is, its culture—and which has always made its presence felt in resistance to the project of "enlightened" or imperial culture.

7. Our popular culture was illuminated at birth by the Christian faith. This Christian faith carries within itself a revolutionary dynamic that pushes for liberation.

8. Faith grows in the people that grows, and the people grows by leaning on its faith. That is why the people always lives in hope while experiencing the harshness of the struggle.

9. Popular culture has found its deepest meaning in the Christian faith, along with the rites and customs in which the people discovers its own identity.

10. Inasmuch as the people liberates itself, it humanizes and evangelizes itself; it carries out its historical project.

11. The Church, through evangelization and catechesis, deposits faith in the consciousness of the people. The people's struggle develops the revolutionary potential of this same faith.

12. The religious acts and gestures of popular culture express and transmit faith.

13. By embracing faith and becoming the people of God, the people bring the transcendent and integral meaning of evangelical liberation to the project that emerges from popular culture. The people of God, for their part, to the extent that they embrace popular culture, identify themselves with the historical people, thus giving it greater unity.

14. This project of liberation is opposed to the non-popular—and often populist—projects promoted by elites who claim for themselves a monopoly over the responsibility for human history and pretend to reduce the people to the role of passive beneficiaries or mere usufructuary "objects."

15. Our peoples came to faith through baptism and preaching. Baptism, which effectively implants the seeds of faith, hope, and charity, also has the virtue of inserting the baptized into the process of liberation of the whole people, in which the historical fate of God's people is at stake.

This is what Argentina's clerical intelligentsia produced on the eve of Juan Perón's return to power, under the benevolent gaze of two bishops. The political context required the reappropriation of the word *people*, so dear to the Peronists. Contrary to widespread opinion, the shantytowns of Buenos Aires did not become Marxized; rather, they yearned for the socialist-nationalism proclaimed by the *"Conductor."*

This presumptuous intellectual construction sought to justify a new form of revolution in society and in the Church. It was presented by the Salvadoran Jesuit Jon Sobrino in 1981, beyond the Argentinian context, under the title *Resurrección de la Verdadera Iglesia. Los pobres, lugar teológico de la eclesiología* (Resurrection of the true Church: the poor, the theological place of ecclesiology).

No longer was it the class struggle that mattered but a direction of history whose sole objective was to change the Church under the guise of defending the poor, using as its instrument tried-and-tested dialectics (*praxis*) known as popular pastoral care.

However, at this stage of our analysis, we still do not know who invented the label "*theology of the people*." The most truthful mention the Uruguayan Jesuit Juan Luís Segundo as the discoverer of the formula. In a work published in 1974, *Liberación de la teología* (Liberation of theology), he indeed used the expression, which was later generally attributed to him. But Segundo fiercely criticized its use. As a true Marxist, he ridiculed the expression: people only repeat what they have been taught and cannot be at the origin of a theology: they only reproduce what they have been taught and have received from prevailing politics.

This supposed origin, coupled with the criticism expressed by this self-professed Marxist Jesuit, made it difficult to use the said label. For this reason, commentators confined themselves to referring to "the inventor," without mentioning his criticism. To our knowledge, the only author who dared to give the "Segundo" explanation was Phillip Berryman in his book *Liberation theology*.[85]

It was not until 1993, and the first edition of Sebastian Politi's dissertation, *Teología del pueblo*, edited by Lucio Gera who also contributed a preface, that the most comprehensive study of the subject was published and Caesar was given his due.

Since Politi's thesis was published, all the leading authors have classified their works under this heading, the most prominent being Scannone. But Cardinal Bergoglio never got involved in these debates, even though he was a Peronist.

Politi shows that the inventor of the formula was in fact Fr. Ernesto López Rosas, SJ.[86] This once and for all lifts the veil on the mystery

---

[85]   Phillip Berryman, *Liberation theology* (New York: Pantheon Books, 1987), pp. 86–87.

[86]   Politi, *Teología del pueblo*, pp. 321–23.

of the never-quoted origin of people's theology and also provides the Argentinian key to what reveals itself as an authentic *liberation theology*.

This Argentinian Jesuit wrote in 1974: "In Argentina, thanks to the Peronist phenomenon . . . a 'theology of the people' has been created, under the general orientation of 'liberation theology.' "

His article was published in the CIAS (Center for Information and Social Action) Jesuit magazine, n°231, under the following complete title: *Teología de la liberación. Su profundización a partir de la experiencia peronista* (Liberation theology: an in-depth approach based on the Peronist experience). It should be remembered that the CIAS were reformed under orders from Father Arrupe with a view to developing actions for social justice and that just a few weeks later, Fr. López Rosas published an article in *Mundo* on the Christian values of Peronism. At the time, Fr. López Rosas belonged to the privileged group that propelled Father Bergoglio to the head of the Jesuit province of Argentina. The group included Fr. Miguel Angel Fiorito, who "has particularly developed the 'theology of the people,' " according to jesuits.global, and who was Bergoglio's spiritual father, and Fr. Andrés Swinnen, who had already worked with Bergoglio in Chile. Fr. López Rosas was still alive in 2023 and was received in Rome by Pope Francis.

It should be pointed out that in *La teología argentina del pueblo* (The Argentinian Theology of the People), the book she wrote about Lucio Gera in 2015, Virginia Azcuy does not present a single text by Lucio Gera that contains the expression "theology of the people."

Ultimately, the answer to the question of the complex relationship between the pope and people's theology was given on October 6, 2016, at the *Interpelaciones del papa Francisco a la teología hoy* Congress (Pope Francis's Challenges to Theology Today), by the liberationist priest Eduardo de la Serna, whose great intellectual honesty we have already commended.

He quoted and commented on a statement made by Leonardo Boff to the Argentinian newspaper *Página 12* on July 24, 2013: "Before being elected Pope, Cardinal Jorge Bergoglio 'was a follower of a branch of liberation theology peculiar to Argentina, which is the theology of the people or the theology of popular culture.' 'Liberation theology had many currents. In Argentina, the one that prevailed came from *justicialism*,' Boff added. Francis always considered himself a Peronist, a justicialist. He was in favor of getting the poor to become active participants [in their liberation], asserting that there could be no solution without their own participation."

In his lecture, quoting the Jesuit Victor Codina whom we mentioned earlier as a member of the conquering elite who serve the pope, Eduardo de la Serna pointed out that the aim was to create a "neo-Christendom," "a Christian and popular civilization."

It should be noted in passing that these terms were also a means of escaping the inquisition of the military, who saw the liberationists as political enemies.

Eduardo de la Serna reiterated traditional teaching to assert that the Church is the new People of God. But in his conclusion, he recalled that Pope Francis considers that "clericalism" has ossified the Church, People of God, and that he has made the theology of the people his own, as appears from a letter to Cardinal Ouellet, president of the Pontifical Commission for Latin America: "Let us trust in our People, in their memory and in their 'sense of smell,' let us trust that the Holy Spirit acts in and with our People and that this Spirit is not merely the 'property' of the ecclesial hierarchy" (March 19, 2016).

This is faux "*gaucho*" talk. The herd does indeed have a certain sense of the pasture, but it remains well and truly under the watchful guard of the *gauchos ovejeros* (the guardians of the flocks of sheep) and of dogs imported from the Pyrenees! Yet it is with phrases such as these that the people is "deified," in defiance of the true Argentinian culture of which the theology of the people so deceptively babbles. Using images such as these, the pope substitutes his distorted vision of pastoral reality for the true vision of the Gospel: "I know my sheep and my sheep know me. They know my voice."

Anyone who has had firsthand experience of flocks of sheep knows that there is nothing more unruly or "sheep-like" than a sheep. Everyone knows the story of the sheep of Panurge throwing themselves into the sea. In Argentina, the word *borrego* refers to the same reality.

In the same vein, the epitome of the grotesque was reached in the tenth paragraph of the previously mentioned 2017 Boston Declaration: "We support a theology that attends to the reality of social conflicts and makes its way through the peripheries. *Just like the shepherds who live with the smell of sheep, theologians must smell like their people and their streets*; thus, the need to pay back the pastoral debt that professional theology still has with our poor people" (emphasis in original).

Sheep are the most foul-smelling of all animals due to their natural grease. Its smell is penetrating and pervasive. The participants at the Boston meeting were the pope's "fan club": they are like him and know nothing about sheep or flocks. Never forget that their style is that of propaganda, in which ideological discourse has to be made to look evangelical. Combine this nonsense with the Holy Spirit, who hovers over the people like the Spirit of God in the first days of creation, and you will have some idea of the degeneracy of current theological thinking.

As Father Scannone and Jon Sobrino, two key participants at the Boston meeting, pointed out, such a theology has ecclesiological consequences. Little attention has been paid to this, even though it lies at the heart of Bergoglian action, leaving far behind the rantings of liberation theology—a "revolutionary Marxist" model according to Gutiérrez! The Italian historian Loris Zanatta tallied the number of times the pope used the word *people* in his first trips to Latin America, Cuba, the USA, and Africa: he counted as many as 356.

The final word must be left to the Jesuit Father Pierre de Charentenay: "Pope Francis moves beyond the theology of the people in order to propound a theology of human globalization, of integral humanism in the line of Paul VI. His three speeches at the World Meetings of Popular Movements (2014-2016) set out a plan of action. If the Pope speaks as a prophet, he also urges believers to engage in politics."[87]

NOTE. We have selected six works from the wealth of literature dealing with the theology of the people: *Le pape du peuple*, Juan

---

[87]   Charentenay, "La théologie du people."

Carlos Scannone, ed. Cerf, 2015; *Theology of the People: The Pastoral and Theological Roots of Pope Francis*, Juan Carlos Scannone, Paulist Press, 2021; *Pope Francis and the Theology of the People*, Rafael Luciani, Orbis, 2017; *Teología del pueblo: una propuesta Argentina para Latino-america*, Sebastian Politi, ed. Docencia 2015; *La teología argentina del pueblo*, Virginia R. Azcuy, ed. UAH Chile.

The theology of the people and the dream of Maritain

How on earth could things have come to this? We could not have hoped for a more compelling conclusion to our research than that of Father de Charentenay. His phrase, "integral humanism in the line of Paul VI" is what will lead us to the original source of this theology of the people.

The reader will have recognized the title of one of Jacques Maritain's most famous works, *Humanisme intégral*, of which Pope Paul VI was an admirer and an attentive reader. At the close of the Second Vatican Council on December 8, 1965, he presented Jacques Maritain with the message he was sending "*to men of thought and science*." He clasped the philosopher—and above all the author of *Humanisme integral*—in his arms, having known him since 1945, when Maritain was appointed ambassador to the Holy See. Paul VI had a Christian Democrat background, and his convictions had been reinforced by his reading of Maritain and exchanging ideas with him. Maritain was also behind the pope's profession of faith at the end of the council.

More importantly—and this is a clear indication of how the thinking of Maritain was incorporated into the council—Paul VI asked him to provide a text for "The Apostolate of the Laity," the final part of the dogmatic constitution *Lumen Gentium*. In one of his memoranda to the pope, Maritain wrote: "I'd rather say spiritual mission than apostolate."[88]

---

[88] See Jacques Gadille's *Fondement d'une théologie du Laïcat selon Jacques Maritain* for more details.

Maritain's influence continues to this day. In his book *Christianisme et démocratie* (*Christianity and Democracy*), Maritain told believers and non-believers alike: "It is by working in the density of the life of the world, in an attempt to transform temporal existence, that this spiritual renewal, whatever be the irreducible division that it involves on the dogmatic and religious plane, will exercise a common action and will bring forth common fruits."

It is not possible to describe here all the inspirations drawn from this in Paul VI's speeches, and those of Pope Francis, who once went so far as to say that all men would be justified. In this, he followed Maritain's lead in his posthumous work *Approches sans entraves* (Unshackled Approaches), which was quoted by the celebrated Prof. Romano Amerio in *Iota Unum* (p. 698): "One day, all the inhabitants of Hell . . . all the reprobate will be pardoned."

It was Prof. Amerio who provided the best analysis of the council's fascination with democracy and its crass errors regarding "the people" in his chapter on "Democracy in the Church,"[89] but he did not mention the theology of the people, a post-conciliar Argentinian invention.

Jacques Maritain's encounter with Argentina was truly bizarre. Its first episode, when he arrived in Argentina in August 1936 to great acclaim, only to leave again in October, hated by those who had praised him after he sided with the "Reds" in the Spanish Civil War, was discussed in a previous section. Maritain made a reappearance at the council and emerged as the inspirer of the mission of the laity (and of the future Argentinian pope).

But it was an Argentinian priest, Fr. Julio Meinvielle, who wrote the finest refutation of the theories expounded by Maritain in *Humanisme ntegral*, in *De Lamennais à Maritain*, published in 1945 and translated into French in 1956. This seminal book was distributed throughout Latin America. Regrettably, the historian Olivier Compagnon, who in 2003 wrote an account of Jacques Maritain's trip to South America, was so biased as to portray Meinvielle as an anti-Semitic freak and a misuser of private correspondence.

---

[89]   Amerio, *Iota Unum*, p. 698.

One cannot understand the tidal wave of theologies underlying the council, or South American theologies for that matter, without reading Maritain. He did not inspire the entire dialectical apparatus involved, but with *Humanisme intégral* (1935), *Christianisme et Démocratie* (1943), and *Principes d'une politique humaniste* (1944), he fueled every revolution and fostered the loathing of the Tridentine Church. He was surpassed only by Emmanuel Mounier in *Feu la Chrétienté*, one of the latter's last great texts in which he set out his "clean slate" policy.

Pastoral theology

The essential principle of all liberationist literature is that of a new world or, to use Father Arrupe's words, *the Church of the future*. Everything in it is focused on the future. The great movement that is rocking the Church and the entire Latin American continent is the equivalent of the classless society of the world revolution—the radiant tomorrow after centuries of obscure night.

Pope Francis has coined a phrase to sum up the action that governs all things: "Open paths." Christ teaches: "I am the way and the truth and the life." This is a static approach that refers back to the past. The fifteen principles on which "popular pastoral care" is based clearly indicate that from now on, pastoral care will obey new criteria. The word *pastoral* has survived, but it has been stripped of its catechetical content. It no longer has any connection with traditional evangelization.

The new pastoral care masquerading as the "new evangelization" is all the more ambiguous in that Popes Paul VI, John Paul II, and Benedict XVI used these terms in a traditional sense, albeit always with a touch of novelty.

Its model is beyond doubt the apostolic exhortation *Evangelii Nuntiandi* of 1975, in which Paul VI delivered a masterful instruction on Catholic evangelization. In paragraph 58, he expressed an excellent criticism of liberationist "base communities." But in paragraph 38, he had already provided all the arguments justifying the

Church's collaboration in the "liberation" of mankind: "The Church strives always to insert the Christian struggle for liberation into the universal plan of salvation which she herself proclaims."

With John Paul II, the problem was different. In Port-au-Prince in March 1983, he forcefully condemned the continent's revolutionary undertakings, but he was caught in the meshes of Vatican II. Having stressed the shortage of priests, he called on the CELAM Assembly to make room for the laity in the Church in Latin America. He added that CELAM served as a reference point and a space for pastoral coordination: "A light that can guide the new evangelization . . . should be that of the Puebla document, which is dedicated to this theme, insofar as it is impregnated with the teaching of Vatican II and consistent with the Gospel. In this sense, it is necessary to spread and possibly to restore the *integrity* of the message of Puebla, without warped interpretations, without distorting reductionisms nor undue application of some parts and the eclipse of others."

However, by 1983, the official Church no longer had any control over what was happening on the continent. Everything was under liberationist command. This became clear with Cardinal Ratzinger's two documents of 1984 and 1986. While highly instructive, they had no impact whatsoever on their recipients, who had by then moved far beyond the Marxist phase of their struggles.

The cardinal's first letter made a distinction between the Marxist and the non-Marxist tendencies of liberation theology—*the theology of the people* would enthusiastically embrace the latter.

The result was a flurry of dizzying back and forths. No pope can erase the extraordinary story of the evangelization of this immense continent. John Paul II's homily on the theme in Santo Domingo the following year, on October 11, 1984, is well worth a read. It offered a precise and moving account of the epic missionary journeys of Spain and Portugal, and of the preservation of the faith over five centuries. The pope was himself enthralled by the story, for he knew what it meant to be attached to one's homeland and to one's faith! He was acutely conscious of the heroism and blood of the martyrs, having himself commemorated Poland's thousandth anniversary in 1966.

But those who still preserve this burning faith in Catholic America are now but a handful. John Paul II hoped to resurrect the soul of this continent—in vain. The last to have revived it was the papal nuncio Eugenio Pacelli in 1932, at the continent's first Eucharistic Congress in Buenos Aires. But in the past, this Christendom was handed over to masonry, and today it is a prey to liberationism. Pope Bergoglio's letter to the Argentinians, which he addressed to them through the local bishop on the occasion of the five hundredth anniversary of the first Mass in the country, is worth reading in this context. In sharp contrast with what was happening in the world with the COVID crisis and lockdowns, Francis focused on the people:

> Let's not allow the feast to fade away.... Today, as yesterday, the Lord's words resonate.... It is his priestly people that continues to multiply the loaves, so that no one lacks the food that gives life. It is his priestly people that knows how to "love one's neighbor as oneself," ingeniously and creatively ensuring that no one is left by the wayside.... It is the memorial of [the Lord's] hope that grants us the possibility, starting from all the things that make us different, to feel that we are a living part of a people, of his people.

A brief history of pastoral theology

"Pastoral theology" has flooded the world, particularly the Latin American continent. But it is neither theology nor pastoral care. The fifteen principles of Argentinian pastoral theology show that it is "pastoral care" without the Church and without doctrine, sacraments, or catechism. It has a long history that has gone hand in hand with all liberationist theological developments. For brevity's sake, we will follow below a study by Ramiro Pellitero, from the Faculty of Theology at the University of Navarre, *Evolución del concepto de "Teología Pastoral"* (Evolution of the concept of "Pastoral Theology").[90]

---

[90] Ramiro Pellitero, *"Evolución del concepto de 'Teología Pastoral,'"* Scripta Theologica no.° 32 (2000 /2).

Its earliest formulation as a theological science in its own right comes from Austria, Pellitero explains. In 1774, Empress Maria Theresa asked a Benedictine priest to undertake a reform of theological studies. In a chapter he called "Pastoral Theology," he defined it as "the systematic teaching of the duties of pastoral ministry." Three years later, he created a "practical course" outlining the three duties of priests: teaching, administering the sacraments, and edifying the faithful.

The bishop of Regensburg, J. M. Sailer (1751–1832), considered by many to be the father of pastoral theology, published his *Lessons on Pastoral Theology in Munich* (1789–1820) with the aim of training priests who would be able to foster the faithful's personal relationship with God in Christ. The Protestants, for their part, developed the discipline of "practical theology" with Schleiermacher (1768–1834); under the influence of Romanticism, this evangelical theologian focused on "the religion of feelings." He saw three disciplines as helping to guide souls: philosophical, historical (dogmatic), and practical theology ("the 'crown' of theology").

Turning back to the Catholics, Pellitero mentions A. Graf (1814–1867), a disciple of J. A. Mölher of Tübingen. Graf conceives of this practical theology as the "scientific self-awareness of the Church in its own self-edification," with a view to improving future ecclesial action and sees it as including transcendental factors (God, Christ, grace, etc.) and institutional factors, along with personal and social factors. In the footsteps of Graf, Franz Xaver Arnold (1898–1969), who was also inspired by Mölher and taught in Tübingen, specified that all the baptized are the responsible subjects of ecclesial activity. This is how pastoral theology became the theology of ecclesial action: word, faith, sacraments, and liturgy.

Karl Rahner later took up their ideas with the expression "self-realization of the Church."

The council used these words only once, but by calling it a "Pastoral Council," Pope John XXIII gave universal prominence to the concept; through it, everyone understood that the assistance of the Holy Spirit was not restricted to the institution but extended to the Church operating in the world. The council was a call to a charismatic, committed Church that did more than simply repeat formulas. Hence the life of the Church became a "theological place," requiring a theological praxis and a science of ecclesial action in relation to anthropology, to the socio-cultural, politics, and culture—a multi-purpose science, in short, capable of entering into dialogue with the modern world. Revelation was demoted to the last place.

Pastoral theology finally developed into an empirical science of action with two main components: a new, critical hermeneutic of the Church's work and a new ecclesial praxis.

In 1974, Protestant "pastoralists" defined practical theology as "the critical theory of praxis" in their publication *Théologie pratique*. This led to political theology, which was to have a direct influence on liberation theology. France and Italy entered the process, as did the United States and Canada.

One of the criteria for a valid pastoral theology is the recognition of the "signs of the times," which enable the discovery of divine will in human history, and thus the constant readjustment of theology to the contingencies of praxis, with a view to illuminating the lives of men.

This suggests that, outside the Church, there exists a superior, or at least different, and more useful mode of believing. The people, as the more "efficient," is here positioned as facing the Church, and the faithful people naturally imposes itself on the Church *docens* thanks to its status of "people *discens*."

The following egregious error was condemned by Pope Saint Pius X in his decree *Lamentabili* of July 4, 1907: "The 'Church learning' and the 'Church teaching' collaborate in such a way in defining truths that it only remains for the 'Church teaching' to sanction the opinions of the 'Church learning.' "

CHAPTER 8

The Amazon Synod, a Defining Expression of Pope Francis's Policy

The Synod on Amazonia that took place in October 2019 in Rome at the initiative of Pope Francis had been well prepared over an extended period of time. The wailings that accompanied it were truly shocking when it was only years of general indifference that allowed it to come as such a surprise. Yes, the pope did "bless" a statuette of a pagan divinity, the "Pachamama," in the Vatican gardens, surrounded by delegates from the Amazon. But the truth of the matter goes much deeper than that.

It lies in the collapse of the Catholic religion in the last remaining Christendom, the Christendom of the Hispanic New World that resisted Freemasonry in the eighteenth and nineteenth centuries and paid the price in blood, particularly in Mexico.

This Christendom was unable to withstand the Second Vatican Council. It collapsed because priests and religious, led by cowardly bishops, abandoned their faithful. These poor faithful simply could not understand the new religion of social struggle, let alone liberationist Masses. So they walked away, abandoning the Mass and the sacraments in which they had placed their faith. In Mexico, Archbishop Felipe Esquivel, archbishop emeritus of San Cristobal de Las Casas, a worthy successor to the liberationist Bishop Mendez Arceo, declared at the time of the synod that the Amazon was a theological place—that is, a place where the new faith is being shaped.

The collapse of the Catholic Church in Guatemala, El Salvador, and Brazil was the result of the council, to the benefit of religious sects. The number of baptized Catholics dropped from 90 percent to 50 percent or even less. As early as 1978, Ricardo Falla, a Jesuit specializing in religious sociology, had predicted what Sylvie Pédron-Colombani, a social anthropologist, would observe in 2001: "For several decades now, Guatemala has been undergoing a religious transformation of the very highest order, as part of a process of diversification, competition and internationalization. One of the main forces behind this process of change is Pentecostalism, whose numbers and influence are obvious to all" (*Pentecôtisme et diversification religieuse au Guatemala*).

I was a personal witness to this situation on the ground; in Brazil, I saw "show" Masses, in Nicaragua, Sandinista Masses, and in El Salvador, guerrilla Masses led by a Belgian priest and ending with the Communist Party anthem. The faithful were well aware of all this and decided to leave their parishes where they no longer understood to which church their parish priest actually belonged. They joined friendly congregations where no one asked them if they belonged to the church of social struggles. They fled from the mindset so well described by Jesuit missionary James Guadalupe Carney, who in 1987 ended his account of the social struggles in Honduras with a chapter called "To be a Christian is to be a revolutionary!"

The staircase of the "House of Works" in São Paulo, Brazil, where activists from the Amazon used to meet, was decorated with posters praising Communist fighters in the Vietnam War and Fidel Castro's regime, as I also personally observed in 1986.

The Peruvian Communist Party had been involved in the political struggle for the "Indios" since before 1940, but without success. It was only when the Church transformed herself into an army dedicated to social struggle, and dressed up revolutionary rhetoric in evangelical language, that a breakthrough was finally achieved. The faithful of Hispano-American Christendom, who had resisted every kind of anti-Catholic and Masonic subversions, were perverted by the conciliar clergy and the reforms of Vatican II. Argentina is a case in point. It should be remembered that the first Eucharistic Congress held in Latin America was an immense triumph for this Marian people, but nevertheless, Argentina became the testing ground and spearhead of the revolution which is still ongoing in our time.

In the middle of the Amazon Synod on October 20, 2019, Cardinal Hummes, symbolically wearing a "relic"—the stole of Dom Hélder Câmara—highlighted this conciliar legacy in his homily on the occasion of the renewal of the Pact of the Catacombs. His words were based on a recently-published interview of the superior of the Society of St. Pius X, in which the latter mocked those who criticized the synod. Cardinal Hummes quoted from memory: "You can't be against the Synod, that would be meaningless. How can you be against the Synod, since the Synod is a legitimate fruit of Vatican II? We are not in that position. We are against it because we were against Vatican II: you cannot be against it." Cardinal Hummes added: "As for us, we must give thanks to God for this beautiful fruit of Vatican II" (*Nos damos graças a Deus por esse fruto belo do Vaticano II*).

Although it is true that the "Pachamama" statuette business was an act of incredible idolatry at the Amazon Synod, Catholic commentators would have done better to educate the faithful about the origins of this disaster. They should have looked beyond the synod "show," which was nothing more than the visible expression of an abysmal state of disorder: "Because of you, the name of God is reviled among the Gentiles" (Rom 2:24).

The Argentinian pope had been in office for over six years, but when it came to the synod, little thought was given to whether there might be something "Argentinian" about it. They forgot that the cardinal of Buenos Aires was the principal drafter of the final text of the 2007 CELAM Assembly, and that this text was the pope's plan of action.

Simplistic explanations were sought. It was the fault of the Germans and their funding; it was the fault of the Germans and their bishops. It was the fault of Hélder Câmara, of John Paul II and Benedict XVI, of Leonardo Boff, of Obama and Angela Merkel. And, of course, the cardinals now installed in Rome, the Jesuits, and the whole machinery of government put in place since 2013.

Given the impact made by the Amazon Synod, it is therefore necessary to look for the root causes of this "synodal birthing."

The place to go is the renewal of the Pact of the Catacombs at Sancta Domitilla in Rome, on October 20, 2019: the updated text of this pact provides the initial clue. By signing it, the attendees pledged the following: "To assume, in the face of extreme global warming and the depletion of natural resources, the commitment, in our territories and with our attitudes, to defend the Amazon jungle. From it come the gifts of water for much of the South American territory, the contribution to the carbon cycle, and the regulation of the global climate, an incalculable biodiversity and a rich socio-diversity for humanity and the entire earth."

The updated pact concludes with this statement: "We celebrate this Eucharist of the Covenant as 'a pact of cosmic love.' "

As mentioned above, the Pact of the Catacombs, which was signed on the sidelines of Vatican II in 1965, gave birth to the Revolutionary Church of Latin America and coined the slogan "The Church of the poor." Because it was renewed at the Amazon Synod, the latter was viewed as the logical continuation of the 1965 pact.

It is worth mentioning that alongside Cardinal Hummes, the Jesuit Father Pedro Barreto, a cardinal recently created by Pope Francis, also took part in this solemn ceremony. In 2020, he took over as head of REPAM (Pan-Amazonian Ecclesial Network), created in 2014, and that had since been chaired by Cardinal Hummes. It was REPAM that was responsible for organizing the Synod on Amazonia, including—most importantly—on the ideological level.

On January 31, 2022, on the fiftieth anniversary of the meeting of Amazonian bishops in Santarém, Brazil, a press release from REPAM made the connection with Vatican II:

> The Second Vatican Council made a decisive mark on the life of the Church, particularly in Latin America, which has committed itself to implementing the reflections of the most recent Council in the history of the Church into local reality.

Medellín can be viewed as the Vatican II of Latin America, and in the same vein, Santarém could be viewed as the Vatican II of the Brazilian Amazonia. The year 2022 marks the 50th anniversary of the IVth Pastoral Encounter of Amazonia, which took place from May 24 to 30, 1972, and brings to mind the words of Pope Paul VI declaring that "Christ points to Amazonia." Those words led the Church in the region to search for Lines of Priority for Pastoral Care in Amazonia. . . .

By 1972, the bishops were already sounding the alarm about the limitations and dangers of the Amazonian reality, anticipating problems that have worsened over time. At this stage, the Church in Amazonia has identified "four priorities and four series of pastoral services, in the light of these two fundamental lines of action: incarnation in reality and liberating evangelization."

Incarnation in reality is a fruit of knowledge of the people and of living with them; it was intended to lead to insights that were subsequently taken up: "Overcoming any paternalism, any ethnocentrism, any imported, prefabricated or artificial model of life." But it also became the starting ground for a liberating evangelization, without dichotomies, mindful of "the signs of place and time, of cultures and groups, of nature and man," which seeks to build awareness with a view to human liberation.

Seen like this, the synod clearly emerges as the outcome of an earlier revolution, and not merely an incidental effect of present-day anarchy.

In order to identify the link between the Second Vatican Council and the synod, it is important to recall four main drivers of the ideology prevailing in the Vatican in general, and at the synod in particular. These can be identified as modernism, conciliarism—the role of Argentina and Latin America which we have already discussed at length—and globalism, together with the network of NGOs promoting it. This is all fueled by intellectual, editorial, clerical, operational, and financial networks that are by no means limited to Germany. In Managua, the names of associations, including Swedish and Swiss groups, which financed the Sandinista revolution and the revolutionary movement throughout the continent, appear on a roll of honor. From France, the CCFD (Catholic Committee against Hunger and for Development) is on the list, immediately followed by the CGT.[91] The Catholic Church—that is, the universal Church—would appear to have shifted into a revolutionary globalist mode.

I. Modernist and conciliar causes

We have already discussed at length the role of modernism, abetted by the sudden incursion of its proponents at the Second Vatican Council, along with its experts Yves Congar, Henri de Lubac, and Karl Rahner. Modernism, and its "direction of history," was served equally well by the Jesuit army and their real "Great Reformer," Father Arrupe, and by the liberationist theorists, all of whom studied in Europe.

II. Argentinian and Latin American causes

We saw in chapter 4 how the CELAM Assembly in Medellín in 1968 was manipulated thanks to its long-term preparation, as was the Amazon Synod some fifty years later, in which nothing was left to chance. Laurent Dandrieu remarked in *Valeurs actuelles*: "You get the impression that everything was pre-planned, pre-chewed, pre-digested."

The two CELAM assemblies in Puebla (Mexico) in 1979, where Lucio Gera played a key role, and in Aparecida (Brazil) in 2007, where Cardinal Bergoglio was the mastermind, both benefitted from a similarly thorough preparation. Here, dissent has no voice; it is eliminated either before, during, or after the meeting. Anything that might hinder the march of the liberationist Church is reduced to silence.

In 1969, the bishops of Argentina published the "Declaration of San Miguel" on the adjustment of the conclusions of Medellín to the country's realities. The forty-two-page document showed an attempt at resistance, only to be overwhelmed by Lucio Gera's indictment that

---

[91]   Translator's note: General Confederation of Labor, a French communist union.

was published in Uruguay the following year, in which he also promoted liberation theology, as shown in chapter 6.

It marked the beginning of the breakdown of Argentinian church structures. Recurring themes took root: the Church of the poor ("The poor are the sacrament of Christ," Pope Paul VI told the peasants of Colombia in 1968!) and the integral promotion of man through the education of consciences, mental renewal, and prophetic denunciation. As shown above, the Church was henceforth to understand its liberating action in terms of the people and their interests, since the people are the subject and agent of human history, which itself is intimately linked to salvation history.

These ideas led to a conquest of power that Leonardo Boff clearly presented in 2000 in *¿Qué Iglesia queremos?* (What Church do we want?).

For Boff, base communities are an alternative to ecclesiastical power. His assessment was illustrated by a picture in which the old clerical powers were being replaced by the new powers emerging from the People of God. The base communities, he argued, had gained their ideological autonomy and were "developing a consistent theological conception," albeit still very imperfect, but moving toward a "new, networked way of being Church": "It is fragile, but it has the strength of the very delicate roots extracting the deep sap that nourishes the majestic Amazonian walnut tree. Base communities are so charged with promise and hope that an alternative to ecclesial power is not an impossibility." According to Boff, the pauperist and Protestant movements of the sixteenth century also seized historical opportunities to challenge Rome's power. If these remarks are associated with the action of the Holy Spirit, the true author of the synod, the connection is clear!

But Boff went even deeper in his analysis. He rejected the idea of a clergy subject to canonical rules that would identify it with the old. Base ecclesial communities were not meant to be "merely a new configuration of power and another way of being Church, but also a spirit of 'communion' (*comunional*) and participation capable of permeating all ecclesial and social spaces." Boff was very sure of himself:

he proclaimed that this reform was supported by cardinals, bishops, priests, religious, and so on.

Seen in their relationship with the synod, these words indicate that demands for a new form of priesthood are not intended to make up for the shortage of priests or to flatter feminists but to establish the new clergy of the new Church.

In one of his personal testimonies, Boff described how, on his return from Germany where he had just received his doctorate in theology, he was sent to the Amazon; that is where he was converted to the "Church of the poor."

Behind its humanitarian and ecological façade, the Amazon Synod was firmly rooted in the Argentinian "theology" of 1969. And following the example of the people, the Amazon was declared a "theological place." Sixty years on, it is clear how far we have come; by coincidence, it was exactly sixty years ago that Father Bergoglio was ordained a priest on December 13, 1969.

The working document for the Synod of Bishops on Amazonia, the *Instrumentum laboris*, explicitly connected the synod with the Argentinian theology of 1969:

> Furthermore, we can say that the Amazon—or another indigenous or communal territory—is not only an *ubi* or a where (a geographical space), but also a *quid* or a what, a place of meaning for faith or the experience of God in history. Thus, territory is a *theological place* [our emphasis] where faith is lived, and also a particular source of God's revelation: epiphanic places where the reserve of life and wisdom for the planet is manifest, a life and wisdom that speaks of God. In the Amazon, the 'caresses of God' become manifest and become incarnate in history."[92]

On the eve of the synod, Leonardo Boff gave an interview to cath. ch, the Swiss Catholic Portal. Asked about his views on the significance of the convening of the Amazon Synod, he replied: "I see this as a unique opportunity for Pope Francis to bring about the changes

---

[92]   *Instrumentum laboris*, no. 19.

that the center of religious power in the Vatican has never managed to implement. Firstly, the synodal nature of the meeting must be emphasized, meaning that decisions depend on all participants, including the indigenous peoples. The text is clear: the point is not to convert cultures, but to evangelize them, so that a new Church is born, with a native face, with its ancestral wisdom, with its rites and customs."

On the subject of the "conservatives" who from the outset had "raised their voices against certain important contents" that were about to be discussed, Leonardo Boff stated: "Those in Europe and the United States who accuse the Pope of heresy because of certain passages in the preparatory text for the synod are the same ones who are hostage to the European paradigm, forgetting that Christianity today was born of the incorporation of Greek, Latin and Germanic cultures. Why not allow our peoples to do the same? . . . There is a very real 'ecclesiogenesis' here, this is the birth of a real Church, that is Catholic and has a different face."[93]

Clearly, the Amazon is a state-of-the-art base community!

Boff added: "Pope Francis represents this new kind of Church, offering a different vision of the exercise of sacred power, one that is simple and evangelical, placing the emphasis not on doctrines and dogmas, but on the living encounter with Jesus."

In response to a question about "threats to our planet's ecological balance," he explained why Pope Francis had chosen the Amazon as the focus of the synod: "The Amazon has a decisive role to play in determining the future of life. This is why he wanted the Synod to be held in Rome, so that all of mankind could follow the discussions and become aware of the grave crisis facing the Earth-system and the Life-system."

Preparations for the Synod on Amazonia were already in full swing in December 2018 when Pope Francis sent a letter of congratulations to Leonardo Boff on his eightieth birthday, which the latter published on his blog:

---

[93]   Leonardo Boff is here referring to his book *Eclesiogênese. As communidades de base reinventam a Igreja* – Petrópolis, 1977.

Dear Brother,

Thank you for your letter sent through Fr. Fabian. I received it with pleasure and thank you for the generosity of your comments.

I remember our first meeting in San Miguel, at a CLAR reunion, sometime between '72 and '75. I've been following you ever since, reading some of your works.

In these days you will be celebrating your 80th birthday. I wish you all the best.

Please don't forget to pray for me. I'm also praying for you and your wife.

May God bless you and may the Blessed Virgin protect you. Fraternally yours,

Francisco

Commentators interpreted this as a recognition of the defrocked liberationist (and now an environmentalist) theologian's struggles.

The next synod, in 2023 and 2024, has as its subject the Synodal Church.

NOTE. The Medellín, Puebla, and Aparecida Assemblies were presided over by Popes Paul VI, John Paul II, and Benedict XVI respectively. Their speeches were, of course, perfectly orthodox, perhaps even unexpected in a liberationist context. However, it seems that at no point did they actually assess the realities of the situation. But it must be said that in Rome, there were not only cardinals such as Silvestrini but also a powerful team of liberationists including men like Cardinal Pironio and Father Arrupe, who were present at all levels of government and influence in the Church. Later on in this investigation, we will discuss another agent who has been active since 1972.

III. Globalism

Shortly after Pope Francis had "blessed" a pagan statuette during the Amazon Synod, Alexander Tschugguel, a twenty-six-year-old man from Vienna, seized five identical statuettes of the Pachamama that were on display in a church on the Via della Conciliazione and threw them into the Tiber.

His deed was hailed by Bishop Athanasius Schneider as one that would go down in Church history. It was the starting point for concerted action and prayers of reparation for the sacrileges that had been committed in the precincts of the Vatican, in the presence of the pope and with his active participation. Tschugguel has given several interviews. In addition to the fact that he is a convert from Lutheranism with a profound knowledge and informed judgment of Catholic doctrine, his testimony is of interest to us precisely because of a point that other commentators had failed to note.

He made it quite clear that he is a layman, not a cleric, and that in a situation like this, everyone, having prayed and reflected, must act.

Thanks to his good knowledge of the synod's context, he gave two precise, overlapping indications: one in English, in an interview published by LifeSiteNews on November 4, 2019, and the other published in French by Jeanne Smits on her blog, on the same day.

"The synod goes hand in hand with the globalist agenda, too," he told LifeSite. To Jeanne Smits, he explained that he had asked Brazilian participants about the theological aspect of the synod: "They told us point-blank: 'That's not what the synod is about at all. The synod is a political matter.' "

So far, all the comments on Alexander's deed focused on the legitimacy of his act and on the sacrilege that took place in the Vatican. If the synod is solely a political affair that has long been in tune with a change in the Church desired by Cardinal Bergoglio, then the lay faithful really should understand at last what is their place in today's battles.

Cardinal Bergoglio and his informant of more than fifty years

According to the definition given by its specialists, the *"globalist agenda"* is the plan to bring all the world's inhabitants under the control of a single state (or of a single "governance"), the New World Order.

Alexander Tschugguel's first remark reminded me of a book I read a few years ago: *Globalisation et Humanisme chrétien* by Guzmán Carriquiry Lecour, translated from the Spanish, with a preface by Cardinal Marc Ouellet. The author was no stranger to me. I had met him among the editors of the Uruguayan magazine *Víspera* in 1970. This magazine featured almost all the writers who contributed to liberationist literature on the Latin American continent. The editorial secretary was also a Carriquiry.

The magazine was circulated in sixteen Latin American countries, the United States and Canada, and in Europe via Brussels. Forty-five years later, I discovered that Guzmán Carriquiry had become undersecretary of the Pontifical Council for the Laity shortly after the election of Pope John Paul II. His path from a "leftist" magazine to a position at the heart of the Vatican called for some serious investigation.

In Rome since 1971

Guzmán Carriquiry Lecour was born in Montevideo on May 20, 1944. He was very active in the Catholic University Youth movement and in the faculty members of the University of Montevideo, and he held a doctorate in law and humanities. He was both a teacher and a lawyer and also worked as a journalist. As a young graduate, he was appointed director of the Uruguayan Church's National Center for Social Communications. His involvement with *Víspera* brought him into close contact with one of the great inspirers of Lucio Gera and Father Bergoglio: the theologian, philosopher, and historian Alberto Methol Ferré. Carriquiry developed a close friendship with Methol Ferré, whom he still regards as his master. On December 1, 1971, following a joint initiative by the archbishop of Montevideo, Bishop Carlos Partelli, and Cardinal Cardjins' first successor, Bishop Marcel Uylenbroeck, secretary of the Pontifical Council for the Laity that had just been created by Paul VI, Carriquiry became a member of the said council.

His function was to accompany, encourage, and direct the particulation of the lay faithful in the life and mission of the Church. After three years, as the first layman to hold this post, he was appointed head of office of the dicastery. By the time Pope John Paul II was elected, Carriquiry was already well-known to Karol Wojtyla, who maintained his appointment. On December 12, 1991, John Paul II appointed him undersecretary of the Pontifical Council for the Laity—again, he was the first layman to hold this post. On May 14, 2011, Pope Benedict XVI appointed him secretary of the Commission for Latin America. On May 2, 2014, Pope Francis named him secretary in charge of the commission's vice-presidency. On April 20, 2019, at age seventy-five, Carriquiry tendered his resignation but did not give up his personal collaboration with the pope; he was appointed ambassador of Uruguay to the Holy See in July 2020 and presented his credentials to Francis the following January.

We have chosen to present the essential elements of this exceptional life story because Guzmán was always Father Bergoglio's informant in Rome, and he remained so when Bergoglio became bishop and cardinal-archbishop of Buenos Aires, and finally Pope Francis: in the course of over half a century, he came to know not only the Curia but all the structures and men associated with it.

The direct testimony of Carriquiry himself, presented by Nicolas Senèze, a journalist from the French daily *La Croix* who did an interview with him, is conclusive.

> Hailing from the opposite banks of the Rio de La Plata, the Argentinian and the Uruguayan have known each other for a long time. . . . At the time, Fr. Jorge Mario Bergoglio was the young provincial of the Argentinian Jesuits, and between these two men, who were both steeped in the same culture of an effervescent post-conciliar Latin America, the chemistry flowed instantly. "*Whenever he came to Rome, he would spend his first evening at our home. Every time I visited Buenos Aires, I went to*

see him," Carriquiry recalls. *"In my dealings with Father, Bishop, and then Cardinal Bergoglio, every time he spoke to us about the great problems of the Church and the world, I was a witness to his profound spiritual discernment and to the way he put us in the presence of God when he was discussing them."*

Guzmán Carriquiry knows Cardinal Bergoglio so well that, when the 2013 conclave opened, he shared with a few friends his conviction that the archbishop of Buenos Aires would emerge from it as Pope. *"The situation in the Curia was such that someone from the periphery, with a strong pastoral and missionary experience as well as great determination was needed to assume the succession to Peter,"* he remembers. *"In Aparecida, I had seen his wisdom and determination in leading a far-reaching ecclesial event, and I was well acquainted with his temperament, forged by spiritual exercises and a strong discipline of prayer."*

When he became Pope, Francis knew he could count on this loyal friend, an expert on the mysteries of the Curia where he first arrived in 1971.[94]

During this interview, Carriquiry said not a word about Cardinal Ratzinger's election in 2005, although during that conclave, the latter had faced Cardinal Bergoglio in the last ballot. Nor did he mention Pope Benedict XVI's resignation. Senèze didn't even question him on this point.

Guzmán has been everywhere, seen everything. He took part in four General Assemblies of the World Synod of Bishops as an expert; he was a member of Holy See delegations to UN conferences; he prepared papal trips to Latin America; he was the organizer of the World Youth Days in Rome in 1985 and in Madrid in 2011; he selected the associations, movements, and ecclesial communities that were allowed to have a representation in Rome; he was an expert at the three CELAM Assemblies in 1979, 1992, and 2007—Medellín, Puebla, and Aparecida. He has lectured widely: for example, he was one of the speakers at the Milwaukee, Wisconsin symposium, *Discovering Pope Francis*, on

---

[94]   *La Croix*, December 16, 2016.

October 8–11, 2018. He is a Commander of the Order of Merit of the Italian Republic; a Knight Grand Cross of the Order of Saint Gregory the Great (Holy See); Grand Cross of the Order of Bernardo O'Higgins (Chile); Grand Cross of the Order of May (Argentina).

The geopolitics of Francis

In order to grasp the significance of all this, it is necessary to turn to Marcelo Gullo, one of the leading experts on the pope's political thinking and his conception of globalization.

First of all, Gullo points out that there is an "inescapable need to understand the deep geopolitical thinking of a man who will hold in his hands the destiny of one of the most important players on the world geopolitical stage."

Gullo believes that the deepest roots of the pope's political thinking lie in the popular nationalism of Manuel Ugarte, José Vasconcelos, Juan Domingo Perón, and Alberto Methol Ferré.

According to Marcelo Gullo, the pope's key concern is to oppose the "imperial conception of globalization" (the Anglo-Saxon conception) by "building the Unity of South America" within the framework of a "multipolar world." Citing Bergolio's writings, he observes that the pope's aim is to build the political unity of the Latin American "Patria Grande" through "Social Justice."

This demonstrates that the Amazon Synod not only involved shameful and idolatrous fooling around but, more importantly, a political project. To understand the thinking of the future pope, Cardinal Bergoglio, one must turn to the preface he gave in 2005 to Carriquiry's book *Una apuesta por América Latina* (An Appeal for Latin America) which bears a different name from its French "translation," *Globalisation et humanisme chrétien*, due to a number of differences between the two texts.

It is common knowledge that the pope is no theologian. He never answers purely theological questions put to him, preferring to brand his "opponents" with a variety of labels more suited to the simplistic nature of political life.

On the other hand, Cardinal Bergoglio enthusiastically set out on the path of globalist politics. In his prologue to Guzmán Carriquiry's book, he underlined the author's passion and intelligence. While admitting that he lacked "the political and technical competence to deal with many problems—this is not the task of a Pastor of the Church," he stressed the educational value of the book and the opportunity it offered to "build paths of hope."

This aspect is dear to his heart, and he therefore resorted to an expression favored by the Peronists: he proclaimed the necessity of "a vast endeavor of education, mobilization and constructive participation of peoples—that is to say, of individuals or families, of the most varied communities and associations, of an *organized community* [emphasis added]—that sets in motion the best resources of humanity hailing from our tradition." He wrote that this great movement should be grounded on "a Catholic and Latin American self-awareness" and a "Catholic understanding of Latin American development."

The cardinal underlined another of the book's merits: it "reveals the confidence and power of the Catholic faith of our peoples, both from the point of view of intelligence and the transformation of reality, and as a response to the aspirations for truth, justice and happiness that beat in the hearts of Latin Americans and in the authentic culture of its peoples, which bears the imprints of evangelization. Here we find the seeds of a new creation in a world torn apart." Such eloquence! This sounds like a whole new evangelization!

In the next paragraph, however, this bombastic mood gave way to a new and unexpected political realism. Bergoglio described two opposing forms of globalization. The first was imperial globalization, a "perfect, polished sphere" that merges peoples "into a uniformity that cancels out the tension between particularities": he called it "the most dangerous totalitarian globalization of postmodernity." The second was "true globalization, which must be conceived of not as a sphere, but as a polyhedron" preserving each person's identity and particularities "which unite in harmonious tension, seeking the common good." The cardinal expounded his thoughts in an expression he had coined to illustrate the ability of peoples to live in harmony with their particular facets: "the idiosyncrasy of peoples."

Fourteen years later, on October 8, 2019, the pope would use the same expression in his opening address to the Special Assembly of the Amazon Synod. "Let us approach the Amazonian peoples on tip-toe," he said; according to the pontiff, it is necessary to flee the "'homogenizing' and 'homogenative' centralism" that has "not allowed the peoples' authenticity to emerge." Any ideological colonization that "destroys the idiosyncrasy of peoples" is therefore to be avoided at all costs, said Francis.

Note that the term *idiosyncrasy* is the one used by the pope in Spanish; it has been translated as "characteristics" in the official English version of the speech.

The terms *polyhedron* and *idiosyncrasy of peoples* belong to a very specific vocabulary, from which Bergoglio has borrowed both as cardinal and pope. They belong to the keywords of his politics.

From whom did he borrow the extraordinary phrase "idiosyncrasy of peoples"?

The word *idiosyncrasy* crops up in scholarly treatises on the characteristics of specific populations or groups. It can also be used to indicate the particularities of an individual. The Bergoglian language extends its meaning to "peoples." It occurs twice in Lucio Gera's work.

The question is: Who was using this expression in Argentina in 2005, or before?

There is in fact only one possible source: Paul Verdevoye, arguably the best French connoisseur of nineteenth-century Argentinian history. A prolific author, he wrote in Argentinian Spanish, whose linguistic variations he had meticulously scrutinized. He delved into the nooks and crannies of successive migrations to discover, in the sediments of the waves that populated Argentina, the constitutive elements of the Argentinian people, and indeed of the Argentinian nation.

In a five-hundred-page compendium, published by his family and friends a year after his death in 2001, some thirty studies were compiled that retrace his brilliant career as a researcher. The volume is entitled *Literatura Argentina e idiosincrasia*. The word *idiosyncrasy* was used by Verdevoye only in the last text of the book, "The first two generations of Argentinian-Jewish writers," in which he observed: "Ever since I became familiar with, or rather was familiarized with, Spanish-American idiosyncrasy, I noted that one of the most constant obsessions in Spanish-speaking America was the search for and expression of national or continental identities."[95]

It's fair to say that all his work and his extraordinary investigations were at the service of this aspiration. Among other things, Verdevoye is the most outstanding translator of Martin Fierro, Argentina's defining national poem. He has inspired research into the idiosyncrasies of Mexico, El Salvador, and Peru, as each of these countries seeks to distinguish itself from the others while at the same time finding common ground to form the "*Patria Grande*."

But this research has shown that there is no such thing as the idiosyncrasy of peoples and that Verdevoye totally ignores the only factor that unites these peoples: the Catholic religion.

For their part, Jewish writers for a time found in Argentina something like a new Jerusalem. But as they settled in, they made their mark on their own territory, setting themselves apart from any idiosyncrasy. Verdevoye married one of his Jewish students. José Isaacson, one of his loyal followers, wrote the preface and created the title of the book *Literatura Argentina e idiosincrasia*. Isaacson repeatedly stresses that Verdevoye was a humanist and also completely alien to any form of methodological fundamentalism.

As mentioned in our study of his references to Romano Guardini, Bergoglio, both as cardinal and pope, overreached the author he was referring to, since in Verdevoye's view, there is no such thing as the idiosyncrasy of peoples in general. On reflection, this is not so strange, since by virtue of the law of the polyhedron, peoples are all different and irreducible to each other in a utopian, planetary vision.

Guzmán Carriquiry's aforementioned book, *Globalization and Christian Humanism*, released in French in 2007 with a preface by

---

95   Verdevoye, *Literatura argentina e idiosincrasia*, p. 471.

Cardinal Ouellet, belongs to a highly politicized genre in which, starting with the title, the Christian ideal no longer really stands out. It is essentially an analysis of the economic situation and of the influence exerted by the United States on Latin America. Carriquiry argues against the globalization of US culture, highlighting the economic and cultural elements of the Southern Cone that could enable it finally to become a true continental and global partner in the concert of nations.

Carriquiry presents Mercosur, a kind of common market created in 1991 between Argentina, Uruguay, Brazil, and Paraguay (joined by Venezuela in 2012 before its suspension in 2019), as a first positive move in this direction. So doing, he follows the opinion of Alberto Methol Ferré, the Uruguayan thinker whom Cardinal Bergoglio so much admired; he was the author's teacher and friend. "The small homelands get by thanks to the Great Latin American Homeland of the South American Union, which must pass through the difficult and necessary main avenue of Mercosur," wrote Carriquiry.

A large number of magazines and institutions worked at fostering the illusion that this coming together of Latin American countries would actually take place. As Brazilian sociologist and political scientist Hélio Jaguaribe put it in 1999: "Mercosur is a passport to history."

But North America was quick to respond. NAFTA, the free trade agreement between the United States, Canada, and Mexico, was created in 1992, followed in 1994 by the FTAA, the Free Trade Area of the Americas from Alaska to Tierra del Fuego. The latter organization has been inactive since 2005. In 2011, a new entity came into being: the Pacific Alliance, comprising Chile, Peru, Bolivia, and Mexico.

Brazil broke away the same year, in 2011, by joining the BRICS (Brazil, Russia, India, China, and South Africa).

Using the *lex mercatoria* to unite peoples is part of the wild dream of globalization.

A bit of history

Since the South American states were established between 1800 and 1820, every dictator in power has dreamed of uniting with his neighbor on the model of the North American States. Unfortunately, neither

Bolivar nor any other founder succeeded. On the contrary, through-out the nineteenth century and the first third of the next—it was in 1930 that all Paraguay's neighbors sought to annex this impoverished country—wars proliferated. The only thing these new states had in common was Freemasonry. The only non-Masonic head of state, García Moreno, president of Ecuador, was assassinated out of hatred of the Catholic faith in 1875.

These continuous wars are evidence of the feudalists' determina-tion to assert themselves at any price.

Argentina was no exception. Freemason Domingo Faustino Sarmiento, who was president from 1868 to 1874 after two years as ambassador of Argentina to the United States, applied the formulas of the "Conquest of the West" to his own country. He ordered the massa-cre of over 150,000 Indians, whom he considered as barbarians and an obstacle to Argentina's entry into the modern world of European nations.

"Will we succeed in exterminating the Indians? I have an invinci-ble repugnance for the savages of America, one that I find impossible to overcome. These scoundrels are nothing more than a bunch of dis-gusting Indians whom I would hang without a moment's notice if they were to reappear. Lautaro and Caupolicán are filthy Indians, because that's what they all are. They are incapable of progress, and their exter-mination is providential and useful, sublime and great. They should be exterminated, without sparing even the smallest, who already possess an instinctive hatred of civilized man," he wrote in *El Nacional* on November 25, 1876.

In a letter to General Mitre in 1861, Sarmiento advised: "Don't try to save the *gauchos'* blood. This is fertilizer that must be made useful to the country. Blood is the only human thing about them."

Sarmiento instituted free, compulsory secular education modeled on that of Jules Ferry with the aim of securing a population committed to progressive ideas. He was totally focused on imitating Europe and the United States.

General Perón was to take up the same idea of a mythical Latin-American "great fatherland" and even sought to join forces with Fidel Castro to this end.

As globalization advances, this far-reaching agenda has, in turn, been taken up by Pope Francis, who preaches to the whole world about dialogue, encounters, and conflict resolution. It was on his initiative that a World Day of Universal Fraternity was instituted on February 4, 2020.

Ever since the council, the Society of Jesus has steered Latin American states toward liberation struggles against economic and cultural dependency. The idea is still the same; only the ideological driving force has changed.

Guzmán Carriquiry wrote about religious inculturation in 2005: "The privileged religious expression of Ibero-American crossbreeding is the Marian devotion. It holds the real key to interpreting the Baroque.... The images of Pachamama (Mother Earth) and Tonantzin (mother of all men) . . . have found in Mary the possibility of being understood, of integrating and of enhancing the real experience of the encounter of peoples who were beginning to know each other."[96]

In 2011, in *El bicentenario de la independencia de América latina*, Carriquiry used the same refrain and was once again praised by the future pope. In his prologue, Cardinal Bergoglio condemned "godspray," a vague theism with no historical incarnation, at best the creator of "Masonic ecumenism."

In 2012, during his acceptance speech as honorary doctor of the Pontifical Catholic University of Argentina, Carriquiry again spoke on the same theme, with a damper because of his audience: "No Latin American symbol is more inclusive—far more inclusive than the so-called mother earth in which indigenous traditions mix with pantheistic ecologies and new age sensitivities—than Marian images, especially that of Our Lady of Guadalupe, and the suffering, patient faces of the Christ of Esquipulas in Guatemala, the Lord of Miracles in Peru and other Latin American Christs. They symbolize both cultural crossbreeding and enculturated evangelization."

With the arrival of Francis, the world has once again become bipolar. Sarmiento's modernity is matched by the pope's, which is radical

---

96   Carriquiry, *Globalisation et humanisme chrétien*, pp. 184–85.

and ruthless: a popular tyrant, to borrow a phrase from Fustel de Coulanges.

Today's enemies of globalization are the Indians of yesterday. They are "executed" as Pharisees, neo-Gnostics, or Pelagians. In times gone by, ignorant Indians were an obstacle to globalization; today, the obstacle is made up of "elitist minorities" in the pay of "political oligarchies," old clerics, and the like, parked in reserves from which it is hoped they will never emerge. They are the advocates of a "globalization of exclusion and indifference," in the words of Francis in his 2015 speech to popular movements in Bolivia. They are nothing in the face of holy ecological globalization.

So what are the Amazonian Indians? They are like a new Cuba, where all the miraculous innovations of a polyhedral Church will be thoroughly tested!

The pope's globalization is a conjunction of the myths of *La Patria Grande* and universal peace, through the eradication of poverty and the struggle of the poor against the rich. These struggles are as old as the hills, if Fustel de Coulanges is to be believed. The question then arises as to whether the myth of *La Patria Grande* and universal peace (including the existence of all religions "willed by God in his wisdom," as the Abu Dhabi Document signed by Francis asserts), is the path chosen by the pope to change the Catholic Church. Or has the Church of Francis already yielded to the third temptation and, having made the choice to deny the Church of Christ, is it preparing to rule the world, spiritual and temporal? Has this been Jorge Mario Bergoglio's personal choice for a long time? Is it a choice shared with others who brought him to power? Will Rome become the second UN?

IV. The globalist plan invoked by Alexander Tschugguel does exist: proof from the NGOs

Rather than going back to the ancient Greeks, we will start with a seminar organized in Rio de Janeiro in May 2008 by the Forum for a New Global Governance (FnGM) and iBase (the Brazilian Institute for

Social and Economic Analysis). The title given to this meeting was in itself a blueprint: *What Amazonia does the world need?*

The forum's presentation brochure immediately answered this question: "In this dawning of the twenty-first century, it is poised to become one of those essential places where humankind will find the biological, political, and cultural resources of a new relationship—with the biosphere and among all peoples—founded on dignity and solidarity. This is the challenge: to place Amazonia at the heart of the debate for the construction of another world, a world of social and sustainable justice, of equality and diversity, of citizens' rights and shared responsibilities."

This is not the place to present a comprehensive overview of this organization, now known as the World Democratic Forum, whose website is called world-governance.org. This website seems to have been inactive since 2016. The FnGM had partners in Brazil, Chile, Mexico, China, India, the Philippines, Mauritania, South Africa, France, Spain, and Lebanon. With its website in four languages—French, English, Chinese, and Spanish—the forum covered entire regions under the patronage of Gandhi, Mandela, Martin Luther King, Confucius, and Flora Tristan.

In its view, the Amazon was not the only region of the world to raise questions: there were also Colombia, Palestine, China, and Europe. Specialists monitored all sectors, from the sharing economy to global nuclear governance and terrorism.

The FnGM also created a global governance index, the WGI, whose latest report dates back to 2011. French contributors to the site included Lieutenant-Colonel Renaud François, lawyer William Bourdon, General Jean-René Bachelet (UNPROFOR, former army inspector), and Brigadier General Hugues de Courtivron, consultant to the Geneva Centre for the Democratic Control of Armed Forces.

Last but not least, Matthieu Calame, who liaised with the Swiss-based Charles Léopold Mayer Foundation for the Progress of Humankind, was also in charge of programs at the foundation. The latter continues to fund alter-globalists, environmentalist, immigrationist, and "negative growth" movements, as well as the high-profile "Extinction Rebellion" association.

Charles Leopold Mayer was a French chemist born in 1881. A philosopher and financier, he made his fortune for the cause of human progress. He died in 1971. His foundation is based in Lausanne.

In Brazil, FnGM's action was given a voice by iBase, which is still active today. Its former director, Cândido Grzybowski, was also a member of the committee that launched the WSF, the World Social Forum in Porto Alegre in 2001. For many years, he was one of the driving forces behind this annual global event (see our book *Terrorisme pastoral*). One of the vehicles for the launching of the WSF in 2001 was the CCFD (Catholic Committee against hunger and for development), whose funding by French Catholics was encouraged by the episcopate.

Among the attendees at the FnGM Forum in 2008 were two other Brazilian members of the WSF, and a large number of NGOs were also represented: ATTAC, the Ford Foundation, FASE (*Fédération pour une alternative sociale et écologique*), the H. Böll Foundation, Greenpeace, and Social Watch, not to mention French journalist Patrick Piro from *Politis*.

Also in attendance were UNIPOP (the Popular University of Brazil) attached to Abong, the Brazilian Association of NGOs, associated in turn with *Brot für die Welt* (Bread for the World, the relief organization of Germany's regional Protestant and Evangelical free churches that wields an annual budget of 290 million euros), the French Agency for Development, and the French Embassy. The Amerindia agency, a CCFD partner agency financed by the latter, was also present, as was Francisco Whitaker, a CCFD project manager from 1968 to 1970 and winner of the alternative Nobel Prize.

This list is by no means complete, but it does give a glimpse of the globalization of networks on which François's globalist policy is based.

The 2009 World Social Forum (WSF)

Since it was founded in 2001, the WSF has held near-annual meetings. The ninth World Assembly took place in Belém, Brazil, from January 27 to February 1, 2009, with 150 countries represented, 2,400 workshops, and 100,000 participants. The presence of ATTAC economist Marilza de Melo Foucher was particularly noteworthy.

Its main theme was Amazonia, and countries that would be included in the Roman Synod ten years later were also represented: Colombia, French Guiana, Venezuela, and Argentina.

The ideology is always the same, as are the participants. The CRID (Centre de Recherches et d'Informations pour le Développement), for instance, was founded in 1976. It brings together over fifty associations and movements, including CIMADE, CCFD, *Frères des Hommes*, *Ligue des droits de l'homme*, *Secours Catholique*, and *Union juive française pour la paix*. Among CRID's partners are ATTAC France, *Coordination Sud*, and *Les amis de la Vie*. CRID also has some twenty partner countries, ranging from Burma to Georgia, India and Mexico, and so on.

The CRID is financed by its members, including the French Ministry of Education and Youth, AFD (the French Development Agency), the Fondation de France, the Charles Leopold Mayer Foundation, and Open Society Foundations.

Back in 1986, in our book *L'Église et la subversion*, we pointed out the collusion between CCFD and CRID. We also discovered and outlined the actions of a subversive agent, Henryane de Chaponay.

This lady was welcomed on April 6, 2018, by Pope Bergoglio, who received her with the following words: "I salute your mission as founder of the Center for the Study of Development in Latin America (CEDAL). Your unflagging creativity has borne fruit through '*Dialogues en humanité*,' whose meetings aim to refocus policies on humankind, in order to build a citizenship that protects our 'common home.'"

CEDAL was created in 1975 by Henryane de Chaponay together with Paulo Freire, the inventor of the revolutionary literacy-critical consciousness method mentioned earlier, from a CCFD branch for interventions in Brazil. Francisco "Chico" Whitaker, future co-founder of the WSF, was at the CEDAL meeting; he was also an active agent of the CCFD.

Henryane de Chaponay is not your everyday girl. She is "the red countess," daughter of the Princess of Orleans, a descendant of King Louis-Philippe. According to former CCFD general delegate Bernard Pinaud, she was "an incredible weaver of networks." "Not only did

Henryane create bonds, she also made the exchange of knowledge between people in the network so much easier," he said.

She took part in every edition of the World Social Forum until 2017—this time in a wheelchair, aged ninety-three. She died on October 9, 2019. She had publicly declared herself an agnostic in 2013 and extolled the "capacity for revolt."

The Pan-Amazonic Social Forum (FOSPA), a regional-themed version of the World Social Forum, held its ninth edition by video conference in November 2020. Its aim was to promote the cry of the Amazonian peoples in the light of the synod. On this occasion, the operational structure modeled on Father Arrupe's CIAS, mentioned above, was once again in place. The Xth edition of FOSPA was held at the end of July 2022 in Belém, Brazil, with the presence of the World Social Forum and several Catholic organizations: the *Commissão Pastoral da Terra* (Pastoral Commission of the Earth) born out of a 1975 meeting of Amazonian bishops, Fundación Jubileo, and REPAM, the pan-Amazonian ecclesial network mentioned several times in these pages.

Those who believed that *Querida Amazonia*, Pope Francis's post-synodal document, would bring the synod adventure to a welcome close are in for a rude awakening.

The synod emerges as a highly political act, with links to all subversive globalist apparatuses, be they areligious or professedly Catholic. It marks the climax of a conciliar revolution that seems to have yielded once and for all to the third temptation: to reign over "all the kingdoms of the world and their glory."

CHAPTER 9

The Four Principles: A Political Scam

"**P**rogress in building a people in peace, justice and fraternity depends on four principles related to constant tensions present in every social reality. These derive from the pillars of the Church's social doctrine, which serve as 'primary and fundamental parameters of reference for interpreting and evaluating social phenomena.'"[97]

What are these four principles? Chances are that even without having read *Evangelii Gaudium*, where they appear in paragraphs 221, 226, 231, and 234, you have already heard them, given that Francis is wont to repeat them:

1. Time is greater than space.

2. Unity prevails over conflict.

3. The whole is greater than the part.

4. Reality is more important than ideas.

But contrary to what the pope has often said, these principles have nothing to do with the social doctrine of the Church.

A look at the reference given by the pope (*Compendium of the*

---

97   Pope Francis, apostolic Exhortation *Evangelii Gaudium* (November 24, 2013), no. 221.

Social Doctrine of the Church, no. 161) will immediately show that this text does not mention them in any way.

On the other hand, the previous number, no. 160, mentions "the permanent principles of the Church's social doctrine which constitute the true foundations of Catholic social teaching," namely:

1. The principle of the dignity of the human person ... which is the foundation of all the other principles and content of the Church's social doctrine.

2 The principle of the common good.

3 The principle of subsidiarity.

4 The principle of solidarity *(numbered by us)*.

The *Compendium* further specifies: "These principles (are) the expression of the whole truth about man known by reason and by faith." It adds, "In the course of history and with the light of the Spirit, the Church has wisely reflected within her own tradition of faith, and has been able to provide an ever more accurate foundation and shape to these principles, progressively explaining them in the attempt to respond coherently to the demands of the times and to the continuous developments of social life."

The intellectual and philosophical discrepancy between Francis's "principles," which he presents as "related to bipolar tensions," and those of the *Compendium* is glaringly obvious.

This discrepancy was pointed out by Fr. Giovanni Scalese who was, among other things, professor and rector at the Collegio Querce in Florence: "It is hard to grasp the derivation of the four postulates of '*Evangelii Gaudium*' from the aforementioned 'permanent principles' of the social doctrine of the Church."[98]

Father Scalese quotes the pope himself from *Amoris laetitia*: "Since 'time is greater than space,' I would make it clear that not all discussions of doctrinal, moral or pastoral issues need to be settled by interventions of the magisterium. Unity of teaching and practice is certainly necessary in the Church, but this does not preclude various

---

98   From Sandro Magister's blog, May 19, 2016.

ways of interpreting some aspects of that teaching or drawing certain consequences from it. This will always be the case until the Spirit guides us towards the entire truth (cf. Jn 16:13)."

There is a very strong connection between this comment by the pope on the one hand and liberation theology and theology of the people on the other. This makes it possible perfectly to understand the meaning of these words, which directly relate to modernism. According to the Chilean Jesuit Jorge Costadoat, "considering history as a '*locus theologicus*' is the most important preconception of Latin American liberation theology."

This can be clearly seen in the expression "until the Spirit . . ." These words constitute a coarse identification of a "*telos*" or direction of history that leads to relativism; relativism is indeed at the very heart of the four principles.

What does this mean? Giulio Meattini, a learned Benedictine monk, explains it as follows: "It therefore comes as no surprise that these postulates should be the object of critical analysis today, in part because they do not stem in any way from divine revelation, nor do they have any foundation in the Sacred Scriptures; they are a mere product of the human mind, which Pope Francis however is audaciously elevating as driving principles of the life of the Church."

Indeed, according to Meattini: "One gets the impression that the affirmation of the superiority of time over space serves an interest: that of starting processes." He notes, further on: "In any case we can say that, under the banner of this principle, the effect has taken hold: following the post-synodal exhortation on the family, a series of 'processes' have made their appearance: debates, controversies, diametrically opposed interpretations, polarizations, perplexities of faithful and priests, uncertainties in the episcopal conferences."[99]

To this we can now add the Synod on Amazonia, the destruction of the Catholic Church in China, and so on.

But first of all, it is necessary to return to the source of the "four principles" provided by Francis himself. In the *Courrier de Rome* No. 600 of June 2017, Fr. Renaud de Sainte Marie wrote:

---

[99] From Sandro Magister's blog, August 23, 2016.

When reading the 2004 *Compendium of Social Doctrine* referred to in the excerpt we just quoted, you will literally not find a single one of the four principles enunciated by the pope. The implication is that these four principles are intellectual syntheses that are the brainwork of Francis himself. The one remarkable correspondence between the two texts that can be identified with precision is the reference to the concept of time. We can already note the following: the Pope relies on the authority of a text published by one of his predecessors to give these four principles a reference value that would be identical to those of the *Compendium*. . . . The principles of Francis, on the other hand, are proclaimed out of the blue and it is difficult to incorporate them into the relatively coherent whole of the *Compendium*. . . . We do not believe that the principles are in fact drawn from the *Compendium*.

This raises two questions. Why does the pope hide behind the authority of his predecessor? What does he want to conceal that he should need this kind of cover, even at the risk of committing an obvious anachronism? Father de Sainte-Marie alone risks indicating of a date (note 11, page 2): "If we are to believe the words of an Argentinian Jesuit, Scannone, his confrere Bergoglio was already using these four principles in the 1970s."

Like so many others, we have wandered about trying to identify the source of these four principles. But after extensive research, we can confirm that they are a scam that provides a pseudo-framework for a large part of the first papal exhortation. Father Scannone was correct: Pope Bergoglio embraced this pretense of intellectual coherence revolving around "four principles" as early as 1974.

Before such a much-needed return to their roots—where do these principles really come from?—it is necessary to understand the pontifical strategy as a whole, in the way it is being expressed today.

Grabbing power through the people

Coming in the wake of the decolonization wars and class struggle, the revolution within the Church had a Marxist character that was overly conspicuous.

In its bid for power, the modernist party needed recruits to spread the ideology according to which spiritual power and temporal power are not distinct but belong to the clergy and the laity, since these act together in a single struggle for justice and for the poor. We should remember in passing that in political parties that claim to be the champions of "social justice," the proletariat is in reality the mass of maneuverers that is entirely subject to the party.

In this context, the ideologists in Argentina invented a sociological category born of their national experience, a "proletariat" that they would call the people of God. They claimed the Second Vatican Council as their source of inspiration and constituted this "people" as the leading edge of the new Church. This people would subsequently be declared infallible *in credendum* because it carries a higher sense of social and political justice than any other institution.

In 1974, in line with this approach, Father Bergoglio pronounced the separation between the Magisterium of the Church and the devotion of the faithful to the Virgin Mary, and between the faith of the Church and its historical interpretation. This unheard-of innovation further radicalized the theology of the people and established it, so to say, as a *"primary theology."*

It reappeared as soon as Bergoglio had become pope. In July 2013, in an article published by the Brazilian newspaper *Estadão*, Leonardo Boff perfectly encapsulated the novelty of the pontificate, under the title "Pope Francis, toward a new springtime for the Church." It listed seven changes: *From the winter of the Church to springtime, from a fortress to an open house, from the pope to the bishop of Rome, from the palace to the guesthouse, from doctrine to experience, from exclusion to inclusion, from the Church to the world.*

It is clear that those who have argued that Pope Francis is not a proponent of liberation theology (they were trying to reassure themselves on the cheap), would do well to seek the opinion of this Brazilian ex-Franciscan who is one of its major representatives.

This brings us to one of the most essential points of this reflection. While the couple liberation theology-theology of the people moved forward under the cover of theology, philosophy, and culture, the party of the theology of the people, like all political parties, aimed at achieving the conquest of power. It therefore sought, especially in Argentina, the political means to win over the people: in Argentina it had only to scoop up the people that Perón, whether present or not in Argentina, had turned into a sacred category since 1945.

On September 29, 2016, Eduardo de la Serna, whose honest insights we have already mentioned, published the text of a conference he gave at the Jesuits' in Bogotá. It is a theological demonstration of the liberationist character of the "people of God" that substitutes itself for the Mystical Body of Christ. In this conference, he stated that in his youth Pope Francis was always close to "the Iron Guard" and to Juan Perón, and that because of this closeness, some have described him as a populist. Obviously, this word does not have the meaning that is has in French politics: it simply means paying special attention to the people as an electoral force.

But that is not the most important thing.

The most extraordinary thing here, and this is what makes Eduardo de la Serna so eminently likeable, is that he does not just assert a fact; he actually gives proof of it, and that changes everything! The truth is that biographers of Pope Francis simply copy each other, asserting that the pope has a certain affiliation with Peronist ideas. But these are always mere allusions and they insist that he did not join the movement, or recall how young he was at the time.

Here below is note no. 11 published by de la Serna following the text of his conference; it is this note that put us on the right track.

"His (Pope Francis's) assertions regarding time and space, reality and ideas, unity and conflict, are characteristic of groups like the Iron Guard. As Archbishop of Buenos Aires, he repeated them in every conference he made in 2005 (VIIIth Day for Social Ministry,

June 25) and in 2010 (Bicentenary of Justice and Solidarity 2010. We as Citizens, We as People)."

It was this footnote that opened the door behind which the source of Pope Francis's *political practice* was hidden. It has nothing to do with theology or philosophy but with rules borrowed from a political party for the conquest and retention of power. These rules, once transposed to the liberationist fight, are applied not only in order to change the Catholic Church but more importantly, on the longer term, to give it new synodal foundations.

Argentina and General Perón

The better to understand what this is all about, it is important to enter into the Argentine mentality, into the spirit of the Argentine nation.

The Argentinian character is unique; there is nothing like it in any other Latin American country. The Argentinians are a recognized exception among other Latin American nations. Their way of pronouncing the Spanish language is also distinctive.

The Argentinians' devotion to General Perón exceeds all reasonable measure. Eleven years after his exile in 1955, a truck driver told me: "In Perón's time, workers were kings!"

More recently, in 2002, it was still not uncommon to see Argentinians weeping at the memory of Evita Perón while listening to the iconic song "*No llores por mi Argentina, mi alma esta siempre contigo*" (Don't cry for me Argentina, my soul is always with you). Only lately an Argentinian told me that when a politician doesn't know what to say, he quotes Perón and gets a huge round of applause! Proud and tender, the Argentinian is still sustained by the dream of Perón's "justicialism," and—fifty years after her death—by the woman who embodied it.

It could be said that Peronism is consubstantial to the Argentinians and that the speeches of the "conductor" (not the *conducator*) and those of his wife enchanted them, in a magical sense. The very word *people* brings back all past glory. Peronism is both anti-Marxist and anti-capitalist; it was revolutionary and socialist before being called justicialist (justice + socialism).

The agents of subversion in the Argentinian Church had only to draw on a body of political doctrine to adapt liberation theology to the Argentinian people.

It is beyond the scope of this book to present Peronism as a whole. Our aim is simply to situate it in the history of contemporary Argentina in order to highlight its relevance to our topic. We will be content with quotes taken from a doctoral thesis presented in 2011 by Alicia Poderti: *Perón, the construction of a political myth, 1943–1955*, at the National University of La Plata.

Her first observation is that "the semantic inventions" of Perón's speeches "have spilled over into the sphere of the symbol, creating a vocabulary and an imagery that will be difficult to erase from the memory of Argentinians."

Elsewhere, she speaks of "the ideological metamorphosis of words." Their emotional impact was so strong that when Perón was ousted from power in 1955, as noted earlier, the new government passed laws and decrees prohibiting the use of any words, images, and so on, related to Perón and punished violators very severely. They say that the father of the young Bergoglio forbade him to wear Perón's insignia.

The social, popular, cultural, and trade-unionist substance of Peronism would be fully absorbed into the "theology of the people." On May 9, 2001, the Argentinian newspaper *La Nación* published an article titled *Curas villeros: predicadores de la Teología del Pueblo* (The priests of the slums: preachers of the theology of the people). After pointing out that Cardinal Bergoglio was the driving force behind their success, she highlighted the links between the first "'third-worldist' priests," of whom the shantytown priests are the successors, and the "left-wing Peronism" of the 1970s.

These so-called "*villero*" priests defined the theology of the people as follows, according to the cited article: "It is based on popular wisdom, not on categories or diagnoses imposed from above. It can be seen . . . as a hermeneutic of the poor people, who lack wealth, but not knowledge."

Perón invented popular culture in the face of official culture through laws similar to those of the Popular Front in France. "The great difference between the Argentina we have received and the one we will hand over to future generations is very simple and also very profound: in the New Argentina, the people will determine their own destiny," he said in his speech on May 1, 1951. Perón also invented the *patria feliz*, the "happy homeland" which is still very much alive in Argentinian memories.

As for Evita, she compared her husband to Jesus: "Why don't the humble men of my country, the workers of my country, react like ordinary men, they who understood and believed in Perón? The explanation is simple: they only had to see Perón to believe in him, in his sincerity, in his loyalty, in his honesty. They saw him and they believed. Thus, what happened in Bethlehem 2,000 years ago is renewed. The first to believe were the humble; not the rich, nor the wise, nor the powerful."

This is language understood by all: *"Cada uno en su casa y Dios en la de todos"* (Everyone in his own home and God in the home of all), said Perón, but we would be sadly mistaken should we imagine that his was a Christian party! It was socialist and revolutionary. It appealed to the heart rather than to the mind. The *"descamisados"* (the "shirtless people") were its electors.

The "conductor" led his people like Moses. He was the law and the prophets. He was by no means uneducated. He was passionate about the history of the great soldiers, from antiquity to the present day.

In February 1947, Perón made his first great speech to the delegates of the General Constituent Congress of the Peronist Party. Here, politics were presented as being at the service of the nation, and the party appeared to be intelligent, idealistic, and humanistic. Perón described it as gathering men of good faith "to collaborate with our project" and "to move forward along the path of truth and reality."

"Peronism is humanism in action: unity, tolerance, loyalty, sincerity," he proclaimed, while presenting a 288-page comprehensive political program.

On July 16, 1947, Perón presided over the UN Security Council and appealed to the peoples of the world in favor of "justicialism," a "third position" between the two "imperialisms" that had emerged from World War II.

On April 9, 1949, he delivered his speech on "The Organized Community," the philosophical and historical foundation of what would become Peronism.

But he was at his most outstanding in lectures he gave at the Superior Peronist School, starting on March 1, 1951, the day of its inauguration. The school had been created to train Justicialist Party leaders. In this series of lectures, Juan Perón explained the art of "political conduct." One year later, they were collected in a book, *La conducción de la política*.

As was his wont, he offered a demonstration of his amazing historical and political knowledge. He quoted Plutarch and Clausewitz, Lycurgus and Darius, Alexander the Great and Alphonsus the Wise, not forgetting Seneca. But also Scheler, Husserl, and Heidegger; Michelangelo, Murillo, and Raphael! And, of course, Napoleon. His methods of presentation were essentially military, based on strategy and tactics.

The quest for the origins of the "four principles" could only begin with the art of warfare. Juan Perón had read the histories of all the great captains, and he had a deep admiration for Napoleon, whom he readily quoted in his advice to party members.

Putting these words and their use in the sphere of strategy together, we find that Napoleon wrote to Stein, a Prussian minister, on January 7, 1814: "Strategy is the art of making use of time and space. I am less sparing of the latter than of the former. We can reconquer space, but never lost time. The loss of time is irreparable in war."

And indeed, it is in the collection *La conducción de la política* that the pair "time and space" appeared for the first time.

It appears as such on page 33 in the very title of chapter II, "The Characteristic of Modern Leadership" (the political art par excellence of conducing the nation towards its unity and greatness): "Time and space in political leadership."

"In the same way as history, leadership (*conducción*) must have, as one of its first requisites, a perfect framework of time and space;

conduct must evolve together with the evolution of man, with the evolution of science and with the evolution of the arts. Each new discovery alters and modifies conduct. For this reason, to be able to understand conduct it is necessary to position oneself in conditions of time and place. Of time, because of evolution; and of place, because of the characteristics of conduct itself, in its own environment."

These essential concepts were taken up again in the substantial chapter on "Doctrine, theory and forms of execution." The concept of time was here enhanced by a comparison with the preparation of the "French Revolution, which was meticulously and wonderfully prepared by the encyclopedists for forty years."

Perón's articles, signed *Descartes*, also included the pair "time and space" in February and April 1951.

Perón's determination to regain power had remained intact since his eviction in 1955. In 1969, he was faced with the task of reconstituting the great popular movement that had brought him to power in 1946. Its activists were scattered across the Argentine political spectrum from the most militaristic portions of the right wing to the most revolutionary part of the left. The bulletin *Las Bases* collected General Perón's thoughts and guidelines for the year 1968–1969. Confronted with the chaos into which the union sector had fallen and the disorganization of the political branch, the "Comando Superior" (this refers to Perón and the leaders of the movement), decided to favor the political branch, while making sure at the same time that contacts could be maintained with the labor union groups that remained united and loyal to Peronism.

The thirty-six guidelines set out by Perón were, as always, ordered according to the classic military concept: strategy and tactics. Number 30 stated: "The organ of execution of the strategic conduct for the country is the one devolved to the Delegate of the Superior Peronist Commando."

In 1974, Perón reprinted all the party's theses in a 238-page work called *Conducción Política*, with explicit reference to his speech to the Escuela Superior Peronista on March 1, 1951. As in the 1951 edition, there are repeated references to the pair "space and time": the first is on page 26, others appear on pages 59 and 130. On pages 75 and 157, under the title *Solución de los conflictos: la unidad* (Resolution of Conflicts: Unity), the principle absent from the 1951 version is developed: "Unity prevails over conflict."

We have now established with absolute certainty the origin of the superiority of time over space in the Peronist doxa and, as a consequence, in the statements of Father Bergoglio. These dates are noteworthy, as well as the date of July 1969, when Perón addressed the women's branch of the party with regard to Eva Perón's action: "Every one of us has the obligation and responsibility to perpetuate it in time and to extend it in space as the best school from which we can draw inspiration."

More recent testimonies bear witness to the fact that these principles are to be found exclusively among the survivors of Peronism.

On February 27, 2016, during the Party Congress, Gustavo Menéndez told Radio Real Politik FM 89.5: "At every moment of our meeting, we understood the need for unity and took into account that unity always prevails over conflict, and that the whole is superior to the parts."

When the pope received Peronist trades unionists on September 14, 2016, one of them stated, "Peronism is our backbone and only unity prevails over conflict." A union representative from the group then thanked the pope for having "opened the door to the divorced," no doubt thinking of Perón who had legalized divorce. The delegation presented the pope with a copy of the Peronist Doctrine edited by the youth branch of the Argentine CGT labor union.

On October 13, 2016, the *Laudato si'* support group quoted the statement of one of its members, Fernando "Pino" Solanas: "We have come here to say that unity prevails over conflict. It was General Perón who established dialogue."

What, then, of Francis's four principles or causes or "hooks" or criteria or postulates or cornerstones or axioms or priorities? How can it be that the pope was able to quote three of the four "principles" in 1974 if, by his own account, he only developed them from the work of Romano Guardini in 1986? The claimed existence of these two "production" dates reveals an inconsistency that cannot escape the gaze of objective analysis.

February 18, 1974

Father Bergoglio, provincial of the Jesuits since July 31, 1973, instructed his brothers in the new religion: the religion of the society, the religion of the theology of the people, the religion that corresponded to his personal vision. The transcription of his remarks of February 18, 1974, was published twice: in *Meditaciones para religiosos*, pages 47 and 48, and in the *Boletín de Espiritualidad* (Bulletin of Spirituality, Charism and Institution of April 1978, number 55, Society of Jesus – Argentina). In his opening address to the 14th Provincial Congregation on February 18, 1974, he referred in particular to the three Peronist recipes at the service of what he called "our liberating projects."

The lead article in this issue was written by Father Arrupe himself. It was followed by the entire conference given by Bergoglio in 1974. In it we find these words: "*The great criteria* for conducting processes are these: unity prevails over conflict; the whole is greater than the part, time is superior to space; these are the criteria that must inspire our work. Only in this way can we obtain unity of *execution*."

Father Bergoglio again took up the notions of space and time in the continuation of a talk in 1978 in a similar setting.[100]

There is absolutely no doubt that the only source of these four principles is to be found in General Perón's instructions to his supporters. Three of them were reproduced without change; the fourth, "reality is more important than ideas," did exist but in a different form; we shall see why Perón did not express it as such at the time.

Considering that their Peronist origins are so obvious, how is it that universal misinformation took hold and continues to this day?

The "four principles,"
a mantra of Bergoglian thought

During his first homily as archbishop at the *Te Deum* for Argentina's national holiday in Buenos Aires Cathedral on May 25, 1999, Archbishop Bergoglio said: "Let us persuade ourselves, once again, that 'the

---

[100]   See pages 54 and 57 in *Meditaciones*.

whole is greater than the part, time is greater than space, reality is more important than ideas, and unity prevails over conflict.' " He repeated this again in 2005 and 2010 (see above).

In 2010, Bergoglio—by now a cardinal—delivered a speech on the occasion of the "Bicentenary of Justice and Solidarity," in which he provided a new explanation of the concept of time being greater than space based on the Gospel story of the encounter between Christ and the mother of the sons of Zebedee. She asked him that one should sit on his right and the other on his left. The cardinal pointed out to his audience that the mother was asking "that when the time came for sharing, he should give them a large piece of the cake," in Spanish "*un pedazo grande de la pizza.*" He continued: "She asked for space, and Jesus replied: 'This is not the time.' " But this response does not exist in the Gospels.

The cardinal went on to quote the Gospel once more: "Can you go where I am going, can you suffer what I am going to suffer?" He then commented on this quote, saying "It means that it is time that decides" (*es decir, le marca el tiempo*).

First of all, it should be noted that neither Matthew nor Mark speaks of going and suffering but that both evangelists quote the same words: "You know not what you ask. Can you drink of the chalice that I drink of?" I have verified in the *Catena Aurea* that none of the commentaries collected by Saint Thomas Aquinas on this episode include any talk about space or time. Nor do the texts of two Spanish bibles, including a pastoral bible used in base communities, contain such references.

In order to get this so-called principle across, the cardinal actually "tinkered" with the Gospel, with no regard for the text. Using the mother of the children of Zebedee and the Evangelists to certify the organizational concepts of General Perón is quite a feat.

But since 1974, cardinal Bergoglio had read extensively. In 2010, he also had in mind the problem of universals, the idealists and the nominalists, and he simply quoted Plato in *Gorgias* and reduced the issue to aesthetics and rhetoric in order to justify that "unity prevails over conflict."

How the scam was concealed by fabrications

The most remarkable thing about the explanations supplied by Jorge Mario Bergoglio is the absence of the one that commentators later provided by referring to a letter from a former Argentine president, Manuel de Rosas (known for his laws and massacres), whom they unearthed from nineteenth-century history. He never made the slightest allusion to it, not even in 2010 under the exceptional circumstances of the bicentenary.

But when Bergoglio was elected to the See of Peter, their aim was to hide, at any price, that he had borrowed the "four principles" from Juan Domingo Perón.

1. The first book to spread a "fable" about the four principles is *The Great Reformer*, written by the pope's official historian, Austen Ivereigh. Although well aware of page 47 of the *Meditaciones*, he deliberately separated it from page 48. He gives the impression that he is well acquainted with Peronism, and curiously, he discusses the contents of page 47 on page 111 of his own book but does not quote page 48 until page 200 of his own book. It is as if the two pages of the *Meditaciones* were completely unrelated.

Ivereigh linked the pope's principles to Congar's principles and to his *True and False Reform in the Church*. Austen Ivereigh also considers them to be Christian principles of government ("*a series of governing 'Christian principles'*"): "In 1974, when he addressed the provincial congregation, they were three: unity comes before conflict, the whole comes before the part, time comes before space. By 1980, he added a fourth, anti-ideological principle: reality comes before the idea. They were principles deduced from various of his heroes—the early companions of Saint Ignatius, the Paraguay missionaries, even the nineteenth century caudillo Rosas—and one major source; what he called 'the special wisdom of the people whom we call faithful, the people which is the people of God.' "[101]

The reader obviously has no way of accessing all these sources of inspiration, spread as they are over four centuries.

---

[101] Ivereigh, *The Great Reformer*, pp. 200–1.

2. Fortunately, Fr. Juan Carlos Scannone had a brilliant idea that Austen Ivereigh had not dared develop. Scannone would repeat it many times, in Spanish, Portuguese, and French. Here are a few examples:

> People say they were taken from a letter on the national organization of Argentina written by Juan Manuel Rosas, Governor of Buenos Aires, to Facundo Quiroga, Governor of La Rioja in Argentina, from the Figueroa hacienda in San Antonio de Arceo (December 20, 1834). Although Rosas did not mention them explicitly, he did express them implicitly. Later—as Pope—Francis would introduce the last two principles in his four-handed encyclical *Lumen Fidei* (nos. 55 and 57). Finally, he developed and elaborated on them in *Evangelii Gaudium* (nos. 217-237), presenting them as a contribution of Christian social thought to "the building of a people (primarily for the peoples of the world, but also for the people of God)."[102]

For the record, the text from *Lumen Fidei* to which Father Scannone was alluding is the following: "Space hardens processes, whereas time propels towards the future and encourages us to go forward in hope."

In 2015, in an interview he gave to Ihu.unisinos in Brazil, Father Scannone said the same thing about Juan Manuel Rosas's "implicit" observance of the four principles: "*Segundo se diz*" (people say). Later on in the conversation, he mentioned Romano Guardini regarding the unity-conflict principle, as well as some vague inspiration relating to the "culture of encounter," in which one should "not ignore the reality of conflict."

All this was again taken up again in Scannone's book *La théologie du people, racines théologiques du pape François* (*Theology of the people, the theological and pastoral roots of Pope Francis*) which was released in France in 2017 and in the United States in 2021, and again surfaced when FactorFrancisco.org republished an interview on the occasion of the theologian's death in December 2019: "These are criteria for discernment. . . . The Pope adopted them when Fr. Tito Lopez Rosas

---

[102]   Scannone, *Razón y Fé*, 2014, t.271, no. 1395.

identified them in a letter from Juan Manuel Rosas to Facundo Quiroga. He communicated them to *Bergoglio, who was enthusiastic about them and developed them* [emphasis added]. Alcira Bonilla told me that this letter was kept in I don't know which archive, stained with blood: the blood of Facundo Quiroga who received this letter days before he was murdered. He had it on him in the battle of Barranca Yaco."

During the same interview, Father Scannone also answered the question: "Is it too risky to say, however, that Rosas is now mysteriously present in the magisterium of the universal Church?" He replied: "If this is true, we must make clear today that his principles were first implemented in politics. They were guidelines for organizing the nation. But now they are principles of universal value. And this shows that reality is better seen from the periphery than from the center."

Fr. Ernesto "Tito" López Rosas published an article on the "Christian Values of Peronism" in the August 1974 issue of CIAS (Jesuit Center for Information and Social Action), in which he wrote, among other things: "We experience our 'national being' and our 'Christian being' in close synthesis, because Christianity in no way inclines us to step outside space and time, but instead makes us see Christ in the immanence of our own personal history and that of the Argentinian people.... Our integration into the people of God is intimately linked to our integration into the Argentinian people" (p. 16).

There was only one way to confirm the accuracy of Fr. López Rosas's account of the origin of the four principles: to scrutinize the contents of that famous letter. It was reproduced in *Correspondencia entre Rosas, Quiroga y López.*[103]

Having read it through very carefully, it is impossible to affirm that any expression or situation whatsoever could have given rise to any "principle" at all. When Rosas refers to "time," he is talking about an undetermined time.

Two French authors have distinguished themselves in providing "information" regarding these principles.

The first is Nicolas Senèze of *La Croix*, the unofficial daily of the

---

[103] Barba, *Correspondencia entre Rosas*, pp. 94–105.

French episcopate: he says the principles "are drawn from Argentine history, in particular Juan Manuel Rosas."[104]

One year later, the second, Nicolas Tenaillon, who specializes in political theology, sheltered behind Father de Charentenay, SJ, to claim the following: "He drew from his readings of Guardini the few principles he set forth in *Evangelii Gaudium*; by the way, they are not social principles, but ontological principles."[105]

The fourth principle

One final issue remains to be elucidated. Why did Father Bergoglio ignore the fourth principle in 1974: "*Reality is superior to the idea*"? Had Perón perhaps omitted to use this brilliant expression?

The truth is that Perón did not say this because he was not a philosopher. He was a leader of men who analyzed history, politics, and economics. He was teaching leadership to the members of his party, people who would never have stopped to think about the relationship between reality and ideas.

The *Boletín Informativo Perónista* No. 7 of March 1972, under the heading "*Preparatory Archives and Preliminary Documents*" referred to a letter written by General Perón which appeared in number 7 of the magazine *Las Bases* of February 16, 1972: *La única verdad es la realidad* (Reality is the only truth).

It appeared with the general's handwritten signature.

In this letter, he provided a critical assessment of the economic situation in Argentina shortly before his return from Spain. He made no show of complacency and spoke out against those who had miracle solutions that he said were sure to be ineffectual.

At the end of his letter, he wrote: "I do not feel that I am infallible, and even less a 'prophet of truth,' but my great experience makes me sense an urgent truth for which we will pay dearly if we fail to seize the opportunity to put it into practice."

---

[104]   Senèze, *Les mots du Pape,* p. 12.
[105]   Interview with the author, *Dans la tête du pape,* p. 49, note 2, published in May 2017.

The subtitle of the letter was in effect: "*La única verdad es la realidad*." The only reality here was the catastrophic economic situation, which Perón presented as the only truth in the face of denial on the part of those who were incapable of dealing with it.

By this point, the pope's own account is definitely disturbing: "Even though I was not able to complete my thesis, the studies I did at the time helped me a great deal with what came afterward, including the apostolic exhortation *Evangelii Gaudium*, seeing that the whole part on social criteria in it is taken from my thesis on Guardini."[106]

Massimo Borghesi, Father Bergoglio, and Romano Guardini

Massimo Borghesi is the Italian author of an "intellectual biography" of the pope, *Jorge Maria Bergoglio. Una biografia intellettuale*. The third part of his book deals mainly with the theory of bipolar opposition in the work of Romano Guardini and its supposed use by Father Bergoglio.

With the intention of showing his command of the timeline of the pope's encounter with the German theologian, he transcribed a recording of the pope himself, from January 3, 2017: "At the beginning of '86, I first became interested in Guardini as a source for spiritual reading, in his books *The Lord*, *The Mother of the Lord*, etc. My readership took another turn when I came across *Der Gegensatz* (polar opposition), Guardini's philosophical anthropology work published in 1925."[107]

Twice, Massimo Borghesi certified that this was indeed a discovery at that date. Similarly to Austen Ivereigh, he explained that for Bergoglio, this book was a revelation that made it possible to avoid the Hegelian dialectic, since Romano Guardini both preserves oppositions and overcomes them in a confrontation which leads to a "fertile tension" that in turn builds a "concrete unity." Massimo Borghesi referenced two speeches delivered by Cardinal Bergoglio in 2005 and 2010.

---

[106] Quoted by Sandro Magister on his blog under the title, *The four hooks on which Bergoglio hangs his thought*, May 19, 2016.
[107] Borghesi, *Jorge Maria Bergoglio*, p. 117.

Such an attempt to link Romano Guardini with the four principles does not hold water, nor does the suggestion that they were elaborated by Bergoglio, whether as a priest, a cardinal, or pope.

In an article published on guardiniromano.blogspot on October 6, 2014, Professor Carlos Alberto Sampedro wrote: "Therefore (unless if Francis is able to provide us with explicit indications of Guardini's role in his formation or magisterium), it is impossible for now to find a direct and structuring influence of Guardini on Francis's thinking."

The professor gave four examples of quotes of Guardini by the pope. He added a comment from one of the pope's followers, Marcelo Larraquy, who had suggested Guardini was a visible source of "Bergoglio's teachings on freedom and obedience in the exercise of authority."

Sampedro concluded: "However, this is insufficient evidence to determine that there was a decisive influence, as one might have thought on the basis of his interest in completing a doctoral thesis on the theology of Romano Guardini."

Massimo Borghesi presented the Portuguese translation of his book in 2018 at a conference entitled *The Thought of Jorge Mario Bergoglio. The Challenges of the Church in the Modern World*, at the Brazilian Jesuit Institute UNISINOS, one of the major hotbeds of modernist subversion on the Latin American continent.

First, there was a reference to Denzinger, where Father Bergoglio claimed to have discovered, in 1974, the notion that "the people of God" are "depositaries of the faith": that reference is nowhere to be found. It was followed by an impossible reference to Rosas's correspondence. And finally, he referred to a thesis that no-one has ever seen or read.

Two assessments of the principles by Catholic thinkers

However, two other papers shed a definitive light on the philosophical content of the pope's principles. They were published by the journal *Courrier de Rome*.

1. *"Axes de lecture philosophique de textes du pontificat actuel"* ("Directions for a philosophical reading of texts of the present pontificate") by Professor Giovanni Turco, November 2016, no. 593.

This assessment is essential reading for every cleric and lay person, so many insights does it contain into the entire intellectual and moral crisis of our time. It includes all the elements needed to respond to all the deviations that we describe in this book.

> In every field of thought, the attitude towards truth is decisive, not only from the intellectual, but from the moral point of view. From an intellectual perspective, the consideration of truth reveals the relationship between thought and being, as well as the internal relationship between act and content within thought itself. The precedence of thought over being, like that of the act over content, reduces truth to being the result of an activity that is always in the process of becoming, in other words, it empties it of any inherent consistency. Conversely, the fundamental character of being, and similarly of content in relation to the act, brings out the priority of truth, both as substance and as criterion.
>
> When considered globally, these assertions, and not principles, appear in reality as presuppositions, that is to say, assertions that have been posited, but not discussed in themselves. Basically, they appear as points of view. These are points of view for their own sake, and that are not verified, be it from a philosophical or from a theological perspective.
>
> From all the texts we have mentioned, the notion emerges that truth consists in a relationship, comes from a relationship, and never exists without a relationship. As such, it is not the criterion of relationship, but the product of relationship. It does not distinguish between relationships, but rather originates in and returns to relationships. In this sense, truth, precisely insofar as it originates in relationships, can never be anything but relative. . . .
>
> These points of view are neither intrinsically nor extrinsically self-evident, and are asserted only for the sake of the consequences that can be drawn from them. They are not principles of a metaphysical, gnoseological or ethical nature. They do not

pertain to being as such, they are not significant in terms of the very nature of thought, they do not affect the bases of action. They themselves do not refer to truth or goodness. The question of their truth is not addressed, but their explicitation is developed in relation to praxis. Ultimately, they emerge as postulates of praxis, designed to achieve the goals of praxis itself. In other words, they are not, strictly speaking, principles, i.e., objective criteria for understanding reality, but functional points of view, insofar as they simply enable us to operate (*E.G.*, 223). *In the end, such an attitude does not correspond to a theoretical attitude, but to ideological behavior.* [Emphasis added.]

2. *Time greater than space. Analysis of Pope Francis' latent Heracliteanism,* by Fr. Renaud de Sainte Marie (*Courrier de Rome*, June 2017, no. 600, cited above).

Analyzing of Francis' words and understanding the extreme seriousness of what is happening before our eyes cannot be successful without discovering something of the content of the philosophy that drives the current pontificate. Indeed, many still refuse to see the truth, so we felt the need to draw attention to the abyss towards which we are being led by soothing words and seemingly fertile aphorisms. . . .

For Heraclitus, the fixity and stability of the elements of the world were a delusion, a mere appearance. Reality only resided in becoming, and nothing that was could abide. . . .

Without dwelling on the present similarity between the sayings of Heraclitus and those of the Pope, our reflection will focus on *the principle of space and time.* From our point of view, this principle is the most important, since it relates to the problem of being and becoming. The whole metaphysical question is therefore at stake, and ultimately the capacity of the human intelligence to know God. . . .

. . . Associating God with movement, with evolution *ut sic,* almost necessarily leads to pantheism, since any form of specific worship, or of a dogmatic content that is exclusive of its opposite, is a sort of betrayal of divine dynamics, of its original polymorphism. Far from revealing God, such an intellectual position makes Him incomprehensible to us, and associates Him with all the possible delusions of humanity when it comes to theological affirmation. In keeping with such phraseology—it is hard to put a name on such thinking—you could say that letting time do its work enables us to conquer new spaces; and woe betide he who seeks to preserve the legacy of the past, woe betide he who delineates God in any way, shape or form, or under any dogmatic definition? What is left of the revealed deposit when such principles are adopted? What can be said of God if such a position is adopted in all rigor? Nothing . . .

Heraclitus in fact fully accepted dialectics as being the essence of the world, with chaos as the father of all things. The Pope does not assume this legacy, but in a way, he does shoulder its consequences. We do not deny that the Pope's intentions are pacific. But he cannot escape the logic of destruction and chaos of the thinking that he has—consciously or unconsciously—embraced. There is no peace in Heracliteanism, there is no place for a God who would be love.

The "four principles" and the theology of the people

When considering this grand cover-up of the origins of the "papal" principles, always keep in mind Emilce Cuda's expression: "Theology of the people is the national and popular mode of liberation theology."[108]

For all their efforts and attempts at reformulation, the proponents of the theology of the people have not succeeded in disengaging themselves from the "Hegelian direction of history." What they were trying was to hide their "Heracliteanism" behind the nation or behind culture.

---

[108]   Cuda, *"Teología y política en el discurso del papa Francisco,"* *Nueva sociedad* no. 248, nov-dec 2013, a periodical connected with the German Friedrich Ebert Socialist Foundation.

The system's leading theoretician, Father Scannone, gave a name to this school of thought: *liberation theology based on cultural praxis*. When the members of COEPAL (Episcopal Commission for Pastoral Care in Argentina) met with the advanced wing of liberation theology, they were immediately contaminated with the most politicized of theological categories, that are also those of shantytown parish priests and the Movement of Priests for the Third World.

While it is true that the theology of the people distinguishes between proletariat as a class and the people, in practice this does prevent the people from covering the same reality. The theology of pastoral praxis does not differentiate the identity of these two kinds of discourse: the revolutionary discourse and that of cultural praxis.

Considering the origin of these principles, the following remarks need to be made:

1. When Father Bergoglio addressed his confreres in February 1974, he was thirty-eight and had been serving as provincial for six months. He had evidently fallen under the spell of the conquering language used by General Perón in Madrid as he prepared his troops to reclaim power in 1973, but Perón died on July 1, 1974. Despite the "four principles," the latter's successors never succeeded in establishing civil peace in Argentina.

2. The Society of Jesus that Father Bergoglio was tasked with leading was divided for both religious and political reasons. In Perón's teachings, he found the concepts that he felt would be most effective in bringing his Jesuits, and later the Argentine nation, together once more.

3. Bergoglio's governorship of the Argentine province proved so divisive that he was sent to Córdoba for two years in 1990–1991. He acquired a taste for power at a time when the temporal-spiritual distinction was being blurred by the confusion generated by the theology of the people.

4. He would go on to implement these principles in the political-religious turmoil of the time in Argentina, first as auxiliary bishop, then as cardinal archbishop of Buenos Aires. He had neither the

theological, philosophical, nor political culture to be a good judge of these principles. He had been directly shaped by Peronism and the theology of liberation and of the people.

5. In his new role as pope, Francis knew nothing other than what he had already put into practice. His apostolic exhortation *Evangelii Gaudium* is a barely distinguishable rip-off of what he used to tell the people of his diocese and the whole of Argentina. This can be easily seen in its construction as a political manifesto that names the enemies who have infiltrated the camp of the People of God: see paragraphs 93 to 104 of *Evangelii Gaudium*, from "spiritual worldliness" to "demands for the legitimate rights of women." It is also a political and economic agenda, coupled with a "*mystical* fraternity, a contemplative fraternity, . . . capable of seeing the sacred grandeur of our neighbor" (§ 92). Remember that Francis set out the "four principles" in this exhortation.

6. What Perón failed to achieve in Argentina, the pope is determined to accomplish in the Church of which he has become the leader. He is still convinced that the principles, which have so clearly failed to save any society to date, are actually effective. The massive philosophical error of these principles is totally at odds with Aristotelian-Thomistic metaphysics. They are principles for a specific political action stemming from Peronism, not from the Church's social doctrine.

The four principles are in reality a means for Pope Francis to maintain and extend his power to transform the Church into a temple of the theology of the people.

The four principles: the bottom line

In our view, the Jesuit Father Ernesto López Rosas, who was bent on rallying the faithful to Perón and keeping them away from liberation theology, committed a falsification that amounts to an intellectual scandal, as did his extravagant interpretation of a letter written by Juan Manuel Rosas in 1834.

But that Jorge Bergoglio, as priest, cardinal, and pope, should have adopted it for the "benefit" of his confreres, the people of his diocese, and the faithful of the universal Church represents a major fraud—one that was accredited by Father Scannone and journalists, writers, and biographers hailing from all over the world.

It was only Italians such as Prof. Turco, Fr. Giovanni Scalese, or Fr. Giulio Meiattini, as quoted by Sandro Magister, and the June 2017 issue of *Le Courrier de Rome* with Fr. Renaud de Sainte Marie, that exposed the intolerable intellectual stupidity of these so-called principles, which in reality stem from second-rate Heracliteanism.

The Ancient Greeks were well aware that Chronos devours his own children. Time has devoured Napoleon and Perón and will also devour the Great Reformer who seeks to transform the Church of Christ thanks to the organizational skills of General Perón.

Contemporary clerical scholars are spinning endless essays about the principle "time is greater than space," ranging from a lengthy article by Fr. Giulio Maspero published in 2014 by the Pontifical Academy of Theology under the title *Il tempo superiore allo spazio, un principio teologico fondamentale per l'agire Cristiano* (Time is greater than space, a fundamental theological principle for Christian action) to a theology conference at the Parisian Collège des Bernardins on April 6, 2017.

This is where we stand today: through the Jesuits, Juan Domingo Perón has been elevated to the rank of theologian of the people's theology. Fraud and deceit are the pillars of this Church of the poor, the Church of mercy, of encounter and dialogue!

NOTE

Saint Thomas Aquinas, S.Th., 2a 2ae, q.33, art.4 ad 2 m.

"Whether a man is bound to correct his prelate?"

Answer: "Yes, but privately and respectfully." "However, if the faith were endangered, a subject ought to rebuke his prelate even publicly."

Canon Law 1983, Book II: Title I, can. 212 §3

§ 3. According to the knowledge, competence, and prestige which they possess, they [the lay faithful] have the right and even at times the duty to manifest to the sacred pastors their opinion on matters which pertain to the good of the Church and to make their opinion known to the rest of the Christian faithful, without prejudice to the integrity of faith and morals, with reverence toward their pastors, and attentive to common advantage and the dignity of persons.

CHAPTER 10

The Liturgy as a Powerful Channel for Liberation Theology and Theology of the People

The extent to which the new liturgical forms have spread conciliar theses among the Christian faithful is well-known. This also applies to Latin America. Thousands of photographic records of the phenomenon exist. They are easy to come across in Argentina, especially in the "peripheries," with cardinal Bergoglio himself—who never celebrated the "Tridentine Mass"—as the celebrant.

It is all too easy to forget that when the pope was elected, we were told in no uncertain terms that the Church was to receive a new impetus, a new theology, and a revitalized pastoral ministry, the model for which was precisely Latin America. But what is the Latin American liturgical model that the pope is allegedly implementing, both for the Amazonian and the universal Church?

The great momentum created by the Second Vatican Council had far-reaching repercussions throughout Latin America. It was—and still is—driven by liberationist currents, who freely made use of the Mass as a means of promoting social and religious revolution. At the time, all the NGOs in the USA, Canada, and Europe, including the French CCFD, were funding these movements.

The continent's liturgy was also greatly influenced by the charismatic and Pentecostal groups that proliferated in the wake of Catholicism's decline. There are American sects everywhere.

I remember one such Mass I witnessed in May 1987 in the guerrilla zone of the Morazán mountains in El Salvador. It was the Belgian priest Roger Ponseele who celebrated the Mass, which retained something of its sacred character, as the consecration was carried out according to the official canon. On the other hand, the presentations and the "homily" were calls to arms. The final hymn did not lack grandeur, but it was the anthem of the Salvadoran Communist Party.

I saw much the same thing in Managua, during the same trip, except that the closing hymn was the Sandinista anthem.

Also in Nicaragua, I attended a memorial Mass for an American priest who had died in a car accident: he had given up the priesthood and got married. His wife was there with their children, and we were treated to a sermon on commitment to serve President Ortega. Incidentally, these Masses always used the same Gospel from Saint Luke 4:18, where Christ reads Isaiah's prophecy: "The Spirit of the Lord is upon me, because he has anointed me to bring glad tidings to the poor. He has sent me to proclaim liberty to captives."

In Brazil, the ideological background was the same, but the mood was less dramatic, especially with Bishop Casaldaliga, a revolutionary poet. There was constant cheering and rhythmic swaying. His poetry was similar to that of Ernesto Cardenal: both wrote psalms and hymns for the new religion.

What looked like evangelical "shows" were held in specially equipped meeting halls; whatever remained of the sacrifice was completely lost in the reigning, joyful anarchy.

At the same time, the faith and sacraments were weaponized. A brochure entitled *The Eucharist in Base Communities* was distributed in those "grassroots" groups. It read (pp. 26-27):

> Formalism and legalism have reached extreme levels. The Eucharist is celebrated in a language no one understands. The priest makes a series of gestures that, likewise, no one understands.

It was necessary at the Second Vatican Council to recon-
sider this absurd situation that had arisen within Christianity.

Celebrating Hope . . . today's struggles are signs that
the kingdom is coming and that tomorrow men will truly
be brothers.

In South Africa, "contextual theology" took advantage of funerals
to trigger active nonviolence protests.

The influence of the theology of the people in Argentina proved
decisive. "Critical religious conscience" would not accept a liturgy that
belonged to the politico-military powers linked to the episcopate. In
protest, one politically committed parish abolished Midnight Mass
on December 25, 1968.

In line with this rationale, each country and each people should
have its own "inculturation" and its own protest Mass combining social
demands with liturgy. One study identified fourteen such Masses:
Misa panamericana, Misa Andina-Altiplano Chile, Misa Pimpa, Misa
a la chilena, Misa peruana, Misa Tepozteca, Misa Criolla, Misa cam-
pesina nicaragüense, Misa popular salvadoreña, Misa cubana, Misa
dos quilombos, Misa Mesoamericana, Misa de Chiapas, and Misa del
Tercer Mundo.

Each has its own music. While there is no great respect for the
accuracy of the Creed, the Gloria is often outright fanciful: "Glory be
to God in heaven and on earth, which is so ill-treated . . ." As for the
Liturgy of the Word and the Universal Prayer, they vary *ad libitum*
with the degree of revolutionary awareness.

By way of an example, here is the Mass composed by Father
Mugica, (a member of the Movement of Priests for the Third World;
see chapter 4) who was murdered in 1974. All the political messages
that this type of Mass carries were incorporated into his text. The
entire liturgy was rewritten with the struggling community in mind;
this is called liturgical inculturation. In the same way that there is a
contextual theology, there is also a contextual liturgy. On the anniversary of Father Mugica's death, Pope Francis underlined his priestly
determination but failed even to mention this sacrilege.

These new liturgical texts that strike us as excessive are new "theological places" that embed the new faith and the new Church in the minds of the faithful.

Text of the Mass for the Third World (excerpts)

"Señor ten piedad de nosotros. Señor ten piedad de nosotros."
Lord, have mercy on us.

"Tú que has nacido pobre y has vivido siempre junto a los pobres para traer a todos los hombres la liberación. Tú que estás a nuestro lado fuerte y resucitado para empujarnos en la lucha contra la injusticia y la explotación. Señor, piedad, Señor."
You who were born poor and who always lived among the poor to bring liberation to mankind. You who are at our side, strong and resurrected, to urge us to fight against injustice and exploitation, have mercy, Lord.

"Gloria a Dios que es el amor y en la tierra paz a los hombres que luchan por la justicia."
Glory to God who is love and peace on earth to men who fight for justice.

"Te alabamos, porque luchamos para que nuestros niños hambrientos coman. Te glorificamos, porque queremos destruir ya los instrumentos de tortura."
We praise you because we are fighting so that our starving children can eat. We glorify you, because we want to destroy the instruments of torture, now.

Liberation theology and theology of the people authors have written little on the subject of liturgy or the Mass. Here are some elements from a text by Leonardo Boff in *Church: Charism and Power*, which set the tone for the reflection on which all liberationists have drawn.

Liturgical creativity is also given its place in the community. The people appreciate the canonical, official liturgy but they also create their own rituals, spontaneously enacting the word of God, organizing great celebrations that center around the Bible and include significant regional objects or foods. It is at these times that faith is given its finest expression. A people that knows how to celebrate is a people with hope. They are no longer a wholly oppressed people but a people who march toward their liberation. (p. 130)

The liturgy becomes an expression of faith and not the carrying out of a sacred ritual. The word is no longer the private property of the priest; the people share it. Tithing becomes the expression of commitment to the community. (p. 134)

Living the primary sacrament, the Church, is the previous condition for receiving the seven sacraments. One might imagine a hand with seven fingers; it makes no sense to want the fingers without wanting or implicating the hand. (p. 134)

Happily, Vatican II brought things back into perspective, recovering its theologically threatened health. The Church is fundamentally the People of God. All share in the magisterial role of Christ, even the laity. The hierarchy, as a part of this people, enjoys an official role but always in service to the entire Christian community. (p. 155)

For liberation theologies, *Ecclesia docens* and *Ecclesia discens* are no longer separate. The people is the sole interpreter of God's will.

Conclusion

B oth before and after the Second World War, the section of the clergy that campaigned against fascism and Nazism found itself at the forefront of the Church's democratic transformation. In France, noteworthy examples include the growing popularity of the *Revue Esprit*, a magazine founded in 1932, and the release of *Echec de l'Action Catholique?* (Was Catholic Action a failure?) by the Belgian priest Joseph Comblin in 1961. Comblin worked alongside Dom Hélder Câmara in Brazil from 1958; he died in 2011.

Before the council, the modernist revolution formed its leaders within the Catholic Church in religious orders and congregations— mainly the Jesuits and Dominicans. Nowadays, they are supported by a number of bodies such as NGOs and Catholic movements, and they enjoy universal media coverage thanks to these numerous agencies.

At the other end of the political-religious spectrum, in 1956, Jean Madiran launched the monthly *Itinéraires*, a copy of which he sent to all the bishops of France; only one, Bishop Le Couëdic of Troyes, wrote a friendly reply.

The proclamation in January 1959 that a council was to be held triggered a major structuring campaign within the modernist party. It arrived at the council ready for battle, enabling it to wipe out the defenders of Catholic orthodoxy. Vatican II became the occasion to implement all the modernist ideas that had been brewing in Europe for over fifty years.

In 1981, *Paradoxes* magazine published a special issue: *30 ans de bouleversements. Les grands débats du catholicisme. Le renouveau théologique. L'Eglise en France* (30 years of upheaval; Catholicism's key debates; Theological renewal; The Church in France). With only a few exceptions, the issue contains more than two hundred pages of conciliar and utopian clichés. Of the thirty-five contributors, only two addressed the subject of Latin America, which was summed up in a few words. Bishop Poupard (the future cardinal) noted: "We are all aware of the tensions that arise in bishops' assemblies on a continental scale, such as CELAM in Latin America." Sister Françoise Vandermeersch, the daughter of a prominent industrialist who in her youth was attracted by the demands of the leftist Front Populaire, wrote: "We also have the experience of Nicaragua. Sisters from my community are there. In Nicaragua, the revolution was truly extraordinary. It was bloody at the start, and that is absolutely true, but what would have happened if it hadn't taken place?"

Since 1962, the revolution has taken hold in Latin America, the world's largest Christendom, and France knows nothing about it beyond what the staunchest progressives in the religious-political sphere have to say. Our Italian neighbors are in a much better position, since a Bologna-based institute has precise information about the Latin American continent, which it circulates. Prof. Roberto de Mattei gave a lecture in Rome during the study day on "Old and New Modernism—The Roots of the Church's Crisis" in Rome on June 23, 2018, which provided a remarkable synthesis. But he said virtually nothing about Latin America, with the exception of a mention of the book *François philosophe* (Francis the Philosopher) written by friends of the pontiff.

Yet while modernism indeed originated from France, Germany, Belgium, Spain, and Italy in the mid-nineteenth century, its ultimate and operational development took place in Latin America, starting from Europe and, to a lesser extent, from the United States.

The long struggle that raged in the Church, especially since 1907, came to a head in 2013 with the election of cardinal Bergoglio as Pope Francis. Earlier, the Second Vatican Council marked a major intermediate phase in the process of destabilization of power in the Church and served as a powerful catalyst for all the errors launched with the devastating slogans of Saint John XXIII: "the springtime of the Church" and "the new Pentecost."

This is a battle for identity whose primary and ultimate objective is to alter the identity of the Catholic Church received from the apostles.

Virtually everything unfolded in broad daylight. There was no conspiracy. The few underground Jesuit operations in Teilhard de Chardin's time were short-lived: hiding was no longer a necessity; power was at hand.

The acceleration and structuring of the modernist movement occurred under the reigns of John XXIII and Paul VI. John Paul II and Benedict XVI were somehow fascinated by the council. They thought they could remedy its shortcomings, but in reality, they were powerless, ignorant as they were of the organized forces confronting them. It was not that they failed to teach, but they had no idea of the realities that were taking shape. Their rebukes in the face of the war waged by the Jesuits went unheeded. Cardinal Ratzinger's two instructions on liberation theology did not address its real causes, because they oversimplified the origin of the crisis to Marxist penetration.

This lack of perception of reality led to the appointment of bishops and cardinals who were to become agents of the revolution in the Church. The Argentinian cardinal Eduardo Pironio, whom we have mentioned on several occasions, is a typical example.

This prolonged and victorious subversion can only be compared to Masonic subversion in eighteenth-century Europe.

It takes money to carry out a revolution. Global networks of Catholic NGOs, official bodies, Europe, the United States, and Canada have been funding all these propaganda platforms for over fifty years. They have colonized charity and branded it with the seal of social and political revolution. They intertwine across the globe.

It would be a mistake to think that such ruin does not exist in France.

At the 1974 French JOC (YCW) rally, the guest of honor was Georges Marchais, general secretary of the French Communist Party, and ten thousand "Jocistes" sang the communist song *l'Internationale* in front of fourteen bishops: "*Il n'est pas de sauveur suprême*" (No savior from on high delivers). In 1972, Archbishop Marius Maziers of Bordeaux published a letter in which he praised socialism and communism. In 1990, Cardinal Decourtray, archbishop of Lyon and primate of the Gauls, was publicly accused by a priest of the Mission de France and Catholic Worker Action for having declared in *Le Figaro* that certain priests had become involved with dialectical materialism.

The political grooming of "the people" has taken different forms in Latin America and France. With total disregard for the wisdom of nations, the people have been assigned powers and a goodness which they never had. The pope's "polyhedric humanity" is nonsense. It never existed, as every historian well knows. All of history, be it sacred or profane, reveals that peoples have always been objects of manipulation. In his last speech, Robespierre railed against "the oppressors of the people." Saint Matthew (18:20), for his part, clearly indicates that the high priests and the elders bribed the crowd to bring about Christ's condemnation. Saint Mark, who was equally specific, confirms that the high priests stirred up the crowd so that Pilate would grant them Barabbas's release.

In view of all this, one can only shudder at the words of the Roman Pontiff on Spanish television on March 23, 2020, at the height of the COVID pandemic: "I have put my hope in humanity, I have put my hope in the men and women who are part of this humanity, I have put my hope in the peoples. (Some peoples) will learn from this crisis and undertake a revision of their lives, and we will come out of it better."

Liberation theology uses the people as a tool to spread a "Catholic" religion without Original Sin, Redemption, Creed, or Church, and ultimately with a "Parousia" that will crown the efforts of social and political struggles whose themes are those of the World Parliament of Religions held in Chicago in 1893.

As a priest, an archbishop, a cardinal, and now as Pope Francis, Jorge Mario Bergoglio has embraced and fostered all the errors of modernism. In a word, he "peronized" and then "argentinized" the Church, burdening it with a political-religious model that failed in the very place where it was born. Fr. Ernesto López Rosas, the famous "discoverer" of the four principles, exalted Peronism. He invented "cultural nationalism," enabling priests and religious to work in the political arena without leaving their priesthood. Perón's doctrine is intended to "save" Argentina and to extend to the Latin American continent, becoming a model for the universal Church. "*El viento de Dios sopla en y desde el sur del Sur*," wrote Carlos Maria Galli in 2013: "God's wind blows in and from the south of the South" (meaning Argentina).

Pope Francis's revolution can be summed up as follows: in the Bolshevik revolution, everything is related to the "proletariat" and its subsequent forms; the theology of the people relates everything to the people, a new *proletariat*. This people is baptized the "faithful people" and becomes the measure of all things.

Pope Francis gave his definition of new evangelization at the plenary assembly of the Pontifical Council for Promoting the New Evangelization on September 29, 2017: "It is necessary to discover ever more that it by nature belongs to the People of God. In this regard, I would like to underline two aspects. The first is the contribution that the individual peoples and the respective cultures offer to the journey of the People of God."

One month earlier, on August 24, 2017, Francis told participants at Italy's National Liturgical Week: "Liturgy is life for the whole people of the Church. By its very nature, in fact, liturgy is 'popular' and not 'clerical.'"

This was all carefully planned; nothing was left to improvisation or spontaneity. The whole business of Mary's "mestizaje" was announced at the end of Cardinal Bergoglio's January 2008 conference in the wake of the CELAM Assembly in Aparecida: "As the Pilgrim People of God in Latin America and the Caribbean, we entrust the missionary disciples to the tenderness, beauty and joy of God's love manifested in the mestiza face of the Mother of God, the Virgin of Guadalupe."

Pope Francis's adulation of the people knows no bounds. In the same 2008 conference, the cardinal quoted at length from his master, Lucio Gera. The bishop of San Nicolás de los Arroyos, Domingo Castagna, had consulted the said theologian about a Marian experience in his diocese. Lucio Gera responded with a letter that became known under the title *El pueblo es como el agua* (The people are like water).

Like water, the people are fickle, and Lucio Gera pointed out that it is the bishop's task to "recanalize" the faith when it strays into imaginary phenomena. Bishops, he said in substance, have a duty to distinguish between Catholic practices of the faith and those that are "fanciful" to the point of being "extravagant" (*"hasta el barroquismo"*). These two caveats were omitted by Cardinal Bergoglio, no doubt in the name of the people's inherent virtue. But in our view, his deliberate omission of the remarks is also an unmistakable sign of a rejection of hierarchical authority within the Church.

In *François philosophe*, the pope's admirers—Monsignor Philippe Bordeyne, Juan Carlos Scannone, Giovanni Ferretti, Miguel Garcia-Baro, Bishop Pascal Wintzer, together with Emmanuel Falque and Laure Solignac, the book's editors—presented a summary of his unorthodox thinking.

These writers all adopt Massimo Borghesi's tactic of legitimizing the pope's "philosophy" by linking it to Paul Ricœur and Maurice Blondel, among others. What they fail to mention is that Father Scannone wrote his thesis on *Sein und Inkarnation. Zum ontologischen Hintergrund der Frühschriften M. Blondels* (Being and Incarnation. Concerning the ontological background of Maurice Blondel's early writings), and that it was he who "introduced" Jorge Mario Bergoglio to Blondel's work.

Father Scannone clarified his own point of view in this book: "We should not overlook Reifenberg's suggestion regarding the mediating role of Vatican II between Blondel and Bergoglio, given his view that the French philosopher from Aix had an influence on the Council, not least through the theologies of Lubac and Karl Rahner, while Bergoglio is a son of the Council and seeks to implement it fully as part of his mission as universal pastor."

In a synthesis of the contributions, Bishop Paul Wintzer wrote:

> Prof. Ferretti prompted us to reflect on the question of truth. Luigi Pareyson and Francis, taking two different paths, have opted for truth as an act that is continually coming into being and that needs to be deciphered. Pareyson's path is that of

hermeneutics, while Francis's is that of discernment. How can we fail here to remember the words of John (14, 6): "I am the way, the truth and the life"? But we can read these words either as being always connected to one another: "I am the way and the truth and the life", or by placing them side by side: "I am the true and living way": the major is then the way, while the truth is movement and advent.

This is nothing new: once again, it leads back to Heraclitus.

Ultimately, Father Bergoglio arrived at the head of the Catholic Church powered by conciliar modernism and the ideologies that derive from it. Father Arrupe, the Society of Jesus, and their European and Latin American allies—including the ex-Franciscan Leonardo Boff—developed the "doctrinal" apparatus of the new Church. Endorsed by the Sankt Gallen mafia, Francis was elected successor to Peter in 2013 after an unsuccessful attempt in 2005. Over the years since 1974, as priest, archbishop, and cardinal, he has masterfully absorbed and spread the worst fake version of Catholicism in twenty centuries.

APPENDIX 1

Clericalism

The pope's political theology has its own language and vocabulary. A flood of commentary swept the Catholic world after the pope used the word *clericalism* to label the source of sexual perversion within the Church.

We are understandably gripped by the sheer volume of investigations into events that are dramatically affecting our Church, but we need to look beyond the facts to understand what is really taking place. These facts only make sense when associated with the ultimate aims of the Vatican's political agenda.

This specific language has its own vocabulary and implies a particular *forma mentis*, a turn of mind. People attribute to the pope's words a meaning they do not possess. Most fail to realize that they cover a reality altogether different from the one ordinarily assigned to them. The term *clericalism* is a case in point.

The pope has clearly stated that the cause of sexual abuse is "clericalism." Cardinal Müller and the French bishop Aillet focused on this word. However, its meaning has nothing to do with clericalism according to the "*Petit Père Combes*,"[109] nor with the term's dictionary definition.

Long before his accession to the throne of Saint Peter, and especially during the Social Pastoral Days in Buenos Aires, Cardinal

---

[109] Translator's note: "Little Father Combes," the French secularist politician who engineered the radical separation between Church and State that would become law in 1905.

Bergoglio bemoaned the plight of those who were victims of political, economic, and religious power. He called these deviations "spiritualist abstractionism," "functionalist methodologism," or "abstract ideologies." He targeted parish priests with their hypocritical morality, "*moralina de los curas.*"

On another occasion, at the closing Mass of the Buenos Aires Meeting on Urban Pastoral Care on September 2, 2012, he expanded this particular catalog of name-calling (for which he has shown a special fondness): "To clericalize the Church is to engage in Pharisaic hypocrisy. . . . No to hypocrisy. No to hypocritical clericalism. No to spiritual worldliness. . . . May God grant us that grace of closeness which saves us from every entrepreneurial, worldly, proselytizing and clerical attitude, and brings us closer to His path: to walk together with God's holy and faithful people."

As pope, he addressed the CELAM Coordination Committee in Rio on July 28, 2013, condemning a mixed array of temptations: ideologization of the Gospel message, socialistic reductionism, psychological ideologization, Pelagian deviations, functionalism, and clericalism.

On the following December 16, he appealed to God: "Lord, free your people from the spirit of clericalism and come to their aid through your spirit of prophecy." The *Osservatore Romano* quoted the gist of his words: "When prophecy is missing, clericalism takes its place, the rigid scheme of legality that closes the door to the figure of man."

On December 16, 2014, he similarly fumed: "We must root out clericalism from the Church."

Rafael Luciani, an expert on Pope Francis's thought, published an article in 2015 on the latter's condemnation of the "chosen one complex"—feeling selected by God and "separated from the world"—whereby clerics or religious feel superior to others and impose their views on them. Francis calls this "the pathology of ecclesial power," and according to Luciani, he is seeking to "change ecclesiastical structures" and "revise the way clergy and religious understand their vocation." The pope took up this theme again in his highly aggressive December 22, 2014, speech on the "diseases" threatening the Curia, Luciani recalled; in turn, the latter criticized "the mindset behind a pyramidal and paralyzed ecclesiastical structure that is unable to discern the signs of the times and seems to ignore the tragedies affecting the great majorities."

Why does Francis indulge in these violent attacks that have so little substance?

The reason behind this is ideological. The papal ideology is applying to the Church—the whole Church—the revolutionary patterns of the conquest of power by establishing an indisputable divide between the "good" and the "bad." And this divide is sufficiently vague for no one to feel safe.

In his book *Yo, argentino. Las raíces argentinas del Papa Francisco* (I, an Argentinian. The Argentinian roots of Pope Francis), the journalist Armando Puente provides the ultimate meaning of this "clericalism," which was not, as can be imagined, invented by Cardinal Bergoglio or by Pope Francis. It can be found in his account of the Second Interdisciplinary Academic Days of Theology, Philosophy, and Social Sciences at the Jesuit Faculty of Philosophy in Buenos Aires in 1971, which the young Father Bergoglio attended. Having outlined the speakers' views on class struggle, Puente explains:

> Gera and Scannone saw liberalism, Marxism and clericalism as contrivances through which the 'enlightened elite' claimed for itself the right to determine how the people should think and act. "It is not a matter of forsaking elitism in the realm of possession and ownership. That is not enough," Scannone argued: "We must also forsake the elitism of knowledge, which exists nowadays among the enlightened elites, be they on the left or the right." He advocated "a bottom-up movement to overcome the entire padlocked Euro-North American space, which regards Latin America as its appendage, dominating and subjugating it; what is needed is a liberating dialectic that allows the people to give birth to an authentically liberating and Latin American project."
>
> Jorge (Bergoglio) did not intervene in this broad debate, but his own vision of national, Latin American and Christian history coincided with this position, which he defined and

still defines as that of the People of God. His position was not conservative; on the contrary, he believed that, in the face of the "truth" that Marxism, liberalism and clericalism dictate to the people, priority should be given to the truth revealed by the Holy Spirit, through a dialogue between "the faithful people, the poor who were the followers of Jesus," and his Church.

Juan Carlos Scannone's theological and philosophical conceptions still resonate with Jorge Bergoglio-Francis, and indeed continue to shape his language.

In reality, "revolutionary clericalism"—for that is what it is—is designed to separate the faithful from the clergy and to propel them towards a new clergy.

This shift in language was one of the ways in which liberationist theology asserted itself. In a 1973 compendium presenting the "Latin American philosophy of liberation" (*Hacia una filosofía de la liberación latinoamericana*), the final article by Juan Carlos Scannone, who was the acknowledged mastermind of the project, bore the title "Transcendence, liberating praxis and language." It called on Descartes, Hegel, and Heidegger to reflect on a "critique of the language of transcendence," which "in modernity, at first took on the character of a *de-substantiation* and *de-objectification* of the image of God, i.e., the character of the negation of God as substance, and as an object of representational thought."

"But later on," Scannone wrote, "postmodernity radicalized this critique, converting it into the '*desubjectification*' and the '*de-absolutization*' of this 'thinking and saying God', thereby arriving at the negation of the absolute god as subject. Thanks to this process, we are now able to encounter in history and through praxis, not the god of metaphysics, but God, the living God of history and praxis."

This "liberation" scheme is being implemented before our very eyes.

It is being applied to the whole Church and the whole world. It is sweeping away the "enlightened elites," in other words, any institutional authority, any hierarchy that does not come from the people.

In the same way as in the Communist Party, the party alone forms the new enlightened elite and provides the people with the meaning of history. For the party, as for liberationist theology, reading the signs of the times "historicizes" all things.

The Catholic Church, its divine constitution and its hierarchy are quite simply referred to by using the word *clericalism*, just as the peasants were the "kulaks" of Stalinism. The bourgeoisie is the class enemy of the proletariat; "clericalism" is the new revolution's assigned enemy.

This ideological status refers to all those who remain in some way committed to the doctrine, sacraments, and discipline of the Catholic Church, who do not, for instance, accept the reforms that lead to Communion given without discernment, the unconditional remarriage of divorcees, the new teaching on the death penalty, and so on.

According to the pope's theology, "clericalism" is the enemy of God's people in the truest sense of the word. In Marxist terms, it is the class enemy. As Father Scannone and others have made clear, there is "the people" and "the anti-people."

To give a concrete example, consider the recent agreement between the Holy See and China: Chinese bishops recognized by the Communist Party do not belong to the "enemy of the people" class. With this agreement, the pope has achieved what the most Soviet-style liberation theology never even dared to dream of: recognizing a church run by the Communist Party and integrating it into a church governed by the pope.

Chinese Catholics and the hierarchy who refuse to belong to the Communist Party are *de facto* categorized as "clericalists."

APPENDIX 2

Networks

Throughout this analysis of the "conquest of power" by Pope Francis, the reader will have realized that since the Second Vatican Council, the full power of the present papal ideology has been supported by a myriad of men and structures. They were not and are not necessarily known to cardinal Bergoglio, and now to the pope, but they worked and still work in unison because they share the same zeal for the birth of a new Church for the world.

On March 17, 2017, the pope received a delegation from the CTEWC (Catholic Theological Ethics in the World Church) network of theologians. This highly active and little-known network on the global level is one of the pope's governing bodies, along with the Society of Jesus from which it originated.

On this occasion, its founder, Jim Keenan, SJ, was interviewed in Rome. The interviewer, journalist José M. Vidal, pointed out that the delegation had been received by the pope in person for over fifty minutes, as well as by cardinals and six congregations.

"Was this an explicit recognition of the network you founded?" the journalist asked.

Fr. Jim Keenan replied that the many Roman meetings had left an impression of "support" for this network which, having grown over the former fourteen years, was now present in eighty countries, constituting a "living network of a thousand Catholic moralists" throughout the world. He added that the delegates had spoken to the pope about the international meetings held by the CTEWC in Trent, Padua, Manila, Bangalore, Berlin, Krakow, Bogota, and Nairobi (the following year, 2018, the meeting was hosted in Sarajevo, a highly interesting city because of its Muslim majority).

Keenan highlighted the "extremely varied nature" of past meetings, noting that the members of the network "were able to debate about diversity without falling into polarization"; they emphasized this during their conversation with the pope. "We build our unity on this capacity for debate, not on a uniform consensus," he said.

Keenan was indeed putting the spotlight on a pontifical approach par excellence: "His Holiness also spoke to us about true unity, which is not found in uniformity but in diversity, taking into account the context without losing sight of what we have in common. Unity in diversity. This was a recurring theme in our conversation."

The Synod on the Family served as a life-size illustration of how the network operates and how effective it is at replicating the papal ideology. Keenan explained:

> For example, to deal with questions about marriage and divorce, he took these issues to the Synod and let the members discuss them for two years! Then, with *Amoris Laetitia*, he waited for the local churches to work and to receive the text, and he is waiting for couples to internalize it so that, after having reflected on it in all conscience, they can bring their lives to the Church. The Pope is respectful of the way in which moral illumination works: through shared perceptions, mutual trust, total honesty and the attention we pay to our traditions and to the Scriptures.
>
> The moral aspect is therefore essential in the Pope's view, but the way in which he tackles it is very inspiring for many of us who work in the field of ethics. In our network, hundreds of moralists reflect and write about his approach....
>
> First and foremost, *Amoris Laetitia* is not an intrusion into intimate spaces. Rather, it is an invitation to rethink how we access the Sacrament....
>
> Secondly, we increasingly see work on sexual ethics and marriage being done by married lay faithful, not priests. [*Keenan*

*here quotes four authors whose commitment to the most radical
ideas I have been able to verify: Lisa Cahill, Flossie Bourg, Julie
Hanlon Rubio, and David Matzko McCarthy.*] Their writings are
more comprehensive, more profound and more significant than
what ecclesiastical moralists have produced in the past.

Keenan called for a Church that is "more welcoming" and open
to young people, adding: "In these times of confusion, obscurity and
total indifference towards the common good, we need a Church that
is a beacon in the darkness. I believe that Pope Francis is in the process
of creating such a Church."

Shedding even more light on the network, Keenan stressed: "We
have no need for individual leaders: we need leaders who know how
to network, how to work as teams and how to inspire others to take
advantage of the great opportunities that are available right now to
address the crisis. This is no time for the mythical lone figure: it is a
time for solidarity-based leadership."

Lastly, it should be pointed out that the network founded by
Father Keenan in 2006 is an extension of the Society of Jesus into all
academic circles, be they Catholic or not. And Emilce Cuda, an expert
on the pope's thinking, is its regional representative.

The Cross, the Sickle, and the Hammer

The real truth!

During Pope Francis's trip to South America in 2015, he made a brief visit on July 8 to the site where, thirty-five years previously, the Jesuit liberationist Fr. Luís Espinal was executed near La Paz in Bolivia. What happened on the heels of this event particularly caught the attention of the media. During a reception by Evo Morales at his presidential palace that evening, Francis was presented by the head of state with "an unusual Christ on the Cross on a hammer and sickle, which was described as having been cherished by Fr. Espinal," reported *La Croix* the following day.

He was also presented with the "Padre Luís Espinal Camps Order of Merit, created in June 2015 by Bolivia's National Assembly: its medal bears the image of Espinal's 'communist crucifix' A month later, at the pope's request, the medal engraved with Luís Espinal's "crucifix" and the Order of the Condor that Morales had also given him were officially deposited at the feet of Our Lady of Copacabana in the Bolivian sanctuary of the same name where the Virgin has been honored since the sixteenth century.

We were astounded by most of the media comments about this "hammer and sickle" crucifix and about Father Espinal's own ideology.

In its Spanish edition on July 13, Zenit reported the words of Pope Francis on his flight back to Rome: "For me, it was not an offense," he said, commenting on the gift from Bolivian President Evo Morales. Zenit pointed out that it was a "wooden crucifix carved on a hammer that was itself supported by a sickle." Clearly, Zenit's journalist Marina Droujinina had no knowledge of Latin America, so she had no idea what she was talking about. Even a cursory observation would have shown her that the figure of Christ was not made of wood.

As for Evo Morales, responding on July 10 to a CNN journalist who asked him whether he had anticipated that his gift might be an embarrassment to the pope, he said: "Father . . . sorry, brother Pope Francis is the most important politician in the world—but the most important politician in the world for justice, for peace with social justice, for equality, for dignity."

By contrast, Bolivian bishop Gonzalo del Castillo, bishop emeritus of the Armed Forces, said that the presentation of the crucifix had been "a provocation, a dirty trick." The Bolivian bishops as a whole expressed surprise.

Marianela Paco, Bolivia's minister of communications, stated: "It's a symbolic gift: the sickle represents the worker and the hammer the carpenter, . . . the two symbols represent the humble, hard-working people." "His drawings and sculptures always had profound meanings," she added with regard to Luís Espinal.

Francisco Zaratti, a leading expert on ecclesiastical affairs in Bolivia, called it an "anachronistic gift." "In the 1970s, this work had meaning as a commitment to socialism," he explained.

Fr. Xavier Albó—yet another Jesuit—compiled and edited the work of Luís Espinal, poet, film-maker, and sculptor, in a book featuring photos of his sculptures. As a friend of Espinal, he had inherited his crucifix, a reproduction of which was offered to the pope. A month before the pope's arrival, Father Albó wrote in *La Razón* (Bolivia): "We reproduce here the new cross of 'Lucho' (Luis's nickname); he combined the Christ of his first vows with a vertical hammer and a horizontal sickle to express the necessary but elusive Christian-Marxist dialogue with the workers and peasants. The fact that he did it with the cross of his religious vows shows just how deeply he felt the pressing need for such dialogue."

During his in-flight press conference on his journey back to Rome at the end of his South American trip, the pope responded to a journalist who asked him about the crucifix by saying that "one could categorize it as a kind of protest art." He went on to mention the work of a "good, creative Argentinian sculptor," "a crucified Christ on a descending bomber. It was a criticism of Christianity allied with imperialism, represented by the bomber."

Referring to Father Espinal in particular, the pope said: "It was a time when liberation theology had many different branches. One of the branches involved a Marxist analysis of reality. Fr. Espinal belonged to this." Recalling that Luís Espinal had been killed in 1980, the pope continued: "In the same year, the Father General of the Society of Jesus, Fr. Arrupe, wrote a letter to the whole Society on the Marxist analysis of reality in theology, helping to restrain this tendency. He wrote: 'it's no good, these are different things, it's not right, it's not correct.' "

Father Espinal died on March 21, 1980. Father Arrupe's letter dates from the following December 8. It provided an excellent analysis of the intellectual disaster of Marxism and, conversely, of the havoc Marxism had wreaked within the society. The only problem is that one of the last paragraphs undermined what went before: "As far as the Marxists are concerned, we must always be ready for dialogue. Furthermore, in accordance with the spirit of *Gaudium et Spes*, we must not reject such well-defined concrete collaborations that the common good may require." To be very clear, Father Arrupe added that it was not because there were reservations about the Marxist analysis that one should "condemn as 'Marxist' or 'communist' the commitment to justice and the cause of the poor."

The company only took heed of the last lines in order to continue its revolutionary action throughout the continent. Fathers who did not follow this line were systematically sidelined.

Pope Francis went on to say: "Espinal was an enthusiast of this Marxist analysis of reality, but also of a theology that uses Marxism. From this, he came up with this art piece. Also the poetry of Espinal was of this kind of protest. It was his life, it was his thought. He was a special person, with so much human geniality, who fought in good faith. Under this kind of hermeneutic, I understand this work. For me it wasn't an offense, but I had to apply this hermeneutic, and I am telling you this so that there aren't any misguided opinions." He added that he was taking the crucifix itself back with him to the Vatican.

The pope calls this "explanation," which is anything but an explanation, "hermeneutics." At this point, it is hard not to think of his famous question: "Who am I to judge?"

All this is actually at the heart of a terrible tragedy.

In most cases, sacrilegious crucifixes retain the cross and replace Christ with all manner of abominations. Another desecration that occurred within the context of a contemporary art exhibition comes to mind: it showed the "work" *Piss Christ,* a crucifix dipped in a yellow liquid presented as urine.

In Father Espinal's case, we are dealing with a different kind of abomination.

What does the Church sing on Good Friday? "*Crucem tuam adoramus*" (we adore your cross); and also "*Dulce lignum, dulces clavos, dulce pondus sustinet*" (Sweet the wood, sweet the nails, sweet the burden which You bear). And "*Dominus regnavit a ligno*" (The Lord reigns from the cross).

This is not Father Espinal's religion. He practiced the religion of the liberationists who, in the name of historical and dialectical materialism, invented a salvation other than that brought by Jesus Christ, the Son of God.

For them, the crucified Christ (they never talk about the cross) is incarnated anew in history. "The crucified people thus has two facets: it is the victim of the sin of the world, and it is also the people that will bring salvation to the world," proclaimed the Jesuit Father Ignacio Ellacuría, SJ, in *Conversión de la Iglesia al Reino de Dios* (Conversion of the Church to the Reign of God, p. 62). We are expected to understand here that the "crucified people" are those who are fighting for their liberation, that the "sin of the world" refers to all the existing powers, including the power of the institutional Church, and that the people "will bring salvation" through their struggles.

Christ on the Bolshevik "cross" represents the "sanctification" of the people's struggles—the consecration, in fact, of the blasphemous alliance between the Revolution and the Redeemer of the world. May God have mercy on Father Espinal. He knew very well what he was doing.

To make sure that history will remember, Evo Morales decreed that the anniversary of Father Espinal's death would be the Day of Bolivian Cinema.

The first blasphemous symbol to appear on the continent, as far as we can determine, is reproduced on page 3 of the book *Los cristianos por el socialismo en Chile* with the following caption: "A symbol that combines the cross with the sickle and hammer reproduced in the private Catholic college Saint George's magazine *The Lance* in Santiago in August 1971."

The Permanent Assembly for Human Rights in Bolivia, a body that is not part of the Catholic Church, asked the Church to open a process for the beatification of Father Espinal and submitted its request to Pope Francis during the latter's visit in 2015. Since then, members of the Jesuit's family have set up an association to that end in Catalonia in the village where he was born. To date, their efforts have been unsuccessful.

APPENDIX 4

Bishop Oscar Romero

O scar Romero was born in El Salvador in 1917. He was close to Opus Dei and known for his conservative approach. Ordained a priest in his native country in 1942, one of his professors in Rome was the future Pope Paul VI, who made him a bishop in 1970. It was in 1977 that he was appointed archbishop of San Salvador, a seemingly unlikely choice designed to smooth relations between the Church and the government in power at the time, which was elected but close to the military.

It was a time of dissent—the 1977 elections were regarded as rigged—and bloody repression, which particularly hit a large number of landless peasants. Faced with widespread poverty and the violence of the authorities, the new bishop set himself up as a defender of the poor without adhering to liberation theology.

In particular, Bishop Romero defended himself as best he could against the rise of the armed revolution, driven and encouraged in the name of liberation theology. But he was no match for it.

On Sunday March 23, 1980, on the eve of his death, Oscar Romero preached a homily in his cathedral calling on the army to put an end to the repression. "My brothers, they are part of our people. They are killing their own peasant brothers. And in the face of an order to kill given by a man, God's law must prevail, which says: 'Thou shalt not kill.' No soldier is obliged to obey an order that goes against God's law.

No one is obliged to fulfill an immoral law. . . . The Church cannot remain silent in the face of so many horrors."

On the following morning, Bishop Romero celebrated Mass in a humble hospital chapel. A hired assassin aimed at him through a window and shot him in the heart. It was rumored that an "extreme right-wing" group had ordered the assassination.

Two years previously, UCA, the Central American Jesuit university based in San Salvador, had published a book bearing the title *Iglesia de los Pobres y Organizaciones Populares* (The Church of the Poor and Popular Organizations). The book is both intriguing and significant.

The first part featured a lengthy "Letter to the Faithful" in which Archbishop Romero upheld the Catholic position, albeit with some concessions to liberation theology and a reminder of the principles of commitment of the Church and the laity to the cause of social justice and the fight against poverty. Bishop Romero also spoke out against violence, no matter where it came from.

The second part of the book, signed by the revolutionary Jesuits Ignacio Ellacuría, Jon Sobrino, and Tomás Campos, presented a thorough rebuttal of Archbishop Romero's letter to the faithful. The title of one of the chapters in this second part ought to attract the attention of historians: *Reflections and Problems of the Church that is being born of the People*. Clearly, the Jesuits and the guerrillas in Central America—the latter included priests, one of whom was Belgian—had no intention of letting victory slip through their fingers.

Poor Bishop Romero! He had said that he was doing his best to create and develop "base ecclesial communities," specifying on page 23 of this two-voiced book how such communities were to be. However, his guidelines had absolutely no chance of being implemented in the Jesuit-Salvadorian context. The bishop was probably unaware that when he called on the base communities to celebrate the Eucharist, they would continue to celebrate another Passover with the same words: that of Moses, who freed the Jews from slavery! This liberation in the spirit of the base communities is prophetically announced by the Eucharist, which is not an obligation, as stated in a brochure for the "faithful" entitled *La Eucaristía en las comunidades eclesiales de base*.

A month before his death, Archbishop Romero had been awarded an honorary doctorate by the Catholic University of Leuven, one of Europe's most prominent centers for the training of liberation theology priests. In his acceptance speech, he adopted a broadly liberationist tone, claiming that the Church was persecuted because of its defense of the poor. He asserted in particular: "The world of the poor teaches us what Christian love must be." He added: "Liberation will come only when the poor . . . have themselves become actors and protagonists of their struggle and their liberation, thereby unmasking the deepest roots of false paternalism, including ecclesial paternalism."

Archbishop Romero was beatified in 2015 and then canonized in 2018 by Pope Francis as a martyr. A martyr, but of what or whom? Of the Salvadoran Jesuit liberationists?

At the time, the guerrilla movement's efforts to expand into El Salvador were unsuccessful. By creating a popular uprising as in Nicaragua, it could have hopes of prevailing. And the assassination of Archbishop Romero could have been a powerful catalyst to that end. But the Salvadorans did not rise up, and they refused to believe that their army was guilty.

Military security had even warned Oscar Romero that his life was under threat. Simultaneously, police were monitoring potential terrorists, who were immediately neutralized within minutes of the assassination.

Fifty thousand Salvadorans attended Oscar Romero's funeral. The faithful were machine-gunned that day by terrorist groups, leaving twenty-seven dead.

APPENDIX 5

Bishop Enrique Angel Angelelli

T he revolutionary Church of Latin America has its martyrs. During major liberationist events or meetings such as those of the Latin American Bishops' Conference (CELAM), a martyrs' tent is set up, where photos of those who died for the people are displayed.

Bishop Enrique Angel Angelelli is one of them; indeed, he was beatified on April 27, 2019, by Pope Francis. He is depicted as a defender of the humble and the poor; he raised his voice against repression in Argentina.

In a collection of seventy-eight "martyr" cards published by the Paulinas Editions in Brazil in 1986, ten years after his death, the bishop was portrayed on card thirteen as having been "martyred on August 4, 1976." In liberationist terms, he was murdered because he believed in the Kingdom of God, meaning the Kingdom of the Church of the poor. It is not the Kingdom whose coming we ask for in the Our Father.

Enrique Angelelli was born in 1923; he entered the seminary at age fifteen and was later sent to Rome, where he received the sacrament of Holy Orders in 1949 before going on to study canon law. On his return to Argentina, he went back to his hometown of Córdoba, where he was assigned a parish ministry; in addition, he visited the *"villas miseria"* (shantytowns) and became an advisor to the local Young Christian Workers.

In 1960, Enrique Angelelli was appointed auxiliary bishop by John XXIII, and he took part in the Second Vatican Council, where he publicly supported modernist positions. This led to his being sidelined for a time—he was not present at the second session. He was later reinstated as an auxiliary bishop and returned to the council in that capacity; in 1965, he took part in the signing of the Pact of the Catacombs.

In 1968, Pope Paul VI appointed Enrique Angelelli bishop of La Rioja, where he played a leading role in the creation of workers' movements and unions. He also helped set up cooperatives and backed the expropriation of large property-owning families—thereby alienating them as well as the province's governor, Carlos Menem, who was a member of one of them.

The facts

Was Bishop Angelelli really killed in hatred of the faith, as his title of blessed martyr would suggest? On August 4, 1976, he was returning from a celebration in honor of two murdered priests. His driver was Fr. Arturo Pinto, and they were traveling along National Route 38.

As they neared Córdoba, their car was hit by one or two vehicles; it flipped over and crashed. Bishop Angelelli was killed instantly. Father Pinto was injured and lost his memory. He would later describe how, when he came to after the shock, he realized that the bishop had been murdered; according to him, Angelelli had been "shot several times in the head."

A thorough investigation was carried out immediately after the accident, including an autopsy, photographs, and a full-scale search for evidence. When questioned at the time, Arturo Pinto could remember nothing.

In 1988, Brother Antonio Puigjané, a guerrilla who had taken part in the attack on the La Tablada barracks, made a statement to the Neuquén police suggesting that Angelelli had been assassinated. The newspaper *La Prensa* reported his allegations. The bishop of La Rioja, Bernardo Witte, expressed his "surprise" that the "mysterious death of

Bishop Angelelli could have been classified as an assassination without sufficient evidence."

The case was referred to a court which declared itself incompetent to obtain new evidence. In 1990, the Federal Appeal Chamber of Córdoba declared that although investigations had been carried out, it was impossible to say whether the accident had been caused with malice aforethought: "Whereas the means used are not sufficient to demonstrate the commission of a crime . . . the court deems it appropriate to declare the present case provisionally suspended."

In 2014, the Federal Criminal Appeal Court of La Rioja instead ruled that the case involved a crime against humanity, making it possible to prosecute not the unknown perpetrators but those who had supposedly issued the orders.

The court sentenced General Luciano Benjamin Menéndez and Major Luis Estrella to life imprisonment for the murder of Bishop Angelelli for a crime that was never proven.

Before being granted house arrest in 2015, Major Estrella told the chaplain of the prison where the two men were being detained that he had never in any way been involved in the case; the chaplain would later confirm Estrella's words.

The current bishop of Mendoza, Bishop Marcelo Colombo, was formerly appointed to the see of La Rioja because he was an unconditional supporter of the assassination theory. It was he who forwarded the request for Angelelli's beatification to Rome in early 2015, recalling that such an honor "is a tribute to the courage of witnesses of the Kingdom of God."

The area in which these events took place, as well as the level of violence that prevailed at the time, are typical of a unique reality. In 1969, violent riots took place in Córdoba (they became known as the "Cordobazo"), a university town that also housed the military academy. In Córdoba, Bishop Angelelli had worked alongside the most radical elements of the armed struggle, all of whom came from the Peronist movement. Photographs of a celebration presided over by the bishop under the Montoneros flag were published by the daily newspaper La Nación.

The bishop's commitment was supported by the Jesuits, who viewed him as a leading figure in the struggle against injustice, dictatorship, and oligarchy.

One month after Bergoglio's appointment as the new provincial of the Argentinian Jesuits in August 1973, the Father General Pedro Arrupe visited Argentina. He came to La Rioja to support the bishop's action and locally concelebrated a Mass with Father Bergoglio, who accompanied him on his trip. La Croix quoted Father Arrupe as saying during the visit: "This is the Church that Vatican II was looking for."

In the same 2015 article announcing the Vatican approval of Archbishop Angelelli's process of beatification, *La Croix* recalled that Cardinal Bergoglio had made the following statement about that visit in 2006: "I met a persecuted Church, in its entirety: the people and its shepherd."

After becoming pope, he remained faithful to this line of thought; indeed, it is for this reason—which is not restricted to Enrique Angelelli's cause—that he promulgated new provisions with regard to the beatification process on July 11, 2017, in *Maiorem hac dilectionem.* Here is its article 1: "*The offer of life* is a *new cause* for the beatification and canonization procedure, distinct from the causes based on *martyrdom* and on the *heroism of virtues.*"

This was an approach that had already been presented by Fr. Gustavo Gutiérrez, who told Vatican Radio in 2015, on the occasion of the beatification of Archbishop Romero:

> I am very impressed by what Aparecida said about martyrdom, in remembering the martyrdom of so many people, as I said, who—again according to Aparecida—offered their lives for God, for the Church and for their people. . . .
>
> This addition of the words "their people" seems very important to me; obviously God and the Church are essential, but I think adding "the people" says a lot. In a broad sense, it is a kind of extension of the motives for martyrdom, and well describes what happened.

The list of new martyrs looks set to grow.

APPENDIX 6

The Pact of the Catacombs

ere below is the full text of the Pact of the Catacombs, several times mentioned in this book. It was signed in the Catacombs of Domitilla in Rome less than a month before the end of the Second Vatican Council at the instigation of Dom Hélder Câmara on November 16, 1965. It called for a new lifestyle for the Catholic hierarchy and, more importantly, a new way of governing the Church. Reportedly, the pact has been signed by five hundred bishops, many of whom joined the original signatories over the years.

The Catacombs' Pact of the Poor and Servant Church

We, bishops gathered in the Second Vatican Council, made aware of the deficiencies of our lives of poverty according to the Gospel; encouraged by each other; in an initiative in which each one wishes to avoid singularity and presumption; united with all our brothers in the Episcopate; counting above all on the grace and strength of Our Lord Jesus Christ, on the prayers of the faithful and the priests of our respective dioceses; placing ourselves in thought and prayer before the Trinity, before the Church of Christ and before the priests and faithful of our dioceses; humbly conscious of our weakness, but also with all the determination and strength which God wishes to give us as grace, commit ourselves to the following:

1. We will seek to live according to the ordinary manner of our people, regarding habitation, food, means of transport and all which springs from this. Cf. Mt 5:3; 6:33s; 8:20.

2. We definitively renounce the appearance and reality of riches, especially regarding to our manner of dress (rich material, loud colors) and symbols made of precious materials (they should in reality be evangelical signs). Cf. Mc 6:9; Mt 10:9s; Acts 3:6. Neither gold nor silver.

3. We will not possess real estate, goods, bank accounts etc. in our own names; if it should be necessary to have them, we will place everything in the name of the diocese, or of charitable and social works. Cf. Mt 6:19–21; Lk 12:33s.

4. Whenever possible, we will entrust the financial and material administration in our dioceses to a commission of competent laity, conscious of their apostolic role, so that we may become less administrators and more pastors and apostles. Cf. Mt 10:8; Acts 6:1–7.

5. We refuse to be addressed, orally or in writing, by names or titles which signify prestige and power (Eminence, Excellency, Monsignor . . .). We prefer to be called by the evangelical title of Father. Cf. Mt 20:25–28; 23:6–11; Jn 13:12–15.

6. In our behavior and social relations, we will avoid anything which may seem to confer privileges, priority or any preference for the rich and powerful (such as: banquets, offered or accepted, class distinction during religious services Cf. Lk 13:12–14; 1 Cor 9:14–19.)

7. In the same way we will avoid the fostering or pampering of the vanity of anyone, in order to seek reward or solicit donations, or for any reason whatsoever. We will invite our faithful to consider their donations as a normal participation in the cult, the apostolate and social action. Cf. Mt 6:2–4; Lk 15:9–13; 2 Cor 12:4.

8. We will dedicate whatever is necessary of our time, reflection, heart, means etc. to the apostolic and pastoral service of people

and groups of workers and of the economically weak and under-developed, without prejudice to the other people and groups in the diocese. We will support those laity, religious, deacons and priests who the Lord calls to evangelize the poor and the workers, sharing the work and life of laborers. Cf. Lk 4:18s; Mk 6:4; Mt 11:4s; Acts 18:3s; 20:33–35; 1 Cor 4:12 e 9:1–27.

9. Conscious of the demands of justice and charity, and their mutual relationship, we will seek to transform assistential activities into social works based on justice and charity, which take into account all that this requires, as a humble service of the competent public organs. Cf. Mt 25:31–46; Lk 13:12–14 e 33s.

10. We will do our utmost so that those responsible for our government and for our public services make, and put into practice, laws, structures and social institutions required by justice and charity, equality and the harmonic and holistic development of all men and women, and by this means bring about the advent of another social order, worthy of the sons and daughters of mankind and of God. Cf. Acts 2:44s; 4:32–35; 5:4; 2 Cor 8 e 9; 1Tim 5:16.

11. Believing the collegiality of the bishops to be of the utmost evangelical importance in facing the burden of human masses, in a state of physical, cultural and moral misery—two thirds of humanity—we commit ourselves:

- to participate, according to our means, in the urgent investments of the episcopates of poor nations;

- to demand that the plans of international organizations, but witnessing to the Gospel, as Pope Paul VI did in the UNO, adopt economic and cultural structures which no longer manufacture proletarian nations in an ever richer world, but which will permit the poor masses to overcome their misery.

12. We commit ourselves to share, in pastoral charity, our lives with our brothers and sisters in Christ, priests, religious and laity, so that our ministry constitute a true service; so,

- We will really try to "review our lives" with them;

- We will find collaborators who will be more animators according to the Spirit, rather than according to the chiefs of this world;

- We will seek to be more humanly present, more welcoming ...;

- We will show ourselves to be open to all, whatever their religion. Cf. Mc 8:34s; Acts 6:1–7; 1 Tim 3:8–10.

13. On returning to our respective dioceses, we will make this resolution known to our people, asking them to help us by their understanding, collaboration and prayers.

"MAY GOD HELP US TO BE FAITHFUL."

Popular Religiosity as a Form of Inculturation of the Faith in the Spirit of Aparecida

T he 5th CELAM Conference that took place in May in the Brazilian sanctuary of Aparecida was a major event for the Church. Its pointed look at Latin American realities is challenging the Church to fulfill its mission of evangelization.

Promoting evangelization as the purpose of its activity is hardly something new in the Church; Christianity possesses an original and founding impulse that leads it to proclaim salvation to all peoples (Mt 28:19).

But the pressing need for mission propounded by Aparecida points to a sense of decline in Latin American Catholicism. For over five hundred years, the Christian faith has permeated the continent's culture, fostering a religiosity that when sincerely embraced, nurtures both personal lives and those of our peoples. However, although Catholics continue to represent a majority, something is changing. Pope Benedict said at the beginning of the Conference: *"One can detect a certain weakening of Christian life in society overall and of participation in the life of the Catholic Church, due to secularism, hedonism, indifferentism and proselytism by numerous sects, animist religions and new pseudo-religious phenomena"* (DA. 2).

We are living in a new era marked by deep and fast-paced change. Such a reality generates insecurity, confusion, and fear in the hearts of the men and women of our time. In the Latin American and Caribbean context, this is even more complex and dramatic because our peoples live in a world where poverty and exclusion are increasing, institution-alized corruption has taken root, and violence of all kinds is spreading together with the growing loss of identity itself.

This situation has developed as a result of the changes foreseen by the Second Vatican Council (GS 4–10) as early as forty years ago. Transformations have become more acute, and this epochal change demands a new way of positioning ourselves in a history that has changed and will continue to change. Things that we thought would never happen or that we would never witness are now taking place, and our future has become uncertain.

We cannot dismiss the phenomena that have arisen in post-modernity, the effects of globalization and so many other processes by thinking of them as a temporary crisis, and just wait for them to pass in the hope that everything will go back to the way it was before. Yet the irreversibility of globalization—which is so unfair in many ways—in its positive dimension as "a network of relationships extend-ing over the whole planet . . . this benefits the great family of humanity, and is a sign of its profound aspiration towards unity" (Benedict XVI, *Inaugural Address*, 2), provides a fresh opportunity for evangelization to reach the whole world and for the Church to work for unity on the continents and among peoples; and to make the cooperation and credibility of Christians more effective.

The Conference has the strong conviction that a Christian cannot fail to be a missionary; on the other hand, this obligation cannot be lived out in depth and in truth in an attitude of discipleship, meaning a personal and communitarian encounter with Jesus Christ. We Chris-tians are disciples of the Master, and therefore, we can only consider reality in terms of mission.

We are not impartial observers, but men and women who are eager to permeate all the structures of society with a love that we ourselves have come to know: a love that is capable of transforming reality into abundant life when the two meet.

In his inaugural address, the Pope said that this is *"the best thing that has happened in our lives"* and *"it is what we have to offer to the world, and countering the culture of death with the Christian culture of solidarity is an imperative for all of us."* (DA 480)

The Church in Latin America and the Caribbean wants to put herself in a position of *"missionary discipleship"* in a concrete way, with critical, sapiential and prophetic openness, with identity and discernment, in order to *"give life to our peoples,"* in Christ.

Discipleship is about discernment: the "humble gaze" (DA 36), listening with attention (DA 366). The disciple does not know what he is, or what he has to do, because he is not a Master: he listens, he pays attention, he does not have an answer. That is the Church of Aparecida: a community of missionary disciples who seek to listen to the Lord. Listening to the Lord also means listening to reality with a humble spirit in order to discern what it is necessary to be and to do.

Like the rest of the world, Latin America is experiencing a cultural transformation; *"the 5th Conference is seeking to establish criteria on how to evangelize culture, and on how the Good News can be brought to the people from the culture of each people"* (Cardinal Paul Poupard).

How Far We Have Traveled

When approaching the reality of Evangelization in Latin America today, it is impossible to do so without taking into account certain terms such as: culture, inculturation, popular religiosity, popular piety. But the realities that are hidden behind each of these words have already been studied and analyzed, and above all, they are today the result of the accumulated experience of history; and history itself, with its constant fluctuations, has progressively determined their meaning and the place they occupy.

In the final document of the 5th Conference, the word "culture" appears about 70 times, and what it is intended to express is totally different from what was understood in the 1950s when the First Assembly of the Latin American Episcopate was held. Likewise, the reality of popular religiosity now has an importance and a positive resonance that is very different from what could be perceived when it appeared in the first writings of the Latin American Church.

We cannot reach a full understanding if we do not read them in the light of the history that gradually shaped them and gave them the scope they have today. The evolution of the Church in Latin America cannot be understood without taking into account the social and political changes that took place there from the 1960s onwards.

When the Council of Trent was concluded in 1563, America had already received hundreds of missionaries, having witnessed the great controversy raised by Bartolomé de las Casas on evangelization and conversion methods; it had about thirty dioceses and had held several local and provincial councils to discuss the American missionary project.

These four centuries were brought to a close by the Second Vatican Council. The diversity of situations and cultures in which the various churches lived, such as the torpid European Christendoms, Eastern churches, communities in India, Japan and China, young churches in Africa and the popular Catholicisms of Latin America, among others, became clearly visible.

These topics "entered through the front door" for the first time, and gave our particular Churches a new light to face old problems and to engage in a cultural dialogue, both within and without. She exhorted that "*through dialogue and collaboration with the followers of other religions, carried out with prudence and love and in witness to the Christian faith and life, they recognize, preserve and promote the good things, spiritual and moral, as well as the socio-cultural values found among these men*" (*Nostra Aetate* 2).

On another level, Vatican II has rediscovered the importance of charisms within the Church (*Lumen Gentium*, 12), and it also urges us to discern the signs of the times (*Gaudium et Spes*, 4; 11; 44). The Council represents a new openness to dialogue with the contemporary world, a degree of reconciliation with enlightened modernity and the recovery of the prophetic dimension of the Church in relation to society. Thanks to this light shed by the Council, it is possible to understand what has happened and been experienced by the Church in Latin America in recent decades.

a) Medellín

Although a wide range of issues were raised, poverty and the need for freedom were the ones that captured attention regarding Latin America and the Caribbean in the post-conciliar period.

The Cuban revolution of Fidel Castro, the attempt to implement developmentalism, and popular social movements in Peru, Chile, Bolivia, and Mexico began to change the scene in Latin America; together with the failed attempt of "Che" Guevara to extend the revolution to the whole of Latin America starting in Bolivia, they shaped the context in which the 2nd Latin American Conference of Bishops was held in 1968. Medellín was not only an application of the Council to Latin America but a creative re-reading of Vatican II from a world of unjust poverty with economic and social "structures of sin." The Church in Latin America is beginning to try to understand itself and discover its mission from the clamor of its poor, the suffering of the people, of indigenous people, women, workers, peasants, children.

Although the cultural question was never directly addressed in Medellin, all its reflections were tinted with the color that social reality was giving to the culture.

The 2nd Latin American Episcopal Conference made a clear choice for the enormous mass of the disinherited of this continent and invested a large part of its energies in the constitution of a "Church that is being born of the people," a space where the poorest gather to listen to and understand the word of God in the light of the awareness-raising about daily realities.

It was thanks to the option for the poorest that the particular churches came into a more direct encounter with the multifaceted religious and cultural reality of this continent. In making room for the poor to have their place and their say, a hidden church is being rediscovered, made up of the memories of more than 2,600 native peoples, with their innumerable languages and traditions, as well as two million people of African descent. It was inevitable that the cultural expressions of these huge segments of the population should find their way into liturgies.

So important was Medellín for Latin America and even for the universal Church that when in 1974 the president of CELAM, Eduardo Pironio, traveled to Rome for the Synod on Evangelization, he took with him three pastoral suggestions that would later have a marked influence on the famous apostolic exhortation of Pope Paul VI, *Evangelii Nuntiandi*. The three suggestions were: base ecclesial communities and the themes of liberation and popular religiosity.

b) Puebla

The Puebla conference found this process of "giving back their voice" to the poor in full swing. The Base Ecclesial Communities and the popular liberation movements considered that social change would only be possible if it were to be taken up by the masses, and be able to speak their language. This conception, with its lights and shadows, contributed to the Church's reencounter with indigenous and Afro-American cultures in a more explicit way.

In Puebla, the cultural theme came in through the portal of popular religiosity and became part of the themes of the 500th anniversary commemorations that culminated in Santo Domingo. Puebla is extensively dedicated to the reflection on popular religiosity. But it only succeeded in contemplating such religiosity as an imperfect realization of the "radical Catholic substrate" of this continent.

The social and ecclesial landscape has changed significantly since 1989. The fall of socialism in the East, neoliberalism which presents itself as the only way of salvation, the rise of the cultural current of post-modernity, have produced a change of horizon in the social and ecclesial conscience of Latin America.

c) Santo Domingo

At the 4th Latin American Conference of Bishops which met in Santo Domingo in 1992, the path of the Church in Latin America was called into question. The challenge of inculturating the Gospel in society demanded that the laity should not reduce their action to the intra-ecclesial sphere, and instead urged them to "penetrate the socio-cultural environment, and to turn into protagonists of the transformation of society in the light of the Gospel." The laity must no longer be "sacristy Christians" in their individual parishes, but should consciously commit to building society in the political, economic, labor, cultural and environmental spheres.

With this background, however, the conditions were already in place allowing for a less narrow vision of the reality of Latin American cultures. The "Unity and plurality of indigenous, Afro-American and mestizo cultures" were discussed and steps were taken in that direction now the reality of our *"multiethnic and pluricultural continent"* was acknowledged, with *"the worldview of each people"*, *"who seek, however, a unity based on Catholic identity"* (SD 244). Cultural and social plurality was thus accepted as long as it did not imply religious plurality.

The conclusions of Santo Domingo revealed an open wound in the relations of the Christian churches with the ancestral traditions of the American peoples: seeking and preserving "Catholic identity" seemed to be in conflict with the challenge of ecumenical and interreligious dialogue. Commission 26, which met throughout the conference, affirmed the *"uninterrupted action of God through his Spirit in all cultures"* (225-1), understanding inculturation as *"a process conducted from within each people and community"* (225-2).

The final version of the document allowed for *"promoting an inculturation of the liturgy, and welcomed with appreciation its symbols, rites and religious expressions that are compatible with the clear sense of faith, while maintaining the value of the universal symbols and in harmony with the general discipline of the Church"* (SD 248).

Culture According to Aparecida

Without question, the new approach to Latin American realities adopted in Aparecida has privileged the concept of culture as an important interpretative key. A very varied approach to the subject was used, but there was no concise definition of the term, although some particular features of this concept, based on the way reality was perceived, do emerge.

... New actors are emerging in within this situation of cultural change, with new lifestyles, ways of thinking, feeling, and perceiving, and with new ways of relating. They are authors and agents of the new culture. (51)

This is a dynamic concept that implies talking about subjects: those who produce it and make it real, as well as about their ways of behaving and the way they represent their surroundings to themselves. This type of connection causes constant change in society. The elements produced in the culture affect each other, thus developing new forms of expression and decision in individuals.

Aparecida brings to light the fact that the social phenomenon manifests itself in a highly complex way. Situations exist that are recognized as unworthy of the human being, and it is necessary to discover how Christianity interacts with this phenomenon. The Church is no longer conceived of as being on the margins of the production of meaning, but as one of the actors of this process. It does not position itself from a critical position, but takes an active part in that which determines the configuration of collective spaces. This positioning allows the Church to avoid the temptation of considering itself as a reality that is apart from society and its contradictions. The Church is a producer of culture, that is, of human behavior, and a promoter of processes. It is only a part of the great spectrum, it is not the only actor. Its ability to wield influence is challenged by the task of convincing of the relevance and possibility of the Christian project, as a project that brings about the integral fulfillment of man and the concrete history in which he develops every day.

One of the underlying principles of Aparecida is the awareness of our responsibility to show that the Good News of Jesus is an effective way of salvation. This has as a counterpart: the need to discover and recognize what role the Church has played and must play in the face of painful and unjust realities that affect a large part of society. Aparecida observed a divorce between faith and the concrete social practice of believers, in spite of the fact that many believers have chosen large-scale options of solidarity. It is the lay world that has as its main task to bear witness to the presence of God in a commitment to transform social structures.

"*The greed of the market unleashes the desires of children, youth, and adults. Advertising creates the illusion of distant make-believe worlds where every desire can be satisfied by products that are of an effective, ephemeral, and even messianic nature. The notion that desires should turn into happiness is condoned. Since only the here-and-now is needed, happiness is sought through economic well-being and hedonistic satisfaction*" (DA 50).

The fundamental cause of this rift lies in a perception of reality that is absolutely linked to personal satisfaction. It is certainly stimulated by social media when they are handled in accordance with market demands. The conception of happiness as the satisfaction of desire is placed at the center of human needs. It is nothing more than the auto-referentiality of a basic narcissism. This is in contrast with the various situations of marginalization and suffering that exist on the continent. The new generations that are growing up in the logic of pragmatic and egomaniacal individualism are hit the hardest by these changes. For them, the past is not something they miss and the future is uncertain. Achieving maximum satisfaction is the reference point of their present reality; it also allows them to forget, if only for a moment, the great conflicts and insecurities from which they suffer. We live in a world where conditions of greater abundance have made it possible to generate a system of behavior that has no concern for social issues.

However, the root of this lack of concern about social life is characterized by the force of disenchantment, to which should be added the phenomenon of globalization, especially in its economic aspect, which affects all sectors, putting at risk the means of subsistence of many people; at the same time, there is a new openness to the influence of novel practices and customs that generate syncretic ideas and ambiguous behaviors, which clash with the ways of seeing and feeling of people who grew up in a different cultural environment. These clashes have been structuring the new society, which has turned change into a permanent reality.

This all helps us to understand that ecclesial life is faced with a series of important challenges, in the face of which the document advocates a life of faith, in which the human richness of the proposition of the Gospel becomes manifest. The community of faith—which bonds people together in a new way and thus becomes a counter-cultural space—is opposed to a conception of social life that places consumerism at its center as the sure and certain path to happiness. For a long time now, we have been witnessing "a kind of new cultural colonization by the imposition of artificial cultures, spurning local cultures and tending to impose a uniform culture . . . which leads to indifference toward the other, *whom one does not need and for whom one does not feel responsible.*" (DA 46). The exacerbated affirmation of individual and subjective rights goes hand in hand with the absence of responsible efforts for solidarity-based social and cultural rights, leaving the dignity of all, especially of the poorest and most needy, unclear. In this cultural situation, the greatest challenge consists in engaging in empathetic dialogue with the different components of culture so that it becomes an effective vehicle for drawing closer to Jesus. A lack of critical reflection and discernment can lead to fundamentalist religious subjectivism or to the syncretism of superficial and washed-up Christians. In this sense, the Assembly of Aparecida has firmly established the need for formation for all the faithful, not as indoctrination, but as a deepening of the journey of faith, which must necessarily go hand in hand with the human process of personal growth.

Culture and Inculturation

Based on the Council, a subjective concept of culture includes everything whereby man develops and perfects his many bodily and spiritual qualities (GS 53). An objective concept of culture includes the cultivation of three basic relationships of man: his relationship with nature, which he modifies, brings under control and uses to acquire goods for consumption and service; his relationship with man, in order to make coexistence more human through the improvement of customs and institutions; his relationship with God, through practicing religion (GS 53): essential to every culture is the attitude with which a people affirms or denies a religious bond with God, because of the values or anti-values that this entails (Puebla 386, 389).

A sociological (ethnological) concept reveals a plurality of cultures in history, different styles of community life (GS 53), with multiple scales of values, diverse manners of laboring, of using things, of expressing oneself, of practicing religion, of establishing laws and juridical institutions, of creating art and cultivating beauty. That this culture is patrimony of each community was made explicit in the reflections of Puebla (Puebla 387).

Evangelizing Culture

In the path we have traveled, a decisive moment was the Synod of Bishops on Evangelization, which was held in Rome in 1974 and culminated in the Apostolic Exhortation *Evangelii Nuntiandi* of Pope Paul VI (December 8, 1975). This document guided all the labors of the 3rd General Assembly of the Latin American Episcopate held in Puebla in February 1979.

While the theme of culture entered the formal teaching of the Magisterium of the Church for the first time in history in the documents of Vatican II with the affirmation of *Gaudium et Spes* stating that man reaches true and full humanity only through culture (GS 53), which has its own value and a legitimate autonomy (GS 55: AA7), only in *Evangelii Nuntiandi* does the theme of the Evangelization of Culture and Cultures appear in the face of the drama of our times, which it describes as the undeniable split between Gospel and Culture (EN 20).

The Pope and Puebla teach that to evangelize is to evangelize Cultures, to bring the "*Good News into all the strata of humanity, transforming . . . from within the personal and collective conscience of mankind (EN 18), values, and models of life which are in contrast with the Word of God and the plan of salvation (EN 19). What matters is to evangelize man's culture and cultures, always taking the person as one's starting-point, and his relationship with others and with God*" (EN 20).

Puebla devoted ample space to this theme (n. 388–56) by asserting that to evangelize is to reach the roots of Cultures, transform structures and the social environment, strengthen the authentic values of cultures, contribute to the development of the *"semina verbi,"* purify disvalues, set aside idolatries and absolutized values, and correct false conceptions of God and the manipulations of man by man.

As a specific point of the evangelization of culture in Latin America, the purification and dynamization of *"popular Catholicism"* by the Gospel (Puebla 457) needs to be stressed, as well as the promotion of the human person according to the social doctrine of the Church, in order to liberate from the servitude of personal and social sin, and to achieve a coexistence worthy of the children of God (472–506).

Puebla expanded on the reflection on culture of *Gaudium et Spes*; it assimilated the proposals of *Evangelii Nuntiandi* on the evangelization of culture and transformed them into a pastoral program for the Church in Latin America: the Gospel must penetrate the values and criteria that inspire our cultures (Puebla 395).

There is in the whole of Latin America *"a Catholic substrate"* (n. 7) *"of a culture impregnated with faith that expresses itself in the religious attitudes of the people"* (n. 413). *"Popular religiosity contains a wealth of values that wisely respond to the great questions of existence (n. 448), but today it is threatened by urbanization, secularism and the structures of injustice that have been imposed on it"* (n. 37).

The importance given by Puebla to socio-economic structures as an element of culture and an object of evangelization constitutes a great contribution and a development of the concept of culture in GS and of the challenges to evangelization mentioned in *Evangelii Nuntiandi*.

Inculturation of the Faith

From a sociological perspective, the term "inculturation" refers to *"the process of transmission and communication through codes, both linguistic and iconic, of values, norms of life and behavioral patterns of a given socio-cultural group to the rising new generations. It is the process*

through which the individual receives, assimilates, reinterprets and
actively assumes the culture in which he/she is born or of which he/she
effectively begins to form part" (A. Do Carmo Cheuiche, *Marco de refer-*
encia actual sobre la problemática de la inculturación, in Medellín 60).

From its beginnings, The Church has always engaged in inculturation in her missionary word. St. Paul put it into practice in the Greek
and Roman world ("*I became all things to all men that I might preach*
the good news," 1 Cor 9:22–23). The work of the great missionaries of
all times has been characterized by the process of inculturation. The
brothers Cyril and Methodius brought the light of the Gospel to the
Slavic peoples and prepared the liturgical texts for them according to
their mentality and in the Slavic language: "Using their knowledge of
their own Greek language and culture for this arduous and singular
work, they set themselves the task of understanding and penetrating
the language, customs and traditions proper to the Slavic peoples,
faithfully interpreting the human aspirations and values that subsisted
and were expressed in them" (Encyclical *Slavorum Apostoli*, June 2,
1985). In the 17th century, the Jesuit apostles of China, Matteo Ricci
and Martino Martini, were able to incorporate Chinese and Malabar
rites into the Catholic liturgy. During the first evangelization in the
Paraguay region, the Franciscan Luis Bolaños wrote the first grammar
and the first dictionary in Guarani, as well as a prayer book in that language; then Blessed José de Anchieta of the Society of Jesus studied the
Tupi language and composed its first grammar, along with a catechism,
poems, and hymns for evangelization.

When Puebla indicated a number of criteria regarding the
assumption of cultures, it spoke of an incarnation (n. 400), but it did
not develop the issue of the inculturation of the Gospel. It was Pope
John Paul II who officially took up the term "inculturation" in his
apostolic letter *Catechesi tradendae* of 1979 and consecrated it, defining its meaning and giving it a universal scope. It was to be one of
the themes he would deal with most frequently in his approach of
Evangelization, highlighting it as one of its important aspects. Just
a few months into his Pontificate, on April 27, 1979, he had already
expounded that "inculturation is a component of the Incarnation":

that is to say, that the inculturation of the faith and of the Gospel are a practical consequence of the Incarnation of the Son of God, who saves all and only that which he assumes (*"quod non est assumptum non est redemptum"*, St. Irenaeus), and that he must therefore assume in the Church all cultures, purifying or eliminating that which is contrary to his spirit, but by the same means preserving it from all self-destruction. Inculturation is the penetration of the Gospel message into cultures, in the manner in which the Word became flesh and dwelt among us (John 1:14).

The Pope began his anthropological discourse on man in his 1979 encyclical *Redemptor Hominis*. Man, in the fullness of his personal and at the same time communitarian and social being, is the path that the Church is obliged to follow in the fulfillment of her mission . . . the path traced out by Christ himself, which invariably leads to the path of the Incarnation and Redemption (n. 14). Speaking to UNESCO in Paris in 1980, he explained: "Man must be affirmed for himself, and not for any other motive or reason: solely for himself." And he continued: "Man lives a truly human life thanks to culture": through culture, man, as man, becomes more man. In an address to the faithful in Bergamo in 1982, speaking on Christian culture and the evangelization of culture, the Pope pointed out, as fundamental axes that would guide his entire Magisterium: a healthy anthropological concept of culture and a theological concept of inculturation of the Gospel.

It is through culture that the Gospel can approach man, man who is the beginning, the means and the end of culture. *"Culture makes man and man makes culture"* (John Paul II at the University of Coimbra, Portugal).

Between Christianity and culture there is an inseparable, harmonious connection, as has always existed between religion and culture. For the Gospel to approach culture and, through it, man, the Gospel must know the language and mental categories of the culture it encounters, its ways of life, its values. This is how it will be able to integrate them into the Christian faith and gradually transform them, until they become a vital incarnation in that culture. Inculturation is, therefore, the process by which faith becomes culture.

In this process, fidelity to the historical experience of God in the context of a particular culture, fidelity to the apostolic tradition and fidelity to universal ecclesial communion are essential. Inculturation can never be reduced to only one of the terms of this triple fidelity. Often, due to lack of clarity, cases of imposition or superficial adaptations occurred, the negative results of which were deplored by Pope Paul VI in *Evangelii Nuntiandi* (20). From these concrete, forced and skin-deep forms of the evangelizing proclamation, no local Churches were born that were capable of transforming their socio-cultural environments or of being missionary in their dynamics; rather, it resulted in cases of superficial Christianization, or a kind of syncretism was produced.

The Church, in her desire to promote authentic evangelization based on a healthy inculturation of the Gospel in a plurality of cultures, faces the challenge of wisely and creatively devising new tools and structures for understanding reality, intercultural dialogue, theological reflection and formation, and collegial communion to safeguard and activate each of the terms of this action.

Salvation must reach all men and the whole of man in his daily and concrete existence, which is why the Gospel, when it comes into contact with the Cultures, incorporates their authentic values and ends up creating culture: "*Faith that does not become culture is not wholly embraced, fully thought, or faithfully lived*," said the Pope in Rome, in 1988. Faith incorporates concrete men and women into the people of God, and this must be done without uprooting them from their own people and culture. All the action of the Church tends to welcome into its bosom those who want to be disciples of Jesus Christ and must accompany them along the path of life they follow day by day with all their cultural baggage lived out in the community. There is constant reciprocity between the evangelization of a people and the inculturation of the Gospel; but for this bond to be fruitful, it is essential to enable culture to manifestly express the signs of the faith, and to encourage it to enter into the process of being purified of the traditions and forms that are not compatible with the Gospel. The Church must also make herself capable of assimilating the values of this people and of understanding how the Gospel is seen from its perspective. In this correct balance, which does not mean that there are fluctuations, it will be possible to communicate the Gospel message to a people with all the authenticity and strength of the word of God, but also with all the authenticity and strength of the cultural reality and of the very being of that people.

Another important moment for the evolution of this line of thought took place after the celebration of the 4th General Conference of the Latin American Episcopate whose central theme was the "New Evangelization, human-cultural-Christian promotion." Chapter III of the 2nd part of the document of Santo Domingo dealt with the theme of Christian Culture, and it includes abundant references to inculturation (n. 230) and inculturated evangelization (n. 248). The crisis of the disappearance of human and Christian values appears as a cause for alarm, and one way to rise to this challenge is the inculturation of the Gospel, in the light of the three great mysteries of salvation: Christmas (the Incarnation), Easter (redemptive suffering), and Pentecost (action of the Spirit that leads to understand in one's own language the wonders of God). We must offer an inculturated evangelization to our indigenous brothers and sisters, respecting their cultural expressions, learning their worldview which, based on the God-man-world globality, forms a unity that permeates all human, spiritual and transcendent relationships. Their symbols, rites, and religious expressions that are compatible with a genuine sense of faith should be received with esteem (n. 248). Modern culture (n. 252–254) and the city demand a new Pastoral Care (255 ff.).

In the Encyclical *Redemptoris Missio*, Pope John Paul II showed that as the third millennium drew near, the need to bring the Gospel to all peoples was becoming even more urgent. Since the close of Vatican II and barely 25 years after the conciliar Decree *Ad Gentes*, the number of those who do not know Christ has almost doubled. The Apostolic Exhortation *Ecclesia in Africa* of 1994 indicates what the ways of the Mission will be: the witness of Christian life, the kerygma or proclamation of Christ who was crucified, died and is risen, conversion and baptism, the formation of Christian communities, inculturation or process of insertion into the cultures of the peoples (n. 52–54), dialogue with other religions, the education of consciences to promote development. This whole program will need to be moved by love.

Inculturation is the intimate transformation of authentic cultural values into Christian values, integrating them into one and the same vision of life, and at the same time rooting Christianity in diverse cultures on the basis of reflection and praxis. This is not an easy process, for it should in no way dilute the characteristics and integrality of the Christian message. To inculturate is to incarnate the Gospel in the different cultures, to transmit values, to recognize values of the different cultures, to purify them, to avoid different kinds of syncretism. This requires periods of preparation and of prudential caution, but above all, of sapiential listening to the voices of the Universal Church, of all the Christian people. It is through the reflection and experience of the Christian people that the genuine sense of faith is attained. Pastors and faithful, the whole people of God, participate in this work (cf. *Lumen Gentium* 12).

For this reason, the inculturation of the faith or evangelization of culture is framed within the logic of the mystery of the incarnation, death and resurrection. It begins in an effort to express the faith in the categories and ways proper to that culture, in an attempt at incarnation. During the second step, the Gospel carries out a discernment of that culture, so that the latter can divest itself of what is opposed to the Gospel. From the death of elements that are not compatible and therefore not possible to assimilate, a new original Christian culture is resurrected. Every culture is a product of man and, consequently, will be marked by sin: culture too must be purified, elevated, and perfected (Encyclical *Redemptoris Missio* 54).

In 1994, in his Apostolic Letter *Tertio millennio adveniente* (n. 38), Pope John Paul II announced two continental Synods: one for the Americas, so different in terms of their history and social situations, and the other for Asia, in which he highlighted the encounter of Christianity with the most ancient of local cultures and religions.

The Church exists to evangelize (EN 14) and the purpose of evangelization is *"transforming humanity from within and making it new."*

Inculturation is proposed as a priority and a requirement for evangelization, a path towards full evangelization, the great challenge on the
eve of the third millennium (EA 59).

Inculturation prepares mankind to welcome Jesus Christ in the
wholeness of its personal, cultural, political, and economic being, sanc-
tified by the action of the Spirit (EN 62). It is not a mere adaptation of
the kerygma or of the liturgy, or a tactic to make Christianity attractive
even at the cost of mutilating Revelation. It is a patient catechesis and a
loving search for those "*seeds of the Word*" which, when they mature,
will produce the fruits of a civilization of love. It encompasses all the
areas of the Church's life: theology, liturgy, life, and structure of the
Church in its twofold dimension, that of transforming authentic cultural values through their integration in Christianity, and the insertion
of Christianity in the various human cultures (*Redemptoris Missio* 52).

An important aspect of inculturated evangelization is to discover
man in the sense of restored human dignity. God restores to man his
inalienable dignity as a person and as a child of God through the Incarnation of his only Son. This ministry of evangelization in the social
sphere, which denounces and combats everything that degrades and
destroys the person, is part of the inculturation of the Gospel (EA 70).

Inculturation as an Action of the Holy Spirit

"*Through inculturation the Church makes the Gospel incarnate in different cultures and at the same time introduces peoples, together with
their cultures, into her own community. She transmits to them her own
values, at the same time taking the good elements that already exist in
them and renewing them from within*" (RM 52).

"*Inculturation is a movement towards full evangelization. It seeks
to dispose people to receive Jesus Christ in an integral manner. It touches
them on the personal, cultural, economic and political levels so that they
can live a holy life in total union with God the Father, through the action
of the Holy Spirit*" (EA 62).

In order to penetrate ways of thinking, feeling, and acting in other
cultures and make them ferment with the leaven of the Gospel, the

action of the Holy Spirit is absolutely necessary: it is He who gives life to history and who can lead it to the "*new creation*" (Rev. 21:5).

This is the same Spirit who made Himself present in the incarnation, in the life, death, and resurrection of Jesus and who is at work in the Church. All that the Spirit works in men and in the history of peoples serves as a preparation for the Gospel, and can only be understood in reference to Christ, the Word who took flesh by the operation of the Spirit, "*so that as perfectly human he would save all human beings and sum up all things*" (RM 29).

Inculturation also has profound links with the mystery of Pentecost thanks to the outpouring and action of the Spirit, who draws gifts and talents into unity. All the peoples of the earth, when they enter the Church and live a new Pentecost, profess in their own tongue the one faith in Jesus Christ and proclaim the marvels that the Lord has done for them. The Spirit, who on the natural level is the original source of the wisdom of peoples, leads the Church with a supernatural light into knowledge of the whole truth. In her turn, the Church takes on the values of different cultures, becoming the "*sponsa ornata monilibus suis*," "the bride who adorns herself with her jewels" (cf. Is 61:10. *Ecclesia in Africa* 61).

"*The event of that day was certainly mysterious, but also very significant*." It allows us to discover a sign of the universality of Christianity and of the missionary character of the Church: the hagiographer presents her to us in the awareness that the message is intended for people of "*all nations*," and also that it is the Holy Spirit who is at work to make every person understand at least something in their own language: "we heard them in our own native tongue" (Acts 2:8). Nowadays, we would speak of an adaptation to the linguistic and cultural conditions of each person. Thus can we see in all this a primary form of "inculturation" brought about by the work of the Holy Spirit. General Audience—Wednesday, September 20, 1989.

God's revelation cannot fail to be inculturated, but cultures are different and changing, just like man throughout history; therefore, the Good News can come alive only under the action of the Spirit, who makes the Word of God resound with salvific power, be challenging and be proclaimed in a language that is appropriate for man to accept in the circumstances in which it is his lot to live. The Spirit is the one who assists so that the plurality of expressions of faith can be recognized. Under the action of the Spirit, God's self-communication is gradually illuminated with the changing circumstances. It is obvious that the many transculturations of the message are progressively enriching its understanding. Moreover, the understanding of the revealed, transmitted, and experienced mystery continues to grow, as the Spirit leads us to the full truth.

Inculturation and Popular Religiosity

Inculturation of the faith is one of the most pressing issues in the Church today. "*The synthesis between culture and faith is not just a demand of culture, but also of faith. A faith which does not become culture is a faith which has not been fully received, not thoroughly thought through, not faithfully lived out*" (John Paul II. *Letter instituting the Pontifical Council for Culture*). Faith is not an idea, a philosophy, or an ideology. Faith proceeds from a personal encounter with Jesus Christ, the Son of God made flesh. A person who discovers God's love in his life is not the same as before. And a people that believes in the living and true God, Jesus Christ, and follows him, is a unique people. Therefore, popular religiosity is the faith of the simple people, which becomes life and culture, it is the peculiar way that the people have of living and expressing its relationship with God, with the Virgin and with the saints, both in a private and intimate environment and, in special way, as a community.

If we are to value popular religiosity in a positive way, it is necessary to work from a radically hopeful anthropology. Man has to be defined in terms of his openness to the transcendent. We must start out from an anthropology that considers man in his unity of body and spirit, and his openness to the infinite. Man discovers God based on what he is and what he does in the concrete reality of his life. The God of Christian revelation manifests himself in these realizations, which he always opens in the direction of their transcendent destiny.

In Puebla, they talked to us about deficient anthropologies that are not compatible with the religious dimension of man: determinism, psychologism, economicism, statism, scientism. . . .

Valuing popular religiosity begins with a conception of man that sees him as the being of the transcendent, of the sacred. Man is the only creature capable of worship, and he manifests his intelligence insofar as it attains a worshipful confession of faith. Christian anthropology starts out with the presupposition of the dignity of man and of all its demonstrations, which also include all the expressions of popular religiosity.

Popular religiosity is quite simply the religiosity of believing people who can do no less than express publicly their Christian faith, with sincere and uncomplicated spontaneity: a faith handed down from generation to generation, and which has gradually shaped the life and customs of all their people.

As part of its process of historical identification and return to its roots, the Catholic Church in Latin America, especially since Vatican II, is rediscovering in a positive way the religiosity that has grown with it ever since the 16th century.

But it has not only been the vitality of popular religiosity in the life of the peoples that has forced intellectuals to reassess its value. Its history has also played a role, in which it has revealed itself as a true repository of the founding cultural synthesis of Latin America, which developed in the 16th and 17th centuries, and jealously guards the diversity and interconnection of its Indian, black, and European substrates.

Giving back its value to popular religiosity is to give back its value to the Church's own past as well as to its historical continuity among the Latin American people.

From this perspective, popular religiosity can be considered as one of the few existing expressions—without discounting others—of the Latin American cultural synthesis which spans all its historical stages and at the same time encompasses all its dimensions: work and production, places of settlement, lifestyles, language and artistic expression, political organization, daily life. Precisely in its role as a repository of cultural identity, it has withstood the attempts of modernity to make particular cultures subordinate to the dictates of reason.

This popular religiosity has been present in Catholicism from its earliest moments. In Latin America, the doctrine brought by the missionaries was syncretized with African or indigenous forms, giving rise in some cases to highly integrated mixed forms.

With the passage of time and with migration to urban areas, popular religiosity, which was once typical of the countryside, spread to the cities.

In large cities, the blossoming of different expressions of popular religiosity is a response to man's urge to recover his socio-religious roots, his natural openness to the transcendent and his search for spiritual values. Faced with modernization, and even more with "postmodernity", it has become a communitarian form of resistance, a "prophetic cry" of man who refuses to reject the mystery and the transcendent as being a part of the horizons of his life. Rural folk who have become townspeople feel uprooted from their land and traditions, and thrown into a world in which only personal achievement and specialized work count. Their natural tendency would be to return to their place of origin, but being unable to do so in reality, they take refuge in that which symbolizes their essence, their land and their traditions. This is when popular urban religiosity would emerge, providing a bridge to unite that which is apparently impossible. They reconnect with their most intimate selves, even though their real situation does not change, thanks to it and to its strong emotional load. Amidst the saints, devotions, and celebrations, they can connect with their own and with that which most deeply identifies them, and make this hostile place their home.

Popular piety as a visible and tangible expression of popular religiosity is a model of the incarnation of the faith in cultural realities, which permeates them and is at the same time enriched by them; in other words, it is a model of inculturation of the faith. It is emotional and related to the senses; it is neither abstract nor rational. It expresses itself in a varied typology of devotional practices in which, by means of symbols, religious and specifically Christian values are experienced and linked to distinct cultural universes, thereby being transformed into a means of self-evangelization. We will only be able to understand popular religiosity if we recognize culture as an interrelated whole.

The experience of faith proper to popular religiosity springs from the actual experience of man and is linked to the expression of symbols, stories, myths, beliefs, and dreams. *"More than words and analysis, it favors symbols, action, ritual, the mythical, movement, kisses, singing, music, eloquent silences, dances, candles and flowers, etc."* (Víctor Manuel Fernández, *Una interpretación de la religiosidad popular*, "An interpretation of popular religiosity").

Puebla sees popular religiosity in Latin America as *"a demonstration of wisdom that combines culture and faith: it is a storehouse of values that offers the answers of Christian wisdom; it is popular Catholic wisdom; it creatively combines the divine and the human.... This wisdom is a Christian humanism that radically affirms the dignity of every person as a child of God, establishes a basic fraternity, teaches people how to encounter nature and understand work, and provides reasons for joy and humor even in the midst of a very hard life. For the common people this wisdom is also a principle of discernment"* (Puebla 448).

Popular Religiosity has a deep sense of transcendence and, at the same time, it is a genuine experience of the closeness of God; it possesses the capacity to express faith in a total language that overcomes rationalisms through contemplative features that define the relationship with nature and with other people; it gives meaning to work, celebrations, solidarity, friendship, family, and a feeling of rejoicing in their own dignity, which does not feel itself to be undermined in spite of the life of poverty and simplicity in which they find themselves.

Popular religiosity has its own mode, which is marked by the heart: here, faith is determined by feelings. Although some do not accept this type of religiosity, arguing that it does not involve the person, nevertheless the feelings of the heart lead faith to express itself in gestures and with thoughtfulness, both with the Lord and with our brothers and sisters. That which is of the senses does not contradict the deepest experiences of the spirit. For this, we need only refer to the great mystics of the Catholic Church, such as St. John of the Cross, St. Teresa, or St. Ignatius of Loyola, who reveal to us this sentient dimension of faith. This would be one of the great values that, in a healthy and enriching exchange, popular religiosity brings to the Church, which is often tempted to rationalize and stop at mere thoughts or formulations that do not engage life.

The expressions of popular religiosity are the *"sign of faith taking root in the heart of the various peoples and of its entry into the sphere of daily life. In this sense, popular religiosity is the first and fundamental form of inculturation of the faith"* (Víctor Manuel Fernández. *Hundir mi camino en esta tierra. Y quedarme.* Vida pastoral, 2002). *Such faith turned into culture is lived spontaneously, as an inseparable part of one's own life, and for this reason it is more than a series of concepts: it fecundates the faith from the heart; it shapes a particular way of living and expressing the dynamism of the Spirit. Not only mass manifestations of piety, but also religious expressions that in a capillary way become part of everyday life, of spontaneous and familiar language, are perceived by the majority as being linked to their identity. This is something that all have in common with the faithful in general, but which is at the same time very personal* (Directory on Popular Piety and the Liturgy. 91).[110]

The experience of faith which is expressed in daily gestures and lived out as a community leads to the love of God and of others, and helps individuals and peoples to become aware of their responsibility in the construction of history and the shaping of their own destiny. Popular religiosity contains a series of very important human and religious values: *"It makes people capable of generosity and sacrifice even to the point of heroism, when it is a question of manifesting belief. It involves an acute awareness of profound attributes of God: fatherhood, providence, loving and constant presence. It engenders interior attitudes rarely observed to the same degree elsewhere: 'patience, the sense of the cross in daily life, detachment, openness to others, devotion, a thirst for God which only the simple and poor can know.'"* (EN 48). From the anthropological point of view, popular religiosity reveals the deepest feelings that M. Eliade calls "arboreal," which are: feeling close to nature, being in touch with life and death, needing to feel safe

---

[110]   Translators note: this is a misquote, the above text comes from an article by Victor Manuel Fernandez: https://core.ac.uk/download/pdf/32624078.pdf.

and integrated in a complex reality. This way in which people situate themselves at the same time demonstrates the need for salvation in the midst of the threats of existence, and the need to give unity to life by means of symbols and narratives.

In Latin America, popular religiosity shapes the historical identity: it is the decanting of a history of evangelization that more or less consciously incorporates a multitude of cultural and religious elements of many peoples, races, and cultures. In the substrate of popular religiosity, we find indigenous contributions (rhythms, dress, music, food, etc.), the Afro-American culture tainted by the experience of slavery, a nostalgia for its origins with its rites of trance and healing, the contributions of the rural environment and the influence of marginalized urban social strata that gather together to maintain their values.

Hence *"the importance of popular piety for the faith-life of the People of God, for the conservation of the faith itself . . . popular piety has been a providential means of preserving the faith in situations where Christians have been deprived of pastoral care"* (Directory on Popular Piety and the Liturgy). In this sense, it is important to highlight the importance of the Christian signs that permeate the culture of the popular classes, creating in millions of people a favorable sensitivity towards God and producing a spontaneous transmission of Christian spirituality. This endearing religiosity of the poor has often turned into a way used by the Spirit to reach the heart and initiate the return of many who were far removed from a life of friendship with God. In other cases, it has sustained a silent but strong adherence to the Christian faith, providing a sense of identity and belonging.

With regard to this transmission, the people is not an anonymous and passive mass, but an active subject. For a long time, the majority of the people was not recognized as a cultural subject. For this reason, Latin American religiosity, on the basis of prejudices that undervalued the people, was considered as something archaic and fetishistic, typical of the ignorant. *"In genuine forms of popular piety, the Gospel message assimilates expressive forms particular to a given culture while also permeating the consciousness of that culture with the content of the Gospel, and its idea of life and death, and of man's freedom, mission and destiny. The transmission of this cultural heritage from father to son, from generation to generation, also implies the transmission of Christian principles. In some cases, this fusion goes so deep that elements proper to the Christian faith become integral elements of the cultural identity of particular nations. Devotion to the Mother of the God would be an example of this"* (Directory on popular piety and liturgy). Aparecida goes so far as to call it *"popular mysticism"* (no. 262).

The challenges facing the Church are many. Today, more than ever, the theme of life is on the table when it comes to proposing that we take up the work of evangelization. It is clear in the conscience of the whole Church that what is at stake is *"life,"* and from it the *"life in abundance"* that Jesus Christ brings us. Hence, the need to concentrate all our efforts on that perspective. Aparecida places before our eyes the reality of a culture of death, some of the most evident signs of which are: the increase of poverty and extreme poverty, the concentration of wealth, lack of equity, the law of the market, neoliberalism, financial paradises, the crisis of democracy, corruption, migration, social discrimination, terrorism, environmental pollution, the crisis of the family, abortion, euthanasia, subjectivism, consumerism, the imposition of modern culture and contempt for ancestral cultures, individualism, the crisis of values, moral relativism, the growing distance between faith and life.

It is painful for the Church to realize that, after having inspired Latin American life and culture for more than five centuries, the religious sense of the people has been eroded (DA 38), and the faith is not transmitted from generation to generation with the same fluidity (DA 39). Aparecida, far from settling into lamentation or condemnation of the situation, humbly recognizes that it does not have the answers to these problems, and that it constitutes an invitation to discern with the light of the Holy Spirit in order to place itself at the service of the Kingdom in this reality (DA 33).

It is becoming vital *"that to bring to the heart of the culture of our time, that unified and complete sense of human life that neither science, nor politics, nor the economy, nor the media will ever be able to provide, we be consumed with missionary zeal. In Christ the Word, the Wisdom of God, culture can once again find its center and depth, from whence one*

*can look at reality in the entirety of all its factors, discerning them in the
light of the Gospel and giving each one its place and its proper dimension"*
(DA 41). Missionary disciples are called to be creative in the fields of
culture, politics, public opinion, art, and science; places that have often
been neglected. *"Assuming with new strength this option for the poor..."*
*(399). "Evangelizing culture, far from abandoning the preferential option
for the poor, actually renews it" (DA 397, 398, 399).* The commitment
to reality is born of a passionate love for Christ, who accompanies the
People of God in their mission of inculturating the Gospel in history,
thanks to their fervent and indefatigable Samaritan charity.

In order to carry out the great project of the Kingdom, following
the style of Jesus, the Church will have to renew her ways of approaching, being in relationship and interacting, as well as rediscovering the
points of anchorage within the existing culture.

*The evangelization of today's postmodern culture is calling for pasto-
ral work both within and outside the Church, that must take into account
words, actions, signs, and symbols, an imaginative context that expresses
the option for the truth about God and man.*

This entails the creation of *a new cultural paradigm*, as the true
alternative to the dominant single thought; it must take into account
the major concerns and poles of interest of today's people: social reality, ecological thought, modern cosmology, ethnicity, peace, the ethics
of care, as well as mercy and compassion.

In this quest, based on the most important assertions provided by
Aparecida, popular piety offers *a privileged path. In the Latin American
people, popular piety is an expression of the Catholic faith, it contains
the most valuable dimension of Latin American culture, it delicately
penetrates the personal existence of each of the faithful and, although it is
also lived out amongst a multitude, it can be developed more deeply and
penetrate ever better the way of life of our peoples; it is an essential starting point to ensure that the faith of the people matures and becomes more
fruitful; it contains and expresses an intense sense of transcendence, a
spontaneous aptitude to lean on God and a true experience of theological
love; it is a legitimate way of living the faith, an expression of supernatural wisdom, a way of feeling part of the Church, and a way of being*

missionaries; it is a powerful confession about the living God who acts in history and a channel for the transmission of the faith. (Aparecida 258, 259, 261, 262, 263, 264).

Through its many lively and significant expressions, religiosity can come to the rescue of man, his identity and his vocation to life. According to the words of the Pope, it is in religiosity that "we see the soul of the Latin American peoples;" it is "the precious treasure of the Catholic Church in Latin America" and "reflects a thirst for God which only the poor and simple can know." Over the course of many centuries, the simple people has developed and handed down practices that are its way of celebrating life. Popular religiosity offers spaces where faith is expressed in a special way *in sanctuaries* that are scattered throughout Latin America and the Caribbean. Shrines play a major role in the history of the Christian faith in America. It would be very difficult for the Church to engage with the large human groups that identify themselves as believers in the Catholic faith—even if they do not always do so in formal expressive forms—without the existence and pastoral action of these shrines. Because of their piety, the simple people go to the shrine and are reminded that their origin is in the Lord and also that the God who loved us once never stops loving us, and that today, in the concrete moment of history in which they find themselves, in the face of the contradictions and sufferings of the present, He ever accompanies the journey of life. In the same way, the Old and New Testaments unanimously testify that the Temple is the place of remembrance of a salvific past and the setting for the present experiencing of grace.

Shrines are the sign of the divine presence, the locus of the constantly renewed actualization of the covenant of men with the Eternal and with one another. When the pious Israelite visited the sanctuary, he would rediscover the faithfulness of the God of the Promise in each and every "today" of history. The Temple is the holy dwelling place of the Ark of the Covenant, the place where the covenant with the living God is made present and where the people of God is aware of constituting the community of believers, "a chosen race, a royal priesthood, a holy nation" (1 Pet. 2:9). The shrine is the place of the Spirit, because it is the place where God's faithfulness reaches the people and transforms them. People go to the shrine first of all to invoke and receive the grace of the Spirit, in order to then carry it forth in all the actions of their lives. The shrine is quintessentially the place of the Word, the preferential place of forgiveness, reconciliation, and thanksgiving. It is there that the faithful, through the sacraments, accomplish the encounter of the living with the One who in consolation and hope, continually provides and nourishes with ever new life all those who hunger and thirst. One comes to the shrine as to the temple of the living God, to the place of the living covenant with Him, so that the grace of the Sacraments may free the pilgrims from sin and give them the strength to begin anew with renewed vigor and new joy in their hearts, so as to be transparent witnesses of the Eternal among men and women. This fidelity of God is what prompts the covenants that are the "promises" of the pilgrim.

In shrines, we learn to open our hearts to everyone, especially to those who are different from us: the visitor, the foreigner, the immigrant, the refugee, those who profess another religion and those who do not believe. Thus, the shrine, in addition to presenting itself as a place in which to experience the Church, becomes a locus of invitation open to all mankind.

"The experience of popular piety constitutes a special way of approaching the simple people, which is so often at a distance from the more traditional forms of pastoral care. It represents an opportunity to communicate the Gospel, expressed, lived out and contextualized in the symbology and rhythm typical of the reality of the people that believes." (Final Declaration of the IVth Congress of Rectors of Shrines of Latin America and the Caribbean.)

Pilgrimages are another expression of popular religiosity related to shrines. They contain a profound symbolic expression that strongly reflects the human search for meaning and for the encounter with the other, through the experience of fullness and of that which transcends us and which lies beyond all possibilities, differences, and times. Through pilgrimages, the experience of searching and openness is socialized by walking with other pilgrims, and it is reflected in the heart, in feelings of profound solidarity.

Feasts occupy another important place, they appear as a closure, as fulfillment, as gratitude expressed in joy, song, and dance. The feast involves all the bodily senses, in an atmosphere of joy and happiness. Here, time is regulated by an alternative rhythm of concentration and inactivity, of religious and non-religious acts. It is not a staged event with spectators and protagonists. Even the spectators are transformed into protagonists. The presence of others, even strangers, intensifies the character of what is being celebrated, since the celebrants feel obliged to show what is being celebrated. The feast also gives its identity to the local community, because its celebration brings together all the neighbors and those who have emigrated, and even attracts newcomers.

Marian devotion, which is deeply rooted in the faith of our people, is one of the main signs of its identity, just as the covenant with Yahweh was to Israel. Israel was aware of being a chosen people, the depositary of the law and the prophets. Because of their relationship with a God who was close to them, they were aware of their uniqueness. By analogy, the Christian people understands that God's protection comes to it through the invocation of an image of Mary, which is personalized and unique; for this reason, Mary personalizes and singles out this particular people.

The people feel a sense of identification with the image of Mary, because it is to her that their own parents had recourse and it is to her that they turn today with their problems. In admiring Mary's personal virtues, popular piety avails itself of her attributes so as to reach God. The miraculous action of Mary is the main sign of the individualized protection that rests on a place and comes from it. Supplication and petitions for favors are a manifestation of the maternal-filial alliance, of interpersonal relationships, of mutual commitment. Even if they are people with limited sacramental practice, they react to sickness or suffering by making a promise. This can consist of walking to the sanctuary, making their pilgrimage in silence, going around the shrine on their knees, with their arms stretched as on the cross, offering candles or donations, but most of the promises remain anonymous and their motivation is kept private to the person or to the family.

The law of the Incarnation is palpable in displays of popular Marian piety. Inculturation of the faith does not only mean that faith is poured into pre-existing cultural molds, but that faith creates signs of identity and molds of social coexistence, expresses them, fills them with life and expresses life. *"The people are like water. Their course is like that of rivers, which are inevitably on pilgrimage. Sometimes, they are like mountain rivers, impetuous and turbulent, falling vertically down to the valley. Sometimes, they are like our rivers in the Pampa, tame, indolent and circuitous, that end up flowing into the ocean after many a playful detour. And lastly, they are sometimes like our Paraná, which borders San Nicolás, and which when it is low, seems tame, but conceals within the force of an unsuspected torrent. The people are like the water of the rivers which being pilgrims, always flow into the ocean. Because they are pilgrims and not merely wanderers, they have their own course and their own goal. Coming from the mountain they go towards the ocean; coming from on High, they go towards the Infinite. To be a river, to be a people, consists precisely in the awareness of having a common origin and in the conviction of having a common destiny. And this conviction is strengthened in the people when, by their Christian faith, they mingle like drops of water with the blood of Christ. For even blood, that is to say, life, Christ's life, and, in Christ, ours, comes from an Origin and, on its pilgrimage through death, flows into Resurrection. This is the faith of our people. But a people, the believing people on pilgrimage in this land, which is water and blood, is always a torrent. A river torrent; a torrent of blood. It is a torrent that shows its vitality by the force with which it seeks the truth, by the force of its love, and by the force that its ideals give it. All these forces regularly concentrate in passion and in fantasy.*

The torrent is the fantasy of the people, which drags with it whatever it finds and whatever it invents, mixing and making indiscriminate. Fantasy is invention. The fantasy of the people is not only the ability to invent stories, but the ability to find truths. These are the truths that lie behind tales, anecdotes and legends; substantial kernels of truth coated with exuberant ornaments by the same playful penchant of fantasy. Birth and death, the meeting of man or of woman, love and loneliness, work and illness, the fact of doing good and of introducing evil, raise the questions of the truth that encloses life in the form of an enigma and a mystery. You try to give answers in the form of divinatory intuitions. From the moment that it encloses in itself something divine, life becomes a divination. In their compelling search for the truth, people grope for the truth by advancing with their fantasy. Because of this, it is easier for them to accept the word of truth, which God reveals to them in Christ. And at the same time, the people will continue to surround the revealed truth with the exuberance of their fantasy." (*El pueblo es como el agua. Escritos teológicos pastorales de Lucio Gera.*)

What was proposed in Aparecida is a call to live this moment of our history as a salvific and ecclesial event. In this light, the mission of the Church reveals itself as the tireless effort to unite in a single message the transcendent with the immanent, the eternal with everyday life, and this is where popular religiosity, as a true and tangible expression of faith, born in the shadow of many sorrows, has much to tell us. "*The greatest nobility of man is to raise his work in the midst of devastation, sustaining it tirelessly, somewhere between brokenness and beauty*" (Ernesto Sábato. *Antes del fin. Memorias*). From the Old Testament until today, in every moment of history in which we have experienced a sense of total failure and fall, we humans have been saved by the most defenseless part of humanity. The Church's mission presents itself as a service to a full, dignified and happy life in Christ and cannot do without the poor and simple people which, in the midst of its daily difficulties, has striven to incarnate this proposal.

As the Pilgrim People of God in Latin America and the Caribbean, we entrust the missionary disciples to the tenderness, beauty and joy of God's love manifested in the mestiza face of the Mother of God, the Virgin of Guadalupe. She holds her people in the pupil of her eyes and shelters them in the recesses of her mantle. Her hands folded in prayer encourage us to cast our nets to bring everyone closer to Jesus, "the Way, the Truth and the Life" (Jn 14:6), because He wants everyone to "have life, and have abundantly" (Jn 10:10).

January 19, 2008
Cardinal Jorge Mario Bergoglio, SJ

Afterword

From the moment of Pope Francis's election, we have been trying to find out who he is. He was unknown to the French faithful. All our research has led us to one certain conclusion: Pope Francis is executing the program of reform of the Society of Jesus as established by Father Arrupe, Father General of the society, the twenty-eighth successor of Saint Ignatius elected on May 22, 1965.

This program has been set out in thousands of books and articles written by thousands of authors who supported, and still support, this ongoing reform.

One might object that it aimed to reform the society, not the Church.

To do so would be to forget the one hundred texts by Father Arrupe published in 1982 under the title *La Iglesia de Hoy y del Futuro* (The Church of Today and of the Future). In his preface to this compilation, Cardinal Tarancón, archbishop of Madrid, wrote: "Its title perfectly sums up and synthesizes the great objective that Fr. Arrupe set out to achieve in his mission at the helm of the Society of Jesus: effectively to assist the Church of the present so that it can adapt itself to the demands of a future which is almost upon us, and which strongly challenges those whose duty it is to proclaim the Gospel message in all its authenticity and integrity, to make it intelligible to the mentality and psychology of the people of the year 2000."

I have invented nothing. All these things were already there in writing. The facts, the people, the speeches, the letters, the testimonies all exist, and they are part of history.

Acknowledgments

I would like to express my gratitude to my wife, who helped me with her prayers and her knowledge of the German language.

To my children Marie-Béatrice, Magali, and Thomas, my knowledgeable reviewers and proofreaders;

To Jacques Camredon, who provided decisive assistance in my search for Spanish-language works and general documentation;

To Federico Müggenburg, an expert on Vatican affairs and the author of a wealth of books and articles on liberation theology;

To Juan Ignacio Terrera for his research in Argentina;

To Sylvia Amick for her research in the USA;

And especially to Isabelle Piot and her husband, François, for their secretarial assistance, proofreading, and technical advice.

Bibliography

French language editions

AFS, *Le mondialisme,* 2011.

Agrikoliansky, Éric, Olivier Fillieule, Nonna Mayer. *L'Altermondial-isme en France, la longue histoire d'une nouvelle cause.* Flammarion, 2005.

André-Vincent, Philippe. *Pour une vraie théologie de la libération, Essai.* Tallandier, 1987.

Antoine, Charles. *Guerre froide et Église Catholique, l'Amérique Latine.* Cerf, 1999.

Archier, Adolphe. *La compagnie de Jésus, esquisse historique.* Delhomme et Briguet, 1892.

Aurenche, Guy and François Soulage. *Le pari de la fraternité.* Éditions Ouvrières, 2012.

Auvray, D. P. *Face à la subversion dans l'Église.* 1975.

Bacani, T. C. *Eglise et politique aux Philippines.* Cr, 1987.

Barthe, Claude. *Trouvera-t-Il encorela foi sur la terre ? Une crise de l'Église, histoire et questions.* F. X. de Guibert, 2006.

Bédarida, Renée. *Les Armes de l'Esprit, Témoignage Chrétien (1941-1944).* Éditions ouvrières, 1977.

Benoît XVI. *Lumière du monde, Le Pape, l'Église et les signes du temps*. Bayard, 2011.

Bigo, Pierre. *Débat dans l'Église, théologie de la Libération*. AED, 1990.

Blondel, Maurice. *L'Être et les êtres*. Librairie Félix Alcan, 1935.

———. *Œuvres complètes II, 1888-1913: La philosophie de l'action et la crise moderniste*. PUF, 1997.

Bordeyne, Philippe and Juan-Carlos Scannone. *Divorcés Remariés, ce qui change avec François*. Salvator, 2017.

Bourdarias, Jean. *Les évêques de France et le marxisme, Histoire d'une connivence*. Fayard, 1991.

Cabestrero, Teofilo. *Des prêtres au Gouvernement, L'expérience du Nicaragua*. Karthala, 1983.

Calbrette, Jean. *Mounier le mauvais Esprit*. Nouvelles Éditions Latines, 1957.

Calvez, Jean-Yves. *Le père Arrupe, l'Église après le Concile*. Cerf, 1997.

Cämara, Hélder (Dom). *L'Évangile avec Dom Helder*. Seuil, 1985.

———. *Le désert fertile*. Desclée De Brouwer, 1971.

———. *Les conversions d'un évêque*. Seuil, 1977.

———. *Révolution dans la paix*. Seuil, 1970.

———. *À force d'amour*. Nouvelle Cité, 1987.

———. *Prières à Marie*. Nouvelle Cité, 1987.

Carriquiry Lecour, Guzmán. *Globalisation et humanisme chrétien*. Éditions Anne Sigier, 2007.

CELAM. *Eglise populaire et théologie de la libération*. Fayard, 1988.

Centre Vincent Lebbe. *Vatican II et l'Amérique latine, journée internationale d'étude, juin 2013*. Cahiers internationaux de Théologie pratique, n°10, 2016.

Christianisme Et Revolution. *Actes du colloque de mars 1968*. Lettre, 1968.

Collectif. *Théologies de la Libération, documents et débats*. 1985.

Comblin, Joseph. *Échec de l'action catholique?* Editions Universitaires, 1961.

Commission Épiscopale Du Monde Ouvrier. *L'engagement temporel*. Action catholique ouvrière, 1958.

Compagnon, Olivier. *Jacques Maritain et l'Amérique du Sud, le modèle malgré lui*. Septentrion, 2003.

Conférence Nationale Des Évêques Du Bresil. *Pour une société dépassant les dominations*. Desclée de Brouwer, 1978.

Congar, Yves. *A mes frères*. Cerf, 1968.

———. *La Foi et la Théologie*. Desclée, 1962.

Conseil Permanent De L'épiscopat. *Libérations des hommes et salut en Jésus-Christ*. Centurion, 1975.

———. Et Paix. *Compendium de la Doctrine sociale de l'Église*. Cerf, 2005.

Cosmao, Vincent. *Changer le monde, une tâche pour l'Église*. Cerf, 1985.

———. *Dossier Nouvel Ordre Mondial, Les chrétiens provoqués par le développement*. Chalet, 1978.

Debray, Pierre. *Les détournements de la Charité*. Kirios, 1987. *Du Christianisme de Hans Küng*. Pierre Viret, 1979.

Dumont, René. *Cuba, socialisme et développement*. Seuil, 1964.

Duquesne, Jacques. *Les catholiques français sous l'occupation*. Grasset, 1966.

Duquoc, Christian. « *Je crois en l'Église* », *Précarité institutionnelle et Règne de Dieu*. Cerf, 1999.

Dussel, Enrique. *Histoire et théologie de la libération*. Les Éditions Ouvrières, 1974.

Falque, Emmanuel and Laure Solignac. *François philosophe*. Editions Salvator, 2017.

Fazio, Mariano. *Le Pape François, Les clés de sa pensée.* Le Laurier, 2013.

Fessard, Gaston. *Eglise de France, prends garde de perdre la Foi.* Julliard, 1979.

———. *France, prends garde de perdre ta Liberté.* 1945.

Folliet, Joseph. *Les chrétiens au carrefour.* Chronique sociale de France, 1947.

Fontaine, Rémi. *Le livre noir des évêques de France.* Renaissance Catholique, 2006.

François, Pape. *C'est tous les jours Noël.* Michel Lafon, 2018.

———. *Je crois en l'homme, Conversations.* Flammarion, 2013.

Francou, François. *L'Eglise au Nicaragua, l'escalade de la violence.* AED, 1988.

Franqui, Carlos. *Vie, aventures et désastres d'un certain Fidel Castro.* Belfond, 1989.

Frères Du Monde. *Chrétiens et marxistes: la Pologne, no 39.* Editions de l'Epi, 1966.

Garrigou-Lagrange, Réginald. *De revelatione I-II.* Ferrari, 1918.

Gaucher, Roland. *Le réseau Curiel ou la subversion humanitaire.* Éditions Jean Picollec, 1981.

Gauthier, Paul. « *Consolez mon peuple* », *Le Concile et l'« Église des pauvres* ». Cerf, 1965.

Groupe Des Dombes. *Le ministère de communion dans l'Église universelle.* Centurion, 1986.

———. *Pour la conversion des Églises.* Centurion, 1991.

———. *Vers une même foi eucharistique, Accord entre catholiques et protestants.* Les Presses de Taizé, 1972.

Guissard, Lucien. *Mounier.* Éditions Universitaires, 1962.

Gutiérrez, Gustavo. *La libération par la foi, boire à son propre puits.* Cerf, 1985.

Hourdin, Georges. *Au pape Jean-Paul II et aux évêques du Synode, Sur la nécessité d'achever le Concile.* Desclée de Brouwer, 1985.

Houtart, François and François Polet. *L'Autre Davos, Mondialisation des résistances et des luttes.* L'Harmattan, 1999.

Houtart, François, *L'Église et le monde, Vatican II,* Cerf, 1964.

Humbert, Colette. *Conscientisation.* L'Harmattan, 1982.

Jean-Paul II. *Centesimus Annus.* Libreria Editrice Vaticana, 1991.

———. *Intégralité des discours au Brésil.* Téqui, 1980.

———. *Novo millenio ineunte.* Téqui, 2001.

———. *Visite à la synagogue de Rome, 13 avril 1986, Juifs et chrétiens pour une entente nouvelle.* Cerf, 1986.

———. *Vivificantem et Dominum.* Homme Nouveau, 1986.

La Bella, Gianni. *Pedro Arrupe, supérieur général des Jésuites, le gouvernement d'un prophète.* Lessius, 2009.

Lassus, Arnaud de. *Un siècle de modernisme, 1097-2007.* AFS, tiré à part n°193.

Le Guillou, M. J. et Louis. *La condamnation de Lamennais.* CNRS, Beauchesne, 1982.

Lubac, Henri de. *Catholicisme, Les aspects sociaux du dogme.* Cerf, 1952.

Madiran, Jean. *L'hérésie du XXe siècle.* Nouvelles Éditions Latines, Coll. Itinéraires, 1968.

Malley, François. *Le Père Lebret, L'économie au service des hommes.* Cerf, 1968.

Marc, Gabriel. *Le développement en quête d'acteurs.* Centurion, 1984.

Marion, Jean-Luc. *Brève apologie pour un moment catholique.* Grasset, 2017.

Maritain, Jacques. *À travers le désastre.* Éd. de Minuit, 1942.

Mattei, Roberto de. *Vatican II, une histoire à écrire.* Muller, 2013.

Maury, Guillaume. *L'Église et la subversion, le CCFD.* UNI, 1987.

Meinvielle, Jules, Abbé. *De Lamennais à Maritain.* La Cité Catholique, 1956.

Mignot, André and Michel de Saint-Pierre. *Le ver est dans le fruit.* La Table Ronde, 1978.

Moltmann, Jürgen. *Le Dieu crucifié.* Cerf, 1974.

Moncomble, Yann. *La mafia des chrétiens de gauche.* Faits et Documents, 1985.

Montcheuil, Yves de. *Leçons sur le Christ.* Éditions de l'Épi, 1949.

Mounier, Emmanuel. *De la propriété capitaliste à la propriété humaine.* Desclée De Brouwer, 1936.

———. *Feu la chrétienté.* Seuil, 1950.

———. *L'affrontement chrétien.* Seuil, 1945.

Pax Christi. *Ils sont tes frères.* Maison de la Bonne Presse, 1957.

Pichot-Bravard, Philippe. *La Révolution française.* Via Romana, 2014.

Plaquevent, Pierre-Antoine. *Soros et la société ouverte, métapolitique du globalisme.* Le retour aux sources, 2018.

Ratier, Emmanuel. *Les chrétiens de Gauche.* Faits & Documents, 1998.

Ratzinger, Joseph. *Église, œcuménisme et politique.* Fayard, 1987.

———. *L'Europe, ses fondements, aujourd'hui et demain.* Ed. Saint Augustin, 2005.

———. *Le sel de la terre, Le christianisme et l'Eglise catholique au seuil du troisième millénaire.* Cerf, 1997.

———. *Mon Concile Vatican II.* Artège, 2012.

Riccardi, Andrea. *Comprendre le Pape François.* Éditions de l'Emmanuel, 2015.

Riobé, Guy. *La liberté du Christ.* Stock/Cerf, 1974.

Rissoan, Jean-Pierre. *Traditionalisme et révolution*. Vol. 1. Aléas, 2007.

Roc Estrello, Les colloques de. *Une génération en marche, Blondel – Teilhard – Mounier*. Saint-Léger Éditions, 2014.

Sagot du Vauroux, Charles-Paul. *L'action catholique au temps présent*. J. de Gigord, 1913.

Sauvaget, Bernadette. *Le monde selon François, les paradoxes d'un pontificat*. Cerf, 2014.

Scalfari, Eugenio. *Carlo Maria Martini, Dernières conversations sur Dieu, l'Église, le Pape, l'éthique et la Foi*. Bayard, 2013.

Scannone, Juan Carlos. *Le pape du peuple, Bergoglio raconté par son confrère théologien, jésuite et argentin*. Cerf, 2015.

―――. *La théologie du peuple, Racines théologiques du pape François*. Editions Jésuites, 2017.

Senèze, Nicolas. *Les mots du Pape*. Bayard, 2016.

Siri, Joseph. *Gethsémani, Réflexions sur le Mouvement Théologique contemporain*. Téqui, 1980.

T.F.P. Collectif. *Allende et sa « voie chilienne »... pour la misère*. Editions Tradition Famille Propriété, 1974.

Teilhard de Chardin, Pierre. *Le Milieu divin*. Seuil, 1957.

―――. *Le phénomène humain*. Seuil, 1955.

Tenaillon, Nicolas. *Dans la tête du Pape François*. Actes Sud, 2017.

Terradas, Jean. *Une Chrétienté d'Outre-Mer*. Nouvelles Éditions Latines, 1960.

Valladres, Armando. *Prisonnier de Castro*. Grasset, 1979.

Vidal, Maurice. *Cette Église que je cherche à comprendre*. Éditions Ouvrières, 2009.

Virion, Pierre. *Mystère d'iniquité*. Éditions St Michel, 1966.

Warnier, Philippe. *Le phénomène des communautés de base*. Desclée De Brouwer, 1973.

Wiltgen, Ralph M. *Le Rhin se jette dans le Tibre, Le concile inconnu.* Cèdre, 1973.

Winock, Michel. *Histoire politique de la revue « Esprit » 1930-1950.* Seuil, 1975.

Yannou, Hervé. *Jésuites et compagnie.* Lethielleux, 2008.

English language editions

Anderson, James. *Sendero Luminoso, A new revolutionary model?* Institute for the study of terrorism, 1987.

Black, Maggie. *A Cause for our Times, Oxfam, the first 50 years.* Oxfam 1992.

Boff, Leonardo and Clodovis Boff. *Introducing Liberation Theology.* Orbis Books, 1987.

Candelaria, Michael R. *Popular Religion and Liberation, The Dilemma of Liberation Theology.* States University of New York Press, 1990.

Carney, J. Guadalupe. *"To be a Christian is… To be a revolutionary",* an Autobiography. Harper & Row, 1987.

Carrigan, Ana. *Salvador Witness, The life and calling of Jean Donovan.* Ballantine Books, 1986.

Cort, John C. *Christian Socialism, An informal History.* Orbis Books, 1988.

Dickinson, Richard D. N. *Poor, yet making many rich, the poor as agents of creative justice.* World Council of Churches, Geneva 1983.

Ellis, Marc H. *Toward a Jewish Theology of Liberation.* Orbis Books, 1987.

Ivereigh, Austen. *The Great Reformer.* Allen&Unwin, 2014.

Kasper, Walter. *Pope Francis, Revolution of Tenderness and Love.* Paulist Press, 2015.

Lefever, Ernest W. *Amsterdam to Nairobi, World Council of Churches.* Ethics and Public Policy Center, 1979.

Lemius, J. B. *A Catechism of Modernism.* TAN, 1908.

Lobinger, F. *Towards Non-dominating Leadership, no 10 Training for Community Ministries.* Aims and Methods of the Lumko Series.

Lumko Music Department. *A guide to the Lumko music tapes.* Lumko Music Department, 1985.

———. *Lumko Song Book, African sung Mass.* Lumko Music Department, 1985.

Mulholland, Catherine. *Ecumenical Reflections on Political Economy.* WCC, 1988.

Neumayr, George. *The Political Pope, How Francis is delighting the liberal left and abandoning conservatives.* Center Street, 2017.

Nolan, Albert, and Richard Broderick. *To nourish our Faith, Theology of Liberation for Southern Africa.* Order of Preachers, 1987.

O'Brien, Niall. *Revolution from the Heart, The extraordinary record of a priest's life and work among the poor of the Philippine sugarlands.* Oxford University Press, 1987.

Oikoumene. *The international financial system: An ecumenical critique.* R. H. Green, 1985.

Pieris, Aloysius. *An Asian theology of Liberation.* Orbis Books, 1988 South Africa Council of Churches, *Hope in crisis,* Sol Jacob, 1986.

Szulc, Tad. *Fidel, A critical portrait.* Avon, 1986.

The Institute For Contextual Theology. *What is it?* I.C.T., 1981.

Wilmore, Gayraud S. and James H. Cone. *Black Theology, a documentary history, 1966-1979.* Orbis Books, 1979.

Witvliet, Theo. *A Place in the Sun, Liberation Theology in the Third World.* SCM Press Ltd, 1985.

Italian language editions

Bianchi, Enrique Ciro. *Introduzione alla teologia del popolo, Profilo spirituale e teologico di Rafael Tello, Prefazione di J.M. Bergoglio – Francesco.* EMI, 2015.

Borghesi, Massimo. *Jorge Mario Bergoglio, Una biografia intellettuale.* Jaca Book, 2017.

Gherardini, Brunero. *Concilio Ecumenico Vaticano II, Un discorso da fare.* Casa Mariana Editrice, 2009.

Loredo, Julio. *Teologia della Liberazione, Un salvagente di piombo per i poveri.* Cantagalli, 2014.

Regidor, José Ramos. *La teologia della liberazione.* Edup, 2004.

Scatena, Silvia. *La teologia della liberazione in America Latina.* Carocci, 2008.

Sorge, Bartolomeo. *Gesù Sorride, Con Papa Francisco oltre la religione della paura.* Piemme, 2014.

Vignelli, Guido. *Una rivoluzione pastorale, Sei parole tali- smaniche nel dibattito sinodale sulla famiglia.* T.F.P., 2016.

Portuguese language editions

Benemelis. Juan F. *Castro subversão e terrorismo em áfrica.* Europress, 1986.

Betto, Frei. *CEBs, Rumo à nova sociedade, O 5è encontro intereclesial das Comunidades Eclesiais de Base.* Paulinas, 1983.

Betto, Frei. *Socialismo e cristianismo.* CEPIS, 1985.

Boff, Leonardo. *O Pai-Nosso, a oraçao da libertaçao integral.* Vozes, 1984.

Casaldaliga, Dom Pedro. *Nicarágua, combate e profecia.* Vozes, 1986.

CNBB. *Terra de Deus, Terra de Irmãos.* CNBB, 1986.

Commissão Pastoral da Terra. *Conflitos de Terra no Brasil.* SEGRAC, 1985.

Corrêa De Oliveira, Plinio, Gustavo Antonio Solimeo, and Luiz Sergio. *As CEBs, Das quais muito se fala, Pouco se conhece.* Vera Cruz, 1982.

Dao, A. and Z. Acarias. *Nostra Luta de 1986: Cantos da Comunidade do Árame.* 1986.

Equipe de Pastoral de Juazeiro. *O Povo descobre a Sociedade, « Capitalismo x socialismo ».* Paulinas, 1986.

Faculdade de Teología N. Sra. Da Assunçao. *A nova emergência da reflexao teologica.* Paulinas, 1986.

Falconi, Antonio Francisco. *A Eucaristía nas CEBs.* Paulinas, 1982.

Fernandes, Dom Luis. *Como se faz uma Communidade Eclesial de Base.* Vozes, 1985.

Formação, Caderno de. *100 Anos de Resistencia e de Libertaçao da Classe Operaria.* Arquidiocese de Campinas, 1986.

Herz, Daniel. *A história secreta da Rede Globo.* Tchê, 1987.

Keller, Pe. Eugenio Dirceu. *A Igreja no Brasil, Das tribos indígenas as comunidades de base.* FTD, 1988.

Piva, Márcia Cruz et Marco Antonio. *Nicarágua, um povo e sua historia.* Paulinas, 1986.

Secretariado Nacional de Justiça e Não-Violencia. *A Não-Violencia Activa, aspectos teológicos.* Paulinas, 1982.

Tarea, Equipe. *Edicaçao popular e sua dimensao política.* CEPIS 1985.

Spanish language editions

Academia de Ciencias de la Urss. *Nuevo orden económico internacional.* Moscú, 1984.

Actes De La Xxiiie Réunión De Amigos De La Ciudad Católica. *¿Crisis en la democracía?* Speiro, 1984.

Aguirre, García de Cortazar, Loidi, and Mardones. *Socialismo, Nacionalismo, cristianismo.* DDB, 1979.

Alas, Higinio and Sergio Cabrera. *Autoeducación Comunitaria de Adultos, Proceso de concientización y alfabetización.* Búsqueda, 1976.

Alfonso, Pablo M. *Cuba, Castro y los católicos.* Hispamerican Books, 1985.

Alonso, Javier Urcelay. *Ecología, Ecologismo y política.* Verbo Speiro, 1984.

Alvarez, Luis H. *Nicaragua sandinista o el refinamiento del engaño.* Instituto democracia y libertad, Argentina, 1985.

Amstrong, Robert and Janet S. Rubin. *El Salvador, el rostro de la revolución.* UCA, 1986.

Amuchástegui, Maria Mercédes. *Lucio Gera y la pastoral popular: una interpretación histórica de sus orígenes.* UCA, 2010.

Arias, Juliana Andrea. *El Grupo de Curas en Opción Preferencial por los pobres: Los herederos del Movimiento de Sacerdotes para el Tercer Mundo.* Universidad de la Plata, 2016.

Arrupe, Pedro. *La Iglesia de hoy y del futuro.* Mensajero, 1982.

Azcuy, Virginia R. *La Teología argentina del pueblo, Lucio Gera.* Centro Teológico Manuel Larraín, 2015.

Barba, Enrique M. *Correspondencia entre Rosas, Quiroga y López.* Hachette, 1975.

Bello, Omar. *El verdadero Francisco, Intimidad, psicología, grandezas, secretos y dudas del Papa argentino. Por el filosofo que mas lo conoce.* Noticias, 2013.

Bergoglio, J. M. *Ponerse la patria al hombro.* Claretiana, 2013.

Bermúdez, Alejandro. *Francesco, nuestro hermano, nuestro amigo.* Ediciones Cristiandad, 2014.

Betto, Frei. *Fidel y la religión, conversaciones.* Oficina de publicaciones del consejo de estado, Cuba, 1985.

Blondel, Maurice. *Historia y Dogma.* Ediciones, 2004.

Boff, Leonardo. *La Fe en la periferia del mundo, El caminar de la Iglesia con los oprimidos.* Sal Terrae, 1981.

———. *Église : charisme et pouvoir.* Editora Vozes 1981, Lieu Commun 1985.

———. *O Pai-Nosso, a oraçao da libertaçao integral.* Vozes Petrópolis 1984.

Cabestrero, Teofilo. *Ministros de Dios Ministros del Pueblo, Testimonio de 3 sacerdotes en el Gobierno Revolucionario de Nicaragua.* Ministerio de Cultura Nicaragua Libre, 1983.

Caceres, Jorge, Andrés Opazo, Rosa María Pochet, and Oscar R. Sierra. *Iglesia, Política y Profecía, Juan-Pablo II en Centroamérica.* EDUCA, 1983.

Cardenal, Ernesto. *Oración por Marilyn Monroe.* Nueva Nicaragua, 1985.

Castillo, Fabio. *Los jinetes de la cocaína.* Documentos Periodísticos, 1987.

Centro de Reflexión Teológica. *Revista Latinoamérica de Teología, n° 13.* Universidad centroamericana, 1988.

Cierva, Ricardo de la. *Jesuitas, Iglesia y Marxismo, 1965-1985, La teología de la liberación desenmascarada.* Plaza & Janes, 1986.

———. *Oscura rebelión en la Iglesia, Jesuitas, teología de la liberación, carmelitas, marianistas y socialistas: la denuncia definitive.* Plaza & Janes, 1987.

Clouthier del Rincón, Manuel J. *Cruzada por la Salvación de México.* Epessa, 1987.

Colegio De Policia. "Gral. José E. Diaz." *Los Mensajes de Juan Pablo II,* Paraguay, 1988.

Comisión De Derechos Humanos de El Salvador. *La Iglesia en El Salvador.* UCA, 1982.

Congreso Internacional sobre la Reconciliación en el pensamiento de Juan Pablo II. *El desafío de la Reconciliación.* Fondo, 1986.

Congreso Internacional sobre Reconciliación y Nueva Evangelización en el pensamiento de Juan Pablo II. *El reto de la nueva evangelización.* Fondo Editorial, Lima, 1986.

Cuda, Emilce. *Para leer a Francisco, Teología, ética y política.* Manantial, 2016.

David, R. *Para una teología y pastoral de reconciliación desde Cuba.* 1985.

Delgado, Mons. Freddy. *La Iglesia Popular nació en el Salvador, Memorias 1972 a 1982,* San Salvador, 1990

Diakonia. *Vivir al modo de Jesús.* Provincia Centroamérica de la Compañía de Jesús, 1986.

Donoso Loero, Teresa. *Historia de los Cristianos por el socialismo en Chile.* Vaitea, 1976.

———. *Los cristianos por el socialismo en Chile.* Vaitea, 1975.

Ellacuría, Ignacio. *Conversión de la Iglesia al Reino de Dios.* UCA, 1985.

Enfoques Latinoamericanos n° 2. *Hacia una filosofía de la liberación latinoamericana.* Bonum, 1973.

Equipe Pastoral. *Dios camina con su pueblo, La liberación del pueblo: clave para entender la testa el antiguo testament.*

———. *Todos se reunían en común, Guía para nuestras celebraciones de la palabra.*

———. *Guía para nuestras celebraciones de la palabra.* San Salvador, 1986.

———. *La liberación del pueblo: clave para entender la fe en el antiguo testament.* San Salvador, 1986.

Facius, Antonio Rius. *Los Demoledores de la Iglesia en México.* Saeta, 1972.

Falla, Ricardo. *Quiché Rebelde.* Universitaria de Guatemala, 1978.

Fernández, Víctor Manuel. *El programa del Papa Francisco, ¿adonde nos quiere llevar?, Una conversación con Paolo Rodari.* San Pablo, 2015.

Freinet, Célestin. *Técnicas Freinet de la Escuela moderna.* Siglo XXI de España editores, 1984.

Freire, Paulo. *Pedagogía del oprimido.* Siglo Veintiuno, 1985.

Gera, Lucio. *La teología argentina del pueblo.* Virginia R. Azcuy, Ediciones Universidad Alberto Hurtado, 2015.

Goddard, Jorge Adame. *El pensamiento político y social de los católicos mexicanos 1867-1914.* Universidad nacional autónoma de México, 1981.

Gonzáles, Marcelo Juan. *Latinoamérica/modernidad/catoli- cismo. Itinerarios interpretativos sobre sus relaciones a partir de la categoría ethos y de la cuestión del quiebre del monopolio religioso.* Universidad Nacional de San Martin, Buenos Aires, 2012.

González Ruiz, J. M., A. C. Comin, etc. *La carta del Padre Arrupe: Requiem por el constantinismo.* Nova Terra, 1968.

Hermandad Sacerdotal Española. *Historia de un gran amor a la Iglesia no correspondido.* HSE, 1990.

Houtart, F. *Del subdesarrollo a la liberación.* PPC, 1974.

Idigoras, J. L. *Liberación, Temas Bíblicos y Teológicos.* Lima, 1984.

INCEP. *Panamá: 15 meses de lucha por la democratización y los derechos humanos.* Incep, 1988.

Iturrioz, Jesús. *Iglesia y democracia.* Biblioteca de Autores Cristianos, 1978.

Laclau, Ernesto. *La Razón populista.* Fondo de cultura Económica de Argentina, 2012.

Larraquy, Marcelo. *Recen por él, La historia jamás contada del hombre que desafía los secretos del vaticano, La puja interna de la Curia Romana ante el fenómeno llamado.* Random House, 2014.

Llach, Juan José et Coll. *Dependencia cultural y creación de la cultura en América latina.* Bonum, 1974.

López Vigil, Maria. *Muerte y vida en Morazán – Testimonio de un sacerdote.* UCA Editores San Salvador, El Salvador 1987.

Luciani, Rafael. *El papa Francisco y la teología del pueblo.* PCC, 2016.

Marins, Trevisan, and Chanona. *Martírio memoria perigosa na America Latina hoje, Suplemento do livro.* Paulinas, 1984.

Martin, Malachi. *Los Jesuitas, La compañía de Jesús y la traición a la Iglesia católica.* Plaza & Janes, 1988.

Meinvielle, P. Julio. *La dialéctica comunista y el 18 de Marzo.* Rioplatense, 1962.

Menjivar, Rafael. *Formación y lucha del proletariado industrial salvadoreño.* UCA, 1986.

Müggenburg, Federico. *La otra Iglesia imposible.* Papiro Omega, 2013.

Mugica, Carlos. *Peronismo y cristianismo.* Merlin, 1973.

Nolan, Albert. *¿Quién es este hombre? Jesús, antes del cristianismo.* Sal Terrae, 1981.

Nuñez, Emilio A. *Teología de la liberación, una perspectiva evangélica.* Caribe, 1986.

Obispos argentinos y Sacerdotes del Tercer Mundo. *Polémica en la Iglesia.* Búsqueda, 1970.

Obispos argentinos y Sacerdotes del Tercer Mundo. *Polémica en la Iglesia.* Ediciones Búsqueda, 1970.

Palacios, Leopoldo Eulogio. *El mito de la nueva Cristiandad.* Rialp, 1957.

Papa Francisco. *Meditaciones para religiosos.* Mensajero, 2014.

Patino, Candelario Moran. *El migrante como lugar teológico: Acercamiento teológico sobre el migrante como una expresión del proyecto salvífico de Dios.* Pontifica Universidad Javeriana, Bogotá, 2013.

Perón. *dijo…, Pensamientos del Sr. General Don Juan D. Perón*. Las Bases, 1969.

Perón, Juan. *Tres revoluciones militares*. Tribuna de la Revolución, 1948.

———. *Discurso, El camino de nuestra Revolución*. 30 julio 1973.

———. *Mensaje del Presidente de la nación al pueblo Argentino*. 12 octobre 1973.

———. *Testamento leído ante la Asamblea Legislativa*. 1 mayo 1974.

Pignatelli, Ignacio Javier. *La verdad sobre la compañía de Jesús*. AGPOgraf, 1974.

Pinell, Jorge Alaniz. *Nicaragua, una revolución reaccionaria*. Kosmos, 1985.

Piqué, Elisabetta. *Francisco, Vida y Revolución*. La Esfera de los Libros, 2014.

Politi, Sebastián. *Teología del pueblo, una propuesta argentina para latino-américa*. Docencia, 2015.

Puente, Armando. *Yo, argentino, Las raíces argentinas del Papa Francisco*. Distal, 2015.

Quevedo, Ernesto Lucena. *Colombia ante la guerra: democracia o totalitarismo*. Democracia Humanista, 1987.

Ramiere, Enrique. *La soberanía social de Jesucristo*. Cristiandad, 1951.

Ratzinger, Joseph. *La teología de la liberación atenta contra la fe católica*. Movimiento cristianismo sí, 1984.

Reunión Para El Dialogo Norte-Sur En Cancún, México. *Estrategia socialista para Latinoamérica*. Kelly, 1981.

Rojas, Javier. *Conversaciones con el comandante Miguel Castellanos*. Andante, 1986.

Romero, Damas, Ellacuría, Sobrino, and Campos. *Iglesia de los Pobres y Organizaciones Populares*. UCA, 1979.

Rubin, Sergio and Francesca Ambrogetti. *El Papa Francesco, conversaciones con Jorge Bergoglio*. B, S.A., 2013.

Sacheri, Carlos A. *El orden natural*. Buenos Aires, 1979.

Satta, Paula. *El movimiento Villero Peronista: una experiencia de radicalización*. Universidad de la Plata, 2015.

Scannone, Juan Carlos. *Religión y nuevo pensamiento, Hacia una filosofía de la religión para nuestro tiempo desde América Latina*. Anthropos, 2005.

Silva, Leelananda de. *Ayuda al desarrollo, datos y problemas*. Lepala, 1985.

Sivatte, Rafael de. *Dios camina con su pueblo*. UCA 1985.

Sobrino, Jon. *Jesús en América Latina, su significado para la fe y la cristología*. UCA, 1982.

———. *Resurrección de la verdadera Iglesia, Los pobres, lugar teológico de la eclesiología*. Sal Terrae, 1981.

Spadaro, Antonio. *Papa Francisco. "Mi puerta siempre está abierta"*. Planeta Testimonio, 2014.

Torres, Rosa María. *Nicaragua, revolución popular, educación popular*. Línea, 1985.

Universidad Centroamericana José Simeón Canas. *Rutilo Grande*. UCA, 1988.

Valdes Morandes, Salvador. *La Compañía de Jesus; ¡AY! JESÚS, que Compañía*. Santiago de Chile 1969.

———. *"La Década INFAME"*, *Navidad de 1972*. Santiago de Chile, 1972.

Vallet de Goytisolo, Juan. *Mas sobre temas de hoy*. Ed Speiro Madrid 1979.

Verdevoye, Paul. *Literatura argentina e idiosincrasia*. Corregidor, 2002.

VERBO, no 221-222. Speiro, Madrid, 1984.

———. no 239-240. Speiro, Madrid, 1985.

———. no 241-242. Speiro, Madrid, 1986.

———. no242. CLC, Buenos Aires 1984.

Vicaria de pastoral. *Vocación y misión de los laicos en la Igle- sia y en el mundo veinte años después del Concilio Vaticano II, versión popular.* Arzobispado de San Salvador, 1986.

Villaseñor, Tarsicio Ocampo. *CIF – CIC – CIDOC, en la década de 1960, un testimonio.* Cidoc, 2011.

Widow, Juan Antonio. *El Hombre, animal político. El orden social: principios e ideologías.* Academia superior de Ciencias Pedagógicas de Santiago, 1984.

Articles

Accaputo, P. Carlos. "La Nacion por construir: Jorge M. Bergoglio S. J.", *evangelizadorasdelosapostoles,* 31 oct. 2015.

Acunto, Agustín d'. "El poder popular y la teología de la liberación en los 70's", *Virajes,* Vol. 14 No. 2, julio - diciembre 2012, págs. 55 – 78.

Albado, Omar César. "Algunas Características de le Teología afectiva según el padre Raphael Tello", *Vida Pastoral 288,* 2010, 20-25.

Albado, Omar César. "La pastoral popular en el pensamiento del padre Rafael Tello. Una contribución desde Argentina a la teo- logía latinoamericana", *Franciscanum, UCA,* 2013.

———. "La teología afectiva como modo de conocimiento del pueblo en la pastoral popular del padre Rafael Tello", *Vida Pastoral 287,* 2010.

———. "La teología de la historia y la categoría de sentido en Lucio Gera", *Revista Nuevo Mundo,* 2007.

Albanese, Pascual. "El papa Francisco, el peronismo y la doctrina social de la Iglesia", *Fundación Atlas,* 2013.

Bergoglio, J. "El Sacerdote en la Ciudad a la luz del Documento de Aparecida", *Charla del Sr. Arzobispo al Clero de San Isidro*, 18/05/2010.

———. "La formación del presbítero hoy. Dimensiones intelectuales, comunitaria, apostólica y espiritual, *Conferencia del Sr. Arzobispo en la conmemoración del 25 aniversario del Seminario "La Encarnación" de la Ciudad de Resistencia*, 25/3/2010.

———. "Nosotros como ciudadanos, nosotros como pueblo", *Conferencia del Sr. Arzobispo en la XIII Jornada Arquidiocesana de Pastoral Social*, 16/10/2010.

———. "Religiosidad popular como inculturación de la fe en el Espíritu de Aparecida", 14 de enero de 2008.

———. Interview by Stefania Falasca, "What I would have said at the Consistory", *30giorni*, 2007.

———. "Ponencia del Sr. Arzobispo en la V Conferencia del CELAM", Aparecida, 2007.

Boff, Leonardo. "¿Que Iglesia queremos? El proyecto popular de Iglesia", en *A voz do Arco-íris, Letraviva*, Brasilia, 2000.

Borghesi, Massimo, entrevista a Luis Javier Moxó Soto. "Biografía del Papa Francisco", *Catholic.net*, 2017.

Bosca, Roberto. "El papa peronista", *Instituto Acton Argentina*, 2013.

Campana, Oscar A. "Rafael Tello, Lucio Gera y el movimiento de sacerdotes para el tercer mundo", *Franciscanum, Revista de la Ciencias del Espíritu*, 2013.

Charentenay, Pierre de. « La théologie du peuple », *Choisir*, 2019.

Cheaib, Robert. "Un'analisi del cardinale KASPER, I fondamenti teologici del pontificato di Francesco", *Zenit*, 13 mars 2015.

Codina, Victor. "Eclesiologia de Aparecida", *Revista Iberoamericana de Teologia*, 2008.

Commission Théologique Internationale. "Le *sensus fidei dans la vie de l'Eglise* », *Vatican*, 2014.

Costa, Marcelo Timotheo da. "Em nome do Pai: o Francisco de Assis de Leonardo Boff", *Topoi (Rio J.)* 2016, vol.17, n.33, pp.444-467.

Costadoat, Jorge. "¿Hacia un nuevo concepto de Revelación? La Historia come 'Lugar teológico' en la Teología de la Liberación', *Revista Teología*, 2017.

Cuda, Emilce. "Actores teológicos como sujetos políticos en los modelos republicanos populistas", *Congreso Uruguayo de Ciencia política*, 2012.

———. "El éxodo laboral como practica mística", *Congreso Continental de Teología. La teología de la liberación en prospectiva*, 2012.

———. "Teología y política en el discurso del papa Francisco, ¿Dónde esta el pueblo?", *Nueva Sociedad* no 248, 2013.

———. entrevista, "El Papa es la única voz política que tiene autoridad moral transversal", *Periodista Digital*, 2017.

Desouche, Marie-Thérèse, « L'histoire comme lieu théologique et fondement de la théologie pastorale », *Nouvelle Revue Théologique* 116-3 (1994), p. 396-417,

Di Marco, Laura, "Curas villeros: predicadores de la Teología del Pueblo", *La Nación*, mayo de 2010.

Fernandez, Víctor Manuel. "Para entender adecuadamente los tres ejes temáticos de la V Conferencie en Aparecida", en *Discípulos misioneros. Un marco teológico-pastoral para la V Conferencia de Aparecida*, 2007, 87-122.

Fresia, Iván Ariel. "Teología del pueblo, de la cultura y de la pastoral popular. A propósito de los primeros escritos teológicos de Scannone", *Stromata*, 2014.

Galli, Carlos M. "Evangelización, cultura y teología. El aporte de J. C. Scannone a una teología inculturada", *UCA*, 1991.

———. "El pueblo de Dios, el pueblo y los pueblos. El papa Francisco y la teología argentina", *Congreso Da Puebla ad Aparecida. Chiesa e società in America Latina (1979- 2007)*, 07/02/2017.

————. "Las novedades de la exhortación Evangelii Gaudium, claves del pensamiento pastoral de Francisco", 2014.

————. "Lucio Gera: In Memoriam. 16/01/1924 – 7/08/2012. Un precursor de le teología latinoamericana contemporánea", *CELAM*, 2012.

Gera, Lucio. "Pueblo, religión del pueblo e Iglesia", *CELAM*, 1976, Bogotá.

Hellenbroich, Elisabeth. "Una iglesia para los pobres – las raíces teológicas de Francisco", *Msiainforma*, 22 de mayo de 2015.

Himitian, Evangelina. "Cambios en la Iglesia: la era Francisco, el fin de los tabúes", *La Nación*, 2013.

Kasper, Walter. "Anticipazione. Francesco, i 'mestri' del papa", *Avvenire*, 2015.

————. Le rapport entre Église universelle et Église locale », *Stimmen der Zeit*, 2000.

Kolvenbach, Peter-Hans. "Sentire cum Ecclesia après le deuxième Concile du Vatican », *CIS, Rome*, 2004.

Luciani, Rafael. "Francisco y la Teología del Pueblo: un nuevo modo de 'ser Iglesia'", *Aleteia*, Ago. 2015.

————. "La opción teológico-pastoral del papa Francisco", *Perspect. Teol., Belo Horizonte*, Jan. 2016.

————. "la Teología del Pueblo: según el papa Francisco", *Aleteia*, Julio 2015.

Maspero, Giulio. "El tiempo superior al espacio (EG 222): un principio teológico fundamental para el obrar cristiano", *Almudí*, 4 junio 2015.

Mattei, Roberto de. "La 'Chiesa povera' dal Vaticano II a papa Francesco", *Corrispondenza romana*, 15 giugno 2016.

Mauti, Ricardo Miguel. "El Concilio Vaticano II: acontecimiento y teología", *Teología, UCA*, 2013.

Pagni, Carlos. "El método Bergoglio para gobernar", *lanacion.com*, 21 de marzo de 2013.

Palazzi, Felix. "'Clericalismo', 'esquizofrenia existencial',... ¿de dónde los saca el papa Francisco?", *Aleteia*, 2015.

Pellitero, Ramiro. "Evolución del concepto 'Teología Pastoral'. Itinerario y estatuto de una Teología de la acción eclesial", *Scripta Theologica*, 2000.

Perón, Juan. "Testamento político: texto completo leído ante la Asamblea Legislativa", 01/05/1974.

———. "Las 20 Verdades Peronistas", 17 de octubre de 1950.

Pikaza, Xabier. "Argentina, lugar teológico del Papa. Con Croatto, Gera y Ferrara", *Periodista digital*, 19 Juil 2014.

Quintana, Julio M. Ojea. "La cultura del encuentro en el papa Francisco: proyecciones políticas y la violencia de los anos setenta en la Argentina", *U.C.A.*, 2015.

Rosas, Ernesto López. "Valores Cristianos del Peronismo", *Revista del CIAS*, no 235, agosto de 1974.

Rueda, José Luis Meza. "La liberación de la teología, tarea pendiente de la teología de la liberación", *Congreso Internat. Teología*, Medellín, 2008.

Scannone, Juan Carlos. "Aportaciones de la Teología Argentina del Pueblo a la Teología Latinoamérica", *Lo Social*, 2015.

———. "El papa Francisco y la teología del pueblo", *Mensaje*, ago. 2014, p. 14.

———. "La filosofía de la liberación: historia, características, vigencia actual", *UCA*, 2009.

———. "La teología del pueblo y desde el pueblo – Aportes de Lucio Gera", *La Civiltà Cattolica*, 2015.

———. "Lo Social y lo político según Francisco Suarez. Hacia una relectura latinoamericana actual de la filosofía política de Suarez", *Stromata*, Vol. 54, Nº. 1-2, 1998, págs. 85-118.

———. "Perspectivas eclesiológicas de la 'Teología del pueblo' en la Argentina", 1997 en mercaba.org/ Fichas/Teologia_latina/ perspectivas_eclesiologicas.htm.

————. "Teología, cultura e interculturalidad", *Congreso Continental de Teología*, octubre 2012.

————. "Un humanismo religioso e interreligioso, de los derechos humanos e intercultural", *Culturas y Fe, UCA*, 1998.

————. entrevista especial, "O Papa Francisco e a Teologia do Povo", *Instituto Humanitas Unisinos*, maio de 2015.

————. entrevista, "A Teología da Cultura não se opõe a Teologia da Libertação", *Ihu Unisinos*, 2007.

Seibold, Jorge R. "La mística popular en la ciudad", *Stromata, UCA*, 2011.

Serna, Eduardo de la. "El Gera que yo conocí", *Editorial San Pablo*, 2012.

————. "El papa Francisco representante de la teología del Pueblo", *Blog de E. de la S.*, septiembre de 2016.

Sinner, Rudolf von. "Leonardo Boff, um católico protestante", 2006.

Tello, Rafael. "El cristianismo popular según las virtudes teologales. La FE.", 1996.

Teología y pastoral andina. "Mensaje final del 25° encuentro de teología y pastoral andina", 2015.

Touris, Claudia. "Sociabilidades católicas postconciliares. El caso de la constelación tercermundista en la Argentina (1966-1976)", *Passagens*, Rio de J., 2010.